# Henry VIII's Bishops

For Ellen and Jake

# Henry VIII's Bishops

## Diplomats, Administrators,
## Scholars and Shepherds

Andrew Allan Chibi

**James Clarke & Co**
**Cambridge**

**James Clarke & Co**
**P.O. Box 60**
**Cambridge**
**CB1 2NT**

**www.jamesclarke.co.uk**
**publishing@jamesclarke.co.uk**


ISBN 0 227 67976 8


*British Library Cataloguing in Publication Data*
A catalogue record is available from the British Library


Copyright © A.A. Chibi, 2003


First Published in 2003 ·

Printed and bound in Great Britain by Biddles Ltd
*www.biddles.co.uk*

# Table of Contents

# Acknowledgements

This book grew out of my earlier works on Bishop John Stokesley and out of my curiosity over the tarnished reputation that Henry VIII's bishops have earned from contemporaries and historians alike. I decided to pursue an examination of who these men actually were, which grew into a series of comparative articles which, in turn, laid the foundations for this book. Throughout the process, guidance has been provided in the form of comments on the text, after-seminar deconstructions, or by exchanges of ideas over coffee, by Mark Greengrass, Terry Hartley, Peter Musgrave, Andrew Pettegree, Richard Rex, Alistair Duke and Kevin Sharpe. I would also like to mention the important contribution of the dozens of students over the years that had asked interesting questions for which, at the time, I could provide merely adequate answers. This book was partially written with them in mind. It must also be said that Adrian Brink has displayed the patience of a saint in his dealings with me, and courage in his support of this endeavour. Thanks also go to Elizabeth Davey for all the work that she put into editing the manuscript.

Of course, little could have been accomplished without the support of my wife Ellen, Jake, my family and my friends, whose shenanigans kept me slightly off-balance but sane nonetheless.

While all of these people can take some small measure of satisfaction at having had a hand in the production of this book, all gaffs, mistakes and errors of judgement fall squarely on my shoulders.

Andrew A Chibi
Sheffield, 2002

# Abbreviations

| | |
|---|---|
| AfR | Archiv für Reformationsgeschichte |
| BL | British Library |
| CSP | Calender of State Papers |
| CSPM | Calendar of State Papers – Milan |
| CSPS | Calendar of State Papers – Spain |
| CSPV | Calendar of State Papers – Venice |
| CW | Complete Works of Thomas More (Yale Edition) |
| CWE | Complete Works of Erasmus (Toronto Edition) |
| Divorce Tracts | The Divorce Tracts of Henry VIII |
| E.E.T.S. | Early English Text Society |
| EHD | English Historical Documents |
| EHR | English Historical Review |
| Foxe | Acts and Monuments |
| Hall | The Union of the Two Noble and Illustre Families of Lancastre & York |
| JBS | Journal of British Studies |
| JEH | Journal of Ecclesiastical History |
| LP | Letters of Papers of the Reign of Henry VIII |
| LJ | Lords' Journal |
| NPNF | Nicene and Post Nicene Fathers |
| OUL | Oxford University Library |
| PG | Migne's Patrologia Graeca |
| PL | Migne's Patrologia Latina |
| PRO, REQ. | Public Record Office – Court of Requests |
| PRO, SP | Public Record Office – State Papers |
| R.H.S. | Royal Historical Society |
| TRHS | Transactions of the Royal Historical Society |
| TRP | Tudor Royal Proclamations |
| SCJ | Sixteenth-Century Journal |
| Strype, EM | Ecclesiastical Memorials |
| VHC | Victoria History of the Counties |

# Introduction
## Who were Henry VIII's Bishops?

The image of the Henrician bishops has never been particularly good. Contemporary opinion itself was often hostile. Hugh Latimer, who had been forced to resign as bishop of Worcester in 1539, was obviously still irritated about it eight years later. He noted in a sermon that some of those Henricians still on the bench under Edward VI were far more concerned with worldly than with spiritual matters. He said that as 'they are so troubled with lordly living, they be so placed in palaces, couched in courts, ruffling in their rents, dancing in their dominions' that they were surely unsuited to the positions they held. In his opinion they were too busy, 'some in the king's matters, some are ambassadors, some of the privy council, some to furnish the court' to be effective prelates.[1] Sour grapes perhaps, but he was not saying anything new.

Throughout the reign of Henry VIII, notably with the onset of religious experiments, the bishops were labelled as 'crafty foxes' and 'romish wolves' by influential enemies. James Sawtry, for instance, reacting against the Act of Six Articles, denounced 'these venomous virulent vipers'.[2] William Turner, likewise, attacked the entire Henrician bench but reserved special criticism for Stephen Gardiner, bishop of Winchester and 'lying limb of the devil'.[3] Of course, John Skelton thoroughly mined the satirical genre in his attacks on Thomas Wolsey.[4]

A century later, the view of the Henricians had not substantially changed. Indeed, an interesting and amusing anonymous pamphlet of 1641 rehashed the old terms. They were 'deceitfull as craftie foxes'. The pamphleteer wrote that they had only pretended to care for the church and for the kingdom. It labelled them 'disingenuous' in that 'they would pretend any thing, and transform themselves into any shape, so they might but hold their livings . . . they are blood suckers'.[5] These rather ugly depictions seem to have stuck and were picked up on by Whig historians in the eighteenth and nineteenth centuries. Only recently have these judgements been questioned by scholars.

Modern historians, less religiously polarised, now tend to view the Henricians in different terms. They are no longer 'unfaithful time-servers', but rather professional bureaucrats and educated lawyers. Not spiritual men or pastoral leaders, but royal administrators[6] with a few idealists and reformers mixed in.[7] The administrative structure of the church abetted this condition as those at the top of the hierarchy seemed to lose sight of parochial concerns. The few idealists have been isolated from the conservative, bureaucratic and spiritually-obstructionist majority for individual study.[8] Finally, Stephen Thompson, in his 1984 Oxford thesis 'The Pastoral Work of the English and Welsh Bishops 1500-1558', permanently dismantled the idea that they were entirely apathetic to pastoral matters.[9] Whether good or bad, one answer still alludes us about them. Why were these particular sixty-nine individuals elevated to the Episcopal bench? That question, their influence on the reign of Henry VIII, and the reign's influence upon them, is the purpose of this book.

Can we uncover the king's motivations? He told Wolsey that the reward of Episcopal promotion was not merely political. He required ' some other great qualities (as profound learning) annexed unto the same'.[10] Testing this claim through an examination of their pre-Episcopal careers reveals that the king was quite serious. Although it cannot be denied that those clerics with substantial crown service records often gained the best positions in the hierarchy, it is also clear that clerics who had not served the crown at all were also elevated to bishoprics (and not just in Wales!).[11] Indeed, it also becomes clear that more serious attention has to be paid to the events of the reign and the king's own responses to them as determining factors.

For example, Henry VIII inherited an Episcopal bench very much dominated by men of politics with legal and administrative backgrounds. Jurists, like Richard Fox and Richard Mayew, dominated the councils in England, while men like Christopher Bainbridge, Silvestro de'Gigli and Adriano de'Castellesi handled problems in Rome (and therefore the pan-European stage). John Fisher stands out as a token divine (appointed by Henry VII under pressure from his mother!). A kind of *status quo* developed as the new king established himself and his style. Administrators, like Charles Booth, Thomas Ruthal or Nicholas West, dominated until they were themselves displaced by Wolsey. He so dominated the court that the bishops were left able to concentrate on spiritual matters once again, while necessity dictated Episcopal nominations. Monastic non-entities, like Edmund Birkhead or Henry Standish, served in the Welsh hinterlands while Jorge de'Athequa, the queen's confessor, was nominated to the see of Llandaff so as not to be a drain on the royal treasury.

Defeating the Scots and the French for the sake of high drama and ego taught the king that warfare was restrictively expensive. Luckily, the Field of Cloth of Gold showed him that prestige could be gained in other ways. He could not match Francis I or Charles V in martial glory or wealth, but perhaps he could outdo them as a man of the Renaissance. Thus, the 1520s witness the elevation of scholars like John Longland, Cuthbert Tunstal and John Clerk. A man of renowned learning, Lorenzo Campeggio, handled the king's international needs. Of course, promoting scholars and humanists came with a price tag: the circulation of new (and sometimes dangerous) ideas and innovative methods of problem solving. Intellectuals and theologians consequently dominated the 1530s – the divorce, the royal supremacy and doctrinal reform were the major issues. As the king liked to keep his options open, it is hardly surprising that these bishops can be divided into religious factions. Such radical thinkers as Thomas Cranmer and Edward Fox counterbalanced doctrinaire conservatives like John Stokesley and Edward Lee. After 1539, as he grew tired of religious experimentation and looked to re-capture past glories, the dominance of theologians waned as the king looked out for effective administrators like Thomas Thirlby, William Knight and George Day (jurists, ambassadors and politicians).

If the king's decisions were influenced by the needs of the day (e.g. theologians in the 1530s), does this mean that the church suffered? Were these good jurists, respected scholars and radical theologians good bishops or not? That some of his most intimate, experienced and employed advisors were also bishops did open the king up to a certain amount of criticism:

> remember for what causes the kinges your noble progenitors in times paste have chosen bishops . . . given their bishopricks to their counsellors, chaplaines which have been daylie attendants in the court, which also have done to them good service, as ambassadors, or to such which have taken paines in their household, as almners, and deans, of the chappel, clarkes of their closet . . . where God's worde doth not approve any bishoprick to be given to any more for any such service done. . . .[12]

The author obviously thought that the church suffered as a consequence. Although Francis Bacon took little notice, David Hume labelled such bishops too 'obsequious'[13] to be spiritually effective.

Of course there were problems in the English church and in the relationship between the Catholic clergy and the laity in England in the early sixteenth-century. All the countries of Europe experienced some tension in the post-1520 period and all the rulers of Europe, spiritual and temporal, reacted and tried to use the church to their advantage.[14] Henry VIII was no exception, but a comparison of the various responses is interesting and illuminating. It reveals that those rulers who were able to take a firm hand and a personal interest (the rulers of France, England, Spain, the states of Italy) were also those who avoided the more extreme social and political disruptions, like those which affected the German states. The responses took many forms.

In Venice, the rulers checked the growth of papal authority with violence (e.g. the War of Ferrara, 1482). In Florence, Savonarola reacted by undertaking a limited reformation of the church. In 1475, the Inquisition was established as an instrument of the Spanish crown rather than of the Spanish church. These reactions failed to fundamentally improve the situation because they did not attack the real basis of the problem - the papal power of ecclesiastical nomination and promotion. Once it was realised that the ruler could take a firm hand in the determination of the character of the national church by gaining a voice in the nomination of bishops and other higher clergy, the way forward became clear.

In England, this lesson had been learned in the fourteenth century and had resulted in the statutes of *Praemunire* and *Provisors*. By Henry VIII's reign he could say, with confidence, that 'we are King of England, and the kings of England in time past have never had any superior but God only'. This confidence would later be enacted in statute form with the royal supremacy. This was not quite the case with regard to England's overseas territories in Ireland. Although, since the reign of Henry II, the English crown had special-relationship status with the Irish Church, until the royal supremacy was imposed this amounted to little more than an over-lordship of the English speaking half of the ethnic division in the four important dioceses of Armagh, Meath, Dublin and Kildare. Until 1534, the crown nominated an English or Anglo-Irish bishop to care for the needs of the English settlers, while the dean and remaining officials were papally provided Irishmen who looked after their own.[15]

The French monarchy also came to a new arrangement when, in 1438, Charles VII, the estates of France, and Pope Eugene's representatives agreed the Pragmatic Sanction of Bourges. This reinforced, at least in theory, French traditions and rituals (e.g. like the right of chapters to elect bishops and abbots) and also limited the power of the papacy to almost a rubber stamp. Of course, some electoral freedoms eventually gave way to force and bribery, legal disputes and lawsuits, as the church was too weak to withstand external pressures. So, while it did increase the power of the French church, it had not, as had the English statutes, firmly increased the power of the crown.[16] By the 1470s, after a series of powerful kings, the nomination of bishops and abbots had very much fallen into the hands of the crown. They pushed the Sanction aside as a mere inconvenience, and royal influence over the church expanded, much as it had in Spain, England and throughout Italy.

This left the bishops in the unenviable position of owing their powers and status to two, often conflicting, masters. In France, England (including Ireland) and Spain (Castile, Aragon etc.), kings and popes vied for supremacy. In Germany and Italy, owing to their unique political arrangements, there were some differences. In the former, bishops and prince-bishops were not simply representative of an ecclesiastical order, the sees having been largely secularised by this time. The bishops appeared to the world rather more like temporal princes and nobles than spiritually-minded ministers.[17] Moreover, the prince-bishops in particular might well have been lured away by their dynastic duties and pursuit of church privileges. Similarly, in Italy, where bishoprics and other benefices were considered the preserve of the noble families, indeed, were treated no better than chattel, the cardinals were also under pressure from dynastic families and expectations from the papacy.

As in the French and Scottish cases, and for a variety of reasons, by the sixteenth century the European crowns were strong enough that the papacy could not ignore their nominations. The results, however, were not particularly good. In most cases, the failure to strike a balance between spiritual, temporal and familial duties was most often the cause of criticisms against the Episcopate (and the bishops themselves did little to assuage their image). Once elected, they generally set out to improve their fortunes and build up the power and prestige of their families. This led, inevitably, to accusations of worldliness, ambition, arrogance, extravagance or ostentation, as abuses such as pluralism, absenteeism, simony and nepotism ran rampant.

That is not to say that there was nothing positive. The bishops of Europe did erect buildings, they wrote books, they patronised scholars and initiated reform. Many took their pastoral duties seriously, visited their dioceses and issued decrees and exhortations. Most, however, only paid lip service to the ideal of ecclesiastical service. In France, Scotland, Italy, Germany, Ireland and the Iberian Peninsula there are some fine examples of pastoral caregivers, but the relative scarcity of the paragons tends rather to reinforce the popular image. The case in England was different. The Henricians stand head and shoulders above their contemporary colleagues as 'conscientious' men. Having said that, it is necessary to understand just what was expected of them.

A bishop in early modern Europe was an extremely important man. He held a central position in the social, political and administrative life of his country. He provided a connection between the spiritual world (as the head of the ecclesiastical hierarchy) and the temporal world (due to participation in government and by virtue of vast property holdings). While it is the case that their individual duties and strengths might be geared more toward one aspect of their position: diplomacy or hunting heretics, it should be remembered that a good bishop did not ignore his other duties. Indeed, a good bishop would, ideally, handle all his duties equally well. What credentials would identify the right men for the position? Was there an ideal against which they might be measured?

When Francis I negotiated the Concordat of Bologna with Pope Leo X in 1516 they agreed certain practical qualifications as a basis for future nominations. Candidates had to be over twenty-seven years of age, suggesting maturity. They had to have a university education to the level of doctor of canon or civil law, or master or licentiate in theology from a 'famous university'. They also had to be legitimate by birth, ordained before their consecration, and they had to have demonstrated good moral behaviour.[18] The delegates to the Council of Trent echoed these requirements. Besides age, education and morality, candidates were forbidden to use their positions to enrich their families, concentrating instead on spiritual matters. They were to ensure that religious life within their diocese was satisfactory, scrutinise the work of priests and dispense discipline. In other words, candidates had to be capable of carrying out their duties by maturity, character and training.[19] Even the royal supremacy, effecting so much else, did not essentially alter this perceived ideal.

Bishops Stokesley and Tunstal wrote, in the late 1530s, that just as the king was the head of the mystical body, ' the office deputed to the bishoppe . . . is to be as eyes to the hoole body' to 'shew unto it the right way of lyving'. Just as the eyes draw power from and translate information to the head, so do the bishops claim a like authority from, and responsibility to, the king.[20] Here, as with the Concordat and Trent, a good bishop is measured by his responsibilities – to advise the king, to exhibit morality, and act as a spiritual model for everyone else.

Such concerns developed because a bishop held a great deal of power, often expressed in the form of patronage (which was an easily corrupted system). Bishops appointed candidates to a wide variety of offices both clerical and temporal, and held the right to examine, accept or reject any clergymen or laymen presented by others for office in their own gift.[21] Such power allowed the bishop to take an active role in determining the character of his clergy and, consequently, the character of religion in the parishes. That said, just how well did the Henrician bishops serve the church? We shall see that they were not mere dilettantes. On average, between first clerical appointment and elevation to a bishopric, the Henricians served sixteen years. They held every office in the spiritual hierarchy and served with low non-residency ratings. Between first post and bishopric, they thus became very familiar with the needs of the church (both spiritual and administrative) and with the needs of the souls in their care.

* * *

Sixteen years training, in any field, suggests not only keen competition but also the high standard expected. For the Henricians, promotion to the Episcopal bench came only after a distinguished pre-Episcopal career. Of course, some did not serve quite so long and some proved their worth only after a considerably longer time. Moreover, non-residence and pluralism cannot be denied, nor should they be, but these problems can easily be magnified out of proportion. Anyway, it is generally accepted now that the parishes were served rather well. Who were the rockets? Paul Bush, Cranmer, Gardiner, Fisher, Thomas Goodrich, John Hilsey, Latimer, Nicholas Shaxton and John Skip all spent less than five years in training.

Bush is neither famous nor infamous, but had gained a reputation as a 'wise and grave man well versed both in divinity and physic'. He was 'a grave orator' among the men of his order, the Austin canons.[22] He served them as provost, corrector and rector of Edington in 1537, was a Salisbury canon (prebend of Bishopston) and had earned himself the patronage of William, Lord Hungerford, who recommended him to the king.[23] He became a royal chaplain and, two years later, first bishop of Bristol. More impressively, Cranmer took only two years, and Gardiner three, to earn promotion. On the way, Cranmer had been rector of Bredon in Worcester and archdeacon of Taunton, whereas Gardiner (who served as private secretary to both Wolsey and the king) had been rector of St Michael's Gloucester and had held three archdeaconries, Norfolk (1528-9), Worcester (1530) and Leicester (1531). Both men had been diplomats, but the overriding factor in their success was their work for the king in the annulment suit (as was the case for Latimer, Goodrich, Shaxton and Skip[24]). Who would question the commitment to the church of a Hugh Latimer, however?

Seven bishops served less than ten years. These were Robert Aldrich, Geoffrey Blythe, Edmund Bonner, Edward Fox, Nicholas Heath, Henry Holbeach and Robert Holgate. Taking Blythe as an example, he served ten years and had been rector of Corfe, archdeacon of Cleveland and a canon of York in that time. Bonner had a more conventional career perhaps, putting in a great deal of diplomatic service while holding four rectorships and the archdeaconry of Leicester, prior to elevation to the see of Hereford in 1538.[25] Holgate, the subject of a monograph by A. G. Dickens, had been prior of St Catherine's without Lincoln (1529) and of Watton in Yorkshire (1536), vicar of Cudney in Lincolnshire and master of St Gilbert's, Sepringham (1534). As master, he was ' indispensable to all legal actions by or against the Order'. Dickens found him to have been a morally upstanding and conscientious man too.[26] If these overnight success stories were worthy clerics, were the men at the other end of the scale less so?

William Atwater served forty years between his first appointment at St Frideswide's, Oxford and his elevation to the see of Lincoln in 1514. He had been vicar of Cumnor and rector of Piddlehinton, Spetisbury and St Nicholas Abington (all Berkshire). He held prebends (e.g. Liddington and Ruscombe in Lincoln), archdeaconships (e.g. Lewes and Huntingdon) and had been dean of Salisbury (1509). Nicholas West put in twenty-nine years.

He had been vicar of Kingston on Thames, Surrey (1502), rector of Yelford, Oxfordshire (1489), archdeacon of Derby (1486) and dean of the chapels royal over that period. He had also served as vicar-general to Richard Fox and as the treasurer of Chichester Cathedral (1507) before his promotion to Ely (27 November 1515). His rise through the clerical ranks was long, not because he was an unworthy cleric but because he was an indispensable diplomat. He had been Henry VII's ambassador to Emperor Maximilian, had served Henry VIII as ambassador (three times) to James IV (1511, 1513) and once to Louis XII (1514) and had been the royal envoy to George Duke of Saxony (1505) and to Francis I (1515).

Outside of Chichester, Robert Sherborne's reputation has been tarnished by the fact that during his twenty-two year pre-Episcopal career he had made so much money. It was also thought that he had forged the papal bulls to his elevation to the see of St David's.[27] As Steer made clear in his monograph, however, Sherborne's preferment had been legitimately earned and, like his colleagues, covered all the available offices. In fact he had one of the most extensive clerical careers among them. He had been a rector, of Childrey, Oxfordshire (1491), had held ten prebends, including Langford Manor in Lincoln (1486, 1494), Alresford, Essex (1494) and Wildland in St Paul's (1489), three archdeaconries (e.g. Buckinghamshire in 1495), and had been dean of St Paul's (1499), treasurer of Hereford (1486) and master of St Cross Hospital in Winchester (1492-1508); quite an interesting cross-section of experiences. The controversy surrounding his provision to the see of St David's (5 January 1505) amounted to little, and there he remained until his translation to Chichester (18 September 1508). But was he a serious churchman?

The fact that he resigned shortly after 25 May 1536 over his opposition to the royal supremacy would seem to suggest it. Moreover, he had used his accumulated wealth quite effectively, encouraging future generations with the foundation of prebends (Bursalis, Exceit Bargham and Wyndham) for the alumni of New College or Winchester, and a grammar school in his hometown.[28] Of course, a time-server could do the same, but 'the records which testify this testify also to his inward piety; and the munificence with which he gave equalled the magnificence with which he lived'[29] – one man's opinion, perhaps, and what about the infamous Wolsey? He founded an Oxford college and a grammar school in his hometown of Ipswich. Did this make him a dedicated cleric too?

Wolsey is an interesting case. The appendix examines his career in full and we find that, while it was extensive, it was hardly awe-inspiring. He was resident vicar of Lydd in Kent (1501) and had been resident rector of Lyminton. His time as vicar was probably short, however, due to the fact that later the same year he became chaplain to archbishop Deane.[30] He had also been rector of Redgrave, Suffolk (1506) and Great Torrington,

Devon (1510), held prebends (e.g. of Pratum Minus, Hereford in 1508), was a dean (e.g. of Lincoln in 1509 and of Hereford in 1512), but had served the church in a number of unusual ways too, having been 'rural dean' of Depwade and Humbleyard, Lincolnshire (1499), for example, taking special responsibility for those distant parts of the large diocese. He had also been parson of St Bride's Fleet Street, London (1510), precentor of St Paul's (1513) and chaplain to Sir Richard Nanfan, the Deputy of Calais (1503), doing good service in this most personal capacity. His later reputation and the many writings of his enemies have blackened his character.

All told, seventeen Henricians had served as vicars of parish churches. They were the men who actually served the parish for the rector. Of course, vicars too could have been non-resident, leaving a curate in their place, but there is little or no hard evidence to suggest that this practice was abused.[31] They did not serve in that position for long, but this should not be taken as an indication that they had not served well. Indeed, between them they held 139 rectorships too, making them responsible for vicars and curates alike. Fisher, a most dedicated churchman, was a non-resident rector (of Lythe in Yorkshire) while we know that Wolsey, at the other end of historical opinion, was resident at Lyminton. To be fair, it is unlikely he ever saw Redgrave in Suffolk or Great Torrington in Devon except on paper. Not to make excuses, but non-residence is not the yardstick of morality it has been taken to be.

For example, Fitzjames took responsibility for the welfare of the souls of two kings, serving both Edward IV and Henry VII as royal chaplain and the latter as royal almoner. Such a burden meant it is unlikely he ever visited Spetisbury, Trent or Aller. Stokesley was non-resident rector of Slimbridge (while vice-president of Magdalen), non-resident at Brightstone (while Henry VIII's confessor) and non-resident at Ivychurch in Kent (while royal almoner). There were nineteen pluralists (four or more rectorships) on the Episcopal bench during Henry's reign, eight of who had been appointed by his father.[32] Moreover, these men also had, on average, pre-Episcopal careers of over twenty-three years. Obviously they were not exclusively engaged in ecclesiastical affairs the whole time. Some were diplomats (e.g. Clerk), court fixtures (e.g. Warham), the sons of nobility (e.g. James Stanley), but some were very dedicated churchmen indeed (e.g. Tunstal).

In general, the Henricians relied more upon prebends than they had upon rectories for their sinecures. They held, on average, two or three (159 in total) each. The prebend was an important position in the diocesan administration, but, as it did not entail a cure of souls, examples of plurality and absenteeism are more frequent. This is only half the story, however. In the fifteenth-century, the average career of a bishop included five prebends, while some held as many as ten.[33] As the office tended to divide the attention and loyalty of the recipient between his patron and the corporate body of the church, it was usually awarded to trusted servants or to men who had already served the interests of the church (as vicars or rectors). Twenty-six of the Henricians (mostly regulars) had held no prebends at all. Although this meant that thirty-eight held about four each, the fifteenth-century aggregate of five was steadily diminished from an average of three and a half in the 1510s to one in the 1540s. This indicates that the king would increasingly brook no divided loyalties.

Take Hugh Oldham as an example of a champion pluralist (he held eleven prebends). Was he more committed to his own personal wealth than to the health of the church? It had been due to the patronage of Lady Margaret Beaufort that he was appointed rector of St Michael's Bread Street, London on 19 September 1485. He resigned this in 1488, in exchange for Lanivet in Cornwall. His first appointment to a prebend was in 1492 for St Stephen's Chapel, Westminster. This marked him as a man with great expectations. Still, he served seven other rectories and ten other prebends before elevation to the see of Exeter in 1504.[34] Oldham's commitment to the church often clashed with the desires of the king who wanted him at court, but Exeter held his attention more often than the national political stage.

Of course, with the right connections, movement up the ecclesiastical ladder need not have been so lengthy a prospect. Edmund Audley, son of James Tucket, fifth Lord Audley, held the prebend of Colwall in Hereford in 1464 prior to his appointment as rector of Machworth and of Berwick St John in 1465. Prior to his elevation to the see of Rochester (7 July 1480) he held only two other rectories, Bursted Parva and Llanaber, Gwynedd, but nine other prebends.[35] James Stanley, sixth son of Thomas Stanley, first Earl of Derby, was likewise first appointed to a prebend, Southwell in Durham in 1477. Only subsequently did he hold five rectories and four other prebends before his election to Ely in 1506 (provided 18 July). But Stanley was heavily involved in extensive educational works and never actually served in the government or at court. We might take him to have been more dedicated to the church, at least, than his noble companion. The dedication of the seculars was matched, or bettered, by the regulars.

It would seem obvious that the reign of Henry VIII was not a particularly good time to have been a monk or a friar, the butt of so much humanist joking. Thompson, however, made it clear that where the regulars served as vicars or held the rectory, they did so with distinction.[36] On average the regulars also held fewer offices than the seculars and served longer. The nineteen regulars represent most of the major orders, starting off as canons, friars or monks, basically as a member of a house of their order, and performed the basic duties of prayer, education, hospitality, alms-giving, annuities and corrodies. It must be said that, generally, the monks performed their functions very well despite the fact that the monasteries were in decline. Their functions, moreover, could be and were being performed by secular clergy, thus monasticism was becoming more a means to a rising social standing than an end in itself.[37] It was thought that men looked to monasticism to pull themselves out of the yeoman ranking, and this is borne out by the fact that fourteen Henrician regulars had been born to that class (see Table 1). While sixteen years was the overall average from first post to Episcopate, for the regulars the average was just over twenty years.

In any case, Rosenthal held that advancement to the higher offices implied some blend of three conclusions. The man was being given 'responsibility for specific actions and decisions', was being rewarded for good services already rendered to the church or, was being marked out for future expectations.[38] In general, the higher office holding of the future bishops is varied, interesting and clearly indicative of an impressive standard. To be an archdeacon, for instance, was to be very administratively active and included responsibility for part or all of a diocese. The archdeacon was responsible for such things as church property, general discipline and possibly even institution and induction to benefice. Only ten of the seculars had not been archdeacons and, those who had, rarely held more than one office and were usually resident.

Thirlby, for example, had made an impact as a junior government official and was rewarded with the archdeacon's office of Ely in 1534.[39] This was no mere political favour, however. He was clearly the ideal choice. As he was familiar with the affairs of Cambridge and experienced in governmental matters he could liase effectively between the two when necessary. Although he got off to a poor start, he rapidly acclimatised and remained resident until he was called away in 1538 on royal diplomatic chores.[40] Those who had been archdeacons had been given the duty because they were capable and had proven themselves, having, on average, already served the church for ten years. They were ready to be tested with the vastly increased duties the office imposed. Note that the future bishops held only twenty-six different archdeaconries between them, hinting that Huntingdon, Surrey and Gloucester, for example, were a standard part of the career, almost a *sine qua non* of advancement.

For the regulars, a priorship had similar career overtones. The prior, either the head or the deputy-head of a monastery or abbey, ranked just below the abbot and was liable for the good order of the brethren and other administrative duties. Take William Barlow as the undisputed champion pluralist. He held the post six times, including Haversfordwest in Pembrokeshire and Bisham Abbey (in 1527 and again in 1535-7), holding the last two *in commendam* consecutively with the sees of St David's and St Asaph.[41] Was Barlow dedicated to the care of his brethren or to collecting offices (and wages)?

According to Geoffrey Baskerville it was the former. When Barlow was prior of Bromehill he strenuously defended the 'excellent state of his house, the morals and behaviour of his colleagues', and claimed 'that all was perfect'; a report accepted by the visitor, Bishop Nix (a principled ecclesiastical disciplinarian), in 1526.[42] What few complaints there had been were resolved by the bishop's injunction that Barlow provide a confessor for his brethren. When Wolsey dissolved the priory over the prior's objections, Barlow was still given a pension of £40.[43] On the other hand, as prior of Bisham Abbey in 1527, he apparently displayed no 'liking for monastic life' and, when the time came, he enthusiastically resigned Haverfordwest and Bisham over to the king. As he held these *in commendam* with his early bishoprics it is doubtful that he ever experienced their regimes[44] and, moreover, could he not have been disheartened by his strenuous earlier dispute with Wolsey? This had initiated a series of heretical pamphlets aimed at the cardinal, for which Barlow was forced to make recompense later.[45] The dedication of Capon, as prior of St John's Abbey in Colchester, seems sure by comparison. He was a strict disciplinarian and took a special interest in the abbey's material conditions. He faced two Episcopal visitations (July 1520 and June 1526) but his accounts were well ordered and he had little or no outstanding debts to burden the members.[46] His attention to detail was repeated as abbot of St Benet's Hulme, Norfolk.[47]

As prior of Bristol, and later of the London Dominicans, Hilsey dedicated himself to the reversal of decline in standards of discipline and numbers. He also tried to 'abolish utterly the physiognomy of anti-christ'.[48] Henry Holbeach was not a religious reformer and, as prior of Worcester (after 13 March 1536), clashed with bishop Latimer over reformation issues. Latimer issued injunctions blaming Holbeach for 'neglect of the king's ordinances for the suppression of idolatry and superstition' as he had not bought a whole English Bible.[49] They came to some kind of agreement, however, as Holbeach was later appointed Latimer's suffragan bishop of Bristol and, on 18 January 1540, first dean of Worcester.[50]

The office of dean was a very prestigious and integral one in diocesan administration and not gifted haphazardly. The dean was the head or principal officer of the cathedral or collegiate church and, with the canons, was responsible for the services, fabric and property of the institution. The dean had to be a senior man of proven ability, devoted, a man who could act independently of the bishop when necessary. An appointment as dean was a good indication of the regard in which a man was held. During the reign of Henry VIII, twenty-three deans became bishops, on average, after over a decade of service to the church and, usually, held only one post.

Were they good deans? Sherborne had been dean of St Paul's and, while his biographer suggests that he had little time for the office, it is interesting to note that he was dedicated enough to spend £550 of his own money making improvements to the fabric of the cathedral.[51] Oldham was the logical choice as dean of Wimborne in 1485 and of St John's Hospital Chester in 1493. He had been deeply involved in Lady Margaret's extensive building projects there, as her legal advisor and as deputy-dean to Smith, and suited to the hospital by his own deep interests in the development of such social institutions as hostels, hospitals and almshouses.[52] Clearly, there were also definite deanships indicative of future success – of the Chapels Royal, of course, or of Salisbury, York and Wimborne. Still, there were very prominent individuals, like John Colet, dean of St Paul's, whom one would think exhibited all of the right qualities for Episcopal promotion but who were never elevated. Similarly, only eleven abbots were elevated after the dissolutions. What set these men apart?

Anthony Kitchin, obscure though he was, and although unable to stem the tide of declining membership as abbot of Eynsham, was, in the 1535 visitation, praised as 'chaste in his living' and as a man who 'looks well to the reparation of the house'. He was not, however, a strict disciplinarian: 'negligent in overseeing his brethren'.[53] Thomas Skevington, as abbot of Waverley, was a 'wise' manager, while John Wakeman, as abbot of Tewkesbury, was praised for his financial acumen having significantly built up the property and wealth of the abbey.[54] Bishop Longland (an upstanding churchman) highly recommended Robert King as abbot of Thame after his good regime at Brewern. While King managed to improve conditions at Thame, his former abbey degenerated without his strong leadership.[55] The abbots were not all gems, of course. William Rugg, who replaced Capon as abbot of St Bennet's Hulme (26 April 1530) was denounced in a visitation report of 14 July 1532 for the considerable debt the house had fallen into and for the degeneration of its material conditions. There were financial difficulties, the members showed 'considerable irregularity and laxity of discipline' and Rugg was himself of 'questionable conduct'.[56] Capon, as abbot of Hyde (28 January 1529/30) was counted among the 'absolutely unscrupulous turncoats and timeservers' who had been placed merely to 'prepare a swift end.'[57]

As can be seen in tables five to seven, the vast majority of the future bishops held some office in the service of the church as a corporate body. As chancellors, they were responsible for the consistory courts and served as the bishop's deputy for 'contentious jurisdictions' or temporal matters. As vicar-generals (the chancellor's spiritual equivalent) they performed duties where Episcopal rank was not necessary. These were the 'gracious jurisdictions' such as dispensations, collection of Peter's pence and first fruits, elections to heads of monasteries and depravations. Sometimes they were both simultaneously (e.g. John Bell). Richard Sampson was vicar-general to Wolsey at Tournai, serving well above the call of duty.[58] Moreover, they were suffragan-bishops, carrying out the official duties of the bishop which required Episcopal rank, and were cathedral chancellors, nominally responsible for the library and educational functions but, more often, acting as principal secretaries to the dean and chapter.

The most common office, and the most advantageous in terms of administrative training was the self-explanatory post of treasurer. Nine Henricians had held this post, including Fisher at St Paul's and Blythe at Salisbury. Robert Vaughan made his reputation as 'a most publick-spirited man' for his great liberality as treasurer of St Paul's. He even built a house there for his successors! Some of the Henricians had been precentors (in control of choir services and acting as the bishop's lieutenant in cathedral matters)[59] and some were chaplains to the great and the good (conducting religious services in their private places of worship and acting as confessors). Stokesley owes much to Richard Fox's patronage in this regard and his good service brought him to the notice of the king.[60] Other such personal duties were performed equally diligently by Warham, as bishop Alcock's proctor (handling his legal matters), by Edward Fox, as Wolsey's private secretary and by Sherborne as cardinal Morton's private secretary. Moreover, the future Henricians had been advocates and advisors, provosts and proctors, wardens and masters.

As stated above, it is a long-established fact that men found favour and advancement in Tudor England by providing good service. Clerics who offered it were promoted to better benefices. Of course, ecclesiastical service was important and, combined with a good civil service record there was no limit to how high a cleric could climb. That said, and considering the ink spilled in criticism, it is interesting that the actual involvement of the future bishops in the temporal kingdom was so limited. At least twelve of them, one in five, performed no specific function in the king's service at all. There is no evidence that they sat on commissions, were chaplains or councillors of any type.

At some unrecorded point, no doubt, the king or some ranking minister spoke to them or was made aware of their virtues. These non-servants might have been asked to opine on some issue of local relevance or might have performed some ordinary and temporary religious function undeserving of wider comment. Lest we conclude that royal service was of no importance it should be noted that most of them were initially nominated to the poorest sees (e.g. Audley to Rochester, Owain to St Asaph, Penny to Bangor), with only Stanley initially promoted to a major see (Ely) and only two of them ever subsequently promoted to wealthier sees (Audley to Salisbury and Penny to Carlisle). It was possible to achieve

Episcopal promotion having rendered no appreciable civil service, but it was unlikely that this would result in any form of lasting impression or higher promotions.[61]

That the bishops served both God and the king is plain. That they served both equally well seems clear. But was this their only qualification for Episcopal promotion? Recall that the king wanted 'some other great qualities (as profound learning)'[62] An examination of their educations and intellectual pursuits shows that the Henricians were also surprisingly multi-talented.

* * *

Historical orthodoxy tells us that the Henricians were primarily lawyers. Many were, and those who were not, at least had extensive legal experience. Should this be held against them? Did legal skills not benefit the church? Recall that contemporary evidence of an 'Episcopal ideal' does not itself disparage legal training.[63] It is clear, therefore, that education (learning, knowledge, wisdom) was key to the Episcopal ideal, and what type less so. Oddly, however, this practical view was largely ignored by many kings of the day other than Henry VIII. In terms of degrees earned, intellectual pursuits undertaken and services rendered to the schools, in order to aspire to the highest clerical positions in England a prospective bishop had to have a university education, wider intellectual interests and experience in academic administration.[64]

Indeed, rare was the English bishop without a university degree. In fact, as early as the eleventh century, a man with a good university education and good academic service record was at least as likely to succeed as was a monastic head, magnate or royal servant. By the mid-fourteenth century education had over-taken all other factors in importance.[65] For example, while only half of Henry III's bishops had some university education[66], at least seventy per cent of Edward III's had traceable university careers. In the pre-Tudor fifteenth century, ninety-two percent of the bishops left traceable academic records, of which seventy had earned degrees. Most had pursued either foreign degrees or additional intellectual credentials as well.[67] Henry VII made forty-three appointments (three to Italians) of which forty (about ninety-percent) had university degrees.[68] Of the Henricians almost ninety-five percent had a traceable university education, with about sixty proceeding to the higher degrees. The Henricians are even more noteworthy when placed beside their continental brethren.

Scholars of early modern France, like Baumgartner, Edelstein or Knecht, have looked at Francis I's bishops and found their educational achievements wanting. A total of some twenty-seven so-called 'humanists' had been created bishops and, while the king may have trumpeted this

achievement, it rather indicates his lack of respect for scholars.[69] At least the
emperor showed somewhat more respect in his Spanish territories.[70] In Castile,
for example, only forty-four percent of the bishops had no traceable university
records.[71] Unfortunately, the Scottish kings followed the French rather than
the Spanish model as the extant records indicate only fifteen of fifty-seven
had traceable educations. Of these, only George Crichton, bishop of Dunkeld,
had undoubtedly earned a degree.[72] Even on the home ground of the
Renaissance, where one might expect a combination of learning and spiritual
virtue, the results disappoint.

 Of the 102 men who held all the bishoprics in papal Italy, thirteen left no
educational record and fifteen left evidence of only a so-called 'courtly'
education, meaning that they had some limited training in the 'military arts,
music and dance'.[73] The Florentines were only marginally 'well-educated'[74],
and education played little role in Venice.[75] Moreover, only papal Italy and
Henrician England even took note of the type of education. Hallman found the
evidence only partially detailed, however, and too sketchy to allow minute
distinctions to be drawn between traditional scholastic philosophy and the
newer disciplines. For the Henricians, however, more detailed analysis is
possible.

 The raw statistics are these: twenty-four lawyers (including Campeggio),
thirty-five divines (including de'Athequa), six generalists and four with no
traceable record. As shown, such details hide the fact that legal training
dominated the pre-1530 period while theology dominated the post-1530 period
(with honours equal in the transitional 1520s). Events, of course, had a very
real impact on the composition of the bench and, as shown, the inverse is also
quite true. What other conclusions can be drawn out of these details? Well,
besides what Henry VIII inherited in 1509 and the obvious need for divines in
the 1530s, it seems clear that the type of education a man had did not in any
obvious way sway the king's nominations. But, just as not every dean became a
bishop, for every divine or jurist who did, a hundred men with equivalent
degrees did not. Why?

 One answer is early recruitment. Being recognised as talented at an early age
is one thing the Henricians share. Wolsey's reputation as a 'boy bachelor' at
least suggests just this kind of notice.[76] Pre-university education is a good
indication of such notice, be it through grammar schools, monastic institutions
or private households. Twelve had grammar school training – seven at Eton
(e.g. Aldrich, Atwater and West), four at Winchester School (e.g. Richard Fox
and Warham), and Heath at St Anthony's School in London. Those with early
monastic training include Barlow, Bird and Capon. Smith, Oldham, Stanley
and Audley were initially educated in private households (Audley at home, the
others in the Stanley household under the direction of Lady Margaret[77]). Early
education aside, all but two (Owain and Salley) of the native born Henricians
can be placed at either Oxford or Cambridge or both (nineteen/twenty-three/

twenty[78]) but it is important to note that many of them pursued foreign credentials as well.

Bainbridge, Booth, Clerk, Edward Lee and Nix went to Bologna.[79] Bainbridge, Knight and Nix went to Ferrara. Richard Fox and Edward Lee attended Louvain.[80] Richard Fox, Sampson and Stanley went to Paris. Stokesley and Tunstal (who also attended Padua) studied at Rome.[81] So, almost all Henry's bishops were educated, almost all had degrees, quite a few had higher degrees and many of their talents were recognised early. Still, many well-educated clergymen did not achieve equal status. What else set them apart were their wider interests.

Simple put, they were an impressive group of intellectuals who could call upon many talents. Stokesley, for example, had impressed no less than Erasmus himself with his philosophy and theology skills[82], and many attested his remarkable linguistic abilities.[83] Edward Fox was a political theorist of no small beer.[84] Fitzjames had interests in astrology[85], Gardiner loved music and drama, as did Sampson[86], both Foxes, Longland and Tunstal were humanists of the highest order, while Barlow was a writer and 'learned wit'.[87] Latimer and Fisher were noted theologians, Tunstal was a mathematician and bibliophile and Ruthal, like Wolsey, was a dedicated patron of the arts.[88] Lacey Baldwin Smith showed that some of them were also dedicated Erasmians, while others, like Edward Lee, were not afraid to challenge the great scholar's ideas. Even as they sought their individual interests, common interests were also pursued. The infamous White Horse Tavern group included Thirlby, Gardiner, Heath, Skip, Edward Fox and Shaxton[89] (not all radical divines), while the men of Doctor's Commons included Bonner, Gardiner, Roland Lee, Clerk, Richard Veysey, Bell, Tunstal, Sampson, Bulkeley and Stokesley (not all lawyers).[90] But there were other ways still in which the future bishops distinguished themselves from their brethren.

Twenty had earned academic distinction as 'fellows' of the colleges[91], while others had been gifted researchers[92] and brilliant teachers.[93] Obviously there were many ways to serve the colleges and gain administrative experience and intellectual prestige. The office of provost, for instance, served the interests of Aldrich, Bainbridge, Day[94] and Edward Fox quite well, while Fitzjames and Rawlins, as wardens at Merton College, became involved in both spiritual and temporal matters.[95] What better pastoral training ground than the mastership of a student hall (e.g. Aldrich, Blythe and Day) or the office of college principal (e.g. Fitzjames, Richard Fox, Skip, Longland, Stokesley and Wolsey)?[96] Certainly, both teaching and pastoral care were good means of gaining a reputation for prudence but, having the ability to absorb knowledge, effectively teach and supervise did not necessarily make a man ideal for later Episcopal promotion, no matter how well regarded his abilities; much more would have been expected. Thus we find that many of the future bishops had also served as functionaries and officials in university administration, serving their schools and, undoubtedly, also their own future interests.

Those with financial talents, like Atwater, Wolsey and Stokesley, served as bursars.[97] For those who had proven themselves in the junior posts, a university proctorship moved them into the higher rankings. As such, Fisher, Mayew, Goodrich, Stokesley and others, supervised the various financial officers, security forces and practically all other related duties (including the arrangement of funerals!)[98] This was good training indeed for responsible senior pastoral positions and these men attracted attention from outside academia because of it.[99] Although the highest administrative posts, chancellor, president and their deputies, were most often held by men who were already bishops, this was not always the case. Mayew (later chancellor of Oxford) had been president of Magdalen College prior to his nomination to Hereford.[100] Stokesley was acting-president of Magdalen in 1510, Ruthal was a chancellor before he was a bishop, and Atwater, Fisher and Day had all been vice-chancellors.[101] All told, over forty Henricians had held some office or other in academia: a strong indication of solid administrative training.

***

There is another way in which the Henricians are unique in early modern Europe. Their achieved status (as bishops) was not the result of their ascribed status. This means that their social positions at birth and, indeed, their regional origins, did not significantly affect their chances of success in the church. In fact, the Henricians are little more than a social microcosm of contemporary England. Though the men themselves had little say in the matter, it is still interesting that the king paid so little attention to what was, on the continent and in Scotland, the overriding factor.[102] However one defines social rank[103] we have reliable information on most of the bishops, so placing them is not as difficult or odious a task as it might seem.[104] It is, in fact, quite rewarding.

Henry VIII (like his father) nominated no blood relatives[105] while Francis I nominated no less than nine princes of the royal blood (taking twenty-three appointments between them!) Edelstein could do little more than conclude that in early modern France the most lucrative sees were the preserve of the royal family.[106] In Scotland, both James IV and James V nominated not only their close relatives but also their illegitimate sons. The former went so far as to nominate Alexander Stewart to the archiepiscopal see of St Andrew's in 1502 when the boy was only nine years old to replace the king's late brother, the Duke of Ross.[107] Such appointments, excused as political gifts, did have the tangible benefit of easing the strain of greedy relatives on the royal treasury. The figures for the non-royal nobility are equally telling.

For reasons of political necessity, Henry VIII had three noble bishops on his Episcopal bench. All had been appointed in the 1520s and all were Italians (Campeggio, de'Ghinucci and de'Medici). They were all of 'patrician' families[108] but were, in fact, bishops in name only, rarely attending to diocesan business. The king had inherited two bishops of noble birth, Stanley and Audley, but these five accounted for less than eight percent of the total.[109] This is impressive when compared to Edward III's fifteen of eighty-five nominations[110] or to the pre-Tudor fifteenth century's seventeen of seventy-nine nominations.[111] Then, of course, Episcopal promotion was an inexpensive and beneficial way to ensure noble support. Henry VIII's record is even more impressive when compared to his European counterparts.

Sixty-eight percent of Francis I's promotions went to noblemen[112] and almost all promotions in the Republic of Venice went to 'trustworthy subjects' (i.e. patricians and relatives of the members of the Council).[113] In papal Italy too, prior to the 1540s (when Trent focused attention on the issue) between thirty and forty percent of promotions went to nobles.[114] In Scotland, at least thirteen of fifty appointments went to noblemen[115] and, while Catalonia might have reflected an English appreciation of factors other than social status[116], the Castilian Episcopate (where thirty percent of Charles V's nominations went to noblemen) is more reflective of the European norm.[117]

Let us consider the nomination of non-noble gentlemen. In England there was a rather artificial two-tier rank of 'esquires' and 'gentlemen'[118], but only three Henricians were of the upper tier, one Italian (de'Gigli), Booth and Cranmer.[119] Twenty-five others are identifiably 'gentleman' by birth.[120] Their appointments were spread evenly throughout the reign (e.g. eight were inherited[121]) and their names are among the most noted, Holgate[122], Skevington, Longland[123], Goodrich and Stokesley[124] included. Perhaps Tunstal can be placed into this lower tier as the eldest (but illegitimate) son of a discredited nobleman[125] and Edward Lee, whose grandfather had been a knight, one-time sheriff of Kent and twice Lord Mayor of London.[126] It is a difficult category to be sure and I have included Rugg as a man from an 'established family', Bainbridge, a man from 'an aunciant house'[127], and Kitchen, a man of a 'fairly well-to-do' family.[128] Others would include the son of the a 'prosperous cloth-maker' of the affluent town of Bury St Edmunds, Stephen Gardiner[129], while others still might include Bulkeley and Owain for reasons of their own.[130] Whatever the criteria used, the comparison with other Episcopal benches makes interesting reading.

In fifteenth century England, only twenty-five percent of the bishops can be identified as non-noble.[131] Francis I promoted only six gentlemen, all of which were noted humanists and intellectuals, but all of whom had also been royal chaplains just prior to new postings (it must be said to insignificant sees).[132] In papal Italy an average thirty-four percent of bishoprics were held by members of the gentry.[133] This figure must be treated cautiously as we do not know the relationship between these men and the Italian ruling classes. In Castile, the emperor promoted forty-eight of his 100 bishops from the non-noble classes[134] but in contemporary Scotland, only nine of fifty-three appointments were to men of the gentry (while twenty-five others had obscure origins).

Henry VIII even nominated men of the lowest social rankings. From the yeomanry[135] he nominated thirty-two men (or almost fifty percent), including the saintly Fisher,[136] the less than saintly Wolsey[137] and several men who fall somewhere between these two in terms of both fame and reputation, like Sherborne,[138] West and Bush.[139] Finally, there were even three bishops of the humblest origins. Adriano de'Castellesi, the Italian bishop of Bath and Wells and younger son of an obscure Corneto man,[140] Knight, and Latimer (who made a positive virtue of his father's humble condition!)[141]

What this tells us, by virtue of comparison, is that the Henrician bench stands out as an example of effective social mobility. Francis I's bench was dominated by nobles, as, of the forty-four bishops with obscure origins it seems highly unlikely that any were of the lower classes. In the Iberian peninsula, where seventeen of Charles V's Castilian bishops had unidentifiable origins, we can perhaps be more generous.[142] In Scotland, only two men are identified as of 'common' social origin – Reid, bishop of Orkney and Elphinstone, bishop of Aberdeen.[143] Even England's healthy foreign population (which cut across the social spectrum) could be said to have representation in the six foreign bishops.[144] Certainly, no other king at the time had so many foreigners on his bench (discussed below).

As they reflected the social structure of England so too did they represent their society in terms of regional origin. The south-eastern regions were dominant in terms of wealth and population, while political supremacy was heavily weighted in favour of the south and the midlands.[145] Unsurprisingly, most of the Henricians were born in these areas. These raw statistics, however, hide other interesting facts. The king inherited a fairly representative bench (two foreigners, two regionally obscure bishops, four southerners, four midlanders, five northerners and two Welshmen), which only marginally over-represented the south. A generation later the overwhelming majority of his nominations went to midlanders, with the Welsh marches (proportionately) well represented. This over-represents neither the most populated nor the richest regions. Also hidden is the fact that there is no significant correlation between the bishops' regional origins and their first Episcopal appointments. This indicates little or no familial influence unlike the Italian and Scottish models.

Yes, thirteen of the bishops were born in their home diocese or at least very near to it (e.g. Bell, a Worcestershire man, became bishop of Worcester, Vaughan, Owain and Bulkeley were all Welsh[146]) but eleven were nominated to sees practically on the opposite side of the country (e.g. Roland Lee, a Northumberland man to Coventry and Lichfield, Oldham, a Lancastrian, to Exeter). Except for those obscure six, the other Henricians neither moved so far, nor were so close to be statistically noteworthy. If nothing else, at least they conform to the patterns of geographical mobility established by social historians[147] and they also compare surprisingly well to other models.

For instance, in his study of the pre-Tudor fifteenth century, Rosenthal discovered that almost a third of the bishops were northerners and, more notably, all of them served southern and midland sees, a trend only evening out under Henry VII.[148] For all of the pluralism and absenteeism of the Italian sees, regionalism is evident. Venetian sees (geographically) went exclusively to natives of the Republic with only the lesser-valued mainland sees ever going to 'foreign' Italians.[149] This was the same situation in Florence, Milan and Genoa[150], and in the Iberian territories, France and Scotland as well.[151] Such factors as social class and regional origin reinforce the proposition that promotion to the Henrician bench was based on talent, a high educational standard, good ecclesiastical service and service to the crown, seemingly unlike the benches of pre-Henrician England or contemporary Europe.

\* \* \*

So, who were Henry VIII's bishops? They were men of all social rankings and diverse geographical origins. The overwhelming majority were university educated, attending the best schools of the day. Most had performed, with distinction, university and college offices. Their administrative skills were obvious, in war and in peacetime, at court or in the diocese. Their record of residence is quite good and their morality is impressive. They had not become bishops through family connections or social status but through early-recognised ambition and a variety of talents. They matched the ideal and met the requirements that bishops of the early modern period were to meet. We should, of course, not deny their weaknesses. Ruthal was greedy, Bonner was arrogant and Wolsey did accumulate offices and titles. All told, however, Henry's bishops must be considered a very conscientious and talented group of men who, in the end, must be held worthy of the high office they had attained and of further research.

## Notes

1. George E. Corrie (ed.), *Sermons by Hugh Latimer, Sometime Bishop of Worcester, Martyr, 1555* (Cambridge, 1845), p.67.
2. James Sawtry, *The defence of the Marriage of Priests, against Steven Gardiner, Bishop of Winchester, William Repps, Bishop of Norwich, and against all of the bishops and priests of that false popish sect* (Antwerp, 1541), as quoted in J.A. Muller, *Stephen Gardiner and the Tudor Reaction* (New York, 1970 edn), p.125.
3. William Turner, *The huntyng and fyndyng out of the Romyshe foxe* ... (Basle, 1543), as quoted in Muller, p.126.
4. E.g., John Skelton, *The Complete English Poems*, ed. by J. Scattergood (London, 1978), p.291.
5. Anon, *The Bishops Manifest* ... (London, 1641), sigs. A2, A4.

6.   e.g. R.L. Storey, *The Reign of Henry VII* (London, 1968), pp.167-9; Susan Doran and Christopher Durston, *Princes, Pastors and People* (London, 1991), pp.124-5.

7.   E.g. Lacey Baldwin Smith, *Tudor Prelates and Politics* (Princeton, 1953), pp.5-6.

8.   E.g. D. MacCulloch, *Thomas Cranmer: A Life* (New Haven, 1994); M. Bowker, *The Henrician Reformation: The diocese of Lincoln under Bishop John Longland, 1521-1547* (Cambridge, 1981); M.J. Kelly, 'Canterbury Jurisdiction and Influence during the Episcopate of William Warham, 1503-1532' (unpublished Ph.D. thesis, University of Cambridge, 1963) and G.M.V Alexander, 'The Life and Career of Edmund Bonner Bishop of London until his Deprivation in 1549' (unpublished Ph.D. thesis, University of London, 1960).

9.   Stephen Thompson, 'The Pastoral Work of the English and Welsh Bishops 1500-58' (unpublished Ph.D. thesis, University of Oxford, 1984).

10.  H. Ellis (ed.), *Original Letters illustrative of English History* (11 vols., in 3 series, London, 1824, 1827, 1846), 3rd. series, i, p.184. D. Bush, 'Tudor Humanism and Henry VIII', *University of Toronto Quarterly* vii (1937), pp.162-7.

11.  See, A.A. Chibi, '"*Had I but served God with half the zeal . . .*": The Career Path of the men who became Henry VIII's Bishops', in *Reformation* 3 (1998), pp.75-136.

12.  Anon, 'A Supplication to our moste Sovereigne Lorde Kyng Henry the Eight' (1544), *The Harleian Miscellany* ix (London, 1812), pp.451-66 (at pp.456-7).

13.  F. Bacon, *The History of the Reign of Henry the Seventh*, ed. by F.J. Levy (New York, 1972 edn), pp.50-4; D. Hume, *History of England* (4 vols., Philadelphia, 1821-2), ii, pp.203, 607.

14.  Richard Mackenny, *Sixteenth Century Europe: Expansion and Conflict* (Basingstoke, 1993), p.79.

15.  Margaret MacCurtain, *Tudor and Stuart Ireland* (Dublin, 1972), pp.22-5.

16.  R.J. Knecht, 'The Concordat of 1516: A Reassessment', in Henry J. Cohn (ed.), *Government in Reformation Europe, 1520-1560* (London, 1971), pp.91-112 (at p.93).

17.  Bernard M.G. Reardon, *Religious Thought in the Reformation* (London, 1981), p.74.

18.  Frederic J. Baumgartner, *Change and Continuity in the French Episcopate: The Bishops and the Wars of Religion, 1547-1610* (Durham, 1986), p.12.

19.  For the Council of Trent, see Keith Randell, *The Catholic and Counter Reformations* (London, 1990), pp.39-67; H.G. Koenigsberger, G.L. Mosse and G.Q. Bowler, *Europe in the Sixteenth Century* (London, 1989 2nd edn.), pp.217-22.

20.  PRO. SP, 1/113, fol. 8v.

21.  Thompson, pp.21-2. This patronage includes ecclesiastical offices from curates to canons and hospital masterships as well as such temporal offices as estate managers, household officers and game wardens.

22.  Anon, 'Paul Bush, The Last Rector of Edington and First Bishop of Bristol, 1490-1558', *Wiltshire Notes and Queries* iv (September 1902), pp.97-107 (at p.98).

23.  *LP*, xiii/i, 1064.

24.  G. Burnet, *The History of the Reformation of the Church of England*, ed. by Nicholas Pocock (7 vols., Oxford, 1865), iv, p.130.

25.  Merrill F. Sherr, 'Bishop Bonner: A Quasi Erasmian', *Historical Magazine of the Protestant Episcopal Church* xliv (1974), pp.359-66 (at p.359). Bonner is also the subject of Sherr's doctoral thesis, 'Bishop Bonner: Bulwark Against Heresy' (unpublished Ph.D. thesis, New York University, 1969).

26.  Dickens, pp.5-10.

27. James Gairdner (ed.), *Letters and Papers Illustrative of the Reigns of Richard III and Henry VII* (2 vols., London, 1861, 1863), i, xxix (pp.246-7); ii, xxx (p.169). The forgery story has been modified as it is clear that he had been canonically provided, the bull of provision is extant though irregular. Bishops de'Castellesi, Smith and Fox and Henry VII himself all defended Sherborne's good name.

28. Steer, pp.3-4; Emden, *Oxford*, iii, p.1686.

29. Stephens, p.184.

30. Gwyn, pp.2-3.

31. To be fair, Day was probably not often resident at All Hallows the Great, London. See, Stephens, p.222; SRO, EP I/52/7, fol. 112.

32. Audley, Bainbridge, Mayew, Nix, Oldham, Smith, Stanley, and Warham.

33. Rosenthal, p.23.

34. Mumford, pp.63*ff.*

35. William Dodsworth, *An Historical Account of the Episcopal See, and Cathedral Church of Salisbury* (Salisbury, 1814), pp.54-7.

36. John A.F. Thomson, *The Early Tudor Church & Society 1485-1529* (London, 1993), pp.220-1.

37. *Ibid*, pp.188*ff*; G.W.O. Woodward, *Dissolution of the Monasteries* (Blandford, 1969 edn), pp.16*ff*; Doran and Durstan, pp.162*ff.*

38. Rosenthal, p.25.

39. *LP*, vii, 257.

40. Shirley, pp.12-9; J.E. Cox (ed.), *Miscellaneous Writings and Letters of Thomas Cranmer* (2 vols., Cambridge, 1846), ii, pp.292-3.

41. *LP*, i/i (Addenda), 1013, 1225.

42. Geoffrey Baskerville, *English Monks and the Suppression of the Monasteries* (London, 1937, 1965 edn), pp.77-8; A. Jessopp (ed.), *Visitations of the Diocese of Norwich, A D 1492-1532* (London, 1888), p.241.

43. William Page (ed.), *VHC: A History of Norfolk* (2 vols., London, 1901, 1906), ii, p.375; Jessopp, pp.242-3; *LP*, iv/iii, 4229 (9), 4755.

44. Stephens, p.247; P.H. Ditchfield and William Page (eds), *VHC: A History of Bershire* (4 vols., London, 1907-24), ii, p.83.

45. SRO, EP I/52/7, fols. 31-3; BL, Cottonian MSS Cleopatra E iv, fol. 121.

46. Page, ii, p.335

47. *Ibid*, i, p.335.

48. *LP*, xiii/ii, 225; Baskerville, pp.232-3, 240.

49. *LP*, xii, 842.

50. *Ibid*, xiii/i, 646 (2); xv, 81; J.W. Willis-Bund and William Page (eds), *VHC: A History of Worcester* (4 vols., London, 1901-24), ii, pp.110-1.

51. Steer, p.4; Stephens, p.185.

52. Mumford, pp.81-83.

53. *LP*, ix, 457.

54. William Page (ed.), *VHC: A History of Surrey* (4 vols., London, 1902-12), ii, p.87.

55. Bowker, p.58.

56. Page, *Norfolk*, ii, p.335; *LP*, x, 364 (at p.143).

57. H.A. Doubleday and William Page (eds), *VHC: A History of Hampshire* (5 vols., Westminster, 1900-12), ii, pp.120-1.

58. Thomas F. Mayer, 'On the road to 1534: the occupation of Tournai and Henry VIII's theory of sovereignty', in Dale Hoak (ed.), *Tudor Political Culture* (Cambridge, 1995), pp.11-30 (at pp.24-7); A.A. Chibi, 'Richard Sampson, His "Oratio, " and Henry VIII's Royal Supremacy', *Journal of Church and State* 39:3 (Summer 1997),

pp.543-60 (at pp.545-6).

59. Rosenthal, p.29.
60. Allen and Allen, pp.120, 161, 163.
61. For their actual office-holding refer to the appendix.
62. Ellis, iii/i, p.184.
63. See, Doran and Durston, pp.124*ff*; Thomson, *Tudor Church*, pp.46*ff*; and Gustav Constant, 'Les Evêques Henriciens sous Henri VIII', *Revue Des Questions Historiques* xii (1912), pp.384-425.
64. See, A.A. Chibi, 'The Intellectual and Academic Training of the Henrician Episcopacy', in *Archiv für Reformationsgeschichte* 91 (2000), pp.354-72.
65. M.D. Knowles, 'The English Bishops, 1070-1532', in J.A. Watt, J.B. Morrall and F.X. Martin (eds), *Medieval Studies Presented to Aubrey Geynn, S. J.* (Dublin, 1961), pp.283-96 (at pp.289-90).
66. J.R.L. Highfield, 'The English Hierarchy in the Reign of Edward III', *Transactions of the Royal Historical Society*, 5th series, vol.vi (1956), pp.115-38 (at pp.125-6, 130).
67. Rosenthal, pp.12*ff*.
68. Thomson, pp.44-6.
69. Knecht, p.97; Michel Peronnet, *Les évêques de l'ancienne France* (2 vols., Paris, 1978), i, pp.487*ff*; Baumgartner, p.33.
70. Elliot, p.103.
71. Rawlings, p.62.
72. Dowden, p.87. Crichton was an M.A. (St Andrew's, 1479) but, as keeper of the Privy Seal, his degree might have been irrelevant.
73. Hallman, p.13.
74. Brucker, p.183.
75. Paolo Prodi, 'The structure and organization of the church in Renaissance Venice: suggestions for research', in J.R. Hale (ed.), *Renaissance Venice* (London, 1973), pp.409-30 (at p.418); Oliver Logan, *Culture and Society in Venice, 1470-1790: The Renaissance and its Heritage* (London, 1972), pp.31-3.
76. G. Cavendish, 'The Negotiations of Thomas Wolsey, the Great Cardinal of England. . .', *Harleian Miscellany* v (1810), pp.123-178 (at pp.123-4); P. Gwyn, *The King's Cardinal: The Rise and Fall of Thomas Wolsey* (London, 1990), pp.1-2.
77. M.K. Jones and M.G. Underwood, *The King's Mother Lady Margaret Beaufort, Countess of Richmond and Derby* (Cambridge, 1992), pp.105, 111, 152; A.A. Mumford, *Hugh Oldham* (London, 1936), pp.32-3. Hibbert, ii, p.3; Malcolm G. Underwood, 'Politics and Piety in the Household of Lady Magaret Beaufort', *Journal of Ecclesiastical History* xxxviii:i (January 1987), pp.39-52 (at pp.45-6); Thomson, *Tudor Church*, p.54.
78. Cardinal, p.15.
79. For details see, R.J. Mitchell, 'English Law Students at Bologna in the Fifteenth-Century', *English Historical Review* li:ccii (April 1936), pp.270-87.
80. For details see, E. Rummel, *Erasmus and his Catholic Critics 1515-1522* (Nieuhoop, 1989), p.95; R.J. Mitchell, 'English Students at Ferrara in the XV Century', *Italian Studies* i:ii, (1937), pp.75-82.
81. Charles Sturge, *Cuthbert Tunstal: Churchman, Scholar, Statesman, Administrator* (London, 1938), pp.9-16; A.A. Chibi, *Henry VIII's Conservative Scholar: Bishop John Stokesley and the Divorce, Royal Supremacy and Doctrinal Reform* (Bern, 1997), p.12; P.S. and H.M. Allen (eds), *Letters of Richard Fox: 1486-1527* (Oxford,

1929), p.161; Robert Coogan, *Erasmus, Lee and the Correction of the Vulgate: The Shaking of the Foundations* (Geneva, 1992), p.1; R. Rex, *The Theology of John Fisher* (Cambridge, 1991), p.51.

82.  *Complete Works of Erasmus*, viii, p.261 (no.1219).

83.  Denys Hay, 'The Life of Polydore Vergil of Urbino', *Journal of the Warburg and Courtauld Institutes* xii (1949), pp.132-51 (at p.150); Denys Hay (ed. and trans.), *The Anglica historia of Polydore Vergil, A D 1485-1537* (London, 1950), p.xi (n. 1); Richard Croke, *Orationes Ricardi Croci Duae* ([London?], 1520), sig. C.4r; Robert Wakefield, *Oratio de laudibus et utilitate trium linguarum* (London, n.d.), sig. Cii; Rex, p.58; G. Lloyd Jones, *The discovery of Hebrew in Tudor England: a third language* (Manchester, 1983), pp.186-7; Richard Pace, *De fructu qui ex doctrina percipitur liber* (Basil, 1517), p.101; *idem, The Benefit of a Liberal Education*, ed. and trans. by Frank Manley and Richard S. Sylvester (New York, 1967), p.127. See also, Allen and Allen, p.161; Francis Aidan Gasquet, *The Eve of the Reformation* (London, 1913), pp.31-2.

84.  G.D. Nicholson, 'The Nature and Function of Historical Argument in the Henrician Reformation' (unpublished Ph.D. dissertation, University of Cambridge, 1977), p.116; *LP*, v, 84.

85.  Damian R. Leader, *A History of the University of Cambridge* (2 vols., Cambridge, 1988), i, p.149.

86.  Glyn Redworth, *In Defence of the Church Catholic: The Life of Stephen Gardiner* (Oxford, 1990), p.10. For more general details on Sampson's career, see BL, Lansdowne 980, fols. 131b, 134-5.

87.  SRO, EP I/52/7, fol. 86.

88.  The intellectual interests of some of the bishops have been examined by Scarisbrick and Masek (as above). Also see, F. Heal, 'The Bishops of Ely and their Diocese during the Reformation' (unpublished Ph.D. thesis, University of Cambridge, 1971); Roger Bowers, 'The cultivation and promotion of music in the household and orbit of Thomas Wolsey', in S.J. Gunn and P.G. Lindley (eds), *Cardinal Wolsey: Church, state and art* (Cambridge, 1991), pp.178-218; Wyman H. Herendeen and Kenneth R. Bartlett, 'The Library of Cuthbert Tunstall, Bishop of Durham', *Bibliographical Society of America Papers* lxxxv (September 1991), pp.235-96.

89.  Smith, pp.25-36; Shirley, p.4.

90.  Smith, pp.42*ff*; Pretor W. Chandler, 'Doctor's Commons', *London Topographical Record* xv (1931), pp.4-20 (at pp.4-5); Eliza J. Davies, 'Doctor's Common, Its Title and Topography', *London Topographical Record* xv (1931), pp.36-50 (at p.37). Also, see G.D. Squibb, *Doctor's Common: A History of the College of Advocates and Doctors of Law* (Oxford, 1977) and Bell C. Coote, *Sketches of the Lives and Characters of Eminent English Civilians* (London, 1804), pp.9-11.

91.  Thomson, *Tudor Church*, p.25.

92.  Cranmer had been common reader in divinity at Buckingham (Magdalene) and reader in divinity at Jesus when Wolsey invited him to join Cardinal College. See Maria Dowling, 'Cranmer as Humanist Reformer', in Paul Ayris and David Selwyn (eds), *Thomas Cranmer: Churchman and Scholar* (Woodbridge, 1993), pp.89-114.

93.  Ridley, *Cranmer*, p.22; Rex, p.13; Muller, *Gardiner*, pp.9-10; Smith, p.27*ff*; Chibi, *Stokesley*, p.13. A survey of the educational details of these men can be found readily enough in John and J.A. Venn, *Alumni Cantabrigiensis: Part One to 1750* (4 vols., Cambridge, 1922-7) and Joseph Foster, *Alumni Oxonienses: 1500-1714* (4 vols., Oxford, 1891).

94.  W.R.W. Stephens, *Memorials of the South Saxon See and Cathedral Church of*

*Chichester* (London, 1876), p.222.

95. SRO, EP I/52/7, fols. 109-10. 'He [Fitzjames] showed himself most worthy of it [the wardenship] by his admirable way of Government which he exercised'.

96. Alfred B. Emden, 'Oxford Academical Halls in the Later Middle Ages' in *idem* (ed.), *Medieval Learning and Literature: Essays Presented to Richard William Hunt* (Oxford, 1976), pp.353-65 (at p.360); A.B. Cobban, 'Colleges and Halls, 1380-1500', in J.I. Catto and Ralph Evans (eds), *The History of the University of Oxford* (3 vols., Oxford, 1992), ii, pp.632.

97. For Wolsey, see T.W. Cameron, 'The Early Life of Thomas Wolsey', *EHR* iii (1888), pp.458-77 (at p.464); A.F. Pollard, *Wolsey* (London, 1929), p.12.

98. C R Thompson, p.5; J.K. McConica, 'The Collegiate University', in J.K. McConica (ed.), *The History of the University of Oxford* (3 vols., Oxford, 1986), iii, pp.96, 104, 164.

99. Anthony Wood, *Athenae Oxonienses: An Exact History of All the Writers and Bishops* (4 vols., London, 1721), ii, p.673.

100. Emden, *Oxford*, i, pp.73-4.

101. Anthony Wood, *Athenae Oxonienses: An Exact History of All the Writers and Bishops*, ed. by P. Bliss (6 vols., London, 1813 edn), ii, p.720.

102. See A.A. Chibi, 'The Social and Regional Origins of the Henrician Episcopal Bench', in *The Sixteenth Century Journal* xxix:4 (Winter 1998), pp.955-73.

103. See, for instance, Elton's interpretation of chapter sixteen of Sir Thomas Smith's *De Republica Anglorum* (1583) where a division of 'gentlemen, citizens or burgesses, yeoman artificers and labourers' was made, or Joyce Youings' stressing of a social structure of nobles, gentlemen, yeoman and commons. Joyce Youings, *Sixteenth-Century England* (London, 1991 edn), pp.110*ff*; G.R. Elton, *England Under the Tudors* (London, 1991, 3rd edn), pp.251*ff*;

104. Useful reference books include A.B. Emden (ed.), *Biographical Register of the University of Cambridge to 1500* (3 vols., Cambridge, 1963); *idem* (ed.), *Biographical Register of the University of Oxford to 1500* (3 vols., Oxford, 1957-59); *The Dictionary of National Biography* (London, 1885-1901); Thomas Fuller, *The Worthies of England*, ed. by John Freeman (London, 1952 edn.); F. Godwin, *A Catalogue of the Bishops of England* (London, 1601).

105. W.A. Pantin, *The English Church in the Fourteenth century* (Cambridge, 1955), p.22.

106. Marilyn Manera Edelstein, 'The Social Origins of the Episcopacy in the Reign of Francis I', *French Historical Studies*, viii (1974), pp.377-92 (at p.380).

107. Ian B. Cowan, *The Scottish Reformation; Church and Society in Sixteenth Century Scotland* (London, 1982), p.51; M. Mahoney, 'The Scottish Hierarchy, 1513-1565', in David McRoberts (ed.), *Essays on the Scottish Reformation 1513-1625* (Glasgow, 1962), pp.39-84 (at pp.41, 46). Stewart blood is found throughout all the Scottish sees accounting for at least nine of 50 appointments in the period. See John Dowden, *The Bishops of Scotland*, ed. by J. Maitland Thomson (Glasgow, 1912).

108. Barbara McClung Hallman, *Italian Cardinals, Reform, and the Church as Property* (Berkeley, 1985), p.12.

109. Thomson, p.49; S Hibbert, *A History of the Foundations in Manchester. . .* (2 vols., Edinburgh and Manchester, 1834-5), i, p.57.

110. J.R.L. Highfield, 'The English Hierarchy in the Reign of Edward III', *Transactions of the Royal Historical Society*, 5th series, vi (1956), pp.115-38 (at pp.120-21).

111. Joel Rosenthal, 'The Training of an Elite Group: English Bishops in the Fifteenth

Century', *Transactions of the American Philosophical Society*, lx:v (1970), pp.5-54 (at p.7).

112. Edelstein, pp.379-81.

113. Prodi, p.418.

114. Hallman, pp.9-11.

115. Cowan, p.49.

116. H. Kamen, *The Phoenix and the Flame: Catalonia and the Counter Reformation* (New Haven, 1993), p.103.

117. H.E. Rawlings, 'The Secularization of Castilian Episcopal Office Under the Habsburgs, c.1516-1700', *JEH* xxxviii:i (January 1987), pp.53-79 (at p.62).

118. A gentleman in England was a man with a recognised position in local society but who was not yet important enough to merit an individual summons to parliament. For details, see Youings, p.115 or John A.F. Thomson, *The Transformation of Medieval England 1370-1529* (London, 1983), p.112.

119. MacCulloch showed that Cranmer's family were of the 'upper reaches of the Nottinghamshire and Lincolnshire gentry' and of a 'very ancient house'. Booth was the younger son of Sir Robert Booth, Lord of Barton and a member of the well-known Lancashire family that already boasted a bishop and two archbishops. See, D. MacCulloch, 'Two Dons in Politics: Thomas Cranmer and Stephen Gardiner, 1503-1533', *HJ* xxxvii:i (1994), pp.1-22 (at pp.1-2); Godwin, p.123; G.W. Marshall (ed.), *The Visitations of the County of Nottingham in the years 1569 and 1614* (London, 1871), pp.70-1; Ridley, pp.13-4; Smith, pp.11-2 and A.T. Bannister (ed.), *Registrum Caroli Bothe, Episcopi Herefordensis AD MDXVI - MDXXXV* (London, 1921), p.i.

120. For how this rank is accounted, see Elton, p.256 and Youings, p.116.

121. William Beresford, *Lichfield* (London, 1890), p.176; Godwin, p.120.

122. A.G. Dickens, *Robert Holgate, Archbishop of York and President of the King's Council of the North* (London, 1955), p.3.

123. Bowker, p.8; Gwenolen E. Wharhirst, 'The Reformation in the Diocese of Lincoln as illustrated by the Life and Work of Bishop Longland, (1521-1547)', *Lincolnshire Architectural and Archaeological Societies Reports and Papers*, i:ii (1937), pp.137-76 (at p.140).

124. A.R. Maddison (ed.), *Lincolnshire Pedigrees* (4 vols., London, 1902-4), ii, pp.414-7; A.A. Chibi, 'Bishop John Stokesley: A Humanist Reformer at the Court of Henry VIII', 2 vols. (unpublished Ph.D. thesis, University of Sheffield, 1993), i, p.10 [Thornton Society, MSS Box 1/2, fol. 25v].

125. Sturge, pp.1-9.

126. For details, see L.B. Smith, pp.11-2; T.F. Shirley, *Thomas Thirlby, Tudor Bishop* (London, 1964), p.1. Smith noted that the pedigree of Edward Lee's father had been traced by Richard H. Manley for *Gentleman's Magazine and Historical Review* [xv:ii (1863), p.337] and that the pedigree of Roland Lee can be found in G. Grazebrook and J.P. Rylands (eds), *The Visitation of Shropshire, 1623* (2 vols., London, 1889), i, pp.189-90.

127. D.S. Chambers, *Cardinal Bainbridge in the Court of Rome 1509-1514* (Oxford, 1965), p.14.

128. Walter Rye (ed.), *The Visitation of Norfolk* (London, 1891), p.229; Godwin, pp.120, 483; E.J. Newell (ed.), *Llandaff* (London, 1902), p.118; W.C. Metcalfe (ed.), *Visitations of Hertfordshire, 1572 and 1634* (London, 1886), p.70.

129. MacCulloch, p.2; G. Scott Thomson, 'Three Suffolk Figures: Thomas Wolsey: Stephen Gardiner: Nicholas Bacon', *Proceedings of the Suffolk Institute of Archaeology*

*and Natural History* xxv (1952), pp.149-63 (at p.156); Redworth, p.8.

130. G. Williams, *Recovery, Reorientation and Reformation Wales c.1415-1642* (Oxford, 1987), pp.135, 303.
131. Rosenthal, p.10.
132. Edelstein, pp.388-9.
133. Hallman, pp.9-11.
134. Rawlings, p.62.
135. This accounting is based on either economic factors [e.g. 40s/year in property] or local recognition as those who employ or those who hold some local responsibility.
136. Brendan Bradshaw, 'Bishop John Fisher, 1469-1535: the man and his work', in B. Bradshaw and E. Duffy (eds), *Humanism, Reform and Reformation: The Career of Bishop John Fisher* (Cambridge, 1989), pp.1-24 (at p.2).
137. Jasper Ridley, *Statesman and Saint* (New York, 1982), p.3. Also see, V.B. Redstone, 'Wulcy of Suffolk', *Proceedings of the Suffolk Institute of Archaeology and Natural History* xxvi (1918), pp.71-89.
138. Francis W. Steer, *Robert Sherburne, Bishop of Chichester: Some Aspects of his Life Reconsidered* (Chichester, 1960), pp.2-3. For more general details of Sherborne's career, see Sussex Records Office, EP I/52/9 (n.f.), Bundels 1-2.
139. Anon, 'Paul Bush', p.98.
140. Hallman, p.12.
141. George E. Corrie (ed.), *The Works of Hugh Latimer* (2 vols., Cambridge, 1844-5), i, p.101.
142. J.H. Elliott, *Imperial Spain, 1469-1716* (Harmondsworth, 1970), p.102.
143 Dowden, p.131.
144. Youings, p.127.
145. Thomson, *Tudor Church*, pp.76-8; G.R. Elton, 'The Body of the Whole Realm: Parliament and Representation in Medieval and Tudor England', in G.R. Elton (ed.), *Studies in Tudor and Stuart Politics and Government (Papers and Reviews 1946-1972)* (2 vols., Cambridge, 1974), pp.19-61 (at p.41).
146. As might have been Barlow. See Barnes, p.2.
147. e.g. Barry Coward, *Social Change and Continuity in Early Modern England 1550-1750* (London, 1988, 1995 edn.), pp.6-8.
148. Rosenthal, p.12.
149. Denys Hay, *The Church in Italy in the Fifteenth Century* (Cambridge, 1977), p.14.
150. Gene Brucker, *Renaissance Florence* (Berkeley, 1969), p.183; Hallman, p.10.
151. e.g. Rawlings, p.61; Marilyn Manera Edelstein, 'Foreign Episcopal Appointments during the Reign of Francis I', *Church History* xliv (1975), pp.450-59 (at p.451).

# Chapter One
# The Legacy of Henry VII, c.1490-1515

The first Tudor was a good son of the church and his policies eventually brought stability to the country and effervescence to the church leadership. Throughout the fifteenth-century it was almost the case that the church did not matter, so many other problems took precedence. By the reign of Henry VIII the church mattered a great deal, but it came at a great price. Bishop Nix, one of the crown's busiest servants, addressed the matter of his non-residence this way; 'we are unable continually to reside in our diocese, for the king's and the kingdom's many affairs and the defence of the church universal [preoccupy us].'[1] Neither he, his patron Richard Fox, nor many of their colleagues were able to preside over their consistory courts very often as bishops, and other high-ranking clerics dominated the government of Henry VII. This was the case because the leading aristocracy had proved itself too unreliable.

Indeed, by entrusting men like Fox, Nix and Warham, the king had been able to break the grip of baronial power and saved money, as clergymen could be rewarded for their services with promotions in the church. This practice also put paid to competition among the noble factions, rivalries which had resulted in and perpetuated the civil strife of the last few decades.[2] As the reign wore on, with each new rebellion crushed, with each noble trouble-maker brought low, with each foreign enemy brought to the peace-table and with each old institution set on a newer and more efficient pathway, the king and his leading ministers were able to restore more and more stability to the kingdom. With stability came peace and wealth.

Although the church was a stable institution, and the threat of the Lollards was nearly forgotten, it could hardly be called spiritually dynamic. Henry VII exacted service to the state as a conscious act of policy and he searched out educated men with both legal and administrative experience for his councils. In so doing he transformed a nearly inconsequential institution into a useful one, both curial (in aspect) and legal (in training). In other words, he moulded (perhaps unconsciously) the Episcopal bench into an effective unit. The appointment of Italians to English sees (a novelty of the early Tudor period) in exchange for services in the papal curia was a natural extension of this sound policy.[3]

These facts are all well understood if not fully appreciated. Elton saw many positive results of the reign. The relationship between church and laity was excellent: the institutions of the church were looked upon with more respect as minor reforms had been carried out and clerics were now able to concentrate on spiritual matters.[4] Other historians, however, wrote that the impact of the king's policy on the church was not so positive. As high-ranking clerics provided the administrative and professional elements of his government, it has been assumed that they necessarily forfeited the impartiality that made them ideal arbiters of the realm's spiritual and moral life. In other words, the church suffered a lack of focused attention. As evidence of this they often refer to Fox's guilt about having been unable to visit his sees of Exeter and Bath and Wells, or they refer to Nix's words (as above). Hume went so far as to describe Warham as obsequious and charged that under his leadership the church had become nothing but a cipher – a mere system of rewards easily managed by the crown.[5]

This is an exaggeration. Henry VII wanted to avoid any conflicts between church and state affecting his ministers. As Elton made clear, minor problems were ignored, by mutual consent, in favour of political stability. Thus, the brilliant but abrasive Fox was twice denied promotion to Canterbury, the primal see going instead to the comparative nonentities Henry Deane and Warham (no Henry II/Thomas à Becket repeats!) The church was, of course, a major stabilising factor. It can come as no surprise that the bishops revelled in their new-found importance. As Knecht opined, the recasting of the Episcopal bench enervated the church's religious leadership. Bishop Smith, for example, repeatedly petitioned the king to be allowed to leave his duties in the Welsh Marches and attend to his long neglected see of Lincoln. Richard Redman paid a series of steep fees to be allowed to remain in his see of Exeter, much against the king's own wishes.[6]

What is not in question is that Henry VII and his bishop-advisors maintained an effective and stable regime. Foreign policies produced net gains, peace was achieved with both Scotland and France, domestic government was placed on a traditional and secure foundation. Moreover, the kingdom's financial institutions were overhauled, the crown was made solvent and the Tudors had earned the respect and acceptance of the continental ruling families. The king and council had learned from experience that although England's influence in Europe was marginal, they could make great gains by a cautious approach. Both historians and contemporary commentators alike placed this success squarely on the shoulders of the king and his Episcopal advisors.[7] They had united both disparate territories and political factions.[8] Henry VII left his son a stable political nation on a sound financial footing.

Unfortunately, but perhaps understandably, Henry VII had overprotected his remaining son. After having been sheltered so long the new king acted as anyone newly freed would; he set about to push the limits which had been placed on him and the country. Between 1509 and 1515, Henry VIII, unschooled in domestic and international politics, famously pushed the envelope of his power. Luckily, the bishops still dominated the government and the new king recognised that he needed these men in order to achieve his own costly ends. What is truly remarkable is the level of effective spiritual leadership that the bishops were able to simultaneously provide. At a time of great potential instability, the bishops rallied to satisfy the new king's desires in the least disruptive manner.

* * *

## 1. The king's good servants

The most serious implication of the new reign was its return to traditional foreign policy; an anti-French stance. The new king swore in public that he would lead his forces in person; a threat not to be taken frivolously.[9] That the war was potentially disastrous for the realm, the treasury and the king's reputation was beside the point. If successful, the aristocracy would have renewed opportunities for glory, plunder and advancement and the king would gain his spurs and a reputation. The details were left to the old royal council. That England did not go to war immediately after the coronation is indicative of the bishops' continued influence and of two serious problems.

Henry's martial policies certainly had the support of the lay peers, led by the Earl of Surrey, and his own intimate companions, Edward Stafford and Charles Brandon.[10] Unfortunately, none of these men were familiar with, or in control of, the minutiae of administration. As the new king was equally indifferent, none of them fully understood the gigantic task which faced them. The administration was in the hands of the old guard – Fox, Warham, Ruthal, Nix and Bainbridge – and they formed a powerful clique at the top of the administrative hierarchy.[11] They are sometimes erroneously called a 'peace' faction because they strove to delay the inevitable.[12] The peace faction was augmented by such men as Wolsey, Longland, Tunstal and the Italians, de'Ghinucci, and de'Gigli.

The new reign presented the bishops with a problem; how to satisfy the king without causing too much real disruption in the kingdom? Henry had laid a torturous diplomatic course at their feet, and that events moved as swiftly as they did is testament to the care with which these men devoted themselves to the project. The immediate problem was that France was in a league (Cambrai) against Venice, a coalition which included all of England's potential allies. In August, however, the king took to insulting the French ambassador, making sport at his expense.[13] Seeing this, Fox advised a more cautious approach.[14]

What was needed was time, both for a build-up of English forces and for the English diplomatic machine to devise a means of revising the international situation and gaining the king a voice in international affairs. Fox pursued a campaign which, at first glance, seemed contrary to Henry's wishes. In reality, however, it was the only possible means of fulfilling them. Bainbridge was sent to Rome to represent England and to work himself into the good graces of the Venetians. Fox, no doubt with Ruthal's and Warham's support, entered negotiations with Venice, France and Scotland. Wolsey, the royal almoner, ran interference between the council, the king and his companions, advising patience. How to reverse the aims of the League?[15] Fox made potential Venetian humiliation his platform. Both crown and country were genuinely sympathetic to Venetian needs based on centuries of good relations and political, commercial and intellectual interaction.[16] Bainbridge was to encourage the Republic's leaders to present their case against the French to the pope.

In co-ordination with Fox, Badoer presented a proposal which would accomplish both their own and the king's ends. The bishops discovered that the League was already weakening and would need only a gentle nudge to collapse. If the pope's attitude could be turned in Venice's favour, a new league could be constructed against France, and the king would have much needed continental allies for his war. This was not a trick of Fox's and Warham's, nor victimisation of Henry by Ferdinand. There was logic in prevarication and the prelates made the king see it that way.[17] The cautious approach also found widespread approval elsewhere.[18]

Letters were dispatched to continental rulers[19] and Bainbridge was given an open commission to work for a truce between the pope and Venice and to push for an anti-French alliance.[20] In England, the king's companions were monitored by Lord Darcy and Wolsey but, always, the diplomatic focus was Italy.[21] On the basis of his legal and administrative abilities, it was assumed that curial intrigues would not be beyond Bainbridge's capabilities. He was, in Scarisbrick's phrase, 'a bellicose jingoist full of animosity towards the French'. He was to win Julius II's affections; the Venetians took to him immediately.[22]

Fox and Bainbridge put forth a plan whereby the Republic would present Henry VIII's letters of support to the pope for his consideration. Bainbridge would not make the first move, but would be prepared to discuss the letters and the king's attitude after papal inquiries.[23] He was summoned to discuss the issue on 1 December 1509. Bainbridge assumed a neutral stance, which the pope appreciated and which led him to seek Henry's advice. Meanwhile, the old peace treaty with the emperor was confirmed and, early in the new year, Fox and Badoer's plan to encourage peace between Venice and the Empire was beginning to reap benefits.[24] As the old League unravelled, Bainbridge proposed a new one around the pope, Venice and its allies, against an obviously rapacious France. The pope was not quite ready to fully commit to the new venture, however.[25]

He no doubt appreciated that he was in a precarious position between France and Venice and feared a spring invasion. Fox was prepared for this and told Bainbridge to use it to the king's advantage. Henry would not consider retributive action against France until he knew most definitely what Maximilian and Ferdinand would do. This dangled a diplomatic carrot before the pope in that it would be to his benefit to head a new league against France. Henry would look favourably on such an alliance if Venice was included, and Bainbridge was to push for this.[26] Fox negotiated with the emperor on Venice's behalf and wrote letters to the pope as well. By 23 February the interdict was lifted.[27] The pope, however, hesitated still as Fox thought he might.

Suspicion was aroused in Rome when a French mission was invited to England in December. Fox's agent, Nicholas West, a resolute and experienced diplomat, was sent to Scotland to undermine the traditional French alliance.[28] A peace treaty was concluded on 29 June and, although it was unpopular with the king's more bellicose companions, it had diplomatic value. Rumours of these activities began to circulate in Rome, as Fox no doubt hoped they would, sending a message to Julius II.[29] In the papal presence, Bainbridge affected an air of indifference about all this, but hinted that he had personally opposed the French alliance, and looked favourably upon curial suggestions of a papal brief to the king meant to disrupt it.[30] As an added inducement, the brief would include the presentation to the king, through Bainbridge, of the Golden Rose, a symbolic papal honour bestowed upon the year's favourite monarch. In the event, the archbishop remained silent at the reception of the Rose. This confused the French cardinals and caused a stir among the Italians.[31] Indeed, soon after, news reached Rome of the signed Anglo-French treaty. What did Fox have in mind?

Obviously, the king himself did not want peace with the French. Luis Caroz, the Spanish ambassador, noted that Henry had earnestly opposed the treaty but had yielded to Fox's arguments, as had a royal council nominally split on the issue. He thought 'many other councillors are Frenchmen at heart. . .' or had been led to believe this anyway.[32] Although the Venetians had doubts about new treaty they were at least not disadvantaged by it[33], and the pope was pushed further towards the camp of the emperor. By 26 April, letters were issued in England to both pope and emperor proposing further peace negotiations.[34] Fox assured Badoer that the 'agreement [the Anglo-French treaty] made will soon die' and it soon become clear that the bishop had been playing for time while Louis XII grew more steadily ill. The treaty was to have been kept a secret as Caroz knew that Henry wanted to conclude a treaty with the Spanish powers. Fox and Ruthal now began work in that direction, the latter as ambassador to Ferdinand.[35]

The diplomatic effort proceeded slowly on three fronts.[36] Badoer reported that Henry considered himself duped by the French, and Louis XII's ally, the Duke of Ferrara, was in dispute with the pope over papal territorial possessions. By the middle of 1510, however, Fox's plans began to reap the desired results. The League of Cambrai was on the verge of acrimonious break up, the pope was prepared to head a 'holy' league against French activities in Italy, and Henry VIII could demand guarantees if he were to abandon the Anglo-French alliance.[37] This in mind, West was sent to France while Fox was working toward the creation of an anti-France league.[38] West was to discuss guarantees from Loius XII, meaning money or a marriage.[39] Soon thereafter, the emperor indicated his own interests and the pope actively pursued an English alliance.[40] In this way, Fox, Ruthal and Bainbridge had succeeded in reversing European diplomatic positions to the benefit of Henry VIII, putting him in a position much stronger than England could have expected.

Louis XII's retaliation against the pope was quick and decisive and played right into Fox's plans. He summoned a local council of the French church and a general council to Pisa for May 1511. The purpose, of course, was to depose the pope, but these actions alienated Henry VIII. In response, the pope summoned the Lateran Council for April 1512 and initiated armed aggression.[41] Henry held back from this, however, as the emperor briefly hesitated. Otherwise, matters moved apace.

Bainbridge had been made a cardinal-legate with responsibilities in the papal campaign against Ferrara.[42] This was a great honour for England and a pleasing inducement to Henry VIII (and put the archbishop at the heart of the action). De'Gigli was sent at the head of an English assembly to negotiate in Rome. This created a rivalry between himself and Bainbridge to Henry VIII's ultimate advantage.[43] Moreover, Fox's agent, Lord Darcy, was sent to Aragon to aid Ferdinand against the Moors (although Fox made it clear that aid was to be used in Africa against the infidels so as not to upset any other English treaties) and Venice was supplied with English bows.[44] Although the Darcy mission proved a fiasco[45], at least the emperor, following these events closely, now declared himself against France too.

If Henry VIII's Episcopal advisors proved themselves able in the manipulation of international affairs to his benefit, they showed themselves equally up to the resulting domestic challenges of war. Even these small-scale military initiatives seriously depleted the treasury. Wolsey wrote to Fox on 30 September 1511 that 'the Kyngis money gothe awey in euery horne'. He also noted the need to send West to Scotland again, blaming Thomas Howard and requesting Fox's attention.[46] Peter Gwyn's reading of this letter is undoubtedly correct. The central issue was the cost that a war with France would entail, but there was no turning back now. The articles of the new League were prepared by 4 October and the king's participation was assured. By November, a dual-alliance with Ferdinand had been negotiated, over Bainbridge's doubts of his sincerity, and the English envoy demanded Louis XII renounce his summonses. He refused. The royal council voted unanimously for war.[47]

Fox, Ruthal, Wolsey and others knew (witness Wolsey's communication) that Scotland presented difficulties. When they attacked France, Scotland would probably invade. In Rome, Bainbridge's initiative to persuade the pope of the formal transference of all Louis XII's rights and titles, including that of Most

Christian King, to Henry VIII, was met with favour. So too was his plan for Henry's coronation as King of France in Paris, two great diplomatic triumphs.[48] A papal brief to this effect was drawn up on 20 March 1512 and Bainbridge negotiated a papal indulgence for all who fought in, or helped pay for, the war.[49] Of course, the brief was secret and only came into effect after Louis XII's defeat.[50] Over the next several months, the clerical peace faction on the council organised a most efficient war effort, including troop movements, shipping, supplies and strategy. The results of Henry's first effort are well known[51], but lessons had been learned.

* * *

On the domestic front, Warham, now lord chancellor, opened parliament in February and advised it of the need for supply which was granted.[52] The rest of the council, now including Bishop Richard Fiztjames of London[53], proposed to the Spanish ambassador a two-pronged invasion plan. The Spanish, financed by England, would attack Aquitaine for the king while the English would invade Normandy or Picardy attacking from the north through the Low Countries. The emperor and the pope would eventually join in, producing an invasion of France on four fronts.[54] From England, Henry would lead the invading forces himself. Fox was given the responsibility of supplying the various fleets and armies and it is clear that he was determined to leave nothing to chance.

* * *

It has been written that this was the campaign which made Wolsey. There is a great deal of truth in this as he had a role in every aspect of the affair. Some historians, however, have used this to write Fox out.[55] Fox's role cannot be ignored as it was he who was negotiating the surrender of Tournai, arbitrating between the king, the emperor and the town's representatives at the Abbey of St Martin. Later, it was Fox who negotiated with Margaret of Savoy to smooth over the emperor's disappointing commitment.[56] In fact, this was probably the greatest diplomatic triumph of Fox's career and the last. The letters exchanged between himself, Wolsey and Dawtrey show us a tired man roused once more by the call of duty. They also evince a man capable in all areas, although it was the younger Wolsey who undertook the legwork.

John Dawtrey, the Southampton collector of customs, wrote on 5 May to advise Fox of the situation there: 'we have here all redy iij shippis . . . whiche wyll bere abowt ccc tonnys of vytayle', and more were expected. Smaller trading vessels and some Spanish ships were carrying in them supplies from London secured by Wolsey, amounting to some twenty-six ships in all.[57] Fox himself arrived in Southampton on 6 May and took control of the effort. A letter of Wolsey's, dated 11 May from Portsmouth, evinces both Fox's skill and his range of knowledge.

Wolsey told Fox that he had a week to find ships and supplies for Charles Brandon's 4, 000 men, having already arranged a month's worth of supplies himself. Although ships were not in ready supply Fox had anticipated the need. Wolsey had wanted the ships at Hampton by 18 May, but the best Fox could do was 1 June:

> Ye knowe well ther must be oon wynd to bryng the ships out of the Themmys into the Downys, and a nother to bryng the ships out of the Downys into Hampton Watre, and the third wynd to bryng the ships out of Westcontrie into Hampton Watre. . . . Thus ye may see ther may be many chauices to retarde the departyng hens of this newe armye.

Fox decided to see to Brandon's needs in person, going first to Hampton and then to the king. He also concerned himself with the communications network, particularly between the west and Dawtrey. He advised Wolsey to keep in constant contact with both Howard and Dawtrey and to take advantage of all opportunities as the winds could not be relied upon. Later, he was also advising Wolsey on troop movements, on how to evaluate the sea-worthiness of ships, on the specifics of the Franco-Spanish truce and on Howard's supply needs. He estimated that at least 10, 000 men would be needed for the new initiative; explained how Howard had got trapped in Plymouth haven by a south-west wind and needed a north-west wind in order to sail out; arranged Brandon's transport on a Spanish vessel, and brought his own experiences to bear on the details of continental fighting as well. Moreover, Fox would accompany the king into France, sending reports back to Wolsey.[58] It seems that Wolsey was too busy to keep Fox abreast of all the details, however. This distressed the bishop as he wanted to spare the younger man the strain and anxieties associated with such a venture, pains of which he himself was all too aware. 'I assure you', he wrote, 'it shall not be possible to furnesshe that army with sufficient beer. I feer that the pursers wool deserve hangyng for this mater . . . Heer can lak noo beer, if ther comme foystes and empty pipes to receyve it . . . This is a daungereux mater'[59]

Events elsewhere changed the international situation. News that the pope was ill was known as early as 30 September 1511. Given their choices, Fox and Wolsey supported Adriano de'Castellesi (the bishop of Bath and Wells and Henry's curial agent) while Ruthal and Bainbridge favoured Cardinal Riario, who was wealthy, on good terms with Bainbridge and a friend to England.[60] Either way, Henry could not lose. When the time came, Bainbridge cleverly backed Fabrizio del Carretto, a layman, purposely placing himself, and by implication Henry, out of papal faction politics. Although Bainbridge painted optimistic pictures of Leo X[61], he knew that the pope was more compromising and equivocal than Julius and that papal affairs would now be secondary to those of Florence. In other words, Leo would not openly invade France. The only real positive in all this for Henry was that his orator, de'Gigli, was in the new pope's favour.[62]

Thus, while in England preparations continued for the war effort against France, Leo X determined to send legates out to the various secular powers to secure peace. Bainbridge warned Henry not to receive the legate until his opinions could be pleaded in consistory and told Ruthal that he had managed to convince the pope to commit the matter to four prelates of lesser diplomatic significance than legates. Henry and the emperor were to be approached by Adriano de'Castellesi whom Bainbridge distrusted 'as parciall a Frencheman as I hame a Ynglishman. I pray God give hymme evyll triste'.[63]

In 1513, Henry invaded France and Scotland invaded England. Although Bainbridge could not push Leo X to enter the lists himself, the victories at Therouanne (16 August), and of the Spurs, put his reputation momentarily in the ascendant. He pushed for the fulfilment of Julius II's brief to have Henry crowned King of France, although for obvious reasons his initiative to obtain a papal bull to ruin James IV of Scotland came to nothing.[64] His star continued to rise when finally, in October 1513, he was to have been named one of the legates *a latere* to deal for European peace. De'Gigli's letter of 11 October made it clear that the pope wanted Henry to agree to this legatine mission as Louis XII was in no position to refuse, but Bainbridge warned against it.[65] He refused the commission, waiting for Henry's approval, and was not displeased when the king refused the papal injunction as premature. Bainbridge played for time until the projected Anglo-Imperial invasion of France, when France would collapse and Louis XII would be disgraced.[66]

The year 1514 was a watershed in the war effort, in diplomacy, in the domestic life of the nation and in the fact that Wolsey emerged to take a commanding position, having been groomed by Fox. In brief, Henry suddenly found himself bereft of European allies once again.[67] As England could not hope to carry on alone, preventing just such a development became the focus of the Fox-Wolsey-Bainbridge network. Wolsey and Fox worked closely to achieve peace and greater English influence abroad, and Wolsey cultivated his own agent in Rome (de'Gigli) much over the indignation of Bainbridge. This is perhaps the first sign that Wolsey's dominance would not be entirely agreeable to others.

Early in the new year, the French Herald made known his desire to speak in private with Henry, Wolsey and Lord Lisle, possibly to propose peace.[68] This makes sense from Louis XII's point of view and would please the clerical peace faction as well. Whether Henry could actually have mounted a new campaign is beside the point; the English had inflicted the most real damage despite fighting well above their weight. Letters to the same effect had been sent to both Fox and Wolsey by the pope. These noted the efforts to influence a peace policy and commended the work of de'Gigli, although both men were still involved in the war effort.[69] This seeming duplicity explains Bainbridge's own difficulties.

He failed to have Henry invested with Louis XII's titles and there was confusion as to the location of the original brief. Cardinal Vigerio said Bainbridge had it, but later admitted to having it himself. He was willing to hand it over but wanted Henry's application first.[70] That application never came, and Bainbridge, now isolated, could not explain why: 'I doo gretlie mervale that I never sithens had worde of your Graces receving theof ne your forsaide pleasour; by cause I never couthe see your saide Oratour'[71] He blamed de'Gigli for his difficulties. Later, he reported certain indiscretions on the orator's part. De'Gigli was a frequent companion of the protector of France and perhaps he had destroyed the brief himself.[72] The real reason was that the English wanted to secure something from France before they would fully consider peace. Bainbridge's appointment as legate also faced opposition in England. Wolsey distrusted his increasingly obstructive aggressive politics while the movement toward peace had progressed. The qualities which had made him valuable a few years earlier, when there was to be war, were exactly those which made him a liability when the objective was peace.[73] Authority in Rome was therefore passed to de'Gigli.

Fox and Wolsey, now described as of one mind on everything, gave the Italian bishop their support and blocked Bainbridge's appointment as legate *a latere* to England and to the Empire as this would have aroused suspicions 'that he ever ordeigned so to doo by the kinges assent'[74] Moreover, although Bainbridge had been *de facto* cardinal-protector since 1511, he was passed over for the official position in 1514 by Giulio de'Medici (who would become bishop of Worcester in 1521 and later Pope Clement VII). This too was the result of the intercession of Fox and Wolsey.[75]

Just as Henry VII had employed Italians to care for English interests at Rome, it made sense now to deploy de'Medici rather than Bainbridge. He was Leo's kinsman and an effective administrator. Bainbridge still had a role to play, however weak his information network had suddenly become.[76] Despite the unexpected cancellation of the Anglo-Imperial agreement and the meeting at Calais to co-ordinate aggression, and the marriage between Charles and Mary, and even though Louis XII and Ferdinand had signed a truce in March, with rumours rampant that Henry VIII and Maximilian would follow suit, Bainbridge denied everything and assured interested parties that massive preparations for war were proceeding. Indeed, as late as May or June 1514, the English were collecting supplies and building up ships. These preparations were raising anxiety in France[77] but Bainbridge affected nonchalance. He was clearly swimming against the tide, however. In late April, the pope addressed letters to Fox and Wolsey commending their efforts to influence the king in the direction of widespread peace; sentiments Fox repeated to Wolsey with regard to the marriage negotiations.[78] Bainbridge was realist enough to reconcile himself to his French counterparts when news confirming the peace finally arrived.

He consoled himself with letters and suspicions about de'Gigli's loyalties: 'he shulde undoubtedlie within short space serve owdre your Grace or me or bothe as untreulie as he hede doon hym [the pope]' and on his own continued efforts in Rome.[79] He noted that should Henry come to terms with Louis and Ferdinand, the pope would undertake to push for the remaining aspects of Fox's and Wolsey's peace plan. While it was perhaps sad that the new peace project required the slow erosion of Bainbridge's position, there can be no denying that through his efforts Henry VIII had a more powerful voice in continental affairs, one which far outstripped his real power. The treaty itself was not prepared until August, and Bainbridge did not live to see it in any case. In the meantime, war preparations went ahead as if nothing else mattered.[80] Thanks to Henry's Episcopal advisors, England was in a stronger position than it had been in 1509 and the king had had his military adventure to boot! They had achieved a worthy peace (which had been Fox's desire all along) and marriage ties with France (which were politically very useful).

* * *

Leaving these political matters aside for the moment, recall Nix's lament over non-residency. He had made it clear that the bishops were responsible for much more than diocesan matters, and this would seem absolutely true if events between 1509 and 1514 are any indication. However, recall that Knecht opined that this secular involvement had the happy side-effect of enervating the churches' religious leadership. Henry VII's domestic stability had forged the Episcopal bench into a strong and politically united group which offered much more than a token spiritual guardianship of the nation.[81] The new reign signalled more than just a new beginning for the state, however. Kaufman drew attention to the fact that between 1499 and 1505, twenty of the twenty-one sees had fallen vacant. This meant that twenty 'elder statesmen' had been removed from the political stage to be replaced by men just beginning their Episcopal careers. In 1509 therefore, not only was there a new king, but he was surrounded by fresh advisors, both Episcopal and conciliar, younger men with perhaps more flexibility and energy than their elders. Still, both old guard – Fox, Fitzjames and Smith – and new blood – Wolsey, Nix and Ruthal – had served the king well. Now we can test whether they served God equally well.

In his letter to Wolsey of 23 April 1516, Fox wrote of the melancholy under which he suffered. This was the result of the realisation of the harm his neglect of his pastoral duties must have caused. He wrote that as he was now 'trowled nyght and daye with other mens enormities and vices' in Winchester, countless souls in Exeter, Bath and Wells and Durham must have gone unserved. He wished to retire from the court 'wherby I maye doo soom satisfaccion for xxviii yeres negligence', for which he alone 'wer greatly to be blamed'.[82] Such feelings of guilt have been used against the Henricians (witness Wolsey's death bed speech in Shakespeare's *Henry VIII*), but had the sees really suffered? In a period where most of the bishops were either diplomats or civil servants primarily, one might well expect this to be true. We need to see clearly that these 'political' bishops were, at the same time, the effective arbiters of the nation's morals and spiritual life.

\* \* \*

## 2. God's Servants in the Country

There can be no denying that affairs of state kept some of the bishops out of their dioceses for long periods of time and some throughout their careers. By the same token, however, others were preoccupied with diocesan matters exclusively. While referring to the Welsh sees (though his observation is more widely applicable) Glanmor Williams noted that to assume a resident bishop *ipso facto* strengthened the religious life of the diocese was quite as mistaken as assuming the contrary. Having a resident bishop sometimes led to serious clashes with the cathedral clergy, and sometimes seriously harmed church life. We have already noted that administrative duties could be carried out by deputies, vicar-generals and registrars and even sacerdotal functions could be handled by suffragans. Williams called such officers 'a permanent civil service in the diocese'.[83] This being the case, we need to inspect individual examples of both resident and non-resident bishops to prove that the spiritual well-being of the country was been maintained by the Episcopal statesmen.

In the case of non-resident bishops we cannot simply assume that the diocese suffered. Recall Fox's guilt over those souls left unserved. Ruthal also felt guilty[84], but need they have? Fox had left the see of Exeter in the quite capable hands of vicar-general William Sykes (a jurist) and acts of ordination and confirmation were carried out competently enough by his suffragan Thomas Cornish, a man of great experience.[85] That said, nothing exceptional happened either; no serious difficulties arose, no heresy problems challenged. Fox's vicar-general at both Bath and Wells, and Durham, was Richard Nix, who proved exceptionally capable and was rewarded in 1501 with the see of Norwich.[86]

In both Exeter, and Bath and Wells, Episcopal non-residency seemed inconsequential and the spiritual life of the dioceses was maintained. The routine work of property management, ordination, induction to benefices, etc., all went ahead in a normal and uninterrupted manner. Indeed, while vicar-general at Bath and Wells, Nix evinced an efficient work ethic. The register shows detailed accounts of the elections of the heads of three religious houses, various dispensations for non-residence and manumissions of serfs on the Episcopal manors; even a detailed grant of non-residence for the vicar of Wembdon so he could pursue three years of university study. The condition and discipline of the clergy and good religion in the diocese had not suffered the bishop's absence.[87] Nor were the people troubled by clerical jobsworths, even if little beyond the active pursuit of the purely routine took place. The disciplining of indecorous and non-resident clergy, the visitation of convents and monasteries and the rectification of abuses carried on as normal.

Of course, a resident bishop might look at other matters. When Oldham replaced Arundel as bishop in 1504, he devoted himself to critical scrutiny and vigorous amendments in Exeter. He recorded, for instance, two examinations for heresy and, although both men were found guilty, their crimes were hardly terrible. One committed the relatively minor offence of talking carelessly and with irreverence, bringing into discredit auricular confession and the doctrine of eternal damnation. His friend had spoken with contempt about the five wounds of Christ. In the event both abjured. Over-enthusiastic perhaps, but the new bishop's vigilance also brought to light certain monastic abuses which Nix had overlooked.[88] Bainbridge, like Fox and Ruthal, was also conscious of his diocesan duties suffering for his non-residency. How could he not when no less a figure than Richard Pace was making the criticisms: 'for having neglected the manors in his diocese so that they became ruinous and unusable for hospitality'.[89] Not as serious as heresy unchecked, but hospitality was still the bishop's duty.

Although Bainbridge had been dispatched to Rome early in the reign, he had anticipated difficulties and left York in the very capable hands of vicar-general John Carver and suffragan John Hutton. Even so, as an additional safeguard Bainbridge had issued a commission to Fox and Nix, giving them full powers to administer York in case of dire emergency. In other words, the archbishop had taken care that his officers and servants would not be over-worked or left in the lurch.

Moreover, he kept as close an eye as he could on the situation from Rome. When it so happened that his commission was not being observed to his satisfaction, he persuaded the pope to order an official investigation. He also vetoed a statute which would have allowed new York canons to be absent during their first term of office, as this would have seriously diminished the Minster's services. Again, the see had not suffered either spiritually or practically in the bishop's absence.[90] Similar cases could be made for Skevington at Bangor and for Mayew at Hereford.

Although the latter was much occupied by affairs of state and by his duties as president of Magdalen College, Hereford was not disadvantaged. It was in the very safe hands of his suffragan Thomas Fowler. Indeed, Mayew did not retire to his see until 20 January 1507[91], and that was only because of conflicts at Magdalen. Even the most serious cases of extended Episcopal non-residency, in the midland dioceses of Worcester, Bath and Wells, and Salisbury (usually occupied by non-resident Italians) the spiritual life of both clergy and people did not seem to suffer. It has been suggested that these sees were in fact better off with non-residents, as that part of the midlands benefited from the ever-improving condition of the Welsh marches.

There can be no doubt that Silvestro de'Gigli, who was the nephew of Henry VII's bishop of Worcester, was best placed to carry on his uncle's work when the latter died on 25 August 1498. Silvestro remained at Rome until May 1504, at which time he was sent to England bearing papal gifts. He spent little or no time in his see because there was no need. His vicar-general and a suffragan carried out the necessary work with great dispatch. Indeed, they handled matters so well that when de'Gigli was next in England (around 1512) he was not summoned to the diocese at all.[92] It is clear that non-residence was less harmful than is often imagined. It can also be shown, however, that Episcopal non-residency was also not a bar to the establishment of a spiritually thriving community.

Skevington, for example, resided at Beaulieu in Hampshire and performed no visitations to Bangor in fourteen years.[93] In that time, no more serious problems arose than there had been at Rochester, a close-knit community and see small enough that Fisher could carry out a very close, in-depth supervisory role. Bangor was in the capable hands of William Glyn, Skevington's vicar-general. The only serious problem arose in 1524 when, over the desires of Wolsey, the bishop named Glyn as archdeacon of Anglesey (a strictly administrative matter). Blythe, also a resident bishop, had serious problems in the much larger Coventry and Lichfield mainly because of the dual function of Lichfield cathedral. It was not just the see's administrative centre but it was also an area of governmental autonomy jealously guarded by the dean and chapter. Indeed, the chapter there was even exempt from taking an oath of obedience to their bishop. Even facing such a potential nightmare, Blythe still performed a small number of ordination ceremonies and carried out the occasional visitation of religious houses.[94] He became a non-resident bishop after 1512 when he was made president of the Council of Wales. A far more significant example is Fox himself.

On 30 July 1494 he was provided the see of Durham and became, for the first time, a resident bishop. In Durham, he was faced with the awesome responsibility (with the bishops of Carlisle, Richard Bell and William Sever) of territorial defence against the ever-invading Scots and with internal government of the region. Sometimes Fox was severely hindered in the latter by the northern baronial families. He had been translated north because the king needed an experienced and trustworthy man in the position of prince-bishop of the Palatinate. Fox was also burdened with a commission to negotiate a marriage treaty for the Princess Margaret to James IV, but he proved equal to the tasks.

Fox took an active interest in the practical forms of defence, for instance, personally supervising the work of his military engineers at Norham Castle and then later successfully holding the fortress against a Scottish siege.[95]

Success here was matched by his successful ordering of the county's ecclesiastical life as well. He carried out his duties in person, ruling with a firm but fair hand. For example, he had made special grants to Thomas Garth and John Hamerton, for their actions during the defence of Norham, over the objection of the prior of St Cuthbert's (the bishop's chapter).[96] Later, when the prior objected against an appointment to William Bettis, Fox patiently assuaged the prior's worries: 'doubte you not, broder, I shall no thyng desyre you to doo that shall be hurt or preiudice to the mitre of that my churche'.[97] Fox's care is evinced in the details of his visitation of the collegiate church of Bishop Auckland on 4 August 1495. From that point onward, or so the canons solemnly promised, half the revenues of the prebends for the next three years would be devoted to necessary repairs and celebrations of masses for the souls of the dead.[98] The bishop also held ordinations, when resident, with regularity.[99]

Time was not always on his side, however. The Warbeck rebellion, troubles with the Scots and his appointment as chancellor of Cambridge (1497) all drew upon his time and attention. After the siege of Norham Castle (5 August 1497), and Surrey's successful counter-offensive, Fox held the governorship for the next six years.[100] Throughout all of this, his ordinary duties were carried out efficiently (if not elaborately). Monitions for non-residency and licences for study-leave were issued, ignorant clerks were examined and pluralists were admonished. Fox, rather cleverly and, indeed, successfully restored order and clerical discipline to the region. This was done by the employment of threats of excommunication against raiders, their English co-horts and bent minor officials, and also with exclusion orders from church rites and ceremonies against their families as well.[101] As Kaufman pointed out, the society of the northern regions of England were largely tribal in make-up and the mere threat of ostracism from one's familial network was often more effective in dealing with criminals and rebels than arrest warrants. Besides, the latter depended on officials who could be equally corrupt.[102] Disorder in the towns was addressed by the church courts, but a commission for the arrest of a fortune-teller is in evidence.[103] Even the smallest details did not escape his attention.

In 1496, Fox instituted *quo warranto* proceedings to examine claims of liberties and franchises. He directed the sheriff to give notice of a general examination of all liberties within the palatinate to be held at a special session before the justices at Durham. Whichever lord, temporal or spiritual, used or claims to use such liberties must appear and make good the claim upon pain of forfeiting them:

> My lord chargeth and straitway commandeth alle maner of persones, aswelle abbottes, prioures, deanes of cathedralles and collegiate churches, masters of hospitalles, persones, vicars and alle other men of the churche; as mayors, bailiffes and burgesses of cites and burches and alle othir lordes, knyghtes and esquyres, freholders and inhabitaunts within the bisshoppriche of Duresme, that clamyth any maner of libertie

or frauches, as waif, stray, foire or market, court baron or lete, wreck
or warren or eny othir libertie or fraunche; shalle come before his
justices at Duresme upon Seynt Lucie day next for to come and there
to putte in their claymes in writyng of their said liberties and fraunches,
such as thei wole clayme, upon payne of forfytyng of the same and
seasour ther off to my lordes handes.[104]

Fox dealt with the problems of crime and baronial complicity as ecclesiastical
matters, the patrons having filled their provisions with less than scrupulous
priests. This created the problem of a church filled with crude, illiterate and
often excommunicate clerics. Fox's register is filled with accounts of these
men. He was fighting both border crime, control of the church and
improvements in the diocese's spiritual condition with a lawyer's tenacity.

Like Fox, Mayew of Hereford was also mindful of the smallest details. In
1505 he argued with the prior of St John of Jerusalem over a small sum owed
him as a result of his triennial visitation. This, noted Kaufman, showed Mayew's
(and Fox's) struggle to restore Episcopal control and order in the aftermath
of civil war.[105] Even Ruthal, busy as he was with diplomatic affairs, found time
to pursue two escaped felons who had fled Durham for Carlisle.[106] Episcopal
administrators such as these laboured against immunists and renegades to make
the church institutionally and administratively sound. As we saw, the more
stability Henry VII brought to the country, the more attention the bishops could
focus elsewhere. Smith at Lincoln acted similarly against advancements without
examinations and licences, but with only a limited degree of success when
compared to his colleagues in the north.[107]

He found signs of neglect and irreverence in his visitation of the
archdeaconry of Leicestershire in 1510. At St Mary's, he found the abbot had
been negligent in his rectorial duty to repair the chancel. Moreover, it was
alleged that the canons were non-resident and that divine services were greatly
lacking. The old chapel of St Sepulchre without the Walls was also in a perilous
state, but it seems Smith's warnings to repair it were ignored. Furthermore, in
the deanery of Guthlaxton, the prior of Lenton was accused of allowing the
chancel of Wigston Church to remain unrepaired and of not exercising
sufficient charity to the local poor. At Bruntingthorpe, Glenfield, Thurlaston
and elsewhere, Smith found that even the cemeteries were disorderly. He was
thorough in his investigations and had cases of immorality, unpaid legacies,
'Sabbath' breaking and several other lesser crimes brought to his consistory
for correction.[108]

As noted, the degree to which the Episcopal administrators held sway over
diocesan affairs depended on how much time they could wrest from
governmental duties and on how well they managed their time.[109] Even before
his retirement, however, Fox had persuaded his vicar-general to conduct
visitations of the religious houses in 1501, 1507 and 1510, and in 1508 had
commanded his archdeacon of Winchester to hold yearly parochial visitations

and to make provision for the vernacular instruction of the people in the fundamentals of the faith.[110] Fox is noteworthy for his systematic supervision of the religious life of his dioceses. This is reflected in many ways. His decision to exact pledges from new parochial incumbents to remain in their parishes secured some spiritual continuity. His moves to amalgamate some poorer benefices in Winchester alleviated the poverty of the incumbents and lowered the overall financial burden. Most notable perhaps was his translation of the Benedictine Rule '. . . into oure moders tonge, commune, playne, rounde, Englisshe, easy and redy to be understande', which he did at the request of four convents:

> For as moche as every persone ought to knowe the thyng that he is bounde to kepe or accomplisshe, we the sayd Bisshop, knowing and consideringe the premisses and rememberynge that we may without like peryll of our sowle suffer the sayd religiouse wemen, of whose sowles we have the cure, to continue in their sayde blindenesse and ignorance of the sayd Rule, to the knowledge and observance whereof they be prefessed; and especially to thentent that the yonge novices may first knowe and understande the sayde Rule before they professe them to it, so that none of them shall mowe afterward probably say that she wyste not what she professed, as we knowe by experience that somme of them have syde in tyme passed.[111]

It has been suggested that his anxiety to retire reflected merely his disenchantment with the prevailing anti-French foreign policy. There is, however, no reason to doubt the sincerity of his concerns over the sins of omission attendant upon his earlier neglect of his Episcopal duties. Truth resonates through the phrases of a letter to Wolsey in which he suggests that he was moved to retire by impulses of an unambiguously spiritual nature. No doubt this attitude infected some of his colleagues.

In the letter of 1517, begging to be excused from renewed attendance at court, Fox not only deplored his earlier neglect of his pastoral duties but also expressed his troubled scruples over past involvement in warfare. Given 'the many intolerable enormytes involve therein', he thought 'that if I dyd continuall penance for it all the dayes of my lyfe . . . I cowde not yit make sufficient recompense therfor'. Indeed, if he were to involve himself again and come to die, 'I thynk I shuld dye in dispeyr'. Even to be summoned to treat such matters had the effect of troubling 'not a littell my spirits', so much so that 'I fere that I shall not by raison thereof be in such quyetnes that I shall dar say masses thies next v or vi dayes'.[112]

Fox was preparing for war on different front. Not for territory or glory, but for the souls in his care. Although the Lollard heresy had run to ground, rumblings could still be heard. Indeed, from the very beginning of the new reign the bishops were as one mind on this problem, which was increasingly manifesting itself in individuals and in literature from the south coast to the

Scottish border. John Colet was certainly clear on this point: 'in this tyme also we perceue contradiction of the lay people . . . we are also nowe a dayes reued of heretykes, men mad with marueylous folysshnes'[113], and heresy provided the central focus of the 1511 convocation. Throughout that year, and periodically into the early 1520s, large-scale examinations and purges were carried out most impressively in Canterbury, London, Lincoln, Coventry and Lichfield, and York.

At Canterbury, Warham was particularly productive despite his other parliamentary and governmental duties and he looked for improvements in all areas. His administration was staffed by first-rate legal minds (e.g. Tunstal) about three-fifths of whom held law degrees, and almost two-thirds of the 135 livings in his gift were filled by university-trained clerics. Kelly thought, however, that the high percentage of parishes (forty-five percent) held by non-residents made doubtful such claims of pastoral concern[114] but, on closer inspection, Warham's actions were wholly beneficial. The see's administration ran smooth in his absences, monastic and parochial visitations went ahead unhindered and heresy problems were acted upon.

His register features the results of his visitations; fifty-four abjurations at which he was personally present at half. One of his successes was the purging of twenty-five heretics from the Tenterden area alone, a Lollard cell which had been spreading heresy since the late 1490s. Such success was the result of thorough investigations and lengthy consistory sessions, nine at least between 2 May and 2 August, at which he was aided by Tunstal.[115] In total, the archbishop's actions and investigations resulted in at least five burnings and, even then, he also found time to carry out widespread monastic visitations with his assistants.[116]

There is nothing particularly noteworthy in the results of these visitations as the usual complaints are most evident. Women were found in the monastery at Faversham, nuns were accusing each other of incontinence at St James's (even though the accused were, respectively, 84, 80, 36 and 50 years old!), [117] and little or no extraordinary cures or disciplines were thought necessary. More disturbing and more ominous for the future, however, were complaints centred on the material aspects of monastic life. Stipends were often too small, grumblings were made over the food and drink available, especially how food was cooked, and problems with lay servants were raised. All indicative of the kind of decay of the monastic spirit to which European humanists were pointing.

Warham personally visited eleven of the seventeen monastic houses included in his second diocesan visitation of 1511-12. This one also included parochial visitations throughout the Canterbury deaneries. The archbishop visited the deanery of Arches in the church of St Mary de Arcubus in London (2 December 1511), the peculiars of Shoreham (30 December) and of Croydon (14 January 1512) and the resulting injunctions were most thorough. Some visitations he left to Tunstal, who thus gained useful experience, visiting Cumbwell on 3 June 1512, the college and deaneries of South Malling and the deaneries of Tarring and Pagham in April 1512.[118]

Once again, the problems encountered were no more sinister than indications of the general decline of monasticism. At the priory of St Martin, Dover there was ill-will between the monks and the townsfolk (who were withdrawing mortuaries). The buildings were in a dilapidated state and there was no grammar master to teach the novices. At Faversham, charity was rarely distributed to the poor, women had access to the cloister and refectory, and stipends were paid in kind. Such things discouraged new membership. The situation in the parishes was also disheartening. There were tithe disputes at Barfreston and Seasalter, anti-clerical incidents at Woodchurch, Kennington and Milton, forbidden English Bible translations were found at Goudhurst and at several places there was nobody deputed to provide care for the ill.[119] Particularly disturbing was Tunstal's discovery at Cumbwell of John Schepy, a brother of some thirty years standing, who had been ill for the last two years, ill-clothed and ill-feed and sometimes beaten by one of his fellows, Roger Maidstone.[120] Such complaints were often repeated and the blame placed squarely on the shoulders of a negligent prior.[121]

There is sufficient evidence to show that most of the bishops were heavily involved in monastic visitation right up to 1540. Some visited in person while others, like Blythe, Nix and Edward Lee of York, issued injunctions after assessing *comperta* from commissary visitations. Like Warham in the pre-1520s, Atwater personally visited eighteen houses in the Lincoln diocese while nine others were left to his officials throughout his Episcopate. Fisher visited the few houses in Rochester and Fitzjames visited some in London. Sherborne, Audley, Oldham and Veysey have all left evidence of personal visitations, as had Blythe, Nix and Longland.

While Warham was thus occupied, Fitzjames was carrying out an equally impressive heresy purge of the London diocese (particularly in Essex), trying some seventy individuals. He personally interrogated over sixty in the 1510-12 period, and about as many again in 1518.[122] The sheer volume suggests that he had little else on his mind. His consistory court would have been in near perpetual session between March and September 1512. Although this initial effort resulted in only two burnings, its real value was inspirational. Prompted by Warham, and with the undeniable devotion to the cause of Fitzjames, bishops Blythe, Fox, Oldham, Bainbridge (at a distance), Nix, Smith and the otherwise uninterested Audley of Salisbury, all hunted down heretics or investigated complaints.

Of these men, Fox was the most staunchly orthodox. Thomas Denys was burnt in the marketplace of Kingston on 5 March 1513, while Thomas and Anne Watt of Dogmersfield, William and Alice Wickham, and Robert Winter of Crondal all appeared before Fox in the parish church of Farnham on 30 September 1514. They all confessed their heresies and abjured.[123] According to Thompson, Audley, partially aided by Veysey, examined some sixty-three cases between 1504 and 1521 (with purges taking place in 1508, 1514, and 1521). Fox and Oldham had bursts of interests in their consistory courts as well, the latter working hand in hand with the mayor of Exeter. Bainbridge showed his concern, as discussed, by appointing Fox and some others as the 'spiritual guardians' of York. In February 1511, the king issued a certificate to the guardians to capture excommunicates and heretics in the north.[124]

Under the archbishop's direction, a sensational array of prosecutions resulted from the discovery of sortilege and the conjuration of spirits. Dickens provides details of a case running from September 1509 to June 1510, which involved three priests and five laymen practising witchcraft at Bingley, evidence of the kind of superstitions still rampant in more isolated parts of the country. The participants found themselves in York consistory on charges of heresy. They had been using the power of consecrated bread to defend themselves against the rancour of any disturbed spirits. They were absolved and did penance[125], but others were not so leniently treated.

In February 1511, for example, a process *de excommunicato capiendo* was initiated against Thomas Cudworth who was suspected of heretical depravity. There was more to the case against Roger Gargrace of Wakefield, however, who was spreading Lollard doctrines.[126] The commission of 8 March 1512, directed by Bainbridge's vicar-general William Melton, was held and charges levelled. Gargrave confessed on 19 March and abjured on 1 April 1512, after which he served a penance. He confessed that his erroneous opinions on the sacrament of the alter had been transmitted to him 'by a certain priest of the county of Lincoln'.[127] Nix in Norwich produced only minimal efforts (one case). Sherborne in Chichester confiscated a French New Testament and later dealt severely with one Thomas Hoth, found in possession of a Tyndale New Testament.[128] Blythe in Coventry and Lichfield, and Smith in Lincoln proved themselves equal to Fiztjames and Warham, and also worked well in co-operation.

Blythe put up a considerable effort against heresy. He initiated physical purges and trials which were the envy of his colleagues, leading the purge of the West Country himself. This was matched by a keen intellectual campaign against Lollard literature, particularly the Wyclif Bible, and he was involved on a royal heresy commission too.[129] The examination of suspects and witnesses continued on a regular schedule from mid-October to late January 1512 and, although Blythe was not always present at these inquisitions, he attended about half of the court sittings and took forty abjurations in person between January and February. This was out of seventy-four examinations, the majority of which were against neighbours or friends of the accused heretics who had not spoken up earlier, too routine for the bishop's personal attention.[130] The most interesting thing to emerge from the Coventry trials was evidence of the widespread use made of books. Illicit translations of scripture (most popularly the Ten Commandments), became the focus of much ecclesiastical energy as the root of the heresy problem.[131] Shortly hereafter, Blythe's efforts were fundamental in several of the articles Fitzjames objected against Richard Hunne. Hunne's own copy and his annotations were keenly examined by Blythe, his marginal notations proving a valuable guide to dealing with other Lollard heretics throughout the country.[132]

What is clear is that the heretical communities of London, Lincoln, and Coventry and Lichfield had access to a wide variety of heretical books. The importation, reading and copying of surviving Lollard manuscripts were popular activities and Lollardy had become a closely integrated and expanding movement against which the bishops put up a surprisingly concerted effort. Although Smith was busy examining heretics in Buckinghamshire (about forty-five cases in the Chilterns area around Amersham)[133], Blythe's anxieties about the number of books becoming involved convinced him to aid in the searching out of a group of heretics 'centred around' a Leicestershire priest. This man had a number of heretical books: 'I praie god ye may cum to the seid books ffor by such ther be many corrupted they will not confess but by payne of imprisonment. And by such means I have gete to my hands right many dampnable books.'[134] That these two bishops were acting in concert is clear in Blythe's report to Smith outlining his discoveries:

> that one John Dauy payntour late of Couentre now dwelling in leicestre and a nother Richard Dowcheman of his occupation abiding with the seid John as they reporte hath been and yet be of ther dampnable opynyons aswell ageinst the sacrament of the alter as pilgremages wurshipping of ymages & other which your lordshipp at more leasure shall mor playnely undrestond and haue sufficient recorde to conuicte them if they will denye . . . ther is also as it is supposed within your diocese one Sir Rafe Kent priste executour to one Master William Kent late parson opf Staunton in leicestre shyre which by his lieff daies was maistre of diuers heretikes and had many books of heresy which of likelyhod shuld cum to the handies of the seid sir Rafe, who had other relatives also of a heretical bent.[135]

* * *

In the early part of the reign of Henry VIII it is clear that the bishops were not only the king's good servants but were also providing an effective spiritual guardianship. Henry VII's earlier successes had allowed them the freedom to concentrate more fully on spiritual and other diocesan matters when times allowed. The homogeneity of purpose which had developed between the church and the crown, and the cooperation between the bishops themselves was, however, briefly undermined by two events. The first was the result of heightened administrative awareness – the conflict in Canterbury province over testamentary jurisdiction – while the second resulted from renewed attentions on contentious matters of church/state authority – the divided Episcopal response to the parliamentary legislation of 1512.

## Notes

1.  Peter I. Kaufman, *The "Polytique Churche" Religion and Early Tudor Political Culture, 1485-1516* (Macon, 1986), p.131.
2.  *Ibid*, p.26.
3.  Margaret Condon, 'Ruling Elites in the Reign of Henry VII', in C. Ross (ed.), *Patronage Pedigree and Power in Later Medieval England* (Gloucester, 1979), pp.109-42 (at pp.111-2).
4.  Elton, *Tudors*, p.69.
5.  Hume, ii, pp.289-93.
6.  Condon, p.111; R.J. Knecht, 'The Episcopate and the Wars of the Roses', *Birmingham University Historical Journal* vi (1957-8), pp.108-131; M. Bowker, *The Secular Clergy in the Diocese of Lincoln, 1495-1520* (Cambridge, 1967), p.17.
7.  E.g., Vergil noted Fox as the most valued minister: '*ob ejus singularem fidem, integritatem, ac prudentiam*' and Warham as 'praiseworthy', as evidenced by his quick eclipsing of the power of several of his 'time-serving' seniors. See Hay (ed.), *Anglica historia*, pp.55-7, 69, 98-9, 121, 130; Kaufman, pp.23, 38-9.
8.  Kaufman, pp.38-9.
9.  *LP*, i/i, 5 (i & ii). Andrea Badoer, the Venetian ambassador, told the Signory that the king was an enemy of Loius XII and a friend of Venice and once his coronation was over he would proceed to invade France. See also, A.F. Pollard, *Henry VIII* (London, 1905, 1951 edn), p.37; J.J. Scarisbrick, *Henry VIII* (Berkeley, 1968), pp.21-2; R.B. Wernham, *Before the Armada: The Growth of English Foreign Policy, 1485-1588* (London, 1966, 1971 reprint), p.78.
10. Vergil, pp.194-200.
11. J.D. Mackie, *The Earlier Tudors, 1485-1558* (Oxford, 1952, 1992 edn), pp.645-54; William H. Dunham, 'The Members of Henry VIII's Whole Council, 1509-1527', *English Historical Review* lix:ccxxxiv (May 1944), pp.187-210 (at pp.207-8).
12. E.g., Scarisbrick, *Henry VIII*, p.25.
13. E.g., *LP*, i/i, 11.
14. Allen and Allen (eds), p.xiii; Mackie, p.232; Gwyn, p.9.
15. More or less a cover for French territorial expansion into the Italian peninsula through an attack on Venetian interests.
16. E.g., *CSPV*, ii, 7, 10.
17. Mackie, p.268.
18. E.g., *CSPS*, ii, 27; Scarisbrick, *Henry VIII*, p.24; *LP*, i/i, 162; Wernham, p.81; BL Vespasian MSS. C.i. fol. 58.
19. E.g., *CSPV*, ii, 17; *CSPS*, ii, 23.
20. Thomas Rymer (ed.), *Foedera* (17 vols., London, 1704-35), xiii, pp.264-5.
21. Allen and Allen (eds), pp.43-4, 54; PRO. SP, 1/229, fol.8; *LP*, i/i, 157, 880.
22. Chambers, p.23; Scarisbrick, *Henry VIII*, p.25; *CSPV*, ii, 20, 21, 23.
23. Roberto Cessi (ed.), *Dispacci Degli Ambasciatori Veneziani Alia Corte Di Roma Presso Guilio II (25 Guigno 1509 - 9 Gennaio 1510)* (Venice, 1932), pp.176*ff*.
24. *LP*, i/i, 148, 268 (ii), 319-20; *CSPV*, ii, 28.
25. *LP*, i/i, 360; Chambers, p.26; *CSPV*, ii, 27; Cessi, p.211.

26. *LP*, i/i, 354; BL. Vitell. B. ii, fol.18.

27. *CSPV*, ii, 37, 45; *LP*, i/i, 383.

28. *LP*, i/i, 402.

29. Of course, there was the financial advantage for England in that Henry VII's pension would be extended and there would be more time to gear up. See *LP*, i/i, 406; *Foedera*, XIII. 270; *CSPV*, ii, 47, 48, 49-55.

30. Chambers, p.30.

31. BL. Additional MSS. 8442, fol.31.

32. *CSPS*, ii, 44.

33. *LP*, i/i, 430, 441; *CSPV*, ii, 61.

34. *CSPV*, ii, 56.

35. *LP*, i/i, 485 (no.51).

36. E.g., *LP*, i/i, 476.

37. *CSPV*, ii, 66; *LP*, i/i, 508; Chambers, p.33.

38. *LP*, i/i, 531.

39. *LP*, i/i, 529; *CSPV*, ii, 74.

40. *LP*, i/i, 545, 617.

41. *LP*, i/i, 816; Scarisbrisk, *Henry VIII*, pp.26-7.

42. L. Frati, *Le due spedizioni militari di Guilio II* (Bologna, 1886), pp.243-54.

43. Ellis (ed.), 2nd series, i, p.226.

44. *LP*, i/i, 734, 825; i/ii, 725, 730, 742; *CSPV*, ii, 102.

45. Wernham, p.8; Hall, i, pp.520*ff*; Scarisbrick, *Henry VIII*, p.28; *LP*, i/i, 837; C G Cruickshank, *Army Royal, Henry VIII's Invasion of France 1513* (Oxford, 1969), pp.3-5.

46. Allen and Allen (eds), p.54; BL. Cottonian MSS, Titus B, i, fol.104v; *LP*, i/i, 880.

47. *LP*, i/i, 889, 942; *CSPS*, ii, 58-9; Hay (ed.), *Anglica historia*, p.163; Chambers, p.38.

48. Chambers, p.38.

49. A. Ferrajoli, 'Un breve inedito per la investitura del regno di Francia ad Enrico VIII', *Archivio della Reale Societa Romana di Storia Patria* xix (1896), pp.425-27; W.E. Lunt, *Financial Relations of the Papacy with England, 1327-1534* (Mediaeval Academy of America, 1962), pp.608-9.

50. Chambers, pp.38-9; Wernham, p.84.

51. Despite a good start, and some limited successes at sea, problems arose for his allies which meant that the king was soon practically fighting the war on his own. On the positive side, the French had been driven from the Italian peninsula and both pope and emperor wanted to press the advantage, justifying a return to France in 1513. See *LP*, i/i, 1182, 1356, 1391, 1511; *CSPS*, ii, 68, 70; Allen and Allen (eds), pp.56-9.

52. Pollard, *Wolsey*, p.17; *LJ*, i, pp.10, 12-3.

53. Dunham, p.208.

54. Scarisbrick, *Henry VIII*, pp.31-2; *LP*, i/ii, 1750, 1884.

55. E.g., Wernham, p.85, Pollard, *Wolsey*, p.108; Scarisbrick, *Henry VIII*, p.41. Pollard wrote that 'Henry and Wolsey were as one' and Wernham stated that 'it was Wolsey who took charge of the reorganization of the fleet and the preparation of a great army' Also, see Gwyn, p.10.

56. Gwyn, p.15; *LP*, i/ii, 2367, 2372; Cruickshank, pp.148-9.

57. Allen and Allen (eds), pp.59; *LP*, i/ii, 1845; PRO. SP, 1/3, fol.197.

58. Allen and Allen (eds), pp.60-8, 71-2; *LP*, i/ii, 1858, 1881, 1885, 1898-9, 1960; PRO. SP, 1/4, fols.19, 22, 29-30, 78.

59. Allen and Allen (eds), p.70.

60. *Ibid*, p.52-3; *LP*, i/i, 880; Cottonian MSS, Titus B i, 104v; Chambers p.42.

61. E.g., *LP*, i/ii, 1984, 2029; Cottonian MSS, Vitellius B ii, fols.42, 43.

62. *LP*, i/ii, 2029.

63. Chambers, pp.46-9; *LP*, i/ii, 2077; PRO. SP 1/4. fol.98.

64. *LP*, i/ii, 2258, 2279, 2283-4 (PRO. SP 1/5, fols.36, 39, 41); Rymer (ed.), xiii, p.376; *CSPV*, ii, 301.

65. *LP*, i/ii, 2353, 2354; PRO. SP 1/5, fol.74.

66. This was not as unlikely as it seems. Henry had secured a marriage agreement between Charles of Burgundy and Princess Mary and, shortly afterwards, a combined Swiss-Papal army defeated the French in Novara in June and in Dyon in September, forcing Louis XII's withdrawal.

67. *LP*, i/ii, 2554, 2544. Late in 1513 Ferdinand began secret negotiations for the renewal of the Franco-Spanish truce (although well aware of English preparations for an even larger force and the plans proceeding for victuals and supply). This came to fruition in March 1514. The emperor followed suit, as did the pope, and the marriage proposal with Charles became increasingly bogged down.

68. *LP*, i/ii, 2556; PRO. SP 1/7, fol.87.

69. *LP*, i/ii, 2558-59, 2572.

70. *Ibid*, 1518, 2363; Rymer (ed.), xiii, pp.379, 387.

71. Chambers, p.25.

72. *LP*, i/ii, 2926; Ellis (ed.), 2nd series, i, p.226.

73. A Tindal Hart, *Ebor: A History of the Archbishops of York* (York, 1986), p.93.

74. *LP*, i/ii, 2611; Cottonian MSS. Vitellius B iv, fol.104. '*qui non solum in hac sanctissima causa verum in omnibus aliis sumus temper unus animi*'

75. William E. Wilkie, *The Cardinal Protectors of England: Rome and the Tudors Before the Reformation* (Cambridge, 1979), pp.41-2, 82-3.

76. *LP*, i/ii, 2644, 2653.

77. *Ibid*, 2877, 2968; 'Letters and Papers Relating to the War with France 1512-13', in Alfred Spont (ed.), *Publications of the Navy Records Society*, x (London, 1897), pp.200-1.

78. E.g., Allen and Allen (eds), pp.75-6; *LP*, i/ii, 2820-22.

79. *LP*, i/ii, 2926-8 (Cottonian MSS. Vitellius B ii, fols.70, 77-8).

80. *LP*, i/ii, 2959, 2974, 3057 or now to Wolsey at *LP*, i/ii, 3026, 3035, 3058.

81. Knecht, 'Episcopate', p.131.

82. Allen and Allen (eds), pp.82-4.

83. Glanmor Williams, *The Welsh Church from Conquest to Reformation* (Cardiff, 1976), p.309. The reader is directed to William's more recent companion volume, *Wales and the Reformation* (Cardiff, 1997) for equally useful materials.

84. *LP*, i/ii, 4523.

85. Howden (ed.), p.xviii.

86. H.C. Maxwell-Lyte (ed.), *The Registers of Robert Stillington and Richard Fox, Bishops of Bath and Wells*, S.R.S., lii (1937), p.1.

87. Howden (ed.), pp.xxvi-ii.

88. *Ibid*, pp.xxvii-iii; Francis Oakley, *The Western Church in the Later Middle Ages* (Ithaca, N.Y., 1979), p.290.

89. *LP*, i/ii, 3261; S Thompson, p.9.

90. Hart, p.92.

91. Williams, *The Welsh Church*, p.310; Bannister (ed.), *Mayew*, p.19.

92. M. Creighton, 'The Italian Bishops of Worcester', *Associated Architectural Societies, Reports and Papers* xx:ii (1840), pp.94-118 (at pp.100-1).

93. *LP*, xiv/iii, 5533; Williams, *Wales and the Reformation*, p.43.

94. S. Thompson, p.72; Tim N. Cooper, 'Oligarchy and Conflict: Lichfield Cathedral Clergy in the Early Sixteenth Century', *Midland History*, xix (1994), pp.40-57 (at pp.41-2).
95. F. Bacon, p.184.
96. Allen and Allen (eds), p.23.
97. Allen and Allen (eds), p.26; Howden (ed.), p.xxxii.
98. Howden (ed.), p.xxxiii, fol. 16.
99. *Ibid*, fols. 11-12.
100. *Ibid*, p.xxxiv.
101. E.g., *LP*, iv, 10.
102. Kaufman, p.127.
103. Howden (ed.), fol. 35b.
104. G.T. Lapsley, *The County Palatine of Durham: A Study in Constitutional History* (London, 1900), p.35.
105. Bannister (ed.), *Mayew*, pp.ivff, 124-5; Kaufman, p.125.
106. Lapsley, p.253; *LP*, i/ii, 1924.
107. S. Thompson, p.126; *LP*, iii, 464 (at p.1125), 822 (at p.1920); iv, 6 (at p.10).
108. *VCH: Leicestershire*, i, p.368.
109. E.g., Allen and Allen (eds), pp.150-1.
110. Howden (ed.), p.xlviii.
111. Allen and Allen (eds), pp.87-8; Oakley, p.292.
112. Allen and Allen (eds), pp.93-4; Oakley, p.293-4.
113. J.H. Lupton, *A Life of John Colet* (London, 1887, 1909 edn), pp.293-304.
114. S. Thompson, pp.19, 24, 45.
115. John Fines, 'Studies in the Lollard Heresy. Being an Examination of the Evidence from the Dioceses of Norwich, Lincoln, Coventry and Lichfield, and Ely, during the period 1430-1520 (Unpublished Ph.D. thesis, University of Sheffield, 1964), p.137; Sturge, p.19.
116. Foxe, v, pp.647-54; *LP*, i/i, 752. Also, see Mary Bateson, 'Archbishop Warham's Visitations of Monasteries, 1511', *EHR*, vi, (1891), pp.18-36; 'Archibishop Warham's Visitation in the Year, 1511' in *British Magazine*, xxix (1847), pp.29-41, 145-63, 297-313, 391-404; 625-40; xxx (1848), pp.23-31, 151-58, 255-69, 518-33, 659-66; xxxi (1849), pp.33-40, 167-78, 267-77, 411-21, 538-51, 637-52; xxxii (1850), pp.41-7.
117. Bateson, pp.22-3.
118. K.L. Wood-Legh (ed.), *Kentish Visitations of Archbishop William Warham and his Deputies, 1511-1512* (Maidstone, 1984), p.xi.
119. *Ibid*, pp.22, 34, 85, 97, 160, 204, 267, 283.
120. *Ibid*, p.49; Sturge, pp.19-22.
121. Bateson, p.34.
122. Foxe, vii, pp.174-5; S. Thompson, p.124; A.G. Dickens, *Lollards and Protestants in the Diocese of York 1509-1558* (London, 1959, 1966 reprint), p.8.
123. *VHC: Hampshire*, ii, p.50.
124. S. Thompson, pp.122-4
125. Dickens, *Lollards*, p.16.
126. *Ibid*.
127. *Ibid*.
128. S.J. Lander, 'The diocese of Chichester, 1508-1558: episcopal reform under Robert Sherburne and its aftermath' (Unpublished D.Phil., University of Cambridge, 1974), p.17-8.
129. *LP*, i/ii, 3289; Arthur Ogle, *The Tragedy of the Lollard's Tower: Its Place in History 1514-1533* (Oxford, 1949), pp.118-9; Fines, p.160.
130. Ogle, p.122 (n).

131. Fines, pp.164-5.
132. Ogle, p.119.
133. Foxe, iv, pp.123-4.
134. Fines, pp.167-8, 171.
135. *Ibid*, p.171.

# Chapter Two
## The Wolsey Era, c.1512-1530

Henry VII had forged the bishops into an effective political and spiritual body. They were active in both church and state matters because they had the freedom to act under a king who took a close personal interest in their activities. They could look to him for good leadership when they needed it. This being the case, when their powers had been trimmed, as in the case of benefit of clergy and sanctuary, they had not complained as nothing but good had resulted.[1] It was clear that the king was acting in the best interests of the country. Henry VII sensibly kept on top of all matters, but the price was that he is remembered as a tired and rather dour man. Moreover, it is a certain truth that political stability, while good for the nation, is hard to maintain and not very exciting in terms of public relations. Henry VIII, freed from a cloistered existence, wanted to see and be seen. He did not want to be burdened by the day to day workings of government. This was not a problem providing that Fox was willing to pick up the slack. His gradual withdrawal from the national stage, and Warham's own desire to focus on church matters, forced the new king into a dilemma.[2] While he wanted to be in charge, he did not want to actually be too involved. Unfortunately, without a firm hand, the bishops, as a unit, found themselves on the verge of collapse. Henry VIII needed another Fox. Luckily, Fox had been grooming a brilliant young protégé, Thomas Wolsey, for just this need and Wolsey played his part very well.

Cavendish tells us that Wolsey, 'perceiving a plain path to walk towards promotion . . . daily attended upon the King in the court', and made himself indispensable to his colleagues as 'their expositor unto the King'. Wolsey was always 'most earnest and readiest among all the council to advance the King's only will and pleasure'. Thus, 'the King therefore perceived him to be a meet instrument for the accomplishment of his devised will and pleasures'.[3] In other words, Wolsey was a godsend to Henry VIII and, in short order, he was made a bishop, an archbishop, a cardinal, lord chancellor, legate, and legate *a latere*. Some of his success was due to the war and its spoils, and some to the papal need for allies. Scarisbrick noted that it is not possible to pinpoint the exact moment when Wolsey eclipsed Fox and Warham for primacy of place, although clearly this had happened by the Anglo-French peace treaty of 1514.[4] The exact moment is unimportant, however.

Our main purpose here is to examine Wolsey's relationship with the other bishops. We shall see that his dominance was in many ways a great benefit to the Henrician bench. As under Henry VII, but to a greater extent, the bishops were freed from political duties and thus able to concentrate on diocesan matters. Thus freed, extensive visitations were carried out, reforms were implemented and the growing heresy problem was tackled. In fact, more so than in any other period of Henry's reign, the bishops were moulded, both by Wolsey and by circumstances, into an efficient body willing and able to effectively deal with both spiritual and temporal matters once again. What is most interesting about this, however, is that the institution could so easily have collapsed into moribundity in this same period, due to internal divisions and external pressures. Wolsey, so to speak, saved the day.

## 1. The problem of testamentary jurisdiction

As Henry VII had solved the national problems facing his reign, the bishops were able to focus their attentions closer to home. Predictably, their success in hunting out heretics and the expansion of consistory court activities, when mixed with increased parochial and monastic visitations, created an atmosphere of anti-clerical suspicion among the laity. The church was becoming more powerful. The temporal authorities thought it was perhaps too powerful and a convocation was held in 1510 to deal with this new threat. The bishops only actually paid lip service to solutions, however, focusing inward instead. After the lead of Fox, they used the meeting to present a litany of complaints against the seemingly unfair administrative practices of archbishop Warham, actions that spilled over into parliament. A committee of reform, consisting of Nix, Fisher, Colet and some others, was assembled to investigate these claims. Its advice was that Canterbury should restrict its use of inhibitions and apparitors in the sees.[5] The evidence of unfair practices by Warham's officers was based on two related complaints. One was Oldham's 1509 tuitorial appeal against the archbishop's interferences in his *ex officio* testamentary jurisdiction; the other was Nix's complaint against the dean of the Arches' undermining of his heresy investigations in Norwich.[6]

The jurisdictional structure of the church was complicated. As Thomson has pointed out, it was sometimes the case that a bishop would have to submit to the archbishop if, for instance, he was himself a party to a suit. Under such circumstances, Warham had judged a case between Oldham and the abbot of Tavistock, and another between Smith and the dean of Lincoln.[7] Jumping ahead, the Hunne case itself provides an example of Warham's interference, as the rector of Whitechapel brought his mortuary suit (a minor case) to the archbishop's court at Lambeth rather than to Fitzjames' London court where it should have gone.[8] In any case, as Oldham stated in his complaint, there was no interference resented by the bishops more than in testamentary jurisdiction, much of the bitterness having spilled over from a twenty-year-old dispute between Bishop Hill of London and Archbishop Morton.

Very briefly, that original dispute arose over the attempts of Hill to restore discipline to the Augustinian priory of Holy Trinity Aldgate over appeals that the prior, Thomas Percy, had made to Canterbury. On 20 October 1491, Hill's visitation uncovered a plethora of the usual monastic problems, but his injunctions were summarily ignored while the appeals continued. On 21 May 1493, a second visit confirmed Percy's ill behaviour and, generally, conditions had not improved enough for Hill's liking. A compromise was attempted when Hill issued new injunctions rather than deprive Percy. The latter, in turn, dropped his appeals. By 10 April 1494, when Percy resigned his office, it had become clear that the second set of injunctions had also been ignored. Moreover, and for whatever reason, Percy returned and disrupted the proceedings of the election for his replacement. He tore up vital letters, acted as if he had not resigned and re-launched his appeals. He violently held up Hill's investigation for which he and his accomplices were excommunicated and the priory placed under interdict.[9]

At some point during these events Percy had appealed against his excommunication to the archbishop's court of Audience, while his associates appealed to the court of Arches, where they received absolution. Morton's officers also began the removal of Hill's bills of excommunication and brought various charges against him. Undaunted, the bishop had these men arrested on a charge of trespass by the city authorities, over which they appealed to the jurisdiction of the chancellor, Morton. Hill also mounted a military-type assault on the priory, capturing Percy and the sub-prior, ransacking rooms and breaking down doors. The two monks were imprisoned, secluded and moved about while Hill installed Richard Charnock as the new prior, a respected scholar and friend of Colet and Erasmus. Of course, Percy's actions were now relegated to second place behind the bishop's violation of Canterbury jurisdiction, which Morton was not prepared to tolerate. A deputation of bishops and government officials, approaching both men in turn, imposed order to the situation. Hill was on the verge of submitting to Morton's penance when another conflict arose between them over the limits of archiepiscopal testamentary jurisdiction.

The long-established customary right to grant probate where testators possessed *bona notabilia* (property) in various dioceses had been confirmed for the church of Canterbury by Morton's proctors in Rome on 4 October 1494.[10] On 20 October it was announced that Hill was appealing to Rome against Morton for having violated his own Episcopal testamentary rights.[11] There were two cases around which the dispute revolved, those of Richard Symson and John Eryk.

By 10 October, the commissary court of London had claimed both cases and Symson's executors found themselves with excommunication proceedings pending for having refused to recognise Hill's jurisdiction. Eryk's executors were summoned before the court to prove their case. Both teams of executors claimed that the testaments and account books proved ownership of property outside London diocese, but the court found the evidence insufficient.[12] Prior to the subsequent hearings of 30 November, the executors appealed to the archbishop, who agreed with them and cited Hill's official to appear before him, threatening a severe punishment. This precipitated Hill's appeal, as it was unfair that Morton should judge a case that involved his own rights. Meanwhile, the London authorities continued to pressure Eryk's executors. At Rome, the litigation commenced on 21 February 1495, Morton represented by de'Castellesi and Ruthal.[13] Hill's proctor, however, was able to get Morton and his officials cited to Rome and had a stall issued to any actions prejudicial to himself. Back in London, Eryk's executors and various officials of the courts were being tossed back and forth between commissary and prerogative, excommunication and other threats hanging in the air.

The papal citation was posted on the doors of St Paul's, on 11 July, and were well guarded against any attempted removals. Indeed, Morton's officials attempted to bribe Hill's officers to remove the notices themselves, but they refused and told the gathering crowd of the citation and that Morton had been excommunicated. Morton now appealed to Rome against Hill's and his men's disobedience to his own authority. Subsequently, Hill and his officials were cited to appear at Rome, first by proctor and then in person when the proctor failed to appear with all relevant documents. Interestingly enough, there seems to have been no definitive settlement at Rome and the case outlived the litigants. In 1510, the situation was much the same, only with Fox and Warham standing *in locum* for Hill and Morton.

Warham had, as bishop of London, opposed Morton's authority. Now, sixteen years later, he rigorously upheld it. He went so far as to threaten Fox with an interdict. Fox, however, believed he was on solid legal grounds and began to bring his considerable political influence to bear on the archbishop and, indeed, recruited some of the other southern prelates to his cause.[14] By 1512, Fox had received from de'Gigli the gift of administration of Worcester (thus signalling his support) and the bishops of London, Lincoln, Exeter, and Coventry and Lichfield, under Fox's leadership, spearheaded moves in convocation against the prerogatives of Canterbury. The bishops demanded a rational explanation for the basis of the arbitrary figure of £5 *bona notabilia*, attacked the assumption that it was somehow cost-effective to have wills proved at Lambeth and called for greater scrutiny of all cases before the prerogative court.[15] There was also a question mark placed over the justification for intervention, based on the fact of a creditor (or debtor) living in a diocese other than that of the deceased.

By 1513, Warham had charged Fox with having induced the other bishops to support his campaign 'by large and greate restitucions made on to them'[16] through his political influence. That is, Fox had bribed Blythe, Oldham, Smith and Fitzjames for support. Warham had the support of Sherborne, Nix and Fisher. Except for de'Gigli, the other Italians, the Welsh prelates, Stanley of Ely and Audley of Salisbury were not drawn into the affair. Mayew of Hereford was no friend of Fox's due to the earlier controversy between them at Magdalen College. Thus were the bishops split into at least three camps, although clearly Fox's support (from a legal point of view) out-classed Warham's. Even so, Fox tried to secure compromises over the probate prerogative before taking the case to Rome.[17]

Christopher Kitching assumed that there were two basic reasons for the bishops' actions. First, they were looking to benefit the family of the deceased by avoiding unnecessary court costs. In theory, this would preserve as much property as possible for the fulfilment of familial obligations. Second, they wanted to 'promote charitable benefactions for the good of his [the deceased's] soul'.[18] Of course, they also acted to preserve their own jurisdictions and financial interests against encroachments by Canterbury. In any case, what Fox had in mind by way of compromise was the establishment of a number of single joint commissions, one for each archdeaconry, an annual pension paid out to the archbishop from each diocese and a total offer of one-third of all probate revenues to Canterbury.[19] In turn, Warham was to abdicate all special probate jurisdictions. Keep these details in mind, they will become important later.

According to Kelly, such unusually comprehensive ecclesiastical probate jurisdiction was peculiar to England. Having developed largely out of convenience, its canonical basis was weak. Fox probably understood this. A difficulty of interpretation over just how far the ordinary's jurisdiction went would be cleared up to everyone's satisfaction. The question of whether authority was vested in the bishop of the diocese in which the testator had died or that in which the testator had normally lived would have been resolved in favour of the former.[20] This claim had become the substance of the bishops' appeal to Rome in 1511. They hoped, moreover, to further undermine Warham's claims in that the title 'legatus natus' uselessly duplicated some metro-political authority while 'legate' jurisdiction was limited to the duration of specific commissions. Warham, jealous of his authority, counteracted this claim with certain archival evidences and protested that his primacy and legateship entitled him to ordinary powers throughout the province. Thus the wills of those dying with goods in several dioceses were rightfully within his jurisdiction.

Evidences were produced in Rome, some good, some dubious. In all, the Fox group launched at least half a dozen separate appeals, including personal processes against Warham's officers.[21] Essentially, on all counts, the tide of opinion and decision was running against Warham but, through Bainbridge, he was able to get the matter referred back to England and to the judgement of the king (reinforcing his right to try clerics and ecclesiastical issues).[22] By April, after having assigned the problem to 'certayne of our counsell', Henry asked the bishops to suspend the process in Rome.[23] Appearances and arguments before the council were made, a compromise arrangement was drawn up, but nothing ever seems to have been concluded. Unlike the earlier example, the case did not die off, it merely died down for a while in light of contemporary events. On 23 February 1513, a royal letter was sent to all the disputants. The king complained that the suit had been divisive of 'the universall Church of this oure realme', had involved his counsellors in a foreign court and noted that it did not 'stande well' with pursuit of the war against France.

The three basic issues of the suits were probate of testaments of hereditaments and rents not chattel, probate of wills where testaments had goods or debts in diverse places and the deputing of 'prayseers' (appraisers). The council's decision was that no bishop was to take cognisance of a will of hereditaments nor appoint appraisers for dead men's goods as, by this means, many extortions had been perpetrated in the past. Warham had authority if a testator or in testate left goods or debts exceeding the value of £10, in more than one diocese. If less than £10 jurisdiction belonged to the ordinary. This judgement was to stand for a period of three years without prejudice to either side.[24]

Although it is clear that this judgement favoured Warham, he alone refused to accept it. In his reply, he agreed to take no probate when the testator left hereditaments or rent not chattel but dissented over apparitors. These, he argued, were necessary officials to guarantee fair treatment. He argued that he was protecting Canterbury's rights, clearly foreshadowing future events. Indeed, after only three or four years the clerical split would be even greater due to Warham's obstinacy. The king's reply to this was short and concise. Warham was to obey without further delay and immediately certify his conformity by letter.

Warham refused to budge, adopting the opinion that the king had not read his first reply thoroughly and that 'the adversaries' had been feeding him malicious reports. He complained that as Fox had the king's ear he could not be impartial, made new charges and demanded a personal audience with Fox present.[25] On 16 July, the king wrote from Calais to have the queen tell Warham to stop bothering Fox's commissary, John Incent, and to explain that royal patience was becoming strained. Warham's reply of 14 August, to Catherine, denied that he had 'vexed' Incent, asserted that he had made perfect answer to the king's letters already and made clear that he would assail anyone who trampled Canterbury's rights. He charged Fox with perjury for his troubling of the king with this matter in wartime. The queen forwarded this letter, adding an explanatory note of the situation to Wolsey.[26] On 16 September, Warham received another letter demanding he conform, to which he replied, but would make no full answer until he could see the king in person. What he hoped to achieve by all this is unknown. His position was weakening by the minute and the split in clerical ranks was becoming serious.

    Indeed, left in London to manage governmental affairs, Warham was eventually outmanoeuvred by Fox, Wolsey and Ruthal and forced to yield. Compositions with Wolsey and Fitzjames in March 1514 and June 1515, respectively, were concluded to the king's terms, and Warham's use of apparitors was limited to one per archdeaconry with regulated fees.[27] The upshot of all this was that much money and time had been wasted through Warham's obstinacy, and both local and provincial administrations had been strained. But more important was the fact that Episcopal faction had appeared, bringing jurisdictional discord in its wake. That this coincided with an expanding tide of anti-clericalism, demands for reform and with the Hunne case itself, caused the king much annoyance. A divided Episcopate could not affect much-needed reform and convocation was paralysed. An undoubted authority was required to avoid this kind of problem in the future. The facts of the Hunne case only brought this message more clearly home to the king (who, remember, did not want to become too involved himself).

## 2. Repercussions of the Hunne case[28]

This *cause célèbre* roused anti-clerical emotion in London and was even discussed in parliament. Indeed, a royal commission was set up to look into the matter. As important as these issues were, however, the Hunne case's real significance was in its timing. We have seen that contemporary events were unfriendly to the clergy. In 1512, parliament had passed an act prohibiting clerics not in holy orders from claiming benefit for certain serious offences. Both Warham and Fox, who tried to prevail upon their Episcopal colleagues in the lords to consent to the measure, promoted the act. They were, however, opposed by Fitzjames and, in order to gain his acceptance, the act was made temporary, to be reconsidered at the next parliament. Between parliaments, the Hunne case captured public attention, bringing churchmen and church authority under suspicion and scrutiny.

    To coincide with the opening of the new parliament, and perhaps to gain an early propaganda victory, Richard Kidderminster preached a sermon at St Paul's Cross attacking the act as against the law of God and the liberties of the church. Moreover, he argued that those who had passed it were all subject to ecclesiastical censure (including, in extreme cases, excommunication) and that, as all clerics were in holy orders in any case, parliament and the civil courts had no authority over them. The clergy, thus inspired by the 'most distinguished English monk' of his time[29], took a decisive stand in parliament. The lords spiritual were in the majority and used their power as a means to frustrate a two-fold endeavour by the commons concerned with Hunne's remaining family and the revival of the act of 1512. The commons were also trying to appeal to the Privy Council in order to frustrate Fitzjames' and the convocation's attempt to reform the '*privilegium clericale*', used to prevent clerks in major orders being brought to secular trials. The prelates were, however, aware of certain abuses and were trying to tie up loopholes.[30] Unfortunately, other matters interrupted their efforts.

The issues raised by Kidderminster, and the inconclusive debate that followed, resulted in open hostility. Warham, Fitzjames, Fox, Nix and Fisher, however, led an effective clerical opposition which, in 1515, resulted in the quashing of the act of 1512.[31] There was an outcry over the defeat and the commons pressured the king into taking action. He called a conference at Blackfriars for a debate on the issue and Henry Standish (a friar, chief of the king's spiritual council, warden of the Grey Friars in London and Franciscan Provincial) naturally took side against the bishops. He argued that the act was valid, not against God's law and was, indeed, in the public interest, a fundamental consideration and thereby acceptable. The outcome of the conference is unclear, but shortly thereafter the commons requested that Kidderminster renounce the views expressed in his sermon. Meanwhile, as Standish continued to express his own views in a series of lectures, he was summoned before convocation to answer for them. Both men stood firm and both camps appealed to the king.

The next session of parliament, and of convocation, saw the continuation of the issue. The bishops again managed to frustrate all actions from the commons on the clerical statute and on a bill concerning heresies[32], while convocation dealt with subsidy demands from both king and pope.[33] These other issues pale to insignificance, however, when compared to the result of Standish's summons on heresy charges.[34] A second Blackfriars conference was ordered with all sides presenting their cases. The king was advised by John Veysey, an adroit lawyer, who suggested that the conventing of criminal clerks was not against divine law or the liberties of the church, leaving convocation's moves against Standish as the real point of this second conference.[35] The judges decided first that the convocation was guilty of *praemunire* for having relied on certain papal decrees (which had not been received by royal assent) in their judgement against Standish and that the church had no real voice in government beyond that given them by the king. The bishops' reaction was to point out that it was their duty to investigate clear or potential heresy issues and that it was unreasonable that parliament could criticise them while the convocation could make no criticisms of the laity without a *praemunire* charge hanging over them. Thus, the basic issue was whether a parliamentary statute could be subordinated to the opinions of a foreign court?

To answer this question yet another conference was summoned, this time at Baynard's Castle, with the king presiding. Wolsey, famously, pleaded on bended knee that 'to all the clergy this matter of conventing of clerks before the temporal judges seems contrary to the laws of God and the liberties of the Holy Church, the which he himself and all the prelates of Holy Church are bound by their oath to maintain to their power'.[36] He begged that the problem be settled at Rome. Of course, to allow this would be to *de facto* admit the power of all the previous papal bulls. The king would have to grant a licence admitting the bull that would contain the curia's decision, and no doubt a confirmation of all previous bulls. Henry opted instead to uphold Standish's view.

Fox retorted that 'Standish will not abide by his opinion at his peril', meaning that if heresy charges were pressed against him he would renege. Moreover, just as Hunne could be implemented in heresy for having supported a known Lollard, the king could also be deposed as a heretic by the pope. Warham remarked that although there had been acquiescence in the conventing of clerks, there had been 'diverse holy fathers of holy church' who had objected, some of whom had suffered martyrdom (a not very subtle reference to Becket). In reply, Justice Fineux told Warham that through the act of conventing clergy, having been accepted by the English church, it could not have been considered contrary to divine law. There were further arguments over the original cause of the 1512 act but, ultimately, the king had to decide the issue.

His well known speech contained four important points: royal jurisdiction would not be diminished; the spirituality had in the past disobeyed papal decrees when it had suited them to do so; the clergy sometimes interpreted canon law according to their own needs and could thus resolve the matter themselves; and, he refused to permit an appeal to Rome.[37] Although Warham asked that the entire matter be referred, the king remained silent. Gwyn's conclusion was that Henry was determined to be the master of his own church just as he was determined to be the master over all temporal matters. Fox and Warham did themselves no favours by arguing against him. While Wolsey had made a conciliatory speech recognising the king's prerogative and the laws of God, Warham had irked Henry with references to martyrdom and Fox had merely inflamed an already bad situation. Despite his long disagreement with Warham over jurisdictional privileges, however, Fox had sided with him against the king in a rather heated manner.

On 10 September 1515, Wolsey was created a cardinal.[38] This was the price Leo X was willing to pay for continued English support at a time when Francis I was looking to gain military glory with an invasion of northern Italy. With his position at court growing untenable in light of recent events, Warham retired from government and handed over the great seal to Wolsey (thinking perhaps that the cardinal could protect the church's interests better than he had done). Thus, Henry VIII had an instrument through which he could oversee both church and state effectively and not be drawn into any more clerical disputes.

## 3. The changing role of the bishops

Obviously, promoting Wolsey to the highest spiritual and temporal offices profited the king but did it also profit the church? His succeeding Bainbridge to York and his promotion as cardinal precipitated a great deal of business at Rome. De'Gigli carried out Wolsey's policies with aplomb, although his gentle hints for promotion to a richer see in England were ignored. Ironically, Wolsey thought that it might not be wise to saddle another important see with a non-resident bishop.[39] The period of Wolsey's dominance saw thirteen new bishops (including himself) promoted to the Henrician bench (including three Italians, a Spaniard and three theologians). How much influence, however, did Wolsey exercise over these new appointments?

There is, according to Gwyn, no direct evidence for Wolsey's involvement at all save in two cases: Tunstal's elevation to the see of London in 1522 and Clerk's elevation to Bath and Wells in 1523.[40] It is unlikely, however, that other future bishops would have been unknown to Wolsey or outside his confidence. Wolsey might have influenced Veysey's appointment as dean of the chapels royal in 1514 as well, although both he and Tunstal had served under other bishops and were ultimately picked by the king. It is clear that, whatever the case might be, Wolsey did not stack the Episcopal bench with his own men. Even Clerk was only nominally a member of Wolsey's household, having served Bainbridge in Rome prior to the latter's death. Wolsey inherited Bainbridge's Roman servants, including Clerk. But Clerk had already made a name for himself having presented the king's book against Luther to the pope in 1521 and having returned on a diplomatic mission in 1523.[41] Longland's appointment to Lincoln in 1521 might also have owed something to the cardinal's influence, but he had already established his theological credentials as a regular preacher at court and was royal confessor. As shown, academic, diplomatic, spiritual and administrative qualifications came before any others, but Wolsey no doubt pointed out the rising stars. That is not to say, however, that his relationship with the bishops was always genial.

The office of legate *a latere* gave Wolsey supremacy over the English church and extensive powers of visitation and patronage. It even allowed him to summon church councils and make new constitutions for the clergy under his own power. All other ecclesiastical jurisdictions were subordinate to his. As one might expect, this authority troubled Warham more so than the others. On 2 December 1518, he summoned the southern bishops to Lambeth for 7 February. This proposed synod was to establish some common positions against potential interference from Wolsey, and to enact reform statutes to precede the inevitable legatine ordinances.[42] Fitzjames, according to Kelly, told Wolsey of the proposed synod and he reacted sharply.[43] Wolsey had been promoted, with Campeggio, to advance a proposed papal crusade in consultation with other bishops and the heads of the religious houses.[44] This being the case, it could be that he simply took over the proposed meeting for convenience's sake.

In any case, in December he summoned the bishops to a council at Westminster Abbey for 14 March 1519, '*pro cleri reformatione*'.[45] What actually happened is unclear, however. The Venetian ambassador noted that Wolsey merely wanted money, a soft option in regard to the proposed crusade.[46] Fox wrote that the main issue was reform, referring to the many possibilities opened up by Wolsey's legatine powers. Bishop Penny, who praised the cardinal's efforts to eradicate vice, confirmed this option.[47] Fox also noted that there would be less difficulty in carrying out church reform because 'our most Christian king who had, I think, exhorted, encouraged, and advised you to undertake the task, will lend his authority and help your godly desires.'[48]

This legatine synod was apparently addressed by Fisher, who concentrated on two issues very much at the centre of church reform – the vanity of costly apparel and 'this vanity in temporal things' which involved the clergy too much in the affairs of state.[49] It seems that this synod was a genuine attempt to look seriously at the current state of the church and at how improvements could be made. Out of it emerged new legatine constitutions (more or less comprehensive restatements of existing canons) and some new rules addressing clerical dress, the conduct of clerics (particularly bishops) and much else.[50] Still, Warham was not pleased by this turn of events and he was not alone.

His chaplain, Thomas Gold, reported that Warham had a supporter in Nix. He wrote that Nix would 'assuredly stick by you' and that should Wolsey proceed with the *praemunire* against him, Nix would 'tell him [the king] that he would forsake him as his leige man'.[51] Although there is no evidence of *praemunire* proceedings against either Nix or Warham, the latter would certainly have perceived the prevailing winds as Wolsey did bring a *praemunire* charge against Standish. Standish was technically guilty of having allowed himself to be consecrated by Warham before he had received royal assent and paid due homage for his temporalities. Warham, therefore, was also technically guilty.[52] In any case, Warham did not appear at the legatine synod of March 1519 until several days after the opening as a kind of protest.[53] There were some other points of contention that we should briefly highlight.

In 1521, after it had become clear that Wolsey was intending to begin the reform of the secular clergy[54], his legatine commission was given fuller authority and extended for a period of five years. Thus empowered, he began to organise legatine machinery. This drew complaints from Warham over the interference of Wolsey's officials in his own testamentary and other jurisdictions. Despite this, a legatine court had been set up by October 1522[55], by which time the two archbishops and their officers had begun talks (Warham wanted to settle the matter).[56] An agreement was drawn up whereby Warham gave up roughly half his own jurisdiction and, in addition, the proving of wills from exempt areas would now be administered jointly and probate fees divided equally. In essence, Wolsey's officials would administer probate valued over £100.[57] Perhaps Warham realised that by acknowledging Wolsey's rights over the probate jurisdiction of the southern province he was, in fact, given a voice in Wolsey's compositions with the other bishops. Indeed, he would be taking half of Wolsey's revenues from non-prerogative wills proved in the dioceses.[58] The sharing of authority was a concession by Wolsey. It made his intention of posting commissaries to every diocese quite clear. Officers were to be used for such things as clerical appeals. Compositions to this effect were negotiated with the other bishops in early 1524.[59]

The upshot of these negotiations was the buying back of Episcopal rights by the bishops (appointments, visitations, courts, probate, etc.) for a third of their spiritualities. While for Booth this meant a charge of about £10, West noted that he would be content to allow Wolsey all of his spiritualities as his major concern was his jurisdictions: 'not for any profit or advantage that I trust or intend to have by the same, but only for quietness and good order'.[60] Even if the bishops were unhappy about these expenses, co-operation had become the norm. Look at the case of a priest named Christopher Nelson. He had brought a case against John Cooke as the latter had reported him to Fox for making indecent advances on a young married woman. This resulted in Nelson's imprisonment and subsequent expulsion from the diocese. Nelson's relative, and Wolsey's auditor William Burbank was contacted, but Fox's letter convinced him that Cooke's case was solid. This reflects well on both Fox's diocesan administration and Wolsey's legatine officers.[61]

Another example of Wolsey's tact was the case of the will of John Roper. As Gwyn reported, this revolved around a small amount of money left to William Roper (Thomas More's son-in-law). Having gone initially before the joint-prerogative court, in February 1525 the widow was summoned to the legatine court of Audience. Warham took issue with this (possibly because of the lost half-share of the revenues) as it contravened the spirit of the agreement with Wolsey. It is likely, however, that Roper himself had brought the case before Wolsey's court in order to resolve a family struggle.[62] Wolsey replied to Warham's letter with grace and sympathy and Warham replied in kind; the case was then returned to the joint court.[63]

In 1523, Wolsey summoned another synod coinciding with the famous parliament of that year. Wolsey was taking advantage of the fact that both provincial convocations had been summoned for like causes on 22 April, but whether the legatine synod ever assembled is unclear. According to Kelly, York convocation met initially at Westminster while Canterbury met at St Paul's and, on 22 April, both transferred to the Westminster chapter house.[64] Assuming that the synod did meet, historians allege that Fox and Fisher put up considerable opposition to Wolsey's plans for a clerical subsidy, although he was eventually able to force through a commitment for five 'tenths' subsidies. Subsequently, Fox and Nix were exempted from the parliamentary pardon as punishment for their opposition, and Blythe was charged with misprision of treason.[65]

Gwyn doubts the seriousness of the charge as Wolsey, thereafter, acquitted Blythe. There is sound evidence for it though. Peter Heath refers to two eye-witnesses, and there was a letter from the Imperial ambassador, Louis de Praet, noting that recently an unnamed bishop had been imprisoned in the Tower in connection with the de la Pole conspiracy. Edward Hall wrote that the bishop in question was Blythe, who was 'attached for treason'.[66] Indirectly related to this was a notation of expenses incurred by the duke of Suffolk and others who had 'examined' the bishop of Chester. Pollard drew a line connecting Blythe to the conspiracy of Francis Philippe at Coventry.[67] There is also the account of the Elizabethan historian William Whitelocke, who noted both Blythe's treason and his acquittal[68], to which can be added an entry from Blythe's own register, an extract from the Lord's Journal for 1523 of all details relevant to his treason charge.

The details are these. On Wednesday, 10 June 1523 (the first day of the second session of parliament), Wolsey informed the Lords that a certain Welshman (suggesting a connection to Blythe's responsibilities on the Welsh marches?) had accused the bishop of treason[69], although later retracted it. Both men were placed in the Tower on 28 March. Blythe was examined by a committee of eleven peers headed by the earl of Surrey, which found that he had been 'falsely and maliciously accused'.[70] There was obviously some opposition to Wolsey's plans although these were neither extensive nor all-inclusive, and in actual fact, he did not interfere with Episcopal jurisdiction all that much after negotiating the compositions.

He faced some additional opposition from Nix over one of his appointments, but in this case it was for his own son Thomas Winter, which looked bad. Between 1526-28, Winter was archdeacon of Suffolk, for which Nix had no complaints, but between 1528 and 1530 problems erupted after his transfer to the archdeaconry of Norfolk. Nix had difficulties with Wolsey's nomination of Winter's replacement (Roland Lee?). Nix tried to prevent that appointment, having already nominated one of his officials to the position (Edmund Steward). As the office was in his gift as bishop, Nix's nomination got the nod.[71] Later, the two faced off again in 1529 over Nix's challenge to Wolsey's right to testamentary jurisdiction in the archdeaconry of Norfolk. As Gwyn wrote, however, Wolsey was only acting to protect the rights of the archdeacon and not in his own interests.[72] That is to say, the cardinal was doing his job.

Other bishops also had problems with Wolsey's exercise of power. In 1518, West had been asked on several occasions to appoint someone of Wolsey's choosing to benefices in his own gift. Wolsey also wanted to make Winter dean of Lincoln, but Longland had someone else in mind as a 'resident' dean. Both Nix and Longland got their way.[73] Gwyn is right to suggest that these examples show us a cardinal merely trying to enforce sound Episcopal discipline. Wolsey was not trying to take on all patronage authority but merely trying to make the bishops consult with him over their appointments. The aim was the improvement of the clerical institution as a whole. Despite the few examples above, an efficient working relationship between the bishops and Wolsey had developed. Note Fox's letter to Wolsey of 1519. He noted that

as far as I can see this reformation of the clergy and religions will so abate the calumnies of the laity, so advance the honour of the clergy, and so reconcile our sovereign lord the king and his nobility to them and be the most acceptable of all sacrafices to God, that I intend to devote to its furtherance the few remaining years of my life.

Thus, despite disagreements, Fox appreciated the fact that Wolsey was on the church's side and his opinions carried a great deal of weight. Serious reform was intended by the cardinal and was much needed: 'in reading your grace's letter I see before me a more entire and whole reformation of the ecclesiastical hierarchy of the English people than I could have expected, or ever hoped to see completed, or even so much attempted in this age'.[74] In this matter, Fox would not be disappointed.

* * *

## 4. Much needed clerical reform

Despite rising incidents of anti-clericalism and a growing list of clerical grievances, when Colet preached to the opening of convocation in January 1510 he placed blame squarely on the materialism of the clergy themselves: 'first unlouse yourselfe frome the worldlye bondage'.[75] Warham took the message to heart and established a committee, including Colet, Nix and Fisher, to consider the full clerical picture.[76] They made some suggestions including new canons allowing ordinaries to suspend inadequate stipendiary chaplains, to help maintain discipline in the lower clerical orders and on clerical dress. Moreover, they made a general exhortation to the bishops for the investigation, submission to purgation and punishment of all simoniacs and other offenders.[77] This rather meagre response to Colet's call for reform must, of course, be viewed in light of the ongoing dispute between Warham and the bishops over probate jurisdiction. All this changed when Wolsey took over.

If his authority interfered with Episcopal jurisdiction in the rather limited ways outlined above, it should be stressed that there was much that was beneficial not least to the bishops' individual reform efforts. Indeed, as Lander pointed out, Wolsey's dominance was so complete that by 1529 only Veysey and Blythe were still involved in political duties for the crown.[78] This suggests that all the others were concentrating on diocesan affairs. We also know that it had been Wolsey's intention to summon a second legatine synod for 9 September 1519, to tackle the strained relations between the bishops and the religious orders.[79] The bishops had many complaints about the exempt houses and Wolsey was going to look for a solution. Although the council was postponed due to outbreaks of plague, Wolsey's commitment carried forward and eventually bore fruit. In fact, the 1515-1530 period is a most impressive one in regard to monastic reform, which can readily be shown by looking at the individual bishops' records of visitation (which were regularly carried out at both parochial and monastic levels). It can also be seen in their effective church courts, diocesan reformations and in their campaigns against heresy. As Gwyn wrote, there was 'a considerable degree of involvement in the health of the diocese shown by the majority of the bishops in this fifteen-year period.

Thompson produced some very useful statistics in his thesis on some of these issues. Fisher, for example, carried out diocesan visitations every year of his Episcopate, save 1527. Of course, he never had any particular political role to play and Rochester was a small see, but Nix, Warham, Oldham and Sherborne also had impressive workloads. Equally impressive were the residency statistics of the Henrician bench. Nix was resident in Norwich at least 75% of his Episcopate, as was Oldham in Exeter and West in Ely. Fitzjames never left London, and Audley was 95% resident at Salisbury. Fisher himself was 90% resident, as were Mayew and Sherborne. Veysey and Fox (both more or less politically active) were only 50% resident at Exeter and Winchester respectively. The worst record was set, not surprisingly, by Wolsey himself. He was resident less than 4% of his Episcopate.[80] Even so, he still managed to carry out both parochial and monastic visitations (by proxy).

Monastic visitation caused the bishops no end of trouble. Thompson noted that Fisher was unique in the attention he paid to his own cathedral prior. In 1508, he chose William Fresell '*per devolutionem*', but showed equal concern for all of his monastic officers, taking their professions in person and even making nominations to monastic posts. Other bishops followed Fisher in taking monastic elections seriously enough to attend to them in person: Oldham and Fitzjames, although sometimes merely to ratify the convent's choice, and even Audley attended elections at Poughley Priory in 1521.[81]

The options for the bishops with regard to reforming their diocese were, however, quite wide. Ruthal and Wolsey both tended to remain at court and delegate, although the former did manage to visit Durham from time to time unlike the latter. His chancellor there, Frankleyne, was archdeacon of Durham and a worthy ecclesiastical officer, and he kept the cardinal will informed of local matters.[82] Of course, Wolsey saw personally to clerical appointments, remaining uninterested in other matters. Likewise, the Italian bishops delegated authority to Wolsey, just as Bainbridge had delegated to Fox. More to the point, Blythe and Fisher concentrated on extensive visitations, Sherborne on church courts and finances, West on heresy, while Longland, Fox and Kite dedicated themselves to spiritual matters above anything else. Kite was a friend of Wolsey's and a firm believer in clerical reformation; an earnest prelate with regard to pastoral care. The see of Carlisle, although no real hotbed of heresy, had its own unique difficulties resulting mostly from its isolation. Kite wrote to Wolsey in 1523 in order to secure his aid with regard to the financial provisions for a priest for the parish of Bewcastle, 'who, since Easter last past, have had neither sacrament nor sacramental that I know of. . .'[83], thinking it unfair that the parishioners should be punished in this way.

Another approach by which the bishops could influence and improve monastic life was through the circulation of annotated or translated copies of the rule of St Benedict. Both Longland and Fox were concerned that ignorance of the rule was being used as an excuse for lax observance. When Fox retired from politics and turned his attentions to the see of Winchester he found all of the usual unsavoury monastic practices. The religious houses were in bad shape as, most disturbingly, was the principal nunnery of the see, Romsey Abbey. Romsey had suffered, over the previous forty years, a succession of inadequate abbesses who had been unconcerned with religious life and clerical discipline, and who had often ignored Episcopal injunctions for improvement. Fox put the problems down to a basic ignorance and lack of education among them, but 1515 proved a turning point.

Anne Westbrooke had been elected at Romsey and, together with the abbesses of Wherwell and St Mary's, and the Prioress of Wintney, turned to Fox for improvements in the religious life of women.[84] The basic problem was a lack of understanding of the *Regula Benedicti*, written in Latin and incomprehensible to most of the nuns. In other words, the nuns did not know what they were supposed to be doing or how to go about doing it except by example. Fox produced an English translation of the rule for them. Significantly, he not only did the translation himself but he made it gender specific for the women and adapted it to specifically English conditions in a 'robust' and 'colourful' way.[85] Fox also bore the printing and distribution costs. Although not all of the bishops were willing to go quite so far, the problem of proper profession was a concern for them as was the lack of proper education for novice monks and nuns.

Fox was clearly determined to make up for the twenty-eight years in which he had been a bishop in name only: 'I haue also many causes in my handis, bothe of correccions and justice, that if I shuld sodenly relinquyshe theme, I shuld vnresonabely and inhonestly disapoynt many maters and persons to my great rebuke and sclaundre', is what he wrote to Wolsey. He went on to write that he visited Hyde Abbey and the cathedral church every fortnight.[86] Fox was not only dedicated, however, but merciless with the unrepentant.[87] In the matter of the election of a new abbot at St Augustine's Bristol, he wrote to Wolsey that

> trawthe it is, my lorde, that the religiouse women of my dioces be restrayned of theyre goyng owt of theyre monasteries. And yet soo muche libertie appereth some tyme to muche. And if I had the auctoritie and powre that your grace hathe, I wolde indever me to mure and inclose theyre monasteries accordyng to thordynance of the lawe.

He went on to defend his actions taken against other nuns, monks and secular clergy:

I trowe there be as litle oponly knowen synne or enorme crymes, bothe in persones spirituall and temporall, as is within any dioces of this realme. And if your grace in haue any information of the contrary, I beseche your grace in the way of cheritie to shewe the same to my said Chauncellar, and God willyng it shalbe spedyly reformed.[88]

Other bishops had similar complaints.

Nix, during his visitations of Norwich, had uncovered the fact that in nine of the sixty-one monasteries novices were untaught. Atwater found ten with the same faults in Lincoln[89] but, for Nix, such conditions were an inspiration to carry out regular visitations of the diocese's monastic houses. He held visitations at least every six years, and each visitation lasted about six months. Visitations were performed in 1514, 1520, 1526 and finally in 1532.[90] In his first visitation of Norwich priory, Nix heard, among the more usual complaints, that there was no schoolmaster and that the number of monks had fallen short of the regulated membership by twenty-two. Even more serious, however, were the unexplained absences of the prior and a profligate sub-prior, and the haphazard manner in which services were carried out.[91] If the cardinal had any particular example in mind when he determined to convene the regulars' council in 1519, however, it might well have been St Mary's Wymendham.

Since its conversion to abbey status in 1448 little or nothing to its credit was ever recorded. Its traditions were said to be bad and its inmates an unruly and insubordinate mob. When Nix visited St Mary's in June 1514 he found that this description an apt one. He discovered fighting in the cloister, that the brethren were at liberty to come and go as they saw fit, a manic prior, insolent servants, decayed buildings, habitual drunkenness and sexual incontinence. His solution was to depose the prior.[92] In the cases of both Norwich priory and St Mary's, his actions produced a much-improved state, noticeably enhanced by his next visitation in 1520. It is clear that Nix had also kept his eye on conditions at both places in the meantime.

Sherborne also personally examined the novices and addressed education issues in his injunctions[93], as had both Fisher and Longland when they could. Lee of York also started to examine novices, but rather late in the day. None were to be admitted to Healaugh Park priory, for example, or to the nunneries of Sinningthwaite and Nunappleton 'without special licence'.[94] Indeed, Wolsey had shown concern over monastic appointments and, in 1526, his officers Dean Higden and the abbots of Rievaulx and Roche examined the abbot-elect of Fountain before the cardinal would confirm him.[95] Sherborne, however, worked under an additional strain.

The bishop of Chichester had no right to visit, and thus reform, nearly half the houses and collages of the see, as well as certain hospitals and almshouses. Like Longland, Booth and Oldham, Sherborne approached the matter of exempt houses through their appropriated churches or through full exploitation of his right to present vicars-by-lapse to even the exempt jurisdictions.[96] His visitation record of 1518 highlighted the usual faults, but his injunctions also included several more general provisions aimed at making long-term improvements and at bringing the orders into better local repute.[97] In his thesis, Lander noted three injunctions as particularly noteworthy. First, that the numbers of regulars should be increased and that individual recruits should be submitted to the bishop personally for approval. Second, that the houses should be administered financially in accordance with the high standards set by the bishop and, third, that priors should provide education for the novices. Later visitation records show that Sherborne's injunctions were successful. In the records for 1521, 1524, 1527 and 1530-31, only one allegation of a sexual failing was made (and there is some doubt about it) and few of the other faults detected were particularly serious. Indeed, they evince an increased number of inmates, which suggests that the monastic life, at least in Chichester diocese, had been rendered more attractive.[98]

Sherborne and his officers, during the 1520s and 1530s, were instrumental in bringing significant improvements to nearly all the religious houses in the see. That these improvements reflect the bishop's preoccupations is revealed by his 1518 injunctions to the prior and convent of Boxgrove. He enjoined the prior to recruit enough monks to bring the total up to its foundation's requirements and he set out regulations for the instruction of the novices in the 'rules, constitutions and ceremonies of religion'. He focused on their diet, attire, extra-monastic movements and discipline. Sherborne was also concerned with the material well being of Boxgrove and ordered the prior to regularly clean the dormitory, repair the boards and pavements and insure that each member 'should have in his own cell a small window'.[99]

Throughout his later visitations (the 1530-31 visitation carried out by deputy as the bishop was then in his 80s) decay of church fabric, unkempt churchyards and lack of education were pinpointed as the most serious problems. His injunctions to the prioress of Easebourne nunnery (5 August 1521) bear this out. His commissary found disrepair in the cloisters and the roof, poor attire for the nuns, monetary problems, a lack of discipline and poor education. Three years later, some of these problems had been resolved but more serious disciplinary problems had sprouted, including arrogance on the prioress's part and too easy access given to outsiders.[100] In November 1524, three other religious houses were cited to appear at consistory to answer for dilapidation of their rectories. In December 1526, the bishop's officers took the unusual step of threatening the parishioners of East Angmering with suspension of their cemetery if they did not repair its walls.[101] Lander made it clear that Sherborne's efforts to give financial aid to those responsible for the upkeep of church fabric were just as serious as his admonitions and corrections to the negligent. He also showed that between January 1520 and January 1521, twenty-one cases involving church fabric had been tried, compared to only five (August 1533 to August 1534) and six (July 1537 to

July 1538) under his successor Richard Sampson.[102] Sherborne had left an impression on the monks (for as long as they remained). His efforts to improve Chichester diocese were much wider than monastic reform, however.

In the period of Wolsey's domination, wherein the bishops were able to concentrate on diocesan matters rather than on court politics, Sherborne's consistory cases against laymen amounted to some 204. This shows that his exercise of spiritual jurisdiction was neither expensive nor particularly cumbersome, but was effective. Penance, for example, was seldom commuted to a money payment, fees were moderate, laymen were not needlessly imprisoned, mostly for heresy[103], nor were excommunications issued for so-called 'small and light causes'. Because Sherborne used it sparingly the very power of the church's censures, in Lander's judgement, were both authoritative and prestigious and, as a result, the courts had little difficulty ensuring the attendance of those cited.[104]

Indeed, Sherborne's Episcopate was also marked by a dramatic increase in temporal values. He not only provided new endowments for the see out of his own pocket, but he also developed a careful leasing policy and reformed the administration of the Episcopal estates and of his own household. As above, his chief concern was the fabric of the church, particularly the palace at Chichester and his favourite manor houses. By 1529, Lander noted, the bishop had spent some £3717 on building and repair works alone.[105] Unfortunately, his careful management was carried on by neither of his immediate successors, Sampson or Day. Lander's calculations indicate remarkable success. By 1536, Sherborne had increased the value of the temporalities of the see by over £60 a year, leaving Sampson a well-ordered and disciplined administration. He also noted a corresponding increase of about twenty-five percent in the spiritual revenues of the see, achieved largely as a result of the bishop's acquisition of new appropriations.[106]

Bishops West and Booth were equally successful in their attempts to increase revenues. Nix, although an extensive builder, left a great many debts. This was a situation avoided by Warham with the introduction of sensible leasing policies.[107] Expenses and repairs were also a major concern for Vaughan who, in 1517, appropriated the church of Llansainfraid in the archdeaconry of Cardigan for the vicars' choral of the Cathedral Church of St David's. He did this in order to increase the number of choralists and to help them meet the expenses of repairs and maintenance of their own houses.[108]

Blythe appears to have had fewer serious problems than Nix with the monastic houses of Coventry and Lichfield, and monastic visitations were performed on an equally regular basis. That is not to say he had no troubles at all. The cathedral chapter at Lichfield had long been immune from Episcopal jurisdiction, based on a 1428 compromise that limited visitations to seven-year intervals.[109] Even then, several of the officers were still immune, subject instead to triennial visitations by the dean. It was also necessary for Blythe to give the chapter two month's notice.[110] Relations with the chapter, because of the compromise and Blythe's frequent absences, were often strained and he faced jurisdictional problems throughout the see as a result. When visitations were carried out it was usually by his vicar-general. At Lilleshall, for instance, the visitor faced the contempt of the members. The problems there were uniquely financial. The abbot could not overcome the arduous debts that encumbered the house. The debt was estimated to have been about fifty percent higher than the house's annual income. Blythe pestered Abbot Cockerell about these debts to such an extent that the abbot left office in 1519. Whether he had addressed the financial issues first is doubtful. Blythe's 1524 injunctions for Burton concentrated on much the same matter.[111]

Lincoln's diocese presented one of the greatest challenges to the devoted bishop due to its sheer size. Although documentary evidence is thin, it is clear that Atwater was a vigorous visitor. For example, between June and August 1519 he carried out eighteen visitations, seventeen in person. His injunctions dealt mainly with residency questions, the letting of benefices and the condition of the fabric and ornaments of the parish churches. At Hertingfordbury, for example, where the rectory was let to a layman, his obligation to repair the chancel had been ignored, just as it had been at Pirton where, moreover, the churchyard was not properly enclosed. Indeed, in the archdeaconary of Leicester, Atwater found no less than twelve chancels in disrepair, thirteen cemeteries in need of fencing, six non-resident rectors, a completely negligent incumbent in Loughborough and four priests who were incontinent. The vastness of Lincoln's diocese meant that Atwater could not be so thorough on all matters, and he came to rely on his vicar-general, John Rayne, and other officers to oversee the parish churches and lay orthodoxy. Atwater intervened only when conditions were particularly troublesome, as those mentioned above.[112] This system worked well, for Atwater and Longland carried on the same way after 1521.

Longland, of course, was much dedicated to spiritual matters, was very active against heresy and also directed himself against financial corruption and clerical ill living.[113] Although he too was a determined visitor, the diocese's 111 religious houses, only some of which were exempt, make it clear why he also depended on deputies. Longland only visited in person where evidence was found of alarming conditions or seriously declining membership. Documentary evidence from Longland's primary visitation exists only for Burnham Abbey on 4 November 1521, and afterwards he visited only eight other houses in person. If the worst example of monastic excess were the canons of de la Pré at Leicester, where there were numerous disciplinary problems, unregulated eating and drinking, laxity in the celebrating of masses and confession, among other things[114], the most interesting and illustrative of Longland's seriousness was at one of the exempt houses, the Cistercian monastery of Thame.

A visitation had been carried out there by the house's regular visitor, the abbot of Waverly. At the time he carried the bishop's reforming injunctions with him. The visitor's record indicates the usual problems of disrepair (particularly in the dormitory) and lax regulations with regard to eating, drinking and religious observances. The abbot also recommended additional instruction in the *Regula Benedicti*.[115] Longland employed other means for investigating exempt houses as well. For instance, as bishop he was the founder and patron of Thame and he listed some twenty-one items that needed explanation or correction in regard to the brethren during the visitation.[116] He charged the abbot, John Warren, with 'negligence and incapacity in business matters, of wasteful administration of property' and with extravagance and neglect of discipline. Moreover, dilapidation of the buildings was far more widespread than merely the dormitory, affecting most of the property, while the house suffered under overwhelming debt.

The list of the abbot's faults is lengthy[117] and common to many of the members. Warren more or less responded to Longland's injunctions with bland denials and equivocation, and there was little Longland could do to force the issue. He appealed to Wolsey to help him affect reform of that house and others, just as Booth had called upon the cardinal for help with regard to the abbot of Wigmore. For whatever reason, Wolsey was less than effective in response here.[118] Later, in January 1528 and with Warren gone, Longland could find no fit replacement and asked Wolsey to consider Robert King (future bishop of Oxford) because of his very good administration of Brewern.[119] He also spent some weeks in Peterborough in 1528 trying to secure the resignation of Abbot Kirton, while also pressing for the resignation of the prior of Spalding. These moves were calculated to revitalise the larger houses, as the example of Thame made it clear they were in decline. That did not stop Longland from concentrating his attentions when the occasion called for it.

From Dorchester in 1528 he received reports of serious disturbances in the performance of offices and in the keeping of religious observances. He appointed William Goldington as the new prior and followed this up with injunctions in June 1529.[120] When he appeared in person in September 1530 he found, unfortunately, that his injunctions had been ignored. Longland suspended the abbot for having failed to exhibit the injunctions for a time, but was never really able to effectively enforce his penances on the brethren. Another Augustinian house, Great Missenden, was similarly intransigent. That house was crippled with debt, fabrics and materials were in grave disrepair, the rule was enforced only haphazardly if at all, the brethren were lacking in discipline, and one canon was found guilty of sodomy.[121] Longland's visitation of 1531, and his subsequent injunctions, concentrated on daily readings of the rule, instruction in Latin grammar, and certain financial and social disciplinary requirements. Slythurste, the sodomite, was imprisoned. Longland's injunctions were often strict and minute and, in some places, could descend into triviality.

In 1531, for instance, Nun Cotham suffered under many problems including insufficient income and heavy debts. This was due, perhaps, to a weak-willed prioress whose relatives freeloaded mercilessly at her burden and also to impatient inmates. Longland's injunctions looked to the heart of this case:

> and likewise chardge you lady priores that ye suffre nomore hereaft'
> eny lorde of mysrule to be within yor house, nouther to suffre
> hereafter eny suche disgysinge as in tymes past haue bene used in
> yor monastery in nunnes apparell ne otherwise. And then frome
> hensforthe te do nomore burden ne chardge yor hiouse with suche a
> numbre of yor kynnesfolks as ye haue in tymes past used.[122]

According to Bowker, Longland had found much the same difficulties at Little Marlow, Studley and Elstow, including ignorance of the rule, financial irregularities and ineffectual prioresses.[123]

Wolsey, despite all his other duties, was responsive to the needs of the spirituality. For example, by virtue of his legatine powers he was able to take some responsibility for the sees administered by the non-resident Italian bishops. Moreover, in the monastic houses, he enforced more rigorous applications of the founders' rules and the retreat from worldliness. Problems in Worcester, for instance, had been building for some time. In 1515, Fox's commissary, Hannibal, wrote of the 'inordinat, hedye and unreligiouse dealying of the chanons of saynct Augistinis besidis Bristoll', and Fox in turn wrote to Wolsey: 'yf I werwithin the diocese of Worcestre, I cowde, by calleng the evill disposed persons byfore me sone remedye the mater'.[124] It took some time, but on 4 March 1525 Wolsey notified Worcester monastery of his impending visitation, having discovered

> that the very persons who should have been an example to the laity
> in life and morals and good works, laid aside the fear of God, and –
> it is with sorrow we say it - lead a life less honest than becomes
> them, to the ruin of their own souls, an offence to the majesty of
> God, the shame of religion, a disgrace and bad example to the clergy,
> and a scandal to the people.[125]

He sent in his commissary, John Alen, on 8 April 1525, and his injunctions were promulgated nine days later. Almost two years hence, however, on 3 November 1526, Wolsey had cause to re-examine the injunctions and made certain changes, noting the improvement of conditions.[126] These changes are interesting and illustrative of his wider concerns and ongoing efforts, so are worth a brief look.

While the second, fifth, eighth, fourteenth and sixteenth through to the eighteenth injunctions were all revoked he made noteworthy changes to the seventh and thirteenth. The seventh had required that, with regard to the 'affixing of the common seal', the consent of the prior and 'the greater and saner part of the chapter shall suffice', all of whose names would be subscribed. The thirteenth injunction dealt with a far more serious problem, the '*proprietarii*'. These were monks who, contrary to the rule of St Benedict, held and retained private property. Those found guilty would 'continuously, during the whole of the year following, in presence of the whole convent, dine and take their food sitting on the ground'. If this humiliation failed, they would be cast out.

What is plain to see is that while the usual charges of sexual misconduct and petty disciplinary problems seem not to have arisen at Worcester, divine services were ill-attended and ill-performed, the rule of St Benedict was openly flaunted, and fasting and silent times went unobserved. The study of scripture and the pursuit of learning, even at this early stage, had begun to decline. The root cause of this rot might well have been the *proprietarii*, and it would be interesting to examine how widespread was this condition. Not only was ownership of private property made a vice under the rule [ca.33] but was also forbidden in canon law. It is apparent that the monks were wealthy, having been paid out of endowment funds, and they were not unwilling to flaunt it.[127]

Such actions evince two depressing conclusions. They indicate that the soul of monasticism was dying out and forced the recognition that the smaller houses were often a discredit to their orders (just as the later dissolution acts would state). Wolsey pursued the idea that their endowments could be better employed elsewhere, serving more appropriate and contemporary needs (as shown by both his and Fisher's dissolutions for educational foundations). In November 1528, he secured a bull empowering him, in combination with Campeggio, to suppress houses with fewer than twelve members and to combine these with larger monasteries. The following May the two cardinals received papal permission to convert abbacies into bishoprics and create new dioceses, to suppress houses worth up to 6000 ducats and transfer these assets to the royal colleges at Windsor and Cambridge, and to unite monasteries that were unable to support as few as twelve members.[128]

Monastic conditions were a key problem area faced by the bishops in their efforts to improve the spiritual reputation of the clergy. With regard to the spiritual well being of the laity, they faced the even greater problem of heresy. Despite the fact that the native heresy, Lollardy, had been in decline since the 1400s, there were still, in the 1510s and 1520s, small pockets of resistance which the bishops looked to eradicate. The Lollards had been clustered into small groups in Essex, Kent, the Chilterns, London, Bristol and Coventry, and only really communicated with each other through the book distribution network of the London-based Christian Brethren. Of course, with the 1520s came new ideas from both continental reformers and their English adherents. These influences spurred the Lollards into new ideological activity and spurred the bishops on to new efforts against them[129], efforts that they could undertake because Wolsey shouldered almost all political problems. One of the most interesting areas targeted by the bishops was the book trade itself.

* * *

## The anti-heresy campaigns of the 1520s

We have seen that bishops Fitzjames of London and Smith of Lincoln were by far the busiest bishops in the pre-1520 period and when Tunstal succeeded Fitzjames he was determined to prove equally worthy. He dedicated himself to the enforcement of lay and clerical discipline and good order but took a conciliarist approach to heresy.[130] He was more concerned with the suppression of heretical books, particularly in light of the rising influence of Luther, than with burnings.[131] In Lincoln, Smith had had some considerable successes but Atwater had been less bothered about heresy. He went so far as to reduce or rescind some of Smith's earlier sentences. As a result, he left Longland with a more serious heresy problem. Such inattention gave the Lollards new impetus, augmented after 1520 by Lutheran ideals. Although some doubts have been cast, the bishops and Wolsey did take the new heresy threats very seriously.

Davis wrote that the reception of Lutheranism in England 'took place more in the imagination of the bishops than in reality'.[132] The bishops certainly remained on guard for heretical opinions, but it is true that the greater threat was from the Lollards. Lutheran ideas were seeping in, concentrated largely in the southern dioceses and, despite the growing furore over the divorce case the bishops remained vigilant. Having worked through some initial doubts about Luther's intentions[133], the campaign against both him, and heresy in general, was publicly opened at St Paul's on Sunday, 12 May 1521.

There, both Warham and Fisher preached and Luther's books were burnt. This was, however, the very public end-product of a rather lengthy campaign which began when Tunstal wrote at least nine letters from Worms warning against Luther[134], and when the king determined to write his own book to win papal approval.[135] Indeed, in March, the pope had even granted Wolsey additional legatine powers to take action against the newly proclaimed heretic.[136] It was after this that Wolsey began to organise. On 3 April, he dispatched some of Luther's works to Warham and made preparations for a synod of theologians at Whitehall to examine further examples.[137] By 16 April, apparently, a meeting of theologians from the universities took place with the king's book prominently featured.[138]

Gwyn doubts that this council ever gathered. Wood maintains, however, that both universities held additional burnings after the main ceremony and that each had sent representatives to the cardinal's council. A synod was perhaps too time-consuming to be effective and the books had already been declared heretical in any case. Synod or not, a short time later Wolsey issued an injunction. The bishops were 'to take order that any books written or printed, of Martin Luther's errors or heresies, should be brought in to the bishop of each respective diocese; and that every such bishop receiving such books and writing should send them . . .' on to Wolsey's officials.[139]

The public ceremony was a great success. The large crowd that had gathered took the occasion very seriously and Fisher's sermon did not disappoint. Even most of the bishops attended![140] This was followed up with the publication of the sermon in all the dioceses, along with instructions on how best the bishops could take advantage of the forty-two errors found in Luther's works. On a more routine note all heretical literature was to be collected.[141] Fisher had inspired the bishops to new energy and they redoubled their efforts, individually and in co-operation. Longland probably benefited the most from the new atmosphere, having been left such a major heresy problem by Atwater.

Longland was concerned that the real threat of Luther to the Catholic Church was as a 'springboard of critical dissent'.[142] In late 1521, he took certain steps armed with a royal letter addressed to various temporal officers charging them to assist him, 'as ye tender our high displeasure'.[143] Thus equipped, Longland began a sweeping campaign in the southern portions of Lincoln[144] rounding up nearly 350 people, most of who had been under suspicion since the days of Smith. Of these, fifty were found guilty, forced to abjure and put to penance or sent into the monasteries, and four were handed over for execution.

He also looked anxiously at the sale of books and tried to impress upon Wolsey the need for further public displays. He went so far as to send lists of suspected heretics to his fellow bishops. Audley's register contains two such lists, one of six heretics and another of six suspected heretics, both of 1521.[145] Theological studies at the universities were also endangered by the thrill of the new, and both West and Longland kept weary eyes upon them. Tunstal, and those with ports in their jurisdictions (Fisher, Warham and Nix) also monitored imports as best they could to intercept new books.

Longland, however, seems to have been the most active, mounting a preaching tour of the diocese too. This initiative bore some fruit later, in

November 1526, with the trial of Thomas Wattes of Grafton. Although only a minor figure, Wattes did evince the threat originating along the Lincolnshire sea-board, and Longland alerted the priests to be extra vigilant against smugglers. It seems clear, however, that major heresy problems did not spread too far outside of the major southeast sees. John Veysey, for example, despite having been appointed president of the Council of Wales in 1526, carried out rather diligent triennial visitations of Exeter but never uncovered any great heresy threat.[146]

Bishop Fisher, despite his tireless efforts in the queen's marriage defence, was never distracted from Rochester for long. His contributions to the anti-heresy effort include both sermons and books, a great deal of which according to Rex were produced with the aid of Tunstal. This aid includes advice and assistance in the composition of the *Confutatio* and the furnishing of Fisher with unorthodox books from continental writers and loans of Greek editions of the early Fathers. The two also co-operated in the related endeavour of book censorship.[147] Fisher also turned to West for commentaries, and the latter helped him write his *Defensio Regiae*. Fisher was, of course, perfectly capable of acting alone.

On 23 December 1524, he charged Thomas Batman, keeper of St William's chapel in St Margaret's parish, with a mixture of Lollard and Lutheran articles. Batman had ridiculed saint worship and advocated salvation by faith alone. He made his second abjuration in February 1525, of mainly Lollard articles and of having preached heresy to his colleagues at St William's. It was not so much Batman himself, or his mild heresies, which set Fisher on edge. It was the implied infiltration of heresy into Rochester's monastic community. Fisher had a clear and deep commitment to the pastoral side of his role as a bishop, 'to help weaker souls whose faith was in doubt'.[148] Rochester too was a small diocese, 123 parishes and twenty religious houses, and it was feared that even mildly unorthodox notions would spread rapidly. So, even at the height of the royal divorce case he was still carrying out visitations and taking abjurations.[149] Sometimes his devotion had unexpected consequences.

Edward Maye, a Rochester official, greatly over-reacted in accusing two hermits named Betes and Kyngeswod, based on the evidence of a list of Lutheran articles found in their possession. These list had been legitimately prepared by Betes for the brethren of St William's to aid them in their struggle against any future Batmans. Later, on 15 June 1528, St William's precentor, William Mafelde, had been found in possession of an English Bible. It was a Tyndale translation that he had bought off William Patenson, Rochester's grammar instructor. Tracing the book's origin, they found that it had come into the diocese through London, having come to the capital via the university of Louvain.[150]

The heart of Rochester diocese was not the only trouble spot, however.

Much like the Chilterns in Lincoln, or Colchester in London, Rochester had its own infamous location in Gravesend. This was a riverside town noted for its 'wild people'.[151] In 1526, William Smyth, a butcher, and Paul Lomleye were charged with Lollard articles. On 16 September 1532, Fisher also charged Peter Durr, a priest, with four articles, Durr having been captured in possession of a forbidden Lutheran text. Others found and charged there include John Pilcher of Cuxton and John Bechyng, rector of Ditton. Both had expressed strong views against auricular confession.

In all the dioceses, books formed a large part of the bishops' efforts. Tunstal began the campaign against Tyndale with the official sanctioning of Thomas More, by Episcopal licence, to read heretical books.[152] Indeed, as early as 1521, the English campaign against Luther had an international dimension in that the Italians were also participating. They were sending copies of the latest anti-Lutheran works printed at Rome to England for the king, Wolsey and the other bishops to use. In March, de'Gigli sent an unnamed polemic and, well before he became tied up in the divorce, de'Ghinucci also performed a web of duties for Wolsey in regard to heresy.

Most of these said duties were in some way tied with Cardinal College. In May 1526, for example, de'Ghinucci was commissioned to seek Roman scholars who would come to England to teach in Oxford and to seek out books and procure transcripts, especially of Greek manuscripts, from both the Vatican Library and from St Michael's in Venice.[153] On 12 July, however, he also presented Wolsey with Cajetan's *Responsiones*. He got this from de'Medici[154], and sent it on to England to help with the anti-Lutheran cause. The cardinal himself handled the publication and distribution of the king's book, and Clerk made arrangements for its presentation, acceptance in Rome, and wider European distribution.[155]

In London, Tunstal was initially more concerned with the book trade than with the simple persecution campaign of his predecessor, but even this policy would change. In October 1524 he summoned two well-known booksellers and ordered them to stop the importation of books from Germany or from selling books containing Lutheran errors. Of course, importations were not the only problems. Unorthodox books were printed in London as well, at least one by the famous Wynkyn de Worde. His case came up before Richard Foxford, Tunstal's vicar-general, on 19 October 1525, along with John Gough. Worde had published a translation of Gough's, entitled *The Image of Love* which, it was alleged, contained criticisms of images and saints. Foxford charged both men to recover all those copies already sold and bring the lot in for examination by Christmas. Those copies that had gone to the universities were likewise recalled. Worde appeared in the consistory on 15 January to answer to further articles concerning suspicion of heresy.[156] Despite such an active interest, however, Tunstal and his officers could not stem the rising tide.

There was an obvious market for such books. Indeed, Tunstal's own actions came back to haunt him in the form of William Tyndale. Tunstal had turned him away some time earlier, refusing to sponsor his plan to translate the Bible. Tyndale took his *New Testament* to Cologne and began exporting copies back. Fearing the impact of an English vernacular translation, Tunstal and Longland urged Wolsey to organise a second ceremonial denunciation of heretical books. Chester noted that reports to the king from Cochlaeus and Edward Lee in Bordeaux helped prompt the official response. The collection and burning of heretical books was set forth in Wolsey's letter to Longland in January 1526[157], from which it is clear that this had been Wolsey's plan all along.[158]

Such events stirred the cardinal into action. He initiated another search for Lutheran books and sent instructions to the bishops of southern convocation to take further action. This included the establishment of a commission of inquiry (featuring Clerk, Fisher, Standish, Tunstal, Gardiner, Adam Islip of Westminster and sometimes Wolsey himself), which sat between 8 February and 26 April. He also called for a voluntary surrender of books and a second ceremony at St Paul's, on 11 February 1526. Once again Fisher would preach, now to an audience of thirty-six bishops and abbots.[159] This ceremonial burning also featured the recantation and public penance of Robert Barnes and the five Hanse merchants.[160]

The Cambridge scholar had been brought before a commission headed by Clerk, while he and Standish examined the merchants.[161] Barnes' real significance has less to do with his unorthodox sermons or his connection to 'German' factions at Cambridge than to his involvement in the book trade. Wolsey also examined the Hanseatic merchants and objected no less the ten articles against them. They admitted to various degrees of heretical activity ranging from an innocent glance through a discovered Lutheran book to the importation and distribution of heretical texts and the holding of banned opinions. At least two of the merchants were required to bear faggots with Barnes at the ceremony.[162]

The second ceremony was followed up in November 1526 when Veysey, Booth, Fisher and others were told to search for English translations of the *New Testament*, and works by Luther and Simon Fish.[163] To counter the threat of clerical heresy, Longland and West employed anti-Lutheran oaths at institutions in suspect cases. West, for example, used such an oath in 1526 on his kinsman Richard West, whom he suspected of harbouring dangerous thoughts.[164] Tunstal also marshalled all of the forces he could to combat the spread of heretical or questionable books, proving ruthless.

On 23 October 1526, he issued letters to his archdeacons, after Longland's example, ordering them to confiscate all copies of the *New Testament* on suspicion of heresy and perhaps excommunication. He also called on city officials to see to their own charges.[165] On the same day he preached that Tyndale's book was 'naughtily translated', having discovered at least 2000 errors.[166] On 25 October, he summoned thirty-one London booksellers to St Paul's, repeated his earlier admonition and told them that new imports would now have to be approved by himself, Fisher, Warham or Wolsey.[167]

Wolsey had other rods in the fire, however. After the second ceremonial burning he put forth a scheme to have books collected and burned in the Low Countries with the emperor's help, and in May 1527, he helped Warham put into action a scheme to buy up *New Testaments* in order to destroy them. This plan prompted Nix to write, on 14 June 1527, congratulating him on doing a 'gracious and a blessed deed'.[168] Earlier, on 12 March, Thomas Berthelet had been summoned to appear at Foxford's residence to answer for his part in the production of *The Treatise of the Paternoster*, a book translated by Thomas More's daughter, Margaret. The book included a translation of one of Fisher's sermons printed at the request of one of Tunstal's chaplains (Richard Sharpe) with one or two other translations. This was Fisher's sermon of 12 May 1521, which he had sent to Wynkyn de Worde to be 'diligently done & trewly printed'. He wanted an English version for the reading public and a Latin version for the pope.[169] It was not a question of orthodoxy; Berthelet had simply not shown the work to the Episcopal authorities. This, at least, shows that Episcopal controls were becoming tighter.[170] About a year later one of those thirty-one printers, Robert Wyer, appeared before the vicar-general over the printing and translation of *Symbolum Apostolicum*. He had to recall all copies and hand them over for examination and destruction. This was 7 September 1527, and Wyer fulfilled his obligations in about a week. Of course, booksellers, buyers and distributors managed to slip through the bishop's nets on more than one occasion throughout the 1520s, but some 130 persons were detected for heresy, of which five had been burnt.[171]

Late in 1527 Tunstal had other concerns. There was a group of Cambridge men preaching in London without his license and his officers had found several Lollards at Colchester working on the fringes of the book trade. This discovery had been made based on information supplied by Longland and some others.[172] Tunstal reacted to the information with a series of tribunals in 1528, from 27 January to 11 May in London, and from 15 July to 15 October in Essex. These tribunals represented what Davis called 'the biggest drive against heresy ever mounted by the English hierarchy'.[173] The bishop uncovered such major figures as John Hacker and John and William Pykas, the latter of whose family grouping spread over two parishes, St Nicholas and St James. Hacker had also disclosed information about a London conventicle that had been in existence for some six years, reading and distributing forbidden texts and Lollard tracts. Tunstal was also able to uncover information relating to the two mainstays of the Christian Brethren book production network, John Stacey and Thomas Philip.

His treatment of the accused was, in the event, rather light, except in the case of William Pykas. He and his brother had distributed books and had taught Lollard doctrine at private houses throughout Colchester and Essex. William was placed in the stocks in Lollard's Tower for three days until he swore the demanded oath.[174] Also, and at the request of Longland, Tunstal undertook an investigation of the potential source of prohibited books turning up in Oxford.[175] On 21 February 1528, Thomas Garrett, a distributor of heretical books, was arrested near Bristol. This was the end result of Longland's investigations at the university.[176]

Longland was ever vigilant with regard to Oxford and worked with the prelates of surrounding dioceses with regard to the trade in illicit books. Bowker wrote that he 'took almost a sportsman's delight' in the successful hunting of heretical preachers, a monk here, two Lutherans there, always writing to Wolsey to broadcast his efforts and hopefully inspire the cardinal to further action.[177] By 1527, he might have thought his work was coming to an end, but up cropped the case of Thomas Garrett to prove just how much more work there was yet to do.

John London, the warden of New College, wrote to Longland on 24 February that Garrett had been uncovered 'lurking' in Oxford with several heretical books, trying to sell them and doing good business. He was part of a distribution chain that spread from Oxford, via the parson of Honey Lane in London, to a bookseller in the churchyard of St Paul's named Nicholas. Garrett escaped Longland's first attempt to capture him but was eventually taken in Bedminster just outside Bristol.[178] Longland wrote to Wolsey about the case and identified another London bookseller named Gough, and five other associates of Garrett who should be rounded up.[179] He suggested that the cardinal examine these men and the prior of Reading too. While Longland (and West) initiated the anti-Luther ordination oath, Wolsey passed the warnings and recommendations over to Tunstal.

The bishop of London had Forman (the parson of Honey Lane), his servant John Goodale and the bookseller Gough all imprisoned on suspicion of heresy and he later interrogated them individually. He came to the conclusion that Gough was an innocent in this affair, Longland perhaps mistaking him for another bookseller, a Dutchman named Theodoryke. Indeed, Tunstal seems to have been leaning towards leniency in any case for the simple reason that 'al my presons by full off other persons out off the fordest parte of my Diocese'.[180] He had been quite busy rounding people up and trying to talk them out of their erroneous opinions with reasoned arguments.

Longland continued to make inquiries at Oxford, based on his findings and information from Garrett's trial, and wrote to Wolsey to license those scholars he had detected 'for having evil books' and that priests should similarly be licensed. The Garrett case shows the bishop to have been a harsh man only when circumstances called for it. In his letter to Wolsey, Longland wanted Garrett, Clarke and Freer 'handled according to the mischief they had done'.[181] Perhaps unfortunately, Clarke died in prison from the plague before his examination. Another important heretic was John Tewkesbury, who had been examined by Tunstal in 1527, when he abjured, and again later by Longland, Tunstal, West and Clerk in April 1529 after his relapse. He abjured again only to relapse again. This third time Stokesley, who was a hard-line conservative who favoured burning first and questions later, captured him. Tewkesbury died at Smithfield on 20 December 1531.[182]

It is quite clear that the bishops could work individually and collectively. They could be effective as members of heresy commissions, on boards of inquiry set up by the cardinal or on their own initiatives. Freed from political and courtly concerns, they had the time to do this properly. Meanwhile, Wolsey himself had serious dealings with Latimer as a result of his controversy with West. This had been in the spring of 1526 when, along with Bilney, Latimer had been summoned to appear in Ely consistory. Later, before the cardinal, Latimer proved himself a skilled theologian in his disputes with several of Wolsey's chaplains, and Wolsey even accepted his exposition on the duties of a bishop. Wolsey concluded that 'if the bishop of Ely cannot abide such doctrine as you have here repeated, you shall have my licence, and shall preach into his beard, let him say what he will', but told Latimer he should have known better than to tangle with West in the first place.[183]

In York's diocese, Wolsey's officers were also troubled by a certain foreign element. A group of cases involving Dutch immigrants with questionable opinions came to light in the late 1520s. One of these, Gilbert Johnson of York, abjured before Brian Higden (Wolsey's vicar-general and dean of York) on 16 May 1528. Anxieties about the spread of heresy meant that Johnson was put to a particularly prolonged and gruelling penance (as described by Dickens), no doubt meant to force others into re-thinking their opinions.[184] Only two months later, Robert Robynson of Hull was hauled up before Wolsey's officers over his criticisms of auricular confession and his doubts on the efficacy of priesthood. He had also made some other Lollard-*esque* mutterings when in his cups. He too was assigned 'prolonged and humiliating penances'.[185] Robynson's friend and fellow sailor Roger Danyell was found in possession of Tyndale's translation, no doubt brought back on one of his voyages. Clearly, further efforts were needed in the north as well.

When Wolsey set out to respond to the heightened threats, however, a conflict with the southern prelates over authority threatened to undermine it. When in November 1527 he had made a formal declaration of his legatine jurisdiction over heresy and undertook an inquiry into charges of heresy within the London diocese, Tunstal objected that as bishop of the diocese wherein the heresy occurred he already had sufficient authority to deal with it. Nonetheless, the cardinal commissioned Warham, Tunstal, Fisher, West, Veysey, Longland, Clerk, Standish and Kite[186] to meet at Westminster. After one meeting, however, a compromise was agreed. The commission was moved to Nix's London residence and Tunstal was put in charge of it.[187] The most interesting case they examined was that of Thomas Bilney and associates, with whom Tunstal carried out a lengthy correspondence.

The Bilney trial was of singular importance. Not only was he a leading preacher, but he was very charismatic and persuasive too. He alone was responsible for the conversion of such men as Thomas Arthur (who preached heretical sermons in London at St Mary Woolchurch), George Marshall (who preached in Danbury[188]), Latimer, Barnes and John Lambert. Bilney's main heresy, among several Lollard beliefs, was denial of the cult of saints as mentioned in West's register. The bishop of Ely had recorded Bilney's licence to preach of 23 July 1525 and later its revocation due to his heresy conviction.[189] Wolsey, in 1526, summoned both Bilney and Latimer to appear before him but took a lenient view. He released Bilney on oath not to preach any more heretical sermons.[190]

At Cambridge, shortly thereafter, Latimer convinced Bilney to go on a preaching tour of his native Norfolk, Suffolk and eventually London. As a result of a sermon in St Magnus's, he was brought before an Episcopal tribunal on 27 November 1527. There he stood accused of breaking his former oath and of spreading heresy. Both he and Arthur were extensively examined and some thirty-four articles were objected against them. Of these we find a curious mixture of Lutheran, Lollard and even Erasmian views.[191] The case revolved around his denigration of saint worship and his advocating of justification by faith alone. A number of witnesses were brought forward to speak against him; people who had witnessed his sermons in London, Ely and Norwich dioceses.[192]

On 3 December, Tunstal (heading the tribunal in Wolsey's absence) produced Bilney's letters and questioned his statements, but Bilney put a number of orthodox spins on his writings and refused to abjure. The bishop had no choice but to judge against him even though he had wanted to avoid the death sentence. On 4 December Bilney was given another chance to abjure but again refused, claiming that he had been the victim of smears and misrepresentations by the witnesses. On 7 December, after a night conferring with his friends, Bilney agreed to abjure, realising no doubt that the witnesses against him were damaging and sufficient for a heresy conviction. Such witnesses had left Tunstal with no other choice in the matter but to proceed to conviction.[193] It seems clear from the oath that Bilney was required to swear that Tunstal was trying to save his life while, at the same time, secure a public demonstration of the fairness of the trial.[194] Both Arthur and Bilney carried penitential faggots at St Paul's Cross as a token of their abjurations, after which the former was allowed to go free provided he preach no more. Bilney, however, was imprisoned at Wolsey's pleasure for about a year before he was returned to Cambridge. Perhaps, as Walker suggested, Bilney's reputation for personal piety, his skilful preaching and his popularity among scholars and laymen alike, explains why Arthur was made to confess to a far more severe oath. No one had been watching Arthur's trial so closely and a voluntary confession was not so dearly needed. In any case, while 1529 was probably not the best time to be at Cambridge, Bilney had returned seemingly a broken man.[195]

Both town and university, quickly embroiled in the divorce matter, were the foci of further ecclesiastical attention by bishops West and Nix. George Joye had been put on trial at about the time of Bilney's return, and sometime earlier Anthony Yaxley had been forced to abjure before Nix. Nix, who was never a friend of the cardinal due to certain monetary disputes and Wolsey's granting of licenses in Norwich diocese without his knowledge, was nonetheless energetic in his hunting out of heresy with or without the cardinal's assistance.[196] Having burnt Thomas Norrice in 1501, Thomas Ayers in 1510 and Thomas Bingey in 1511, Nix carried on his efforts having little real connection to the divorce controversy. By 1530, it appears that he had managed to isolate the heresy problem to certain merchants in those infamous seaside communities, and he placed the blame for the spread squarely on the closeness of Cambridge. Indeed, a number of Norfolk men were numbered among the suspect Cambridge scholars: Arthur, Lambert, Barnes, Nicholas Shaxton and Bilney included.

When Shaxton applied for a license to preach in Norwich diocese in 1531, Nix refused it without a formal abjuration as Shaxton had been accused of preaching heresy and of bringing heretical books into the diocese.[197] Bilney too fell foul of Nix and was caught by his Episcopal officers after starting a private preaching tour of Norwich on 16 August 1531.[198] Nix had also managed to ferret out one of Tyndale's agents in 1530, Thomas Hitton, who had been importing copies of the *New Testament* and Joye's English primer. He had Hitton burnt as a heretic in Maidstone sometime thereafter.[199]

One of the most notorious of the colporteurs was Robert Bayfield, a former monk of Bury St Edmunds and a member of the Christian Brethren. Sometime in 1525 Barnes had provided him a copy of Erasmus's *Novum Testamentum* and later, in 1526, he had acquired two of Tyndale's translations from a book agent named Necton. Bayfield abjured before Tunstal in April 1528 certain articles suggesting the usual Lollard beliefs, like *solascriptura*[200], but fled

England immediately afterwards to become one of Tyndale's book agents. When he was captured and tried again in 1531, it was before Stokesley, whom we shall see was less inclined toward leniency.

\* \* \*

## 6. The end of the Wolsey era

It is clear that the cardinal's once over-riding dominance was beginning to weaken post-1527. Gwyn wrote that this was caused by his attempted reform of diocesan organisation and by the fact that he was not a humanist (and was thus ill-equipped to deal with men who were). The second point is well illustrated by both William Roper and William Tyndale, two contemporary observers who pointed out Wolsey's attempts to oust Stokesley from the court because he did things differently. Tyndale noted that

> If among those cormoraunts any yet began to be to much in favour with the Kyng, and to be somewhat busie in the Court and to drawe any other way then as my Lord Cardinall had appointed that the plowe shoulde go, anone he was sent to Italy or to Spayne, or some quarrel was picked agaynst him, and so was thrust out of Court, as Stokesley was.[201]

As the king turned more and more to these men for advice, Wolsey's obstructionism did him no favours.

With regard to the re-organisation of the dioceses, for which he had solicited no other opinions nor summoned legatine convocations, it was not so much that the idea was ill-founded as it involved a loss of revenue, or potential loss of revenue, to curia officials and that there were also strong objections on the part of the existing bishops. They were bound to lose revenue from fees of various kinds too, as these new dioceses were to be founded on certain monastic lands. Moreover, the bishops would be losing large areas of jurisdiction and there were also several other vested interests among the laity. Colet had recognised the need for this kind of reform in his earlier convocation sermon, and Fisher had agreed with him, but neither would be losing out here. Longland, Wolsey's friend, offered no support either, even though the sheer size of Lincoln had restricted his real involvement in its spiritual life.[202] As the creation of new dioceses would have disrupted clerical unity and discipline, the plans were quietly shelved (for the moment).

\* \* \*

The lessons of 1515, the contested jurisdictions between church and state, the state of the clergy themselves and the rising incidents of anti-clericalism had forced the king's hand. He had made it very clear to all concerned that he expected to preside over a church that was subservient to his will, but still effective. To ensure this he put at its head a man who would do his bidding and, in regard to visitations, reform and heresy, it had proven a good decision. Building up the bishops into a powerful spiritual body had, however, less happy returns.

The late 1520s saw the emergence of the greatest issue of the early reformation period in England, the so-called 'Great Matter'. The Roman church refused to grant the king what he thought was his rightful due. Several English churchmen proved equally lukewarm, or even hostile, to his plight and united against him. Wolsey found himself caught in the middle between his duty to the king and his duty to the church, having finally discovered a royal task that he could not perform. Others, however, were in no such quandary. While the bishops concentrated on the heretics, monasteries and on the book trade, a new group of men captured the king's attention and eventually solved his problems, displacing the 'old' bishops in the process.

We shall see that the divorce, and subsequent related events, split the Episcopal bench once again into rival factions and altered its structure from an assembly of legal-minded advisors and diplomats into a company primarily composed of humanist scholars and intellectual theologians. Initially, this split brought conservative but anti-Roman prelates to the forefront. The role of the bishops had shifted over the 1520s. They still advised the king and shepherded the souls of the nation but they no longer administrated the government (having been displaced by Wolsey and lay officials like More). Pre-1527, the bishops easily combined roles in both diocese and court. Post-1527, the balance was increasingly more difficult to maintain as the needs in one often contradicted the good of the other, particularly with regard to perceived heresy. The intellectual priorities of the kingdom were changing. As the king's search for intellectual support led him to compromise his zeal against Lutheranism, and as his advocates became more and more entrenched in their anti-papal positions, ever more radically anti-papal (and thus anti-clerical) opinions were tolerated and the Episcopate was changed forever.

## Notes

1. Elton, *Tudors*, p.69.
2. E.g., *CWE*, iii, p.233; *LP*, ii, 1552.
3. George Cavendish, 'The Life and Death of Cardinal Wolsey' in Richard S. Sylvester and Davis P. Harding (eds), *Two Early Tudor Lives* (New Haven, Conn., 1962), p.12.
4. See, Gywn, pp.5*ff*; Pollard, *Henry VIII*, pp.352*ff*; Scarisbrick, *Henry VIII*, pp.41-6; G.R. Elton, *Reform and Reformation England, 1509-1558* (Cambridge, Mass., 1977), p.47.
5. Wilkins, iii, p.655. What follows is based on Michael Kelly, 'Canterbury Jurisdiction and Influence During the Episcopate of William Warham, 1503-1532' (unpublished Ph.D. thesis, University of Cambridge, 1963), pp.42-94.
6. DRO. Reg. Oldham, fol.165.

7. Mumford, pp.92-4; Thomson, p.125.
8. Richard Wunderli, 'Pre-Reformation London Summoners and the Murder of Richard Hunne', *JEH* xxxiii:ii (April 1982), pp.209-24 (at p.218).
9. Christopher Harper-Bill, 'Bishop Richard Hill and the Court of Canterbury 1494-96', *Guildhall Studies in London History* iii:i (October 1977), pp.1-12 (at p.2).
10. Wilkins, iii, pp.641-2; Christopher Harper-Bill (ed.), *Register of John Morton, Archbishop of Canterbury, 1486-1500* (2 vols., Leeds, 1987), ii, fols.220v-221.
11. *Register of John Morton*, ii, fols.208v-9v.
12. Harper-Bill, p.7.
13. *Register of John Morton*, ii, fols.207v-8.
14. BL, Additional MS 48012, fols.14v, 25.
15. Wilkins, iii, pp.653-7.
16. PRO. SP 1/1, fols.102-3; *LP*, i/i, 308, 448 (iv).
17. Warham appointed his proctors on 7 April 1511 [BL, Additional MS 48012, fol.22 for Clerk] whereas Fox appointed his on 2 June 1511 [Kelly, p.60].
18. Christopher Kitching, 'The Prerogative Court of Canterbury from Warham to Whitgift', in Rosemary O'Day and Felicity Heal (eds), *Continuity and Change: Personnel and administration of the Church of England, 1500-1642* (Leicester, 1976), pp.191-214 (at pp.193-5).
19. Reg. Oldham, fols.175rv; Wilkins, iii, pp.656-7.
20. Irene J. Churchill, *Canterbury Administration* (2 vols., London, 1933), i, pp.381-90; Kelly, pp.61-8.
21. Kelly, p.71-4; G. Parrish, *The Forgotten Primate* (London, 1971), p.18.
22. BL, Cottonian MSS, Vitellius B ii, fol.22; Wilkins, iii, p.656; *LP*, i/i, 1780; i/ii, 1941, 2019, 2312.
23. J.B. Sheppard (ed.), *Literae Cantuarienses* (3 vols., London, 1889), iii, p.430.
24. *Ibid*, pp.416-21.
25. *Ibid*, pp.429-30.
26. *Ibid*, pp.435-7; *LP*, i/ii, 2269.
27. Kelly, p.91. The composition with Fox was no similar.
28. For the basic details of this infamous case, see J. Duncan M. Derrett, 'The Affairs of Richard Hunne and Friar Standish', in *CWTM*, ix, pp.215-46; Foxe, iv, pp.183-90 and *CWTM*, viii, p.126.
29. M.D. Knowles, *The Religious Orders in England* (3 vols., Cambridge, 1959), iii, pp.91-5.
30. Ogle, p.134; Pollard, *Wolsey*, p.31 (n.1); Rymer (ed.), xiii, pp.532-3.
31. Ogle, p.130; *LJ*, i, pp.21, 25, 38, 41.
32. *LJ*, i, pp.45-7, 53-6.
33. *LP*, ii, 887, 996-8, 1280, 1312; BL, Vit. B ii, fols.97v, 98-99v.
34. PRO. SP 1/12, fols.18-21; *LP*, ii, 1314.
35. Gwyn, p.48; Derrett, p.230.
36. Ogle, p.152.
37. Derrett, pp.234-5; Gwyn, pp.49-50; Ogle, pp.152-3.
38. *LP*, ii, 892.
39. Mandal Creighton, *Cardinal Wolsey* (London, 1891), p.103; *LP*, i/i, 761.
40. See, *LP*, iii/i, 1972 (although somewhat ambiguous); Gwyn, p.295; Phyllis M Hembry, *The Bishops of Bath and Wells, 1540-1640; Social and Economic Problems* (London, 1967), p.52.
41. *LP*, iii/ii, 3594.
42. Kelly, pp.162-3; N. Pocock, 'Archbishop Warham Abortive Council, 1518', *EHR*

viii:xxx (April 1893), pp.297-9. See also, BL. Additional MSS. 48012, fols.53v-4.

43. Wilkins, iii, pp.660-1; *LP*, iii/i, 77 (2).

44. Rymer (ed.), xiii, p.740.

45. E.g., A.T. Bannister (ed.), *Bothe*, pp.iii, 57, 65, 74; Allen and Allen (eds), pp.114-7; *LP*, iii/i, 77, 98, 120, and 127.

46. *LP*, iii/i, 162; Rawdon Brown (ed.), *Four years at the court of Henry VIII* (2 vols. London, 1854), ii, p.263.

47. *LP*, iii/i, 77; iii/ii, 1128.

48. Allen and Allen (eds), p.116; *LP*, iii/i, 1122.

49. Michael Macklem, *God Have Mercy: The Life of John Fisher of Rochester* (Toronto, 1968), p.54; Ronald Bayne (ed.), *The Life of John Fisher* (London, 1921), p.35; F. van Ortroy (ed.), 'Vie du bienheureux martyr Jean Fisher cardinal, évêque de Rochester', *Analecta Bollandiana* x/i (1891), pp.121-365 (at pp.216-7, 257-8); S. Thompson, p.74.

50. Gwyn, pp.267-8, 270; A.T. Bannister (ed.), *Bothe*, p.66; A. Hamilton Thompson (ed.), 'Visitations in the Diocese of Lincoln 1517-1531', in *LRS* xxxiii (1940), pp.148-52; Bowker, *Secular Clergy*, pp.124-6; Heal, 'The Bishops of Ely', pp.51-3; Wilkins, iii, pp.662-82.

51. *LP*, iii/i, 77 (6); PRO. SP 1/18, fol.37; Gwyn, p.290.

52. Gwyn, p.291; George Bernard, *War, Taxation and Rebellion in Tudor England* (Sussex, 1986), pp.96-107.

53. *LP*, iii/i, 129.

54. Rymer (ed.), xiii, p.734.

55. *LP*, iii/i, 98, 127 (wrongly dated to 1519); iii/ii, 2625.

56. *LP*, iii/ii, 2647; Ellis (ed.), 3rd series, ii, pp.41-2; PRO. SP 1/26, fols.40, 271; *LP*, iii/ii, 2767; iv, 1662.

57. Gwyn, pp.278-9; *LP*, iii/ii, 2752; Kelly, pp.182-7; Kitching, pp.191-213.

58. Kelly, pp.184-6; PRO. SP 1/26, fol.120 (*LP*, iii/ii, 2633). See drafts at PRO. SP 6/7, fol.24; 1/26, fols.242, 243-6 (*LP*, iii/ii, 2752).

59. *LP*, iii/ii, 2752. Details of the joint commission can be found in Churchill, i, pp.410-11 and *LP*, iii/i, 599; iv/ii, 5589; A.T. Bannister (ed.), *Bothe*, pp.189-90; Guy, 'Wolsey', pp.482-3.

60. *LP*, iii/i, 599 (PRO. SP 1/19, fol.168); Gwyn, p.281.

61. *LP*, iv/ii, 5095.

62. *LP*, iv/i, 72, 1118, 1518; Gwyn, p.283.

63. Ellis (ed.), 3rd series, ii, p.43 (*LP*, iv/i 1157); *LP*, iv/i, 1518; Gwyn, p.284.

64. E.g., GLRO. MS 9531/10 Register of Cuthbert Tunstal, 1522-1529/30, 313v; Wilkins, iii, pp.700-1; A.T. Bannister (ed.), *Bothe*, pp.142-4; *LP*, iii/i, 3024; Kelly, p.174.

65. E.g., Elton, *Reform and Reformation*, p.92; Guy, 'Wolsey', pp.483-4; Pollard, *Wolsey*, pp.187-91; Hay (ed.), *Anglia historia*, pp.305-7, but there seems to be no real hard evidence in support. See also, Gwyn, pp.286-7; Kelly, p.175. For Nix and Wolsey see, PRO. SP 1/50, fol.20 (*LP*, iv, 4659); for Blythe, see PRO. SP 1/54, fol.34 (*LP*, iv, 5589); Peter Heath, 'The Treason of Geoffrey Blythe, Bishop of Coventry and Lichfield 1503-31', *BIHR* xlii (1969), pp.101-9. See PRO. SP 1/50, fol.165 for the testamentary jurisdiction problem. See also, PRO. SP 1/53, fol.241 (*LP*, iv, 5491), fol.242 (*LP*, iv, 5492); SP 1/56, fol.209 (LP, iv, 6139).

66. Hall, p.655; *CSPS*, Suppliment to vols.1&2, p.219.

67. *LP*, iv/ii, 2751; Gwyn, p.373; Pollard, *Wolsey*, pp.177-8.

68. Henry Wharton, *Anglia Sacra* (2 vols., London, 1691), i, p.456.

69. Heath, 'Blythe', p.108.

70. *Ibid*, p.105.
71. *LP*, iv/ii, 4659 (PRO. SP 1/50, fol.20).
72. *LP*, iv/ii, 5589, 5491, 5492; Gwyn, pp.294-5.
73. *LP*, iv/ii, 4527.
74. Allen and Allen (eds), pp.114-5; *LP*, iii/i, 1122; Gwyn, p.315.
75. Wilkins, iii, p.651. Colet's sermon is STC 5545, 5550; Lupton, p.303.
76. Wilkins, iii, p.655; A.T. Bannister (ed.), *Mayew*, p.10.
77. A.T. Bannister (ed.), *Mayew*, pp.103-4, 106-7; S. Thompson, p.114; Wilkins, iii, pp.586-7.
78. Lander, p.23.
79. Allen and Allen (eds), p.122; *LP*, iii/i, 414; Gwyn, p.270.
80. S. Thompson, pp.231*ff*.
81. *Ibid*, p.153.
82. E.g., *LP*, iv/i, 1289, 1482.
83. *LP*, iii/ii, 3436; J. Wilson (ed.), *VHC: Cumberland* (2 vols., London, 1905), ii, p.46.
84. Allen and Allen (eds), p.110.
85. Barry Collett, 'The Civil Servant and Monastic Reform: Richard Fox's Translation of the Benedictine Rule for Women, 1517', in Judith Loades (ed.), *Monastic Studies; The Continuity of Tradition* (Bangor, 1990), pp.211-28 (at p.215).
86. Allen and Allen (eds.), pp.90, 150-1, 158; *LP*, iii/i, 2207.
87. E.g., *LP*, ii, 730; iv/i, 3815; Allen and Allen (eds), pp.79-80.
88. Allen and Allen (eds), pp.150-1.
89. A. Jessopp (ed.), pp.106*ff*; A. Hamilton Thompson (ed.), pp.72 (for Assherugge), 80 (for Burcestre), 85 (for Burne).
90. A. Jessopp (ed.), pp.65-319; Knowles, iii, p.73.
91. A. Jessopp (ed.), pp.xviii, 73.
92. *Ibid*, pp.xv, 95-100.
93. Lander, p.172.
94. 'Visitations in the diocese of York, Holden by Archbishop Edward Lee (A.D. 1534-5)', *The Yorkshire Archaeological Journal* xvi (1902), pp.424-58 (at pp.439-41); S. Thompson, p.155.
95. *LP*, iii/ii, 1517, 1713; iv/iii, Appendix, 85.
96. Lander, p.165; Knowles, iii, pp.71-2; A.T. Bannister (ed.), *Bothe*, pp.77-80, 132; Mumford, pp.91-5.
97. SRO. EP I/1/5, fols.141-2.
98. Lander, pp.171*ff*.
99. William Turner and W.H. Blaauw, 'Injunctions given to the Prior and Convent of Boxgrove, A.D. 1518', in *Sussex Archaeological Collections*, ix (1857), pp.61-66.
100. W.H. Blaauw, 'Episcopal visitations of the Benedictine Nunnery of Easebourne', in *Sussex Archaeological Collections*, ix (1857), pp.1-32 (at pp.23-7).
101. SRO. EP 1/10/3, fols.31-2, 35-6, 38, 40; 1/10/4, fol.12; Lander, p.67.
102. Lander, p.66.
103. E.g., SRO. EP 1/10/5, fols.5, 7-9, 80-90.
104. Lander, pp.72-7.
105. Steer, p.7; Lander, p.101.
106. SRO. EP, VI/4/1, fols.73-4; Lander, pp.114-6.
107. E.g., A.T. Bannister (ed.), *Bothe*, pp.vii, 149, 285; *LP*, x, 1257; M.E.C. Walcott, 'Bishops of Chichester', in *Sussex Archaeological Collections Relating to the History and Antiquities of the County* xxix (1879), pp.1-39 (at pp.21ff); J.M. Wilson, 'The Visitations and Injunctions of Cardinal Wolsey and Archbishop

Cranmer to the Priory of Worcester in 1526 & 1534 respectively', in *Associated Architectural Societies' Reports and Papers*, xxxvi:i (1921), pp.356-71.

108. R.F. Isaacson (ed.), *The Episcopal Register of the Diocese of St David's 1397 to 1518* (3 vols., London, 1917, 1920), iii, pp.827-9.

109. Wilkins, iii, pp.508-11. See also, Cooper, p.42.

110. P. Heath (ed.), 'Bishop Geoffrey Blythe's Visitations, c.1515-1525', in *Staffordshire Record Society*, fourth series, vii (1973), p.xxiv; *idem*, 'Suppliments to Bishop Blythe's Visitations', in *Staffordshire Record Society*, fourth series, xiii (1988), pp.47-56.

111. Heath (ed.), 'Blythe's Visitations', pp.174*ff*.

112. A. Hamilton Thompson (ed.), pp.223-5; W. Page (ed.), *VCH: Hertfordshire* (4 vols., London, 1902-14), iv, pp.310-11; W. Page (ed.), *VCH: Leicestershire* (5 vols., London, 1907-64), i, pp.368-9.

113. Bowker, *Longland*, p.15.

114. *Ibid*, p.23

115. A. Hamilton Thompson (ed.), p.209.

116. Knowles, iii, pp.70-2; Wharhirst, pp.163-4.

117. George G. Perry, 'The Visitation of the monastery of Thame, 1526', *EHR*, iii (1888), pp.704-22.

118. *LP*, iv/ii, 5121; S. Thompson, p.156; A. Hamilton Thompson (ed.), p.209; *LP*, iv/ii, 5189; Knowles, iii, pp.70-2.

119. *LP*, iv/ii, 5189.

120. G.G. Perry, 'Episcopal Visitations of the Austin Canons of Leicester and Dorchester', *EHR*, iv (1889), pp.310-13.

121. Bowker, *Longland*, pp.22-3; A. Hamilton Thompson (ed.), 'Visitations in the Diocese of Lincoln 1517-1531', in *LRS* xxxiii (1940), pp.18-27.

122. A.R. Maddison (ed.), 'Extracts from Bishop Longland's Register', in *Associated Architectural Societies' Reports and Papers*, xv:ii (1880), pp.167-79 (at pp.174-6).

123. Bowker, *Longland*, pp.25-8.

124. Allen and Allen (eds), pp.79-80; S Thompson, p.151.

125. R.W. Hoyle, 'The Origins of the Dissolution of the Monasteries', *HJ* xxxviii:ii (1995), pp.275-305 (at p.280).

126. Wilson, p.356-64.

127. *Ibid*, p.369.

128. *LP*, iv/ii, 4920-1; iv/iii, 5607; Gwyn, pp.464-9.

129. Doran and Durstan, pp.94*ff*.

130. Sturge, p.130.

131. E.g., BL, Cott., Vit.B xx, fols.218-20.

132. J.F. Davis, *Heresy and Reformation in the South East of England 1520-1559* (London, 1983), p.41.

133. For Erasmus's words of caution see, *CWE*, vi, pp.368-72.

134. BL, Vit.B.xx, fols.217-37.

135. Elton, *Reform and Reformation*, pp.75-6; *LP*, iii/i, 1220, 1233; Scarisbrick, *Henry VIII*, pp.110-16; *CWM*, v, pp.720-1.

136. Wilkins, iii, pp.689-93; Rymer (ed.), xiii, p.742; *LP*, iii/i, 1197, 1210, 1233-4.

137. *LP*, iii/i, 1218.

138. *Ibid*, 1233.

139. Allan Chester, 'A Note on the Burning of Lutheran Books in England in 1521', *Library Chronicle* xviii (1952), pp.68-70; Strype, *EM*, i/i, pp.55-6, i/ii, pp.20-25.

140. *CSPV*, iii, pp.121-5; *LP*, iii, 1275.

141. Wilkins, iii, pp.690-3.
142. A.G. Dickens, *The English Reformation* (New York, 1976 edn.), p.36.
143. Foxe, iv, p.241.
144. *Ibid*, pp.219-46; Fines, p.242.
145. Fines, pp.169-70.
146. D.H. Pill, 'The administration of the diocese of Exeter under Bishop Veysey', *Transactions of the Devon Association* xcviii (1966), pp.262-78 (at p.263).
147. E. Surtz, *The Works and Days of John Fisher* (Cambridge, Mass., 1967), p.97; Richard Rex, 'The English Campaign against Luther in the 1520s', *TRHS*, 5th series, xxxix (1989), pp.85-106 (at p.96).
148. Surtz, p.310.
149. Stephen Thompson, 'The bishop in his diocese', in B. Bradshaw and E. Duffy (eds), *Humanism, Reform and Reformation: The Career of John Fisher* (Cambridge, 1989), pp.67-80 (at p.74).
150. Davis, pp.42-3.
151. Elton, *Policy*, p.366.
152. *LP*, iv/ii, 4028; Rex, 'Campaign', p.97. For further details, see Wilkins, iii, pp.711-2; Guildhall Library, MS 9531/10, fol.138.
153. *LP*, iii, 1916.
154. *LP*, iii/i, 1204, 1411; Rex, 'Campaign', p.98.
155. *LP*, iii/i, 1510, 1574, 1760; Ellis (ed.), iii/i, pp.283-4; Gwyn, p.486; *LP*, iv/i, 2446.
156. A. Reed, *Early Tudor Drama*, (London, 1926), p.167.
157. BL, Cott. MSS, Vit.B.v., fols.11a-12b; Ellis (ed.), i/i, pp.179-84; *LP*, iv/i, 995.
158. Allan G. Chester, 'Robert Barnes and the Burning of Books', *Huntington Library Quarterly* xiv:iii (May 1951), pp.211-21 (at pp.211-3).
159. Susan Brigden, *London and the Reformation* (Oxford, 1989), pp.157*ff*; Ellis (ed.), i/i, pp.179-84; *LP* iv/i, 995, iv/ii, 2607; Chester, 'Barnes', p.216; S. Thompson, 'Pastoral Shepherds', p.127; Wilkins, iii, pp.706-7.
160. James P. Lusardi, 'The Career of Robert Barnes', in *CWM*, viii/iii, pp.1367-1415 (at pp.1382-3).
161. *LP*, iv/i, 1962.
162. *Ibid*.
163. *LP*, iv/ii, 2607; Bannister (ed.), *Bothe*, p.187.
164. S. Thompson, 'Pastoral Shepherds', p.128.
165. Wilkins, iii, pp.706, 727; Guildhall Library, MS 9531/10, fol.45r; Bridgen, p.159; BL, Lansdowne MS 979, fol.41.
166. Sturge, pp.132-3.
167. GLRO, DL/C/330, fol.123r; Strype, *EM*, i/ii, pp.364-5; Foxe, v, pp.213-4; Reed, pp.165-6.
168. David Daniell, *William Tyndale, A Biography* (New Haven, Conn., 1994), p.175.
169. G.J. Gray, 'Letters of Bishop Fisher, 1521-3', *The Library* 3rd series, iv (1913), pp.133-45 (at p.139).
170. Reed, p.170.
171. Bridgen, p.162.
172. Strype, *EM*, i/ii, p.50-65.
173. Davis, p.57.
174. BL, Harleian MS 421, fols.19-20; Davis, pp.60-65.
175. Strype, *EM.*, i/ii, pp.63-5.
176. Guildhall Library, MS 9531/10, fols.136-8; Foxe, v, p.141. For the correspondence between Tunstal and Wolsey on these matters, see *LP*, iv/ii, 4004, 4017, 4125, 4418

(printed in Foxe, v, Appendix vi).

177. Ellis (ed.), iii/ii, pp.247, 252.
178. *LP*, iv/ii, 4004.
179. Foxe, v, Appendix no.vi, letter 4.
180. *Ibid*, letter 7.
181. *LP*, iv/ii, 4017.
182. *LP*, v, 589; Foxe, iv, p.690.
183. BL, Harleian MS 422, fols.84-7.
184. Dickens, *Lollards*, pp.18-9.
185. *Ibid*, p.24.
186. Guildhall Library, MS 9531/10, fol.130.
187. *Ibid*, fols.130v-6; Greg Walker, 'Saint or Schemer? The 1527 Heresy Trial of Thomas Bilney Reconsidered', *JEH* xl:ii (April 1989), pp.219-38 (at p.220).
188. Guildhall Library, MS 9531/10. fol.136r; DL/C/330, fol.136v.
189. CUL., Register of Nicholas West, fol.33r; Davis, p.47.
190. Harold S. Darby, 'Thomas Bilney', *London Quarterly and Holborn Review* v (January 1942), pp.67-84 (at p.75).
191. Foxe, iv, pp.62*ff*.
192. Davis, pp.49-51; Guildhall Library, MS 9531/10, fols.133v-5v.
193. E.g., *LP*, iv/ii, 4029 (2).
194. Walker, p.220; Guildhall Library MS 9531/10, fol.135.
195. Darby, p.82.
196. *LP*, iv/ii, 4659, 5491-2, 5589, 6139.
197. *LP*, v, 297; *VHC: Norfolk*, ii, p.253.
198. Goddard Johnson, 'Chronological Memoranda touching the city of Norwich', Norfolk and Norwich Archaeological Society i (1847), pp.140-66 (at p.144); *LP*, v, 522, 560.
199. Davis, *Heresy*, p.80.
200. Foxe, iv, pp.680-3.
201. William Tyndale, 'The Practice of Prelates' in Henry Walter (ed.), *Expositions and Notes on Sundry Portions of the Holy Scripture* (Cambridge, 1849), p.309; Sylvester and Harding (eds.), p.218.
202. Gwyn, pp.466-8.

# Chapter Three
# The End of the Medieval Church, c.1527-1534

We have seen the Episcopate's development cycle from a solidly political and spiritual block into a faction-ridden institution and, lastly, into an effective ecclesiastical elite. Although dominated by lawyers and administrators up to the mid-1520s, these naturally factious individuals were forged by Wolsey into a solid working synod fighting heresy, reforming the clergy and guarding the souls of the nation. Although they had been successfully moulded into this powerful spiritual fraternity, the king's 'Great Matter', a partially spiritual event, proved not only their downfall but the beginning of the end of the medieval church in England. The reasons for this are, perhaps, obvious enough.

While heresy and reform were largely straightforward matters of legal interpretation, marriage law, annulment and divorce were matters which raised serious and fundamental theological issues. Issues with which lawyers were ill-equiped to deal. Consequently, the 'old' bishops (those created prior to 1527) once again became divided. Warham, Fox and de'Ghinucci supported the king[1], Longland and Wolsey voiced some qualms about the matter and the rest opposed the effort (some quite impressively). The new bishops (those created after 1527), of whom almost all were humanists, theologians and scholars with little or no ties to Rome, entirely supported the king.

It was due to these divisions that the Episcopate was once again weakened. Neither its relationship with the laity nor with the crown were on an equal footing anymore, and consequently, the bishops could not resist the more dire aspects of the royal supremacy (even had they so wanted). Nor could they block key religious changes which brought an end to clerical independence. On the positive side, the divorce made the career of fourteen bishops. Canonists and theologians alike were given an unprecedented chance to prove their value to the king and thus, out of the ranks of the royal chaplains, jurists and other assorted spiritual officers, arose a new breed of bishop. These 'new men' included Stokesley (dean of the chapels royal), Edward Fox (almoner), Gardiner (principal secretary to Wolsey and later to the king), Edward Lee (royal chaplain) and Cranmer (a little known university don turned ambassador). Indeed, every man promoted to the Episcopal bench between 1530 and 1547 can account the divorce as in some way their introduction to court, government and to their ultimate position.

The basic issues and events are at once political and theological, diplomatic and academic, parliamentary and literary. Most of them have been examined in depth, if not conclusively, elsewhere. We therefore need not go over them again in any great detail.[2] Using a chronological framework, however, we can examine how and why those bishops who were involved became so, what they did and how the 'new men' emerged dominant. In the course of events, some were allowed to be ruled by their consciences and some were not, but the outcome had implications for all of them. We shall see, however, that whether involved or not, the state of the church, spiritual and administrative, was still effectively maintained. As in the French wars, and under Wolsey's dominance, the pastoral duties of the bishops were kept up.

* * *

## 1. The king's 'Great Matter' and the rise of the bishop-theologian

Although the origins of the Aragon divorce are shrouded in mystery and speculation, we know that questions about the marriage pre-date the beginning of the reign. In June 1505, for example, Prince Henry complained to Fox that his marriage contract with Catherine was illegitimate and that he refused to honour it. As Fox was known to have been against it anyway, at least until the papal dispensation arrived, the prince may have merely wanted a sympathetic hearing.[3] Later, the marriage went ahead against the better judgement of Warham and, almost in fulfilment of the archbishop's worries, a series of miscarriages plagued it and tormented the king. By about 1518, he was confiding his doubts about his marriage to his confessor, Stokesley. The confessor advised him that 'he could not any longer live with the Queen, his wife, his marriage being certainly null and void, he having married his own brother's wife, which marriage no dispensation could make lawful'.[4] Apocryphal perhaps, this story illustrates that there was some residual anxiety about the legality and morality of the marriage still in the air, even a decade later.

By 1525, Henry's fears of dynastic failure finally overcame his respect for his wife. He began to favour his illegitimate son, making him Duke of Richmond, and recognized Mary as his heir, making her Princess of Wales, and cast his obviously cursed marriage aside. He knew what he wanted to do and he naturally turned to his church and to his chief minister. Wolsey, whose support for the king on this matter has been held in some doubt, opted to pursue a line of inquiry against the impediment of public honesty. That is, he instigated a legal investigation. To facilitate matters he turned to men with legal training.

Warham was consulted and found to be in much the same opinion as before: 'the trowth and jugement of the lawe must have place, and be folowed'.[5] Fox, however, was found to have mellowed from his earlier opinion. When questioned, he wrote that while he agreed that Catherine and Arthur had lived together, he 'could not remember' specific details. He could certainly recollect nothing about consummation[6], although this was the major issue for Wolsey.[7] Based on these and similar opinions, he initiated a series of inquiries. Along with Warham as his assessor, he set out to investigate the matter through an *inquisitio ex officio*. This was entirely appropriate. In their role as legates, the cardinal and the archbishop approached the king at Greenwich on 17 May 1527 and summoned him to appear at Wolsey's Westminster residence for the convening of the trial. Henry was to answer to a charge of incestuous cohabitation with his brother's widow, forbidden by Leviticus.[8] Gardiner, Bell, John Allen, John Cocks, William Clayborough and William Benet (lawyers all) attended, and the trial progressed apace.[9]

On 20 May, Bell (royal proctor) presented his justifications for the marriage. On 23 May he produced Julius II's bull of dispensation and the two judges named 31 May as the day objections would be raised against it.[10] The main objection was that the marriage was contrary to divine law. As neither Wolsey nor Warham were notable divines, they turned to other more learned men to examine the implications of this claim.[11] Among those contacted were bishops Fisher and Longland (recognized theologians) and Tunstal (a humanist jurist). This first consultation, however, was not favourable to the king. Indeed, most of the scholars approached pronounced that the marriage was valid.

Fisher, who it was assumed would not support the king[12], had been consulted earlier and had written to Wolsey twice already. The substance of his letters was that, while there was some question of divine law involved, the fact that the pope had often exercised dispensation for similar marriages in the past was enough for him to conclude that it was well within papal authority to do so.[13] Longland and Tunstal agreed that the dispensation was sufficient.[14] The dean of the chapels royal, Stokesley, had a different opinion. According to two contemporary sources, he became the first and only 'man of learning . . . found to write in his [the king's] favour or defend his unjust cause'[15], still in the minority, however. Despite the weight of opinion, the trial would have gone ahead after 31 May to a successful conclusion. That is to say, the next session would have seen judgement taken against the marriage had it not been overtaken by events elsewhere.

On 6 May, Rome had been sacked by Imperial troops. This is undoubtedly what threw the cardinal's preparations, and hence the marriage question, into confusion. Free, the pope would have been under no pressure to degrade Wolsey's authority. In the hands of the queen's nephew, however, who could be sure what the pope would do? Wolsey decided that it would be expedient to obtain from the pope a confirmation of his authority to try the case in England. He now switched gears from legalities to diplomacy and set off for France. An indication of his plan is supplied by his report to the king on a flying visit to Fisher at Rochester.

After discussions over the papal position and Wolsey's scheme to circumvent the problem with the help of Francis I and the French cardinals, Wolsey questioned Fisher on his knowledge of current affairs. He discovered that Fisher had been approached by some agent of the queen beforehand, who had informed him of 'certain matiers there were, bitweene Your grace and her lately chaunced'. Catherine wanted his council in the matter. Wolsey relayed the well-known story of the bishop of Tarbe's objections to the bull of dispensation and the possible divine law and public honesty objections against the marriage.[16] Convinced that he had made an impression, Wolsey moved on and spent much of 1527 in France proposing to assume some kind of pseudo-papal authority.[17] This made the king wonder where Wolsey's true loyalties lay? His agents warned him that the king had taken the matter into his own hands while casting doubts on Wolsey's commitment. The upshot was William Knight's famous mission to Rome behind his back. Wolsey only got wind of this in September, too late to stop it but soon enough to convince the king to modify it.

If the cardinal seemed distracted there were good reasons. Besides the new diplomatic necessities, he was troubled by the queen's claims of non-consummation[18], and it would fall to him to find the king a new wife. Wolsey wanted a French princess to cement foreign relations, all the while ignorant of Anne Boleyn's presence. The Knight mission, however, surely clued him in. Knight was to get Henry a papal dispensation allowing him to marry a woman related to him in the first degree of consanguinity (of which the candidates were limited). The cardinal could only assume that this meant Anne.[19] Why this should be kept from Wolsey is unclear, but it does indicate his slipping control over events.

Knight reported that the pope had urged the king to take no immediate actions. He feared that a dispensation would only encourage Wolsey to pursue the matter under his legatine authority, which would do Clement no favours with the emperor. He wanted the English to do nothing until he was at full liberty. New commissions, draft dispensations and letters flowed out of England, and diplomatic efforts were enthusiastically pursued on two fronts – Wolsey in France and Edward Fox and Gardiner in Rome. In England, the king initiated a wider theological inquiry on divine law and the Levitical prohibitions.

On the diplomatic front, the emperor countered Wolsey's wider intentions simply by allowing the pope to escape to Orvieto, effectively removing the pretext of his proposed synod. With his options thus limited, the only way the pope could be levered out of the emperor's influence would be through war. De'Ghinucci, now Wolsey's agent in Rome, wrote to him in December to explain that if the French were to advance, the pope would be most grateful.[20] Wolsey instructed English agents in Spain to join their French peers and declare war on Charles V in January 1528 but, ultimately, the English effort was reduced to financing a French army[21], which was good enough. Soon, all of Milan, the western Mediterranean and Rome itself were under French control; the Imperialists were cut off from Spain and pent up in Naples. Safe, the pope sent Campeggio to England to hear the king's cause as senior partner to Wolsey, carrying the famously 'secret' decretal commission with him. When the French occupation ended, so too did the commission's power. How had Wolsey failed?

While he deftly handled the French and tied up the Imperials, Edward Fox and Gardiner had arrived in Orvieto to try to change the pope's mind and obtain an open decretal commission. The focus was on the irregularities in Julius II's bull. By 13 April Fox had left Italy to report to Wolsey that the pope was willing only to issue a fresh dispensation and a general commission sanctioning only the usual type of papal inquisition. Knowing that French military pressure would soon be forthcoming, Wolsey ordered Gardiner to keep pressing for the decretal letter and pursue the public honesty case.[22] The pope held out until the Imperial threat was removed but, even then, well aware of the ever-shifting military position in Italy, granted the decretal bull in June, making its powers secret and thus deniable. Wolsey practically got what he wanted but could never use it. He and Campeggio were to try the matter in England and deliver a just sentence but, ultimately, the Blackfriars trial was meaningless. The impetus now shifted to the theologians.

It cannot be stressed enough how important their work was to become. It would influence the king's thinking from this point far into the future[23], favouring it more and more as the diplomatic and judicial methods broke down. Stokesley, Fox and Gardiner became the *foci* of a panel of scholars. These men dealt with the divergent intellectual questions springing from the king's scruple, produced a number of polemics and books in support (some good, some mediocre) much of which has been examined elsewhere.[24] In brief, they began with Warham's doubts about the dispensation and related divine law.

If the second marriage had transgressed divine law then the dispensation was invalid as papal authority was not sufficient to dispense; a view which was opposed by Fisher, Longland and Tunstal. The scholars, however, could take the position that dispensation of 'divine law' (conveniently ambiguous) was, based on Aquinas, beyond papal authority and therefore useless as the basis of a marriage.[25] What needed to be shown was that Henry's marriage specifically fell under the Levitical prohibitions. That Leviticus represented divine law and that the king's marriage transgressed it went on to become the crux of theological debate (particularly as Deuteronomy seemed to rebut the words of Leviticus). Debating scriptural meaning is often a formidable task and the dean assembled a team of specialists – experts in theology, canon law, Greek, Latin and Hebrew – to bolster the king's arguments. Who were these men and how did they get involved?

At the core of the group were Stokesley (a theologian and linguist) and Edward Fox (a canonist)[26] and, aided by such men as Nicholas de Burgo, Robert

Wakefield and Richard Pace, they approached the matter with keen determination. In fact, only a short time after the Westminster trial, at least three polemics had already appeared, attempting to reconcile the paradoxical verses. These formed the initial drafts of the *Henricus octavus*, the book presented in 1529 at the Blackfriars' trial in the king's name.[27] Gardiner produced part of the draft copy of the *Henricus*[28] and made other contributions to the overall work.[29] The role of the intellectuals was more than theoretical, however.

Both Fox and Stokesley would be sent to Paris on diplomatic missions to gauge support for the divorce among scholars and clergy there. Later, Stokesley, Cranmer and Edward Lee would go to Italy for the same purpose. Moreover, Fox would present the king's case as part of the embassies to the two English universities – at Cambridge with Gardiner and at Oxford with Longland and Bell. It is well known that Cranmer came to the king's attention in October 1529, after a chance meeting with Gardiner and Fox near Waltham Abbey the previous August.[30]

Henry asked the university don to write out his opinion of the matter and arranged for him to stay at Durham Place with the earl of Wiltshire. Cranmer argued that, 'besides the authorities of the Scriptures, of general councils, and of ancient writers . . . the Bishop of Rome had no authority, as whereby he might dispense with the word of God and the Scripture'.[31] Although hardly original, Cranmer had taken his book around Cambridge, convincing several of the learned doctors. This had impressed Gardiner and Fox, as had Cranmer's idea that the king should consult the universities on the marriage question.[32] Thus, after the Blackfriars' trial and with Wolsey's influence waning, the king organized a new initiative. The new spiritual advisors would blitz their opponents, the pope, parliament and finally the church in England, with their learning and power on the king's behalf. What was the reaction to this of the 'old guard' bishops?

Chief among the king's opponents was Fisher, and More would not commit himself. In an attempt to win them over or at least make them reconsider, selections of the new men were dispatched. More, shortly after his elevation as lord chancellor, faced a visit from Cranmer, Fox and Lee, and was later engaged by Stokesley.[33] No more than a year later, Fisher faced a slightly varied band at Warham's residence, of Stokesley, Lee and Fox (with Cranmer now ambassador to the emperor and out of the country).[34] The king grew to depend upon this core group so much that they were moulded into an 'inner ring of political counsellors' advising him on divorce-related matters and practically taking over the privy council.[35] These men continued to centre their efforts on the divorce for some time to come, as indeed did the queen's own champions, several bishops among them. Obviously Campeggio and de'Athequa were both working on Catherine's behalf. Sherborne also initially supported the queen but did not get involved.[36] Tunstal, West, Warham, Veysey, Clerk and Standish, with Fisher, had all been appointed to the queen's council and all, save Warham, took their duties seriously despite her reservations.

Clerk, however, was in a unique position. As Wolsey's agent he was also acting for the king, diplomatically. He was in France in 1527-8 urging Francis I to support Henry and he helped Wolsey with the preparations for Blackfriars. His own book on the subject, entitled *Pro Defensione Matrimonii Henrici cum Catherina*, was circulated in Paris.[37] Standish and Veysey did little more than present themselves as advocates of the queen during the trial, while Clerk was her apparitor and advocate throughout.[38] There was a clear 'generation gap' over the issue among the bishops.

Campeggio reported that both Fisher and Standish also submitted books on the queen's behalf, as had Tunstal, works which impressed him but which were not read out in court.[39] Tunstal never actually appeared in court, having been sent on another diplomatic mission, but his book was enough to earn him the king's displeasure for some time to come. In any case, apart from Fisher, only one bishop in opposition to the king stood by his convictions for any length of time. West had written a reply to one of the many polemics produced in the pre-1528 period. This in turn generated a response and a further reply concerning the basics of the case. His polemics, *In Dei nomine, amen. Cum ex facto . . .* and *In Dei nomine, Amen. Ad ea qua . . .*[40], extensively examined by Henry Kelly, maintained that the marriage was not at all contrary to divine law.

In any case, such materials were presented to the Blackfriars' court and West stood by his opinions and the queen. According to Scarisbrick, the men appointed for her acted in the form of a council body at least twice: once when they witnessed her promise to send for the dispensatory brief of Julius II's from Spain and again when they were all present when she declared her virginity at Bridewell.[41] This council, after 1529, did meet from time to time, but this became increasingly pointless and even dangerous.[42] Apart from the naming of councils, the one idea that seemed fruitful was to make a wider consultation on the issues.[43] Just prior to the trial, therefore, more scholars were dispatched to Paris and rumours of even greater efforts surfaced afterwards.

The queen learned that Stokesley was to be sent, and gossip had it that Fox and Reginald Pole were already hard at work. Meanwhile, in England, Cranmer suggested approaching the other universities, thinking that this would give the king enough assurance of the marriage's illegitimacy to allow him to 'proceed to a final sentence' and annulment in a domestic church court.[44] Neither Oxford nor Cambridge proved particularly obliging in the short term, but eventually both came around. In February 1530, Gardiner and Fox elicited a positive response from about 200 Cambridge scholars[45], although Oxford resisted commenting until April.[46] Interestingly enough, Gardiner's list of supporters includes the names of eight future bishops: Capon, Rugg, Shaxton, Latimer, Skip, Goodrich, Heath and Day. Neither university, however, offered unequivocal support.[47] The king hoped that he might fare better in France and

Italy, and looked to his scholastic envoys for more convincing support.[48] Academic investigations began in Europe shortly after the Blackfriars' trial.

Pole, Thomas Starkey and Thomas Lupset had been sent to Paris, in October 1529, while Richard Croke had been sent to Italy in November. De'Ghinucci doubted the wisdom of consulting individual scholars[49] and, indeed, both France and Italy looked like lost causes until Fox and Stokesley arrived.[50] It should be noted that Stokesley, Fox and Pole engaged in other intellectual pursuits while in Paris which would bare fruit for the king's purposes in the future. These other pursuits evince a back-up plan, should the consultations fail, to gain the king's divorce through an appeal to a general council. Stokesley, Pole and Fox (in Paris by June[51]) were all actively seeking to treat with Parisian conciliarists[52], gaining material later used against papal authority at home.

Although the Parisian consultations are well known and have been examined in depth elsewhere, it is worth noting the work that the king's agents actually did. Opponents, moles and trouble-makers were uncovered and dealt with[53], the French were spurred on to increase their efforts, obstacles were overcome[54], supporters were recruited to the cause[55] and subscriptions were gained from right under the noses of Imperial agents.[56] In fact, Stokesley and Fox were making 'such efforts to procure the divorce as are enough to set the world on fire'.[57] Their success was crowned on 23 May when the Parisian jurists determined against papal power to dispense from divine law[58] and later, on 2 July 1530, when the 'unanimous judgement and consent of the majority of the whole Faculty [of theology]' voted in support of the king's case.[59] Similar votes were held at Angers, Orléans, Bourges, Toulouse, Padua and Ferrara with much the same results.[60] The consultation of Bologna is more interesting for the fact that Campeggio was present as an *agent provocateur* and because of its position under direct papal jurisdiction.

Stokesley had a great deal on his plate in Italy. As part of the Wiltshire embassy he was to explain the foundations of the king's case to the emperor.[61] As the king's chief advocate he was also to explain how the marriage transgressed divine law and to marshal the now familiar arguments against the bull, the brief and the origin of the marriage proposal.[62] If this were not enough he also had to orchestrate the massive academic effort, but he did so quite successfully. Indeed, when on 10 June 1530 the Bolognese theologians declared for the king, the Spanish ambassador, Rodrigo Niño, was flabbergasted. How, he asked, 'in a college founded by a Spaniard, and in a city within the territory of the Church, so unjust a cause could have any partisans'?[63]

* * *

When Stokesley (now bishop of London) returned to England in November, eight of the nine continental determinations were handed over to Warham with an eye to a domestic resolution. Stokesley, Fox and de Burgo finished a Latin version of the king's book while a translation, which included the determinations, was prepared by Cranmer in 1531. At the same time, of course, Fisher had been writing against the king's book and had begun sending finished chapters to Rome by June.[64] It appeared at the same time as the translation.[65] Despite the efforts of the opposition, however, the king's cause rolled on, much of which was now being tied into a burgeoning theory of royal authority in ecclesiastical matters.

Although we will examine that issue more fully later, it should be noted that as the grant of the supreme headship initially gave the king no new powers, it is doubtful that this had been his purpose. Much more likely is the theory that assuming, or forcing, the clergy to recognize his authority was just another means of pressurizing the pope. The title and grant of royal authority over the domestic church was nothing more than one weapon, of many, used in the on-going divorce campaign. Indeed, if the pope would still not act, the king could threaten to have the marriage decided by the church, over which he was recognized supreme head. This makes sense in light of the king's request that the pope elevate Stokesley and Gregory Casali to cardinalships.[66]

It is logical to assume that there was a plan for a third *ex officio* papal trial at which the king would have two sure judges. One English and one Italian, as before, at least hinting at impartiality (Stokesley and Casali *in locum* for Wolsey and Campeggio). Henry also suggested, on 10 July 1531, that the pope commit the case to the judgement of three English abbots (Kidderminster, Islip and Capon) or, alternatively, to allow the bishop of London to oversee a new trial as the king's ordinary. Yet another plan called for the matter to be

> committed to the Bysshop of London, or the Almoner [Edward Fox] whome He knowyth, as named by Us, one other whome the Quene or thEmperor shal name, to the Bisshop of Canturbery, to be named by the Pope as Metropolitane of the Realme . . . and fourth to be named by the Frensh Kyng.

to meet at a neutral sight, Calais or Guisnes.[67] When no reply was forthcoming on any of these, the scholars were sent to sound out parliament.

Officially, this was a damage limitation exercise to put an end to unhelpful conjecture. It had the advantage, however, of showing the pope that Henry was more than willing to appeal to parliament if need be. Stokesley gathered up his research materials, the lists of books, opinions and the university determinations and, with Longland and More, delivered the fruits of the year-long academic crusade to the lords, together with an abridgement of the *Collectanea*, talking up the cause from a number of angles. A neutral commentator praised the bishop's refutation of 'malignant opinions', primarily those of bishops Clerk and Standish.[68] Unfortunately, these two lacked the disputation skills of the queen's other advocates, Tunstal, Warham and Fisher, none of whom were present, and so a long-winded debate was avoided.[69] In the commons, More made much of Stokesley's recent efforts[70], reporting that

If this mariage be good or no many clerkes do doubt. Wherfore the kyng like a vertuous prince willing to be satisfied in his conscience and also for the suretie of his realme hath with great deliberation consulted with great clerkes, and hath sent my Lord of London here present to the chiefe universities of all Christendome to knowe their opinion and judgement in that behalfe. And although that the universities of Cambridge and Oxford had been sufficient to discuss the cause, yet because they be in his realme and to avoyde all suspicion of parcialitie he hath sent into the realme of Fraunce, Italy the Pope's dominions, and Venicians to knowe their judgement in that behalfe, whiche have concluded, written and sealed their determinacions according as you shall heare red.[71]

Hall noted that the writing opinions were well received.[72] Public relations out of the way, the king's men could exploit other options.

As the king's scholars were responsible for defending his cause, it was decided for a number of reasons that a delegation would be sent to the queen on the last day of May. A further delay of the proceedings at Rome might be agreed if she could be convinced of the need or she might even be persuaded to consent to having the cause tried in England again (or at least not at Rome). A rather large deputation of 'mostly reluctant persecutors'[73] was sent, but little was expected or achieved. The duke of Norfolk talked up the political advantages. Lee examined her first marriage and the impediments it brought. Sampson explained how and why a decision at Rome in her favour could easily be overturned. Longland argued that her 'sterility' (i.e. the fact that she had lost so many babies) was a divine punishment for the illicit marriage – a point Stokesley took up in detail. Their main point was that even if they could offer no proof of consummation, legal opinion would favour presumption as she had lived with Arthur and shared a bed with him.[74] The effort came to nothing in the face of the queen's resolution, which left the king's men with the option of determination in a domestic church court.

Warham, however, now refused to co-operate (in a manner reminiscent of his attitude during the testamentary jurisdiction matter). Revenge perhaps? The king was prepared for the archbishop's defiance and a *praemunire* charge was threatened on the basis that, in 1518, he had consecrated Standish without ascertaining whether he had exhibited his bulls of appointment to the king for the restitution of temporalities. Although Warham prepared a speech in self-defence, it was never used. The archbishop died on 22 August 1532 before anything further was done.[75] In the meantime, the king turned to Lee (now also royal almoner), offering him the nomination to York if he would preside over a trial of the marriage in England. The deal was accepted but, once installed in October 1531, Lee inexplicably changed his mind about a trial and about the wisdom of pursuing the case in England altogether. Although the scholars continued to debate, without the archbishops the matter was effectively stalled.

Warham's death was thus like the light at the end of a long dark tunnel. This, and at almost exactly the same time, Anne's announcement of her pregnancy, were taken as signs of divine grace. On 1 October, Nicholas Hawkins relieved Cranmer of his position as ambassador to Charles V so that he would be free to take up his new position as archbishop of Canterbury. Furthermore, as a reward and a celebration for everyone involved, the king arranged a visit to Francis I.[76] Henry trotted out his scholars, Clerk, Stokesley, Longland and Gardiner to their French peers, and Stokesley negotiated with the French academics to gauge support of the king's second marriage.[77] When Henry was satisfied that all that could be done had been done, the English party returned to Dover on 13 November.[78] Almost immediately plans were put into motion for a new ecclesiastical trial.

In February 1533, Henry put pressure on his bishops and others to sign a document giving their full authorisation of the intended procedure. Cranmer, Stokesley and Longland signed immediately while Lee and Gardiner held out.[79] Perhaps as a means of winning them over or to show that he did not really need to, the king determined that it was time to appeal to the clergy themselves on the issue. There was much propaganda and practical value in this approach. As was the case with parliament, there was residual discontent among the clergy over recent issues and the prelates were quite obviously and publicly divided. Clerical leadership had been enfeebled at a time when it was most needed, and the vast majority of the clergy had not been privy to the ways and means along which the marriage had been examined. Their ignorance of the issues made them susceptible to rumours and misinformation.

With Cranmer not yet returned, however, the bishops of St Asaph and London took turns presiding over the southern synod, assembled in January. The opportunity was taken for the divorce issue to be introduced into the fourth session (March 1533) by the presiding ordinary. However, Stokesley must have realized that taking the marriage question to convocation at this time was not without risk; the queen's men would raise objections and cause delays. Convocation would appear unorganised and the king might turn instead to his temporal court. A unified (or as near to) decision in convocation in favour of the king should have been the final necessity before a decision could be taken with confidence on the marriage question by the new archbishop. This in mind, Stokesley thought to forestall needless obstructionism by dealing with the opposition himself. He proposed an *in camera* debate with Fisher on 8 February, thinking perhaps to heal the rift among the senior clergy or, at least, pressure Fisher into silence. The scheme came to nothing, however.[80]

Thus, when southern convocation assembled on 26 March at St Paul's, Stokesley, presiding for the moment, they introduced the marriage question for their final consideration and judgement, all the while anticipating controversy.[81] In a carefully stage-managed way, he produced the results of the university polls and the collected foreign opinions once again. Much over the objections of the queen's advocates, he revealed a papal bull that he claimed allowed the clergy free expression of opinion.[82] Two days later he read the university determinations into the record. He then went on to pose questions to the bishops on the divine laws of marriage and on papal dispensation authority.[83] After a brief disputation, Stokesley, Longland, Standish and thirty-six abbots and priors agreed that the papal power of dispensation was inadequate. Six others would have agreed, but wanted the question of consummation addressed. The next day, Cranmer was installed as archbishop, and on 1 April the bulls were exhibited to the three senior bishops and convocation was recessed to the following day.

Cranmer, now presiding, was unsure how to proceed as the tricky question of the consummation was to be introduced and examined. Between himself and Stokesley it was decided to brave it out and try to divide and conquer the opposition. First, the theologians of the lower house were asked whether it was lawful to marry the wife of one's brother, assuming consummation, after he had died without issue and, if it was not lawful, was the prohibition against it an indispensable divine law? According to Wilkins, fourteen agreed, seven disagreed, one was rather dubious and one other agreed it was a matter of divine and moral law but was still dispensable. On 3 April it was the turn of the jurists in the lower house, who were asked whether the consummation had been sufficiently proven in law?[84] They agreed that it had been. The next day, the jurists of the upper house were asked to consider this opinion. It was endorsed by Gardiner and Veysey but rejected by Clerk. On 5 April, the king, understandably, grew tired of debate and demanded an immediate answer. Was his marriage forbidden by an indispensable divine law or not? Of the seventy-five theologians in attendance, fifty-six said it was so forbidden.[85] The king now felt secure enough to proceed to a church court. Meanwhile, on 13 May, the questions were put to the divines and jurists of the northern synod (long held as more a less a rubber-stamping body for southern decisions). As Tunstal and Lee had proved such disappointments of late (Kite had played no part) Stokesley presented the royal case and debated Tunstal over the details. The result was never in doubt and it had only propaganda value anyway as, by this point the Dunstable trial had already concluded the matter.[86]

On 11 April, Cranmer wrote to the king seeking permission to bring the case to trial. Permission was granted the following day[87], and the pope had been outflanked. The archbishop's court was assembled at the Priory of St Peter at Dunstable on 10 May, sitting with Longland and Gardiner.[88] The queen was unsure and suspicious when the summons to appear at Dunstable came, and she therefore refused to appear in person or by proxy. She was declared contumacious and, as such, was precluded from making further monitions. It was a deceptively easy victory but the trial was a serious event and went on nonetheless.

To the familiar evidences were added the decisions of the recent provincial synod. Stokesley, Gardiner and Clerk (now switched camp) and others also had the opportunity to present their own findings, opinions and determinations.[89] On 23 May, fortified by these evidences, Cranmer declared the marriage null and void '*ab initio*'.[90] This meant, in essence, that the king had never actually been married to Catherine, in the strictest legal sense, just as he had been advised and just as he believed since 1527. He had been, and now was, free to marry. Whether he was free to marry Anne Boleyn specifically was another issue (recall Knight's mission to Rome). Ever cautious of his legal and moral position, the king empowered Thirlby (as his proctor) to petition Cranmer for a judgement on the legalities of the Boleyn marriage.

This new board of inquiry assembled at Lambeth Palace in secret, due to the fact that the king's second marriage was not yet public knowledge.[91] On 28 May, Cranmer deliberated with the experts and declared the marriage to have been validly contracted and solemnized. They were to be regarded as man and wife on his pastoral and judicial authority. The royal couple now approached Stokesley, the royal marriage specialist, making a personal appeal for his re-examination of the archbishop's recent decision. Why he was approached on the matter now is unclear.

Although he could do little more than agree, Stokesley opined that perhaps Cranmer need not have gone so far as to 'give sentence of divorce' for the first marriage as it had been judged never to have existed anyway. Nonetheless, he confirmed the decision and affirmed the king's right to marry again.[92] Whether the king realized it or not, Stokesley had just given him a subtle reprimand. He could not approve the Boleyn marriage for the same reason he could not support the Aragon marriage: to do so would have discredited his academic reputation. He could still play a part, however.

A new ideological campaign was started to secure agreement for the king's second marriage at the London Charterhouse and at Syon Abbey. At both, inmates had proved unwilling to declare officially for the new marriage. Visitations began as early as January 1534.[93] Initially, the bishop of London preached on the illicit nature of the first marriage, wanting the monks and nuns to subscribe his opinions. It was, optimistically, reported to Cromwell that converting the members to the king's will would soon follow. In due course, a first draft of Stokesley's certificate was signed at Syon[94], but the council subsequently altered the wording to make it a clearer statement of approval for the Boleyn marriage. This, Stokesley had never intended. The new draft was submitted, but the brethren of Syon refused to sign it and advised the nuns to do likewise.[95] This obstinacy was soon overshadowed, however, by the decision that the entire English clergy should make a specific declaration of their approval for the Boleyn marriage. Again, Stokesley was approached first, to review the wording of the new declaration.

The problem was that clerical approval would have serious and negative ramifications in that they had made no such definitive statement. The king would actually be ill served by such a document, as it would appear that the agreement of the clergy was based on fear of the king's wrath. Stokesley pointed this weakness out, reminding the king that 'the clergy did not entreat expressly by name of this marriage, but only of the invalidity of the first marriage.' Discussion in convocation had revolved only around the two related questions, amending the document that Bedyll brought for his approval to make it a better reflection of the actual events and thus more readily acceptable to his fellow clerics.

Recall the reactions of the Charterhouse and Syon Abbey to the attempted amendment of his own former document. Had he endorsed the document without those corrections, he thought, 'I should seem to ascribe more of affection, not only this, but other heretofore, then of known or supposed truth, and so bring my learning and conscience in this matter to less estimation'.[96] Should that happen, earlier resolution would be cast in doubt. By following Stokesley's advice to use only the original papers, the king would get clerical support for his decision to invalidate his first marriage and, at least *tacit* approval of the second (and really this was the most he could expect).

Indeed, this actually proved to be a useful middling position. It allowed the bishops to fall in line behind the king without compromising their own reputations. It was such a useful intellectual device that Stokesley used it to his own advantage in two sermons of summer 1535.[97] We see it put to use even earlier on 17 May 1534 when, as reported by Chapuys, a Privy Council meeting was assembled. The ambassador had been invited to attend the meeting to hear certain arguments in favour of recent proceedings. His attendance was sanctioned so that he could take the arguments to the dowager-princess of Wales and the princess Mary. At the meeting, Fox explained why he had been called upon and outlined for him the provisions of the late Act of Succession. Tunstal noted that it was a most necessary device in establishing peace and, for this reason, no one, including the former queen, ought to refuse to swear to it.

Chapuys might have been aggrieved by Tunstal's apparent change of heart, and certainly questioned his sincerity. Nonetheless, Tunstal continued in this vein, speaking against the papal bull and upon the sending of an excusator to Rome. Following Tunstal, Stokesley produced a presentation of the arguments against the legality of the first marriage, recounting various evidences and noting for the ambassador that the king's appeal to the projected general council nullified any new papal actions which might now be taken against him. Chapuys was certainly biased, but he was no fool and produced his own counter-arguments against these opinions[98] and, according to himself, 'manfully' disputed them all. As a renowned lawyer his opinions carried some weight. He opined that if the king appealed to a general council it would be taken as *tacit* recognition that the pope, despite everything else, still retained a certain authority.[99] This gave the king's advisors, now mostly theologians, some pause, and would explain the seemingly endless moves, countermoves and pressures (political, diplomatic and financial) which plagued the late 1530s on this conciliar question.

* * *

## 2. Further matrimonial problems

The king had made good use of the talents of the men recruited for the court. He had wished to build himself a reputation on the backs of intellectuals and scholars and, as an unexpected bonus, escaped a difficult situation. In so doing, however, he destroyed the medieval church and plunged himself, and the realm, into decades of religious controversy. This, of course, gave the bishop-divines much to consider in the 1530s and much work as the king depended on their expertise. The bishops were never again, as a body, however, so central to the king's marriage crises. Where Episcopal co-operation and leadership had been crucial to ending the Aragon marriage, it was practically invisible when the king wished to rid himself of Anne Boleyn, and later of Anne of Cleves. With regard to the former, when the king made up his mind on, or had been convinced of, Anne's faults, there was in practise little else which needed to be done.

Whichever chronology of events one follows with regard to the downfall of Anne Boleyn[100], with regard to the involvement of the bishops only a few notations need be made. When she suffered a stillbirth it proved a reminder to the king of the divine curse under which his other marriage had suffered. This brought to mind the man who had originally pointed it out. Thus, when the time came for a decision, on 27 April, it was not Cranmer but Stokesley to whom the king first turned, in secret, to consider how he might overturn his marriage.[101] One has to agree with Chapuys that this was probably welcome news to the bishop, but as he had seen the rise and fall of the king's affections before, and as he was no friend of Cromwell's (a partisan of the Boleyns) he remained circumspect.

Chapuys told the emperor that Sir Geoffrey Pole (an intimate friend of Stokesley's) had confirmed that an unnamed courtier had asked the bishop whether or not the king could abandon his second marriage. Stokesley wisely refused to be drawn into the affair and would not give an opinion unless the king approached him in person. Sir Geoffrey indicated to the ambassador that even should the king take that action, Stokesley would, before he answered directly, try to ascertain precisely what were Henry's intentions.[102] It all became academic in any case when Anne was charged and convicted of adultery and high treason on 15 May 1536.

Despite his own thoughts on the subject, Cranmer did his duty and convened another *ex officio* court at Lambeth Palace, which met at the same time as Anne's treason trial.[103] The proceedings are familiar enough. The king and queen were summoned and proctors were named (Nicholas Wootton and John Barbour for Anne, Sampson for Henry) with Edmund Bonner acting as a witness. Events moved quickly because they did not really matter, except as the tying up of loose ends. According to Henry Kelly, the archbishop issued a decree of nullity on 17 May, an official copy of which was subscribed on 10 June, introduced into convocation on 21 June and subscribed by both houses by 28 June. Of course, by this point Anne had been dead for nine days. The bishops had a somewhat larger role in the ending of the Cleves marriage, perhaps due to the diplomacy involved.

Henry had married Anne in January 1540 as a purely diplomatic measure, but his true feelings were not long in appearing. On 10 July, Cromwell was accused of, arrested and imprisoned for treason (or at least for having placed the king in such an embarrassing position). On 2 July, a bill reducing marriage impediments (to clear the king's path to Anne Boleyn's cousin Catherine Howard) was introduced into the lords and, after a first reading, was handed over to a clerical committee of Cranmer, Tunstal, Gardiner and Heath (now bishop of Rochester) for examination. The bill passed the lords unanimously on 3 July, and the commons on 5 July.[104] After this cleared the way, the Cleves marriage came under immediate scrutiny.

On 6 July, parliament requested that the king allow his marriage to be examined by the entire clerical estate, both northern and southern convocations meeting together. The mixed convocation met the following day at St Peter's Church, Westminster, and included both archbishops and twelve other prelates. After Cranmer's introduction of the problem at hand, Gardiner outlined the legal arguments in the case and a committee was set up to examine the details and take the depositions of witnesses the following day.[105] Anne had a marriage pre-contract with the son of the duke of Lorraine and, while this had came to nothing, it was enough for the king. Besides which, he had made clear that his marriage had not been consummated and that he had raised objections to it earlier. On 9 July, after some more considerations, the marriage was declared null and void. The ending of a royal marriage in 1540 was not such an occasion for worry and second-guessing as similar events had been in the previous decade. There were no secret consultations, no lengthy searches for precedents and academic opinions and no pretence of embarrassment. Everybody quickly moved on.

The dissolution of the Aragon marriage had cleared the way for rising humanists and theologians to replace jurists as the king's chief advisors and to destroy the clerical estate as an independent institution. The dissolution of the Boleyn marriage allowed an imprecise legal interpretation of previous marriage contracts, while establishing the archbishop's *ex officio* court as the final arena of ecclesiastical dispute. The dissolution of the Cleves marriage reinforced all these themes. The clergy were, by 1540, little more than intellectual puppets, clearing the way for the supreme head's desires; they had become spiritual civil servants. If Cranmer, Gardiner or Tunstal had any misgivings, these were no longer given voice. There were no polemics approving, defending or condemning the king's actions.

* * *

### 3. The king's authority recognized

We noted above that the king's new title of supreme head did not really give him any new powers although, as a weapon against the old guard bishops, it had its uses. It cannot be denied, however, that the accompanying political and ideological moves, aimed at the papacy, inaugurated great changes for the country and altered the nature of doctrinal dispute and religious orthodoxy in England. It also initiated a period of unrest on a now divided Episcopal bench. Men more completely dedicated to the king's causes were rapidly replacing the bishops of the Wolsey era. These 'new' men were, however, of varying religious opinion.

Take the four most powerful positions on the bench as illustration. All four bishops were humanist intellectuals and royal partisans, and none had respect for the papacy. The richest diocese (Winchester), the two archiepiscopal sees (York and Canterbury) and the most metropolitan (London) went to three theologians and a jurist. Put another way, however, three were religious conservatives and one (Cranmer) was a maverick. The Episcopal appointments of the mid-1530s, mostly to radical theologians, sent a clear signal of impending change. These men, radical or otherwise, however, did hold in common an obvious anti-Roman bias. Historical orthodoxy also holds that much of the 1527-34 period was a time of no clear-cut policy direction. The divorce, the supreme headship and, finally, the royal supremacy were *ad hoc* initiatives – re-active rather than pro-active. Studying the pattern of Episcopal promotion, however, makes it clear that this assessment is flawed. There was a clear pattern. The king placed those men who had proven themselves to him into positions of power, after which they began to chip away at papal authority and the medieval clerical order.

* * *

The idea of Imperial kingship and all of the prerogatives this entitled had already been successfully asserted against the papacy at Tournai. This event forms a very useful guide to the king's thinking in the pre-1534 period. Mayer has shown this quite clearly in a recent article, writing that when the king claimed 'supreme power as lord and king in the regalie of Tournai without recognition of any superior', he was claiming the uncontested fealty of the clergy as his due. There followed derogation of the papacy's legal standing and jurisdiction and a corresponding expansion of royal authority. The pattern of financial threats and, ultimately, the hinting that 'he [Henry VIII] might withdraw England's obedience from the pope', found later reverberation.[106] Of course, there had been qualms of conscience from his agents at the time, but the plan ultimately worked (if temporarily). It would work better now as the king had the firm support of both the recently promoted intellectual bishops (who had no ties to Rome) and the members of a parliament whose anti-clerical predilections had been sharpened by Wolsey and recent over-zealous heresy trials (examined below). The king could denigrate the old clerical order, bring ever-increasing financial, legislative and judicial pressure to bear on the pope and he could threaten schism and finally abandon the papacy altogether if Clement did not submit to his desires. Just as had happened at Tournai.

There was a new problem, however. The more spiritual distance the king put between England and Rome, the closer he seemed to move towards Wittenberg. In order to firmly establish a new spiritual order, the further dismantled the old order had to become. This included Episcopal authority, the monastic establishment and ecclesiastical law. All had to be re-examined for change. As a result of this, faction swept through the upper ranks of the church. Initially, the Henrician bishops (those elevated post-1527), much like the king himself, were basically conservative men who acknowledged and even supported royal authority. Stokesley, Lee and Gardiner may be taken as representative of this group. Against them stood what remained of the old guard – Fisher, Standish, Clerk, West and Warham. These men wanted little or no change and resolutely set themselves against innovation under any guise. It is no accident that these two groups had polarised around the divorce.

Events moved even faster after 1532. The rising influence of Cromwell and Cranmer and the more in-depth comparison of royal and papal authority were matched by the king's rising interests in 'empire' and theories of 'imperial power'. This, in turn, brought more so-called 'Erastians' to the bench. These were men who were willing to concede the state's omnipotent power in ecclesiastical matters and hedge their own religious radicalism in exchange for the chance to exercise their reforming aspirations: men like Hilsey, Edward Fox, Latimer and Shaxton. It is clear therefore that the Episcopate was never completely unified in the 1530s and that the evidence of royal nominations makes it clear that the king was maintaining a balance of opinion. While the need for a balance might have solved problems at court, it created difficulties in the spiritual nation. As we shall see with regard to heresy, reform, visitation and preaching, however, both the old and new bishops performed their duties well and most of them learned to become good Henricians very quickly.

\* \* \*

The fall of Wolsey is a well-known and very significant event for which the basic details need not be repeated. What it is necessary to stress, however, is that he had himself acknowledged the reality of the new order at the time of his disgrace. He had made no appeal to the pope for protection, realising the futility of such an action, nor had he submitted himself to parliament. Wolsey had made his submission in King's Bench.[107] Of course he did this to avoid the consequences of a parliamentary attainder that might have cost him his life. King's Bench would strip him of his offices and possessions, true, but it would leave him alive. In so doing, however, there is a *tacit* recognition of the king's right to judge men in holy orders, confirming the precedents set in the Hunne and the testamentary jurisdiction cases in the 1510s.

Wolsey threw himself on the mercy of the man he recognised as the source of his temporal and spiritual powers 'having none other refuge to flee to for defence or succour, in all adversity, but under the shadow of his majesty's wing'.[108] The king could be, and was, merciful, merely exiling the cardinal to York. Although Wolsey's problems were far from over, as a means of dismantling the old order, this was as good a beginning as possible. Bernard speculated that Wolsey's later arrest in November 1530 should also be considered an act aimed at the pope. This was very much in line with other events of the period and, if Wolsey could only have been brought to London, a show trial would no doubt have been staged.[109]

Similarly, in the wake of Wolsey's fall, parliament considered legislation aimed at sending a clear message to Rome and the old bishops. One such piece was the so-called Pluralities Act of 1529, which restrained the practice of clerics holding more than one office and the non-residency this involved. This interesting clause states that papal dispensations from these restrictions would no longer be valid, although new ones might be purchased from the crown.[110] The act neatly curtailed papal authority and advanced the king's power simultaneously, and was reinforced by royal proclamation in September 1530.

According to both the Milanese and Venetian ambassadors, bishops Fisher, Nix and Clerk appealed to Rome against the act. This, in turn, was used to justify prosecutions against them.[111] These three then made further appeals to Rome for support, but this was never forthcoming. While their actions might well have angered the members of parliament (particularly the commons) the prosecutions proved too difficult and were eventually dropped. Instead, *praemunire* informations were filed in King's Bench (from which there was no appeal) against fourteen clerics (including eight bishops) on 11 July 1530. The basis of the informations was that these eight bishops, Blythe, Nix, Standish, Skevington, West, Sherborne, Fisher and Clerk had all abetted Wolsey's papal legacy by having granted him a percentage of their annual incomes. They were, therefore, guilty of *praemunire* by association.

Each of these bishops had entered into compositions with Wolsey: Fisher, West and Sherborne for half their casualties, Blythe for a third, Nix for forty marks, Standish for ten, and Skevington and Clerk for ten pounds each.[112] Of course, this 'association' with Wolsey was a subterfuge. Most of these eight had contested the cardinal's authority at one time or another in the 1520s.[113] Indeed, much ink has been spilled trying to ascertain the real reason why these particular men had been picked out. That some of these men had been supporters of Catherine in the on-going divorce crisis (although some had worked on the king's behalf) and that the king needed money are no doubt contributory factors.[114] Guy suggested that the king picked out 'potentially dissident elements' from the upcoming southern convocation for special treatment. Bernard, however, argues instead that it was a mere continuation of the king's anti-papal programme. Both theories are attractive, but the answer to why these particular men were picked could be nothing more than a simple matter of opportunity.

The remaining bishops of southern convocation were either conveniently absent or on the king's team of divorce scholars (and thus practically holy to him). De'Athequa suffered with Catherine while three others, Campeggio, de'Ghinucci and Stokesley, were out of the country. Even then, the latter two supported the king anyway. Wolsey had been exiled north, Longland was also an advocate of the king, Booth was an enemy of the cardinal, Warham was thought to be on his last legs, and Rawlins, of St David's, was a non-entity. In the end, however, the individual threats came to nothing and parliament was prorogued on 17 December 1529.

When southern convocation re-assembled in January 1531 they had two disquieting but rather ill-perceived threats hanging over them. One was the king's financial need. The cost of keeping up diplomatic pressure on the pope was high. The other was the earlier *praemunire* threat. What had been threatened against a few clerics was now used as a weapon against the entire clerical estate. It was now, apparently, the clergy's exercise of independent jurisdiction through the church courts which upset the king. Obviously, the threat to Rome is clear. The real fear for the bishops was the idea that some kind of parliamentary oversight might be established over them.[115]

Certainly this was a legitimate concern. There were a number of grievances voiced by the members of the commons, including the extent of church liberties, their unique and apparently unfounded authorities, and the disproportionate wealth between clergy and laity. All of these seemed to fester in the minds of the literate laity, having been brashly paraded before them by Wolsey and papal nuncios. However, when parliament was recalled it failed to continue its efforts for clerical reform. The senior clergy had expressed an intention of initiating reform themselves and they were being giving a chance. They met in this tense atmosphere at St Paul's on 12 January without ceremonial. Warham and the upper clergy discussed their situation and did talk about self-reform.

In March, Stokesley read to the upper house a document described as '*quondam famosum libellum contra Clerum*', a prototype for the future supplication against the Ordinaries. The bishops' reluctance to dispute indictments against them is a clear indication that the nature of the institution had changed. This led to a great growth of reform legislation, or at least suggestions for such. Between mid-February and 1 April the convocation debated ideas for over twenty statutory reforms. These ranged from traditional issues like dress, monastic appropriations and simony, three model heresy statutes, and those issues raised earlier in the commons – convict clerks, feast days, excommunications and the conferring of sacraments without fee.[116] Other issues included grammar school education and new canons regulating the admittance of clerics to benefice and holy orders.[117]

The great centrepiece of the effort was a lengthy condemnation of heresy. This listed some seventy heretical books and authors and made the publication of new books dependent upon the approval of the local bishop. Over the next few sessions, four more canons were produced, regulating clerical conduct, lodging, church repair, the setting up of a uniform education system in the sees, and for the proper number of religious members and monastic discipline. The new regulations stressed the work of the prelates themselves. They were to display new energies in the examination and punishment of malefactors and were to make visitations a major instrument of reform.[118] Clearly, the main target of their talks had been heresy, but at least the bishops were responding to lay pressure.

As noted, the bishops spent much more time on combating the spread of heresy and examining suspects than on other issues. It has been suggested that an intensified heresy campaign was one method by which the conservative bishops could combat the rising laxity on the government's part with regard to unorthodox opinion. Thomas More threw himself into just such an effort, as did bishops Longland and Stokesley. In any case, at this first meeting of convocation, Warham commanded strict secrecy of their talks and, at the second meeting, Stokesley reiterated the archbishop's warning. He also tacked on an excommunication threat to ensure compliance. Why is unclear. No real serious business was carried out in this subdued atmosphere anyway as they waited for word of what the king intended for them.[119]

On 19 January Stokesley ordered the session transferred to the Chapter House of Westminster Abbey.[120] This move would facilitate communication with the king and was, no doubt, initiated in the council. In light of the general direction of the king's thinking, such a move also inhibited the convocation's independence to a greater extent. Tracts about headship issues were also delivered and read out to the convocation (to be examined next chapter). The clergy were being primed and this made them nervous. This is evinced by their reaction to a visit from the Imperial ambassador, Chapuys, and a papal nuncio. The mere presence of the nuncio caused anxiety and the clerics refused to receive him. The nuncio was allowed to confer with Stokesley (as the clergy's proctor), but Chapuys doubted the bishop's motives. Chairing convocation though he was, Stokesley was also a member of the council and the ambassador wondered where the conversation with the nuncio would be reported first.[121]

In any case, the king's mind was revealed to the clergy soon enough. As is well known, he wanted southern convocation to purchase a pardon for their illegal exercise of spiritual authorities. That is they were, as a body, being charged with compliance in the cardinal's *praemunire* offence. In return for £100, 000 plus expenses; a very large subsidy modelled on Wolsey's 1523 clerical subsidy[122], the king offered to

> grant to all and singular the prelates and clergy of the province of Canterbury and to all the Registers and scribes of whatsoever prelates which were ministers in the exercising of spiritual jurisdiction within the province of Canterbury . . . generous and gracious pardon of all their trespasses of penal laws and statutes of this Realm.[123]

He also wanted to be recognised as sole protector and supreme head of the Church in England, implying that this would include sacerdotal function. Of course, the king was not the first English sovereign to exploit his position *vis-à-vis* the clergy[124] and they took little notice of the additional title. In fact, within two days of receiving the proposal (22 January), after some intermediary haggling, the convocation voted the entire sum and began to consider a payment schedule.[125] As agreed, they asked the king for the pardon.

It seems that this victory had been too easy and the king was momentarily nonplussed and unsure of his next step. He initially called for the entire sum to be made payable on demand 'in case of war'[126], then bought himself more time by disputing the payment details.[127] Warham took advantage of this window of opportunity to convince the clergy to forward a petition voicing their anxieties about heresy, the 'late raging ayenst the fame and personages of the prelates of the clergie'. Heretics and 'their famous lyes and cursed bokes and workes euerywhere dispersed to thintent to blemisshe and hurte the estimacion of the said prelates & clergie'.[128] He then demanded guarantees of the church's ancient liberties and privileges, a comprehensive definition of *praemunire* and certain modifications to the parliamentary legislation of 1529.[129] Convocation also reminded the king of how he had himself defended the church and its properties against Luther. Clearly, the church leaders were anticipating the general aim of the king's programme and wished to make a pre-emptive defensive strike. It was unlikely any of this would be granted, of course, but the king considered the options.

When he had decided upon the details, he presented parliament with a bill ratifying the subsidy and pardoning the clergy and used a threat of temporal interference to achieve 'instant clerical compliance'.[130] A few days later he presented Warham with a list of conditions the clergy would have to meet before they would be granted the pardon they wanted. He demanded that they recognise him as 'sole protector and also supreme head of the Church of England', and at the same time, denied their earlier request for definitions and guarantees. In return he would, however, pledge peaceful conditions under which the church might attend to 'the cure of souls committed to his majesty' and he would allow a full five years for payment of the subsidy. Moreover, he would confirm such privileges as did not offend his regality and, finally, he would pardon the clergy for all past offences. Warham tabled these and some other articles in convocation himself.[131]

The articles initiated a fierce debate, spread over the next two sessions. The lower clergy could not come to a decision over the issues and Fisher spoke out vehemently against the king's new demands in the upper house.[132] To overcome clerical ill-ease, the king agreed that his new title could be augmented with the words 'after God'. This did not overcome Fisher's opposition so Thomas Audley (now chancellor) or Cromwell suggested 'as far as the word of God allows'. To this Fisher, Stokesley and nine other bishops subscribed on 4 March.[133] The king's claim to spiritual power was dropped just as his grip over the church had been tightened. The pardon was granted.[134]

Northern convocation followed their southern brethren's lead on 4 May, granting £18, 840[135] (roughly proportional by wealth to the southern grant), but not without debate. In the northern synod, however, the government had little effective representation on the issue.[136] Tunstal protested the form of the title, thinking that while *'cujus singularem protectorem unicum et supremum dominum'* would probably not offend most people, he feared its 'misuse by those heretics who strive to diminish the authority of the bishops'. He wanted clarification[137], but did the new title actually give the king any additional authority?

In his reply to Tunstal, Henry made it clear that he remained loyal to the Catholic faith and that he would not interfere in the clergy's sacerdotal functions. This, as far as Fisher was concerned, saved the pope's spiritual headship.[138] Tunstal (a jurist), however, had made a distinction between temporal and spiritual headship. The king replied that the clergy were still bound to obey the prince.[139] Vague perhaps, but what the grant and pardon did was to consolidate the position the king had enjoyed *de facto* since 1515 and which he had claimed over Tournai. Indeed, the king still hoped to pressure the pope on the marriage question, so it could be said that this was little more than another weapon in the campaign. With this business settled, the southern bishops turned to the question of heresy once again. Stokesley read out extracts from Tyndale's *Practice of Prelates* to draw attention to its errors[140], and shortly thereafter (31 March), both parliament and convocation were prorogued.

Having established recognition of his supremacy over the English church, and having become comfortable with it, the next step in the royal programme of papal pressure was a financial one. This was the Act in Conditional Restraint of Annates[141], which also threatened the jurisdiction on which Episcopal promotions were based. From this point on the clergy were to pay no more than five percent of their first year's revenue (to cover necessary costs). Implementation was made conditional on the pope's reaction, and clauses were added which challenged his supremacy directly. If he refused his bulls of consecration, for instance, then the bishop would be consecrated without them.[142] This was a timely threat in that John Capon, abbot of Hyde, had just written to Cromwell complaining that the pope had refused to send bulls for his elevation to the see of Bangor.[143]

The clergy, particularly the prelates, had certain reservations about these measures. In particular, they balked over the mere hint that parliament would have a role in the creation of new bishops. This in turn raised suspicions in the commons. Elton suggested that Cromwell took advantage of these suspicions and the ill feeling over recent heresy trials to jumpstart his own schismatic programme.[144] While this is doubtful, it was still a complex issue obscuring the origins of the commons' supplication against the Ordinaries. The king had a clause added which delayed implementation of the act until he confirmed it by letters patent. Still, the prelates and both abbots in attendance voted against it. As Lehmberg made clear, it also got a rough ride in the commons, but it was eventually passed.[145]

* * *

The suspicions raised by the prelates' difficulties over recent legislation resulted in a parliamentary supplication presented to the king by a common's committee on 18 March 1532.[146] It was, more or less, simply a list of their many grievances against the clergy, the most interesting of which was the very first against the power of convocation to make 'laws, constitutions and ordinances' which bound the laity without royal assent or the assent of the laity themselves.[147] Oddly, the king did not respond to this indictment as the supplicants hoped he would. Rather, he assumed a position as a neutral referee between the two estates.

He said, 'it is not the offyce of a kyng which is a judge to be lyghte of credence, nor I have not, nor wiyll not use the same: for I wyll heare the partie that is accused specke or I geve any sentence.'[148] Possibly as a lesson to the commons, the king delayed action on the supplication for several weeks, proroguing parliament on 28 March for the Easter recess. In the meantime, he passed it over to Warham and requested a formal reply from the clergy.[149] Debate began anew when the convocation reconvened on 12 April. A week later, Gardiner had produced rejoinders to the commons' first articles, subsequently accepted by both houses.[150]

Subsequent moves are unclear. We do know that Stokesley argued a conciliatory position between the king's newfound powers and the traditional privileges of the church (so recently assured in the pardon).[151] Perhaps he feared what Warham and Gardiner (two jurists) might produce, having himself used divine law arguments against the pope. Could the king claim to be the source of spiritual authority? Stokesley went so far as to arrest proceedings in convocation in Warham's absence, in order to establish a period of calm reconsideration. Unfortunately, the archbishop revived the debate unchanged. He was feeling very able after the assumed 'victory' of the general pardon and handed the supplication back to Gardiner for a complete reply. This, it turned out, was a costly mistake for both men.

'We, your most humble subjects, may not submit our charges and duty, certainly prescribed by God, to your highness's assent'. In denying the king, Gardiner referred to the indispensability of divine law, the very argument used against the papal dispensation in 1529. His too clever answer also denied any estrangement between the clergy and the laity, claiming instead the very opposite: 'but only have, as we dare surely affirm, with all charity, exercised the spiritual jurisdiction of the Church, as we are bound of duty, upon certain evil-disposed persons infected and utterly corrupt with the pestilent poison of heresy.'[152] Towards the minor matters, Gardiner gave no indication that the abuses would be reformed forthwith, although a *tacit* acknowledgement of the need is hinted. Unsurprisingly, an even stiffer tone pervades those passages where Warham maintained the privileges of the archiepiscopal courts.

With regard to heresy, the bishops offered up only an oblique defence. They were not justifying or defending the heresy laws (seeing no moral or political need to do so) but saw no better way of handling 'arbitrary citation' except to deal with individual cases of abuse as they became apparent. As for arbitrary imprisonments: 'if any man hath been under pretence of this particularly offended, it were pity to suffer any man wronged; and thus it ought to be, and otherwise we cannot answer, no man's special case being declared in the said petition'.[153] The prelates could not submit their statutes and laws to the king for the royal assent, wrote Gardiner, because the inspiration for them had come from God. They would, however, consider

> what your highness's wisdom shall think convenient, which we shall
> most gladly hear and follow if it shall please God to inspire us so
> to do – with all submission and humility beseech the same,
> following the steps of your most noble progenitors, and
> conformably to your own acts, to maintain and defende such laws
> and ordinances as we, according to our calling and by the authority
> of God, shall, for His honour, make to the edification of virtue and
> the maintaining of Christ's faith, whereof your highness is defender
> in name, and has been hitherto in deed, a special protector.[154]

Their freedom, within the framework of the universal canon law, to make spiritual laws both for the clergy and laity independent of any sort of secular assent, was the most precious of the 'liberties' assured to the *Ecclesia Anglicana* in Magna Carta. It is most surprising that a lawyer of Gardiner's reputation, and an administrator of Warham's experience, should fail to see the danger the clergy were in. That they not only failed to appreciate the inherent harm in the issues raised by the commons, but that they dismissed them as meagre, the grievances and machinations of evil men, is amazing.

The draft answer was somewhat judiciously redrafted over the next few sessions and it placed any blame that the commons might cast on the actions of a few unnamed individuals rather than on the clergy as a whole. It was certainly not a conciliatory report.[155] The king received it on 27 April and handed it on to a commons' committee only three days later, describing it as 'very slender'[156] and encouraging them to discuss it further. The ramifications of his mistake cowed Gardiner into silence and Warham was broken with rumours that a *praemunire* was to be shortly levelled against him. These events brought Stokesley to the leading position in convocation and the duke of Norfolk warned him that the clergy had better promptly produce a more prudent reply. Debate resumed on 29 April and lasted until 6 May.

The king quickly grew impatient. He and his advisors presented the prelates with a set of cut and dried propositions for their signatures four days later. From this point on, the clergy could only assemble at the king's writ, and in future, they could not enact or execute any new canons without royal licence and assent. Indeed, they were to submit all previous canons to a mixed parliamentary commission with annulment powers. When convocation did not immediately submit, the king examined the bishops' consecration oath for further leverage. In his appeal to the commons he said that the bishops were 'but half our subjects, yea, and scarce our subjects' and asked if they could not 'invent some order' in the matter? The very idea hurried the debate in convocation and, on 15 May, all but Clerk gave in to the king's demands.[157] The next day Warham presented the king with the document embodying the 'submission of the clergy'.

* * *

Gardiner's most recent biographer explained that the bishop had been making a stand for the independence of the clergy and for the position and duties of the Episcopate. As late as 13 May, Chapuys had commented that Gardiner and More were trying to keep up the struggle to defend the church's liberties, 'in the face of Henry's evident anger'.[158] Evidence for this view is taken from the letter Gardiner wrote, justifying his opinions after his banishment from court and after Edward Fox told him the king's view. Redworth called it 'bold and defiant', and in some ways it was, but not entirely. Gardiner defended his opinion in this way:

> I beleved, soo gret a numbre of learned men affirmyng it soo
> precisely to be true, that was in the answer alleged concerning
> Goddes lawe; specially considering your Highnes booke against

Luther, in myn understanding, most playnly approvith it; the boke wryten in your Graces cause, and translate in to English, semeth to allowe it.

referring to the *Determinations* (the defence of the Aragon divorce).

In 1528, Campeggio had noted the profusion of Lutheran books and the many calls on the king to take a more personal interest in religious change. He had warned that the sole object of such appeals was to justify the seizure of church property. Henry replied that the church was itself rife with sin and that the papacy had erred in many ways from the divine law, but it was not his place to change it.[159] Gardiner was bold indeed to throw the king's arguments back in his face while defending the clergy's right to declare canons as an inalienable prerogative: 'if it be Goddes auctorite to us alotted, thowe we cannot use it condignely, yet we cannot geve it awaye'.[160]

Gardiner remained in exile for a short time only. A diplomat and lawyer of his calibre could not be allowed to remain out of service for too long. His letter, bold as it might have been, put paid to any chance of promotion to Canterbury (much as Richard Fox had missed out earlier). In the meantime, the lower house proposed to send Stokesley, Longland, the abbots of Westminster and Burton, Sampson (the dean of the chapels royal) and Fox (now almoner) to present a plea to the king to assure the former immunities and privileges of the church and, wisely, to seek his opinion on possible answers to the supplication. Out of this a new reply could be drawn.[161]

The new reply turned on two familiar points. They still insisted that the church had a spiritual authority and a unique judicial power to develop new laws on matters of faith and good manners. Such powers were necessary for the health of the souls of the nation. This had been traditionally recognised by Christian princes and 'most vehemently asserted' by the king himself in his polemic against Luther. Recognition of the need for the king's consent would be incorporated into their new reply, however. They assured the king that there would be no new canons, save on matters of faith, morals, reform and correction of sin, without his prior consent. Ultimately, however, this collection of royal favourites accomplished very little as their proposal was not very much different from Gardiner's. It still contained an element of autonomy.

Lehmberg suggested that the king had used this occasion to demand that the clergy abandon altogether their legislative authority.[162] In regard to existing canons, the bishops conceded that if any contained material contrary to the temporal law and the royal prerogative, 'not being now in use' and not concerning the faith or reformation of sin, they would gladly revoke them.[163] This compromise was also not to the king's liking; it implied that they had a choice in the matter. Henry was determined to have approval over all constitutions, old and new and on whatever subject matter, and he wanted to be consulted beforehand on all new formulations. He also wanted to establish a thirty-two-man committee (half-laity) to examine existing canons. Those acceptable to the majority of the committee would be given the royal assent.[164]

The clergy were compelled to accept the judgement of the king on the issue on 15 May 1532.[165] Stokesley, however, attached a codicil, 'so that the said schedule be not against the law of God nor contrary to the General Councils'. This was a conciliarist opinion to which Longland and Standish also ascribed. As conciliarism was of current royal interest, Henry let this addition go by unchallenged. In the event, both Warham and Gardiner were completely compliant and only Clerk remained intransigent.[166] The upshot of all this is that the theoretical position which had been taken for the crown in the *Censurae academarum* and in the *Collectanea* had now been established in reality.

Convocation could not now assemble without the king's permission, nor could new canons be enacted without his assent. Moreover, all existing canons were to be reviewed by that royal committee, some of which would no doubt be disallowed. The king's position *vis-à-vis* spiritual legislation mirrored his position *vis-à-vis* temporal legislation almost exactly. The pope was now effectively deprived of any legislative authority he might once have exercised over the English church. The 'submission' was both a weapon in the war with the pope over the divorce, and the completion of the legislative stage of the royal supremacy.

After the act of Appeals, events moved rapidly onward: convocation declared against the Aragon marriage; Cranmer annulled it; and Anne Boleyn was crowned on 1 June 1533. The king's international worries were intensified, however, when the pope threatened him with excommunication. Although he still wanted the pope to confirm the annulment and declare the case to have been rightly settled, the excommunication threat effectively closed the door on any future compromise. Then again, Leo X had also threatened the king with excommunication over Tournai and his bluff had been successfully called. There was no reason to suppose Clement VII was made of sterner stuff than Leo.

The king recalled his envoys and broke off diplomatic relations immediately. He then confirmed the Act of Appeals by letters patent and appealed against the pope's threat to a future general council. Next he summoned his senior ministers together, particularly those bishops closest to court (Stokesley, Longland and Gardiner) and asked them to search their various libraries and discover whether the pope was higher or lower in authority than a general council: find out if, in fact, he had any more real power in England than any other foreign bishop. On this latter question he looked especially to his intellectual advisors, Stokesley, Longland, Clerk,

Fox and Sampson for guidance.[167] It was [168] upon the results of these investigations that further action would depend. On a more practical note, Stokesley was now to appoint preachers to St Paul's Cross favourable to the king's position and lean on opponents. In parliament, Cromwell gathered his forces and began to cement the break with Rome through legislation.[169]

The Act of Appeals removed the last vestige of papal authority in England, while the Acts of Succession and Treason recognised the Boleyn marriage and legitimised any issue. The Act of Supremacy put into statute form all the concessions made by the clergy and gave the king the power to decide heresy, to conduct visitations and to amend spiritual jurisdictions. Of course, the international tensions created by the Dunstable decision caused problems as well. Henry turned his attention to securing the domestic situation, starting with the bishops. Between July 1533 and the enactment of the Act of Supremacy in March 1534, four bishops of the old order were brought under pressure, as Warham had been earlier.

On 8 June 1532, Fisher, still a vocal advocate of the queen, preached a sermon in her favour much to the king's displeasure.[170] By 1534 there was an increasing recklessness in his attacks on the king's causes and not a few hints that he would have welcomed a crusade-like invasion by the emperor. Chapuys wrote that he had, 'by a third party', given the emperor's orders to Fisher. What these 'orders' were, if not just Chapuys' wishful dreaming, is not known.[171] Fisher had been passing his divorce-related writings over to the ambassador for continental distribution[172], and had been keeping him abreast of all the latest developments in the divorce suit.[173] It was not until 1533, however, that Chapuys hinted of Fisher's treasonous appeals to Charles V to take 'active measures immediately'.[174] However much trust we can place in the ambassador's reports (and this is never sure), one must wonder if they could have been kept secret.

 Interestingly enough, Henry took advantage of the first opportunity to put Fisher under more intense scrutiny: his otherwise innocent association with the nun of Kent.

The Elizabeth Barton story is well known, and by July 1533 the king had had his fill of her opinions. He ordered Cromwell and Cranmer to handle the problem. The nun was imprisoned and interrogated, and her writings were burnt. The king, however, wanted her, and any followers, condemned and burnt as heretics as well.[175] On 23 November, Capon preached a lengthy sermon at St Paul's Cross as part of the nun's public humiliation and, shortly thereafter, she and her supporters were convicted of high treason.[176] Fisher, Thomas Abel and four others were convicted of misprision of treason at the same time. Chapuys was sure that Fisher was prosecuted at the king's command and there is no reason to doubt it.[177] On

30 March 1534, an act of attainder against him was given royal assent. It was never executed, however, as the oath of succession took precedence.[178]

The next bishop to face royal displeasure was Standish. He too had taken the queen's side (and subsequently the pope's) in the early 1530s. An opportunity arose to put pressure on him through the activities of his vicar-general at St Asaph, Robert ap Rees. In October 1533, Rees had been indicted of a *praemunire* in the Great Leet of Denbigh for having retained 200 persons for six years, for keeping three benefices and farms, and for 'diverse extortions' of the king's subjects. Rees was obviously the main target but Standish was included in a *praemunire* charge as his superior, of whom 'the king should have a great sum without further trial'.[179] Both Standish and Rees choose to fight the charges, going so far as to sue out writs of *supersedes* in Chancery. Salisbury, the steward of the court at Denbigh, refused to process the writs, however, even after the two men swore out *subpoenas* against him.[180] The case against Rees seems to have moved on apace but the fate of Standish in this instance is unclear. Scarisbrick wrote that Cromwell's involvement signalled government complicity in the affair and a veiled crown action against the bishop. Under the circumstances this seems the only logical conclusion.

Next up for treatment was Nix. Evidence against Nix who, as we have seen, was never a man to back down from a fight, had been collected from as early as 1532. In that year, a *quo warranto* indictment had been issued against him. On 10 June 1531, Nix had appointed a coroner to examine the death of a child, an action somehow infringing upon the ancient liberties of Bacton. He was subsequently called into King's Bench to explain himself. He appeared early in 1532 after three summonses.[181] Nix, of course, had a history of trouble similar to this. Indeed, he had taken on the cardinal himself, and nor was this his first summons into King's Bench.[182] Of three previous appearances, however, he won twice.

In Hilary term 1534 the Attorney General, Christopher Hales, appeared in King's Bench to lay a *praemunire* indictment against Nix. This was the result of a petty injury done to the mayor of Thetford, Nix having somehow offended the immunity of that town too.[183] He was summoned into the court, however, for having acted in contempt of the royal jurisdiction and the prerogative of the crown. The case was blown up into a *praemunire* as a result of Nix's persecution of William Hewett (twice charged for heresy in the Norwich consistory). The Hewett matter had been brought to Cromwell's attention due to the bishop's continuous harassments.[184] By February 1534, the case against Nix was in full swing.

Although leniency was to be shown to this ancient bishop, and even though he defended himself with his accustomary vigour, Nix was forced to plead guilty and was placed into custody on 10 February. Shortly thereafter he was released on bail and charged to appear again after Easter.

Scarisbrick found this treatment curious, but we need not wonder too much about it. Nix had surely got the message.[185] Parliament, in fact, passed the Act of Pardon and the court case was finally resolved in Nix's favour, although a 'free gift' to the king of some 30, 000 crowns was extorted out of him.[186] For whatever reason, an observer named Rokewood wrote to Lord Lisle that Stokesley was to be the next target, but he was wrong.

The next target was Tunstal. Tunstal had been given a rough ride since 1530, the result of his over-zealousness in the queen's defence. When Wolsey fell from grace, an opportunity was taken to implicate the bishop and he was forced to surrender his office of lord privy seal to Wiltshire in order to secure the see of Durham.[187] In the period under discussion, Tunstal showed himself in very public opposition to both the divorce and to the supremacy, but the only real punishment he had suffered was northern exile. Like Gardiner, his administrative and legal skills could still be put to good use, even in the north, and he was too valuable a diplomat to be left out in the cold too long. Even though he made the occasional plea to the king for caution in the supremacy matter, he eventually came round to the king's point of view (c.1534).[188]

What was the effect of the bishops' recognition of the king's spiritual authority in the dioceses? Bowker, examining Lincoln, suggested that it was rather small, at least prior to the 1534 metropolitan visitation.[189] This is an accurate reading of the matter, as the evidence of heresy prosecutions, Episcopal visitations and clerical reform shows little or no change from what had gone before.

* * *

## a. Impact on diocesan matters

One of the problems faced by all of the bishops was the adequacy of their clergy, both secular and regular. While they could examine and even reject clergy presented to them, it was rare when they did so, needing copious justifications. A canon of 1529 had gone some way towards alleviating this problem[190], stating that the bishops were to examine the candidate's morals and education and could reject those unworthy. The best example of this was when, immediately upon his return to England, Stokesley initiated a program of clerical reform in London along the suggested lines.

The character of the clergy was a grievance with some of the laity too. While there is blame enough on both sides of the issue[191], the atmosphere in the 1530s made change necessary. London, always an obvious hot spot, was the best place to start. The bishop looked initially at curates, un-beneficed deputies of those beneficed clergy so difficult to remove once established. Curates could be more readily reformed and, with lay grievances against absenteeism mounting, it was a *politique* place to begin. And it was an impressive beginning; an 'unprecedented examination of the curates in their learning, in their capacity for further learning, morals and in their pastoral capabilities'.[192] Like Stokesley, Sherborne, Fisher, Longland and Tunstal were also concern with the image of the clergy, but opportunities for change were rare. Tunstal held some twenty-one ordination ceremonies between 1531 and 1535, in which only 100 secular and thirty-one regulars were ordained. Thompson has shown that even though the bishops were aware of their duties, patronage was limited.[193] This being the case, clerical reform had to come about more through visitation injunctions.

Despite his other problems, Fisher maintained a hectic schedule every year up to the last visitation of Rochester in February 1534, just prior to his arrest. Sherborne, who isolated himself in Chichester in light of events at court, also maintained an impressive visitation record and proved himself a committed opponent of heresy.[194] By 1530, it was well known that the coastal areas of East Sussex were harbouring heretics from the continent, but the bishop's attitude was only fully revealed in the 1533 heresy trial of Thomas Hoth, a canon of New Priory near Hastings.[195] Hoth had said that, 'it were necessary and convenient that the New Testament were in English that every man might read and understand it'. Sherborne's reaction was unusually heated, displaying his distaste for vernacular translations.[196] It was his visitation record, however, that was truly impressive.

He spent several months of every year, up to his retirement in 1536, in visitation.[197] As in his earlier visitation of 1521, that of 1530-31 focused on the decay of church fabric and unkempt churchyards. Sherborne also made an effort to help out financially those responsible for the upkeep of church fabric, while admonitions and corrections were made against the negligent. Lander showed that between January 1520 and January 1521, the bishop tried twenty-one cases involving church fabric and five more such cases in the August 1533 to August 1534 period. In November 1524 there had been three different religious houses cited to appear at consistory to answer for the dilapidation of their conditions, and in December 1526 the bishop's officers took the unusual step of threatening the parishioners of East Angmering with suspensions of their cemetery if they did not repair its walls.[198] Lander thought that Sherborne was well able to affect spiritual reform in this way, having taken the time to thoroughly examine and reform the various, and often conflicting, jurisdictions within the diocese. In the years leading up to his retirement he tackled non-residence, continued to enforce the improvement of church fabric, protected his officers' and the parochial clergy's incomes and corrected immoral clerics.[199]

Longland too carried on much as before. We know that he took a personal interest in only the most bothersome cases, trusting Rayne to carry on in his absences. In the early 1530s the trouble spots for Longland were Little Marlow, Dorcester, Elstow and Missenden. He had visited Little Marlow in 1527, finding ignorance of the rule of St Benedict and an ineffective prioress. When he visited again in October 1530 he found that little had changed. Indeed, the community had been reduced to only six members. Elstow proved to be a much greater problem, however.

The bishop's injunctions are dated 1 October 1530: two months after his visitation. He had found an awkward bailiff, an uninterested chaplain and a poor relationship between the abbess and the nuns. The abbess, it seems, was arrogant and refused to mix with the other nuns, even on official occasions. Here also, as at Dorcester, was found one of Longland's bugbears, buildings much in need of repair and little concern about material conditions.[200] In June 1531, he found little had changed. He removed both the abbess and the prioress for having disobeyed his injunctions and installed others. This caused a rebellion in the nunnery as the inmates refused to accept the new officers, some even walked out in support of the former prioress. Longland reacted swiftly. He deprived the former prioress, isolated the nuns on a ration of bread and water and waited them out.[201] The conditions at Missenden were even worse still.

The bishop had sent his injunctions to them on 27 June 1531: only nine days after his visitation. He had even sent them in English as the abbot and convent were 'ignorant and have small understanding of laten'. He had found the place riddled with debt, a rule only haphazardly enforced (if at all) and poor discipline. The injunctions concentrated on a daily reading of the rule and instruction in Latin grammar 'an hour before prime, an hour after chapter and an hour after none and at other seasons'. The abbot had also allowed himself to be manipulated by a lay steward, John Compton, who did what he liked, 'cutting down trees and woods at pleasure'. The most disturbing discovery was the treatment of six boys there to be educated. They were unsupervised, abused and, as noted earlier, the victims of John Slyhurst's sodomy. Although Slyhurst was imprisoned, his fate is unclear.[202]

An even more serious problem confronting the bishop was the matter of the abbot of de la Pré in Leicester (the roots of which can be found in Atwater's reports). According to Rayne's visitation, abbot Richard Pexsall kept his own table in the refectory and entertained seculars and court figures with lavish dinner parties. But this was only the tip of the iceberg. By 1532-33, Longland was in the process of trying to deprive Pexsall but, subsequent to the threat, the abbot mobilised his political connections. He wrote to Cromwell with a gift of £40:

beseeching your mastership to use it as you shall think best for my

quietnes in Crist, and that I may have of the kinges grace or of your
mastership a protection that myn ordinary have no such stroke in
my house as he hathe had, to the disordre of me and myn.[203]

Cromwell intervened, which prompted Longland to write as well. 'The
place is almost undone by hym [Pexsall], and the longer he tarrieth therein,
the more it shall decay', warned the bishop.[204] Bowker noted that Pexsall
had gone so far as to appear before the royal council in order to circumvent
Longland's authority. It was not until 1534 that the bishop was able to
oust him.

In any case, many such aspects of diocesan administration remained
unaffected by the supreme headship in the early 1530s. The same problems
and pressures existed in the monasteries and in the parishes as before,
and the bishops acted as best they could in response. Likewise, the matter
of heresy was an on-going problem which recognition of royal authority
did not exacerbate or alleviate to any great degree. Ogle speculated that
the bishops used heresy as a means of rallying themselves and, indeed,
they did set out on an anti-heresy campaign of major proportions in the
early 1530s. More effort was spent than in the 1520s, but on much the
same problems.

In 1530, for instance, Warham sent out letters exhorting the bishops
to preach in English against heresy wherever it happened. Studies of the
period make it clear that with regard to the native Lollards, the Episcopal
machinery was set up and active, as it had been earlier. The new danger
was the Lutheran emphasis on reading, preaching and on the wider
dissemination of literature of a questionable nature. Despite past efforts,
the machinery was not yet prepared for the influence that Lutherans were
able to command in this way. While the royal council had issued two lists
of condemned works along with penalties, including heresy charges, in
regard to the book trade the bishops were very much on their own.

Nix was one of the first to signal the new dangers from the importation
of heretical books. He tried to get closer Episcopal control over
Cambridge[205], but he might have been over-anxious. His 1532 visitation
uncovered only ten, non-literate heretics in the town.[206] In 1530, and again
in 1532, lists of proscribed books were produced in convocation[207], but it
is clear that these were not comprehensive enough for some. On 3
December 1531, for example, the bishop of London released his own list
through a sermon at St Paul's Cross[208] including books not on the
government indexes.[209] Stokesley thought that an expanded effort was
necessary because of his recent difficulties with Richard Bayfield and
James Bainham.

The basic details are that Bayfield had appeared on charges before
Tunstal, having criticised saint worship and advocated preaching of the
gospel based solely on scripture.[210] He had later been found in possession

of heretical books and was arrested and examined on three separate occasions throughout November 1531, before bishops Stokesley and Gardiner.[211] He eventually confessed his activities as a reader and colporteur to Lollard audiences and to being in London (on a preaching tour) without Episcopal licence.[212] He was sentenced on 4 December by Stokesley's vicar-general, Foxford, excommunicated, deprived of clerical office and handed over to the temporal authorities for punishment.[213]

Stokesley later questioned Bainham's views on purgatory, saint worship, auricular confession, priestly absolution and the sacraments, but focused most intently on his possession of heretical books. Bainham had been influenced by Bayfield who, he claimed, lived in the 'true faith', and also indicated Crome and Latimer as influential. On 16 November he was offered the choice of abjuration or burning and, after a long delay (to February), opted for abjuration. On 8 February, Foxford ordered him to pay £20 to the king and to do penance at St Paul's Cross, after which he was returned to prison to await Stokesley's final ruling. On 17 February he was released and dismissed from further trial. After only a short time he relapsed and was recaptured. In the case of a relapsed heretic the bishop had little choice but to hand him over to the secular authorities. Bainham was burnt at Smithfield on 30 April.[214] John Foxe related several dozen similar examples from Stokesley's anti-heresy campaigns.[215] In all of them we find the influence of books clearly illustrated.

Stokesley's dealings with men from the book trade were not all negative, however. He was well able to use it to his own advantage and had cultivated a mutual regard with Henry Pepwell, 'a leading member of the trade'.[216] In 1531, Pepwell issued an edition of Eck's *Enchiridion locorum communium adversus Lutheranos* on Stokesley's advice, having secured it in Antwerp with the help of the bishop's agent, Thomas Dockwray.[217] John Bale placed this particular book on a par with Barlow's *Dialogue Describing the Original Ground of these Lutheran Factions* when discussing Stokesley's securing of orthodox texts for domestic consumption.[218]

Pepwell proved his value to the bishop time and again in his heresy crusade and their arrangement was well known. In 1533, Vaughan wrote to Cromwell that 'the Bishop of London, Stokesley, has had a servant [Dockwray] in Antwerp this fortnight. If you send for Henry Pepwell, a stationer in Paul's Churchyard, who was often with him, he will tell you his business'.[219] Stokesley's activities in the book trade, however, did not conflict with those of the government or the court. If anything, it showed that he was eager that the king should go even further. Could such manipulation of the book trade truly be effective?

If nothing else, the bishop's relationship with William Barlow proves that it could. Barlow has been described as 'an ideologue who saw in politics an instrument for the reform of English religious life'[220], much as would his reforming colleagues later. He had, as they would, discovered that it was more effective to affect an Erastian position than try to force through radical reform. In a letter to the king of the late-1520s he freely admitted to having denied the mass and purgatory and to have 'grievously erred against the blessed sacrament of the altar'. In his favour, however, he approved of vernacular scriptural translations, which probably saved his skin.

Eventually, a place was found for him moving back and forth between London, Paris and Rome on the king's marriage business.[221] While in Paris he came increasingly under Stokesley's influence and later, on the bishop's advice, wrote his book against the Lutherans.[222] When Barlow returned to England in 1530 (or 1531), however, he fell back into his old ways, even writing tracts of a Sacramentarian nature.[223] This prompted the bishop of London to give his book against the Lutherans as wide an audience as possible under the shelter of his Episcopal authority.[224] The book provided the first English account of many of the heretical Lutheran and Anabaptists sects and its strong language, frighteningly horrific descriptions and unsympathetic treatment probably scared off many otherwise impressionable individuals. No doubt this was just what Stokesley had wanted and why he promoted the book so vigorously.[225]

Dickens wrote that the real starting point to an examination of the bishops and heresy in the 1530s should be the cases of Crome and Latimer in 1531. On 11 March 1530, Crome's confession to fourteen articles set the tone for several others. It was, by this date, no longer heresy to deny papal supremacy, although it was still heresy to question the cult of saints, purgatory, the seven sacraments and to import, read and possess vernacular scriptures and certain other banned books. Latimer confessed to similar articles on 21 March 1532, the end result of an interesting sequence of events.

Recall that Latimer's radical thinking and preaching had got him into trouble with West in 1525, only to be licensed to preach by Wolsey thereafter. In 1529 he was preaching animated sermons in favour of vernacular translations[226], but his support of the divorce shielded him from any real difficulties. Indeed, after 1530 he seemed to be quite the rising star. He was invited to preach before the king at Windsor on the second Sunday in Lent, 13 March 1530. He must have proved his orthodoxy to the king's satisfaction, as later, between 11 and 24 May, he found himself on a board of inquiry investigating suspected heretical books under the chairmanship of the archbishop. This was the board whose recommendations formed the basis of the two indexes. For his good services he was rewarded with the rectory of West Kington in Chippenham, where he often preached in favour of vernacular translations of scripture.[227]

Between this and 8 March 1531, however, his sermons began to take a cynical view of the legitimacy of praying to saints, purgatory and certain rites and ceremonies. His views were brought to the attention of convocation. He, with Crome, Bilney and Lambert, was set to face heresy interrogations only for these to be superseded by other events. It has been suggested that Warham was behind the charges as an expression of convocation's continued authority over spiritual matters. In other words, these four had been rounded up as a signal to the king. Latimer alone, however, was summoned to appear before Stokesley on 29 January 1532. This was due to a sermon he had made at St Mary Abchurch. He had been trapped and lured to London by the bishop himself.[228] His sermon included passages against pilgrimages, purgatory and an attack on the bishops' use of informants in heresy cases, and Stokesley heard the details through planted witnesses.

After the sermon, Stokesley wrote to Richard Hilley, Campeggio's chancellor at Salisbury, demanding that Latimer be sent to London to answer to charges of preaching without a license and other 'certain crimes and excesses'.[229] Latimer would not go quietly, and replied that his Cambridge license should have been sufficient to allow him to preach anywhere and reminded the bishop that the king had recently affirmed the validity of such licenses. Not content to leave the matter there, he wrote that while he believed in the three creeds and all of Holy Writ, he was willing to be instructed in that which he was ignorant. For, he noted,

> I once thought the Pope Christ's vicar and lord of all the world . . .
> now I might be hired to think otherwise . . . I once thought the Pope's
> dispensation of pluralities discharged consciences, and that he could
> spoil purgatory at his pleasure by a word of his mouth. Now I might
> be entreated to think otherwise.

He also once thought that images of saints could deliver men from their troubles, but was now grieved that the bishop could force people to remain deceived. Moreover, he noted rather wryly that Stokesley himself once believed that a man could marry his brother's widow.[230] In the end, Hilley capitulated to Stokesley's demands. Latimer thought he knew what awaited him and wrote, 'I look not to escape better than Dr Crome'.[231] What really awaited him was an extensive, three month long examination, with periods of questioning three times a week.

The first few hearings took place in Stokesley's consistory but were then transferred to the chapter house at Westminster. Latimer discovered that it had been Stokesley's plan to get him back before an Episcopal board of inquiry all along.[232] In convocation, Latimer faced the full array of staunch conservatives: not only the bishop of London, but Warham, Lee, Gardiner, Fisher, Veysey and one or two lesser churchmen took turns to interrogate him. Latimer described these hearings for us:

> Every week thrice I came to examinations, and many snares and traps

> were laid to get something. . . . At the last I was brought forth to be
> examined into a chamber hanged with arras . . . but now this time
> the chamber was somewhat altered . . . an arras hanging hanged over
> the chimney . . . an aged man [Veysey?] . . . put forth one [question],
> a very subtle and crafty one. . .

and he was asked to speak out loud and clear. Later, he discovered that
there was a scribe behind the array in the unused fireplace recording his
words.

> The question was this: "Mister Latimer, do you not think on your
> conscience, that you have been suspected of heresy?" . . . There was
> no holding of peace would serve. To hold my peace had been to
> grant myself faulty. To answer it was every way full of danger.

Latimer does not tell us his answer and, as this information was related
some twenty years later he might have been using the episode
allegorically.[233] It does show the lengths to which the bishops were now
willing to go or to which they had to go.

The articles finally prepared for his signature were similar to those
received by Crome, save that one on vernacular translation.[234] As he refused
to sign them, however, he was declared contumacious by Warham,
excommunicated and imprisoned at Lambeth for a time thereafter.[235] On
21 March, he was brought out before the commission again and this time
subscribed the charges, which Stokesley noted in his register. According
to Wilkins' sometimes inconsistent record of convocation, however, the
prolocutor of the lower house entered the chamber and, after a lengthy
discussion with Stokesley, it was decided that Latimer would be absolved
from his excommunication if he would confess only that he had preached
indiscreetly. In doing so, he would have to ascribe only articles eleven
and fourteen.[236]

What was this all about? Stokesley probably saved Latimer from the
full wrath of convocation for two reasons. Latimer was a fellow advocate
of the king's divorce and the supplication against the ordinaries had just
been sent over by the king, so time was precious. Moreover, the two
articles would have prevented him from preaching in the London diocese
(which is what the bishop wanted in the first place) and, in any case,
Latimer came to terms at once. He had been tricked again. Stokesley now
postponed the actual signing of the articles until 10 April.[237] Why?

At some point during the hearings a vigorous opponent of Latimer's
named Thomas Greenwood had begun spreading rumours about the rector's
abject submission. Latimer found this out and wrote that he would in no
way alter the substance of his teachings. He admitted to certain
indiscretions in the past, but rather unthinkingly crowed at his triumph in
escaping severe punishments.[238] Greenwood promptly submitted the letter
to convocation and, when Latimer reappeared on 10 April he was shown

the letter and made to subscribe to all sixteen charges after which he was absolved of excommunication. This should have been the end of the matter but Latimer was summoned to reappear on 15 April to face new inquiries springing from the Greenwood letter.

For Latimer this was the final straw. He appealed over the bishops' heads to the king on 19 April. The commission was subsequently adjourned until 22 April at the king's pleasure. The king, however, unexpectedly refused to intervene on Latimer's behalf and, in fact, warned him to submit to the bishops and do the assigned penance, 'as ye have deserved', warning that if he did 'such things again ye sha[ll]' be burned as a heretic.[239] On the appointed day Latimer performed an abject submission, admitting errors in discretion and in doctrine.[240] Stokesley granted absolution from heretical pravity 'at the special request of our lord the king', and warned Latimer that his cards were marked.

The following year Latimer was brought before convocation once again, this time over sermons he had preached in Bristol. His sermons there, in defiance of his convocation oath, touched upon images, purgatory and pilgrimages. His earlier submission was brought out and Stokesley inhibited him from preaching in the London diocese, backing this up with a more general prohibition against all unlicensed preaching.[241] Clearly, the bishops could still act effectively as a body when the occasion called for it, but they also had to act individually from time to time as well.

In the London diocese, on 30 April 1532 and with Bainham's pyre still smouldering, the bishop was accused of mistreating Thomas Patmore, ill treatment brought to the attention of the king. Patmore, who held the London benefice of Much Hadham, had been a rather obscure figure up to 1531 when he preached in favour of clerical marriage. He was reported, subsequently arrested and brought to trial[242], at which many other issues surfaced. It was revealed that he read Tyndale's forbidden works to illiterate Brethren audiences[243], that he had rejected the intercessionary power of saints and images and that he was responsible for arranging the marriage of his own curate, Simon Smith. He refused to abjure, however, and was sentenced to perpetual imprisonment in the Lollard's Tower. Two years later, after several visits from the bishop, Patmore's servant John Stanton brought his case to the attention of parliament.[244]

When the case was forwarded to the lords, however, the chancellor dismissed it as frivolous and sent Stanton to the Fleet prison on 30 April 1532 as an accomplice in Patmore's heresy.[245] Three years after this, Patmore appealed to the king. The shift in royal policy made the conditions right for such an appeal. The Episcopate was now taking second place to the crown's other officers in heresy investigations. His case was re-examined by Audley, Cranmer and Cromwell, who in the end thought they had no choice but to uphold the earlier verdict.[246] What is significant here is that temporal officials had reviewed Episcopal authority in an ecclesiastical matter. After 1534, heresy had become much more a temporal matter, in which the bishops acted as specialist royal agents. This is clearly shown by the later (1537-39) cases where Audley sent heretics to Stokesley for examination (see below).

In the more conservative north of England, however, the three prelates and their officers had more autonomy. In 1537, for example, the archbishop acted alone and presided over his consistory to examine William Senes, who had been found using banned books. In fact, twenty-eight heretical articles were objected and he was imprisoned. By comparison, in contemporary London, the duke of Norfolk had to request that archbishop Cranmer and bishops Latimer and Shaxton examine John Lambert on the crown's behalf. The new arrangement did little to alleviate the problem though.

Like Stokesley, Longland faced a severe heresy problem in the early 1530s. Thomas Harding, a Buckinghamshire Lollard, was arrested in May 1532 in possession of several heretical books (mostly Tyndale). These he had read and taught to his illiterate fellows. He also confessed to several unorthodox opinions concerning purgatory, saint worship, Mariology, holy water and the real presence in the sacrament. The fact that he was a relapse, having previously been tried and found guilty by both bishops Smith and Atwater, meant that his fate was pretty much set in stone.[247] The case of Thomas Alwaye also shows to what lengths Longland had to go in the struggle.

Alwaye had originally been arrested in 1528 as a result of the bishop's implementation of Warham's mandate of 3 November 1526.[248] In 1530 he wrote to Anne Boleyn for help. Alwaye noted the severity of his treatment and pleaded that he had spent 'a yere and more' in the tower at Wolsey's pleasure, his fate having been committed to Tunstal and Longland. As a result, 'my lorde of Lyncolne Inioyned me, payne of dethe, that hereafter I should never come within the cettye of London, neyther the Universytes of Oxford and Cambreg withowt hys specyall lysence'. In 1529 Longland had also enjoined Alwaye that he 'shoulde not departe owte of hys dyoses where as I have bene all thys yere paste, and can gett noo servyce, no not so much as mett and drynke'. When he was able to get service, 'the bysshoppe of Lyncolne hard of yt he commauned hys chaunceler to sende a letter to dyscharg me, whyche was done or I had bene fully VI weks in the servyce'. The point of the letter was that Alwaye wanted Longland's injunctions relaxed so that he could secure himself a living, 'as yt shall please god to sende me'.[249] Longland also played a role in the condemnation of John Frith, which we will examine shortly.

Although heresy was a greater problem in the southern provinces, the northern bishops had their share. Archbishop Lee faced a problem in the form of those Dutch immigrants in York who had earlier plagued Wolsey. One of these men was Lambert Hooke (or Sparrow) who had abjured sometime in late 1533 of some twenty charges, including heretical views of the sacrament, purgatory and pilgrimages.[250] A similar case was examined before Lee's vicar-general William Clyff, who objected sixteen articles against Gyles Vanbellaer. He had been found in possession of a Dutch translation of the New Testament and his trial was held on 27 November 1534. As both Hooke and Vandellaer came from Worksop we might well speculate that there was a small Lollard cell there. A couple of further cases, where the details are sketchy, involved Lee's 5 February 1536 commissioning of Clyff and others to examine Stephen Kendal of Richmond archdeaconry, and the 20 August 1535 abjuration of Richard Brown, vicar of North Cave, of articles based on his preaching against the traditional doctrine of the Eucharist and the efficacy of saints.[251] The diocese of Durham does not appear to have had even this much of a problem. Tunstal had complained to Cromwell that heretical books were being circulated in the seaport towns of the northern parts of the see[252], but this seems only to have resulted in one heresy case. In 1531, Roger Dichaunte, a 'Calvinist' merchant of Newcastle, made a complete recantation and submission before the bishop of any heretical opinions.[253] The real problem remained in the southeast and along the southern seaboard, as earlier.

Sherborne, an opponent of vernacular translations, had his share of these problems in the see of Chichester.[254] By 1530 it was well known that the coastal areas of East Sussex were harbouring several heretics from the continent. The bishop proved himself a stalwart enemy of heresy whenever he found it through his triennial visitations. We referred to the very serious case of Thomas Hoth earlier. The precentor of New Priory Hastings had, in 1533, been found in possession of a French vernacular translation and a Tyndale *New Testament*.[255] Hoth was well known to the bishop, of course. In 1521, he had been a novice of New Priory and six years later he was a canon. In the visitation reports on the prior and two other canons, Hoth was said to have 'withdrew himself from the priory without the prior's licence'. The reason for this is not clear, and no proceedings seem to have been taken against him at the time. It could be that Sherborne kept his eye on Hoth for more damaging evidence.

In May 1533, on another visitation, the bishop found what he was looking for and commissioned his vicar-general, John Worthiall, to begin an investigation of Hoth on heresy charges. Hoth apparently noted that, 'it were necessary and convenient that the New Testament were in English that every man might read and understand it'. Though this was hardly dangerous, Hoth was also charged over his opinions on purgatory, clerical marriage and salvation.[256] In his first appearance before the bishop, Hoth confessed to the articles and agreed to abjure, thereby avoiding a long drawn-out heresy trial and undue publicity.[257] His heretical opinions seemed to have originated at Cambridge, 'a certayn bachiler of Divinite named master Stafford, redyng the lector of Divinte in cantrige' was named. His trial followed the usual procedures. Two witnesses – lay associates of the priory – had identified him as 'predyaux and out maister t'gater', and a suitable penance was set. He was imprisoned for a time in the Bishop's Palace awaiting final judgement and was, eventually, ordered to remain within the precincts of his priory for a year with other restrictions attached. It is interesting to note that when New Priory was dissolved, Hoth was not given a benefice, as had the other priest-canons.

Another case involving heretical books in Chichester was that of Thomas Whit of Rye. On 5 June 1533 James Jonson, an Augustinian friar, accused him of heresy.[258] Acting on the bishop's commission, Worthiall considered Jonson's articles against Whit and singled out those stemming from his possession of certain unnamed heretical books. These books had been uncovered in his possession by John Segar, rector of West Blatchington, and witnessed by the mayor himself. In his own defence, Whit claimed that he had been left the books by a merchant of Norwich whom he did not know, that he had never read them and that he was unaware of their contents. Worthiall allowed that Whit was probably innocent and could purge himself of heresy charges in his own parish church; no need for the bishop's involvement.[259]

* * *

As noted above, the ever-widening breach with Rome created a need for a widespread employment of anti-papal preachers to publicise the supremacy message. Combined with the attack on the church's legislative authority, the clergy and laity alike both began to question the viability of canon law and, thereby, the role of ecclesiastical courts. Indeed, Cranmer would carry out a massive re-examination of canon law at a later date. The new scrutiny extended to the *ex officio* powers of the bishops, the authority under which heresy trials were conducted.[260] While the number of heresy trials remained fairly constant, more and more involvement was undertaken by temporal figures. Such events also inspired more complaints that innocents were being cited for heresy 'out of clear clerical malice'. There were complaints that key testimony was being buried and that defence witnesses were being barred from making presentations.[261] Such a charged atmosphere surrounded the highly publicised cases of Thomas Philips and John Valey.

The bishop of London had accused Philips for his heretical views of purgatory, images and the sacrament. The latter, he claimed, was nothing but 'a remembrance of Christ's passion and a signification and token of better things to come', a Zwinglian or even Karlstadtian point of view.[262] When arrested he was also found in possession of several heretical books. Despite the accusations and an admission of ownership, Philips thought himself immune to a heresy charge for lack of witnesses. Only when it was too late did he discover his error. John Stacy, already convicted of heresy, had pointed the finger at Philips and according to More, there were 'diverse heretics' willing to do the same.[263] The bishop dismissed Philips' objections and required him to make a public abjuration in light of this, but was rebuffed.

Instead, he too appealed to the king against the bishop's authority, the trial and against his imprisonment, charging Stokesley with malice. This, matched with his refusal to do penance, forced the bishop to pronounce excommunication against him, describing him as 'a preacher, a teacher, a schoolkeeper . . . and a reader of damnable lectures'.[264] As had been the case with Latimer and Patmore, the king refused to hear his appeal. Philips then turned to the commons, as had Patmore, on 4 February 1534.[265] He asked them to intercede on his behalf with Audley.[266] The commons forwarded a petition to the lords on 7 February, but More dismissed it as frivolous two days later. On 2 March the commons raised the issue again, requesting an answer from Stokesley alone but the lords responded 'una voce' against it.

Such trials and complaints had resulted in the new Heresy Statute of 1533. Trials were to be initiated only after an indictment at common law or by the accusation of two credible witnesses. The meaning of heresy had also been changed but, so long as witnesses were called, the consistory courts could function more or less as before.[267] This can be illustrated with a brief reference to the case of John Valey (*alias* Faley). Valey, parish clerk of St Peter's Colchester, stood trial for heresy along with four others. Stokesley wrote that while the others had been co-operative, after which he sent their answers and confessions to Audley[268], Valey had refused to answer to anyone but the chancellor. After some delay, however, he submitted to the bishop and was released on sureties. Valey subsequently abjured, but later voiced doubts on the value of auricular confession and was retried as a relapse.

After 1533 the emphasis at trials changed from abjuration or death, to conversion to a less extreme Erastian position. This was the case, at least, for those who were of potential use to the government. This can be illustrated with the famous case of Thomas Frith. The bishop of London's spies had led him to this key Brethren leader who was of official interest for three reasons. Not only was he a friend and close associate of Tyndale, but he had also provided the Brethren with the leadership denied them by the deaths of Bayfield and Bainham. More important than this, perhaps, was the fact that he was a gifted writer.[269] If Frith could be captured and convinced to abandon his more extreme views he would make a useful addition to the government's publicity machine.

Frith had been arrested in July 1532, but had escaped and fled to Antwerp. He returned following the deaths of Bainham and Bayfield, having heard of the abjurations of Latimer and Crome. He was back around 25 July 1532, and was able to avoid the bishop's officers for quite some time. He was finally arrested in October, the result of a joint effort between Stokesley's agents and the king's officers.[270] Frith might still have been saved from burning had it not been for the sermon of a Doctor Curwen. Curwen, in his Lenten sermon before the king, noted Frith's Sacramentarian views. The allegation was enough to seal Frith's fate. In the course of his June examinations before Cranmer, Stokesley, Gardiner (for the spirituality), Suffolk, Audley and Wiltshire (crown agents), he was interviewed on several occasions, sometimes by the archbishop alone, other times by the entire commission.

Cranmer noted after one interview, on 17 June, that Frith insisted there was 'no corporal presence of Christ in the host and sacrament'. He concluded that '[Frith's] opinion was so notably erroneous that we could not dispatch him, but was fain to leave him to the determination of his ordinary'.[271] He was again brought before Stokesley at St Paul's on 20 June 1533, sitting with bishops Longland and Gardiner[272] and, once again, he refused to modify his views.[273] Even at this late date Stokesley was convinced to give Frith another chance, this time by Gardiner. Gardiner had been Frith's tutor and wanted to speak with him in private, hoping perhaps to convert him for sake of shared academic experiences. When this failed, Frith was condemned with Andrew Hewet, on 3 July 1533. The two were passed over to the temporal authority, Stephen Peacock, the mayor of London[274] and burnt together at Smithfield on 4 July 1533.[275]

* * *

There were not many famous heresy trials in the rest of the 1530s as it was less and less clear precisely what constituted heresy at any given time after 1534. We shall see that, in fact, the heretics of the early 1530s became the bishops of the mid-to-late 1530s. Men like Latimer and Shaxton had more value to the king as ecclesiastical authorities than they had as heretical martyrs. This attitude caused a massive wedge to be driven between conservative members of the Episcopal bench and their more radical colleagues, at least until attitudes changed again later. Of course, the king was running his new church pretty much by the seat of his pants, and teething pains must have been expected.

# Notes

1. BL, Vit.B xii, fol.123v.
2. See, Virginia M. Murphy, 'The Debate over Henry VIII's First Divorce: An Analysis of the Contemporary Sources' (unpublished Ph.D. dissertation, University of Cambridge, 1984) or Nicholas Harpsfield, *A Treatise on the Pretended Divorce between Henry VIII and Catherine of Aragon*, ed. by N. Pocock (Westminster, 1878).
3. J.T. Sheppard, *Richard Croke, A Sixteenth Century Don* (Cambridge, 1919), p.8.
4. *CSPS*, iv (ii), 967 (p.472). The confessor could have been Longland. Cf. Wharhirst, p.156; *LP*, ii (ii), 4340 and Bowker, *Longland*, p.8.
5. *CSP*, i (i & ii), cx (p.197).
6. *LP*, iv/ii, 2588; iv/iii, 5791; Maria Dowling, 'Humanist Support for Katherine of Aragon', *Bulletin of the Institute of Historical Research* lvii:liii (May 1984), pp.46-55 (at p.49).
7. If consummated, the first marriage established a possible divine law argument against the second. If not, then the bull of dispensation was defective in not covering public honesty. See Scarisbrick, *Henry VIII*, p.194; PRO, SP 1/54, fols.362-3.
8. For an overview see, 'Letters and Papers, Foreign and Domestic, of the Reign of Henry VIII', *The Quarterly Review* cxliii:cclxxxv (1877), pp.1-51.
9. Parmiter, pp.11*ff.*
10. H. Kelly, pp.23-5.
11. *LP*, iv/iii, 3231.
12. *Quarterly Review*, p.15.
13. *CSP*, i, 189 [*LP*, iv/ii, 3147; Pocock, *Records*, i, pp.9-10].
14. PRO, SP 2/1, fols.22-3 [*LP*, iv/iii, 3140]; Raphael Holinshed et al (eds), *Chronicles* (3 vols, London, 1586), iii, p.906; *LP*, iv/iii, 3231.
15. R.S. Sylvester and D.P. Harding (eds), p.321; *CSPS*, iv/i, 160, 168, 241, 244. For Stokesley's involvement, see A.A. Chibi, '"*Turpitudinem uxoris fratris tui non revelavit*": John Stokesley and the Divorce Question', *Sixteenth Century Journal* xxv:2 (Summer 1994), pp.387-97.
16. *CSP*, i/i&ii, cx (p.201).
17. He expected to convince Francis I to summon all the 'independent' cardinals to a conclave at Avignon, where Wolsey would be appointed papal vicar-general. See, *LP*, iv/iii, 3186 (v); *CSPV*, iv, 365.
18. *CSP*, i/i&ii, cix (p.195). To Wolsey, the king's marriage was groundless because the original dispensation was insufficient.
19. E.g., J. Block, *Factional Politics and the English Reformation 1520-1540* (Woodbridge, 1993), p.14; Parmitre, p.21. Henry had had an affair with her sister.
20. *LP*, iv/ii, 3682.
21. *Ibid*, 3930; Wernham, pp.118-9.
22. Pocock, *Records*, i, p.150.
23. See Nicholas Harpsfield, *The Life and Death of Sir Thomas More*, ed. by E.V. Hitchcock (London, 1932), p.49; R.S. Sylvester and D.P. Harding (eds), p.218; BL, Cott. MSS, Cleo. E, vi, fols.148rv; Guy, *England*, pp.153, 155; Virginia Murphy, 'The Literature and Propaganda of Henry VIII's First Divorce', in Diarmaid MacCulloch (ed.), *The Reign of Henry VIII. Politics, Policy and Piety* (St Martin's Press, 1995), pp.135-58.
24. E.g., Scarisbrick, *Henry VIII*, pp.163*ff.*
25. Thomas Aquinas, *Summa Theologiae* (60 vols., London, 1969), xxix, p.154 (I-II,

Q.97, a.4, ad.3).

26. PRO, SP 1/94, fol.98v [*LP*, viii, 1054]. Much of the following is based on the theses of Murphy [pp.15-48] and G.D. Nicholson.

27. SP 1/63, fols.244-407v (at fols.303-13v, 360-84v); *LP*, v, 5 (viii).

28. PRO, SP 1/54, fols.130-229v; *LP*, iv/iii, 5729; Murphy, 'Debate', pp.88-9.

29. PRO. SP 1/63, fols.314rv, 315-58; James Gairdner, 'New Lights on the Divorce of Henry VIII. Part One', *EHR*, xi:xlvi (October 1896), pp.673-702 (at p.674).

30. Ralph Morice, *Narratives of the Days of the Reformation*, ed. by J.G. Nicholas (London, 1860), p.242; Foxe, viii, pp.7-8; D. MacCullock, *Thomas Cranmer* (New Haven, 1996), pp.45-6.

31. Foxe, viii, p.9; Burnet, iv, p.130.

32. Cf. Erwin Doernberg, *Henry VIII and Luther: An Account of Their Personal Relations* (London, 1961) p.69 and Ridley, *Cranmer*, pp.35-7. For his role as a translator see SP 1/94, fol.98v [*LP*, viii, 1054].

33. BL. Cott. MSS, Cleo. E. vi, fols.148rv; R.S. Sylvester and D.P. Harding (eds), p.118.

34. *LP*, v, Appendix no.3; *CSPS*, iv/i, 547.

35. John Guy, 'Thomas Cromwell and the Intellectual Origins of the Henrician Reformation', in A. Fox and J. Guy (eds), *Reassessing the Henrician Age: Humanism, Politics and Reform 1500-1550* (Oxford, 1986), pp.151-178 (at p.154).

36. Scarisbrick, 'Conservative Episcopate', p.73; PRO, SP 1/93, fols.67, 71v.

37. *LP*, iv/ii, 3340, 3382, 4744; Scarisbrick, 'Conservative Episcopate', pp.74-5. Clerk argued, after Fisher, that the levitical prohibitions were applicable but only to a living husband.

38. *LP*, iv/iii, 5613, 5694, 5732; *CSPV*, iv, 482; Stephen Ehses (ed.), *Ehses Römische Dokumente zur Geschichte der Ehescheidung Heinricks VIII von England, 1527-1534* (Paderborn, 1893), p.117.

39. H. Kelly, p.112; *CSPS*, iii/ii, 411; PRO, SP 1/54, fol.262.

40. Lambeth MS 2341, fols.1-44v, 46-179v; H. Kelly, pp.68*ff*; PRO, SP 1/54, fol.262; BL, Vit.B xii, fols.123v*ff*.

41. Pocock, *Records*, i, pp.181*ff*; ii, pp.431*ff*.

42. E.g., *CSPS*, iv/ii, 168, 211.

43. *CSP*, iii/ii, 829-30. Indeed, on 21 October 1528 the theologians of the University of Paris supported the king by a simple majority. This was seen as a good omen.

44. *LP*, iv/iii, 6111; Foxe, viii, pp.7-9; H. Kelly, p.175.

45. Burnet, iv, pp.130-1.

46. *Ibid*, p.39 (the king sent them three angry letters).

47. H. Kelly, p.176. They agreed that it was 'more probable' that the king's marriage transgressed divine law depending on whether or not the earlier marriage had been consummated but neither judged it contrary to natural law or beyond papal dispensation.

48. For dissenting views see Ehses (ed.), no. 170 (at p.172); Parmiter, p.124; H. Maynard Smith, *Henry VIII and the Reformation* (London, 1962), pp.29-30; BL, Harleian MSS 6382, fol.42; Ronald Bayne (ed.), *The Life of Fisher* (London, 1921), p.55; J.J Scarisbrick, 'Henry VIII and the Vatican Library', *Bibliotheque d'humanisme et renaissance* xxiv:xxv (Geneva, 1962), pp.211-16 (at pp.211, 214); Rex, *Fisher*, pp.163, 183; Scarisbrick, *Henry VIII*, pp.255-8; *LP*, x, 34.

49. For de'Ghinucci's doubts see *LP*, iv/iii, 6205. For other information, see 'The Divorce of Catherine of Aragon', *English Review*, clx:cccxxvii (July, 1884), pp.89-116 (at p.90).

50. For Pole, Fox and Stokesley in France see Thomas F. Mayer, 'A Fate Worse than

Death: Reginald Pole and the Parisian Theologians', *EHR* ciii:ccccix (October 1988), pp.870-91. For further details on Fox and Stokesley see *CSPS*, iv/i, 124, 160, 194; *LP*, iv/iii, 5945, 5983 [*CSPS*, iv/i, 194]; PRO, SP 1/56, fols.103r-4r [*CSP*, vii/v, cclxiv (pp.219-22)].

51. *LP*, iv/iii, 6481.
52. Fox was collating material for the *Collectanea satis copiosa*, including extracts from Jacques Merlin's *Conciliorum quattuor generalium tomus primus*. Pole studied the writings of Jean Gerson and Stokesley made contact with Jean Mair, a prominent nominalist theologian and conciliarist thinker. For details see, G.D. Nicholson, p.116 and Mayer, *Starkey*, pp.79*ff.*
53. *CSP*, vii/v, cclxvii (p.227) [PRO, SP 1/56, fol.211r].
54. *CSPS*, iv/i, 250; *CSP*, vii/v, cclxvii (pp.227-8); *LP*, iv/iii, 6164, 6449; James K. Farge, 'The Divorce Consultation of Henry VIII', in Heiko A. Oberman et al (eds), *Orthodoxy and Reform in Early Reformation France: The Faculty of Theology of Paris, 1500-1543* (Leiden, 1985), pp.135-43 (at p.136).
55. *LP*, iv/iii, 6147 [*CSP*, vii/v, cclxvii; SP 1/56, fol.211rv].
56. *CSPS*, iv/i, 249; Farge, p.136; *LP*, iv/iii, 6199; *CSPS*, iv/i, 285. See Farge, pp.137, 139 (n.112 for a list of names). Also see James K. Farge, *Biographical Register of Paris Doctors of Theology, 1500-1536*, (Toronto, 1980).
57. *LP*, iv/iii, 6321.
58. *LP*, iv/iii, 6394, 6400.
59. For the full text of the theologians' determination see, *Divorce Tracts*, pp.12-5; Hall, ii, p.776; Rymer (ed.), xiv, p.156.
60. PRO, SP 1/63, fol.248rv; James K. Farge, 'Paris Partisans of Henry VIII and of Catherine of Aragon', in Heiko A. Oberman et al (eds), *Orthodoxy and Reform in Early Reformation France: The Faculty of Theology of Paris, 1500-1543* (Leiden, 1985), pp.143-50 (at pp.145-8).
61. *CSP*, vii/v, cclxviii (p.230 n.1) [Vit. B, xiii, fol.11]; Holinshed (ed.), ii, p.913.
62. *LP*, iv/iii, 6111; Chibi, *Stokesley*, p.66.
63. *CSPS*, iv/i, 375 [*LP*, iv/iii, 6479; BL. Add. MSS. 28, 580, fol.202].
64. *LP*, v, 342, 378.
65. *Ibid*, 546; H. Kelly, p.181.
66. *CSPV*, iv, 639.
67. *CSP*, vii/v, ccci (p.310).
68. *CSPM*, i, 861. This was Augustino Scarpinello, the Milanese ambassador.
69. Stanford E. Lehmberg, *The Reformation Parliament 1529 - 1536* (Cambridge, 1070), pp.128-9; Gustave Constant, *The Reformation in England*, trans. by R.E. Scantlebury (2 vols., London, 1939-42), i, pp.350-1.
70. *LP*, v, 171.
71. Hall, ii, pp.774-80 (at p.775), as quoted in Lehmberg, p.129.
72. Hall, ii, p.775, but see *LP*, v, 171.
73. H. Kelly, p.191.
74. *LP*, iv/iii, 739.
75. *CSP*, v, 245; J. Moyes, 'Warham, An English Primate on the Eve of the Reformation', *Dublin Review*, 114 (1894), pp.390-420 (at pp.401-15); Ogle, pp.353*ff.*
76. *LP*, v, 1256; *CSPS*, iv/i, 986.
77. Muriel St Clare Byrne (ed.), *The Lisle Letters* (6 vols., Chicago, 1981), i, p.249 [*LP*, v, 1642].
78. *Ibid*, pp.250-1 [*LP*, v, App. no.33].
79. Muller, *Gardiner*, p.50.

80. Cf. Pocock, *Records*, ii, pp.369-70 [BL. Cott. MSS, Otho, C, x, fol.161rv] and Burnet, iv, p.239.
81. Wilkins, iii, p.756.
82. Compare H. Kelly, p.199 and Constant, *Reformation*, i, p.351.
83. Wilkins, iii, p.756.
84. *Ibid*. Cf. Pocock, *Records*, ii, pp.443-4; Burnet, iv, p.216.
85. Sixteen were opposed, including Fisher and de'Athequa. Stokesley, Longland and Standish approved (casting proxies for five other bishops, including Campeggio). Of the total 197 votes cast by proxy, only three were opposed. The results from the jurists, forty-seven in attendance, were much the same, all but six approving. Of the bishops, only Clerk opposed Gardiner, Veysey and their three proxies (including de'Ghinucci). See, Pocock, *Records*, ii, pp.444, 446-59; Burnet, iv, pp.216-7; H. Kelly, p.202.
86. *LP*, vi, 653; Dickens, *Lollards*, p.161 (n.7); 'The Records of the Northern Convocation', *Surtees Society*, cxiii (Durham 1907), no. lxxi, pp.207-17. The final vote was forty-nine to two in favour among the divines, and forty-eight to two among the jurists. See, Wilkins, iii, pp.767-8; H. Kelly, p.203.
87. BL. Harliean MSS 283, fol.4 [*CSP*, ii, viii; *LP*, vi, 327], fol.97 [*CSP*, ii, ix].
88. *CSP*, i, x, xii, xiii; *CSPS*, iv/ii, 1057, 1072; C.H. Williams (ed.), *English Historical Documents 1485-1558* (London, 1967), pp.719-20; Pocock, *Records*, ii, p.473.
89. C.H. Williams (ed.), pp.719-20; Pocock, *Records*, ii, pp.475, 476, 481-2.
90. BL. Cott. MSS. Titus B, i, fol.71 [*LP*, vi, 461, 495-6, 525-9]; Rymer (ed.), xiv, p.462; Burnet, i, p.120.
91. Rymer (ed.), xiv, p.467; Parmiter, pp.237-8; *LP*, vi, 661; Hall, ii, p.222.
92. PRO, SP 1/82, fol.12 [*LP*, vii, 15]; H. Kelly, p.212.
93. I have examined this elsewhere see, Chibi, *Stokesley*, pp.109-11. Also see G.H. Cook, *Letters to Cromwell and Others on the Suppression of the Monasteries* (London, 1965), p.32.
94. *LP*, viii, 441.
95. PRO. SP 1/82, fols.12 [*LP*, vii, 15], 40 [*LP*, vii, 22]; *LP*, vii, 8, 12; viii, 229; ix, 332; M.D. Knowles, *Religious Orders*, iii, pp.215-7.
96. *LP*, vii, 15 [PRO. SP 1/82, fol.12]; H. Kelly, pp.212-3.
97. E.g., A.A. Chibi, 'Henry VIII and his Marriage to his Brother's Wife, the Sermon of Bishop John Stokesley of 11 July 1535', *HR* lxvii:clxii (February 1994), pp.40-56.
98. *CSPS*, v/i, 58.
99. *LP*, vii, 690.
100. E.W. Ives, 'The Fall of Anne Boleyn Reconsidered', *EHR* cvii:ccccxxiv (July 1992), pp.651-64, and George Bernard, 'The Fall of Anne Boleyn: A Rejoinder', *EHR* cvii:ccccxxiv (July 1992), pp.665-74.
101. Warnicke, p.211; MacCulloch, *Cranmer*, p.156.
102. *LP*, x, 752.
103. H. Kelly, p.244.
104. *Ibid*, pp.261*ff* for additional details.
105. *Ibid*, p.267; Wilkins, iii, pp.851-2. The committee was Cranmer, Lee, Bonner (now bishop of London), Tunstal, Gardiner and Bell (now bishop of Worcester) and others, including Thomas Thirlby, from the lower house.
106. T.F. Mayer, 'Tournai and Tyranny: Imperial kingship and Critical Humanism', *HJ* xxxiv:ii (1991), pp.257-77 (at p.266-7).
107. Pollard, *Wolsey*, pp.244-5.
108. George Cavendish, *The Life and Death of Cardinal Wolsey*, ed. by R.S. Sylvester

(London, 1959), p.231.

109. G.W. Bernard, 'The Pardon of the Clergy Reconsidered', *JEH* xxxvii:ii (April 1986), pp.258-71 (at p.264).

110. Tanner, pp.13-4; *The Statutes of the Realm* (11 vols., London, 1810-28), iii, p.293.

111. *CSPM*, i, 831; *CSPV*, iv, 629, 634.

112. Scarisbrick, 'Conservative Episcopate', p.117.

113. J.A. Guy, 'Henry VIII and the Praemunire Manoeuvres of 1530-31', *EHR* xcvii:ccclxxxiv (July 1982), pp.481-503 (at pp.485-6).

114. H. Kelly, pp.124-5; J.A. Guy, 'The Pardon of the Clergy: a Reply', *JEH* xxxvii:ii (April 1986), pp.283-4.

115. There are many interpretations of these early events. Besides Bernard and Guy, interesting reading comes from J.J. Scarisbrick, 'The Pardon of the Clergy, 1531', *Cambridge Historical Journal* xii:i (1956), pp.22-39 and M. Kelly, 'The Submission of the Clergy', *TRHS* xv (1965), pp.97-120.

116. Wilkins, iii, pp.725-6.

117. Kelly, 'Warham', pp.227-9.

118. Wilkins, iii, p.717-24.

119. Haigh, *Reformations*, p.106; Lehmberg, p.109.

120. Wilkins, iii, pp.724-5.

121. *CSPS*, iv/ii, 615; *LP*, v, 62.

122. Kelly, 'Warham', pp.312-3.

123. *LP*, iv/iii, 6047 (iii) [PRO, SP 1/56, fols.84-7v].

124. Kaufman, pp.13*ff*; Scarisbrick, 'Conservative Episcopate', pp.347*ff*; Elton, *Reform*, pp.140*ff*.

125. Guy, 'Manoeuvres', p.491.

126. *CSP*, iv, 635; *CSPM*, i, 850.

127. *LP*, viii, 1490; *LP*, xiii/ii, 1217.

128. Bernard, 'Pardon of the Clergy', p.278.

129. *CSP*, iv, 619; *LP*, v, 721 (iii).

130. The two clerical pardon bills of 1531 are discussed in Guy, 'Manoeuvres', pp.492-4.

131. Wilkins, iii, p.725; *LP*, v, 928; Lehmberg, pp.112-3.

132. E.g., Haigh, *Reformations*, pp.107-8.

133. PRO, SP 6/2, fols.94-6; *LP*, v, 1022.

134. *Statutes*, iii, p.334; Elton, *Constitution*, pp.174-6.

135. Wilkins, iii, p.744.

136. Cf. BL, Cott. Cleo. E vi, fol.257; Burnet, vi, p.52.

137. Wilkins, iii, p.745; 'The Records of the Northern Convocation', pp.218-20.

138. Wilkins, iii, pp.762-5.

139. 'The Records of the Northern Convocation', pp.221-34.

140. Lehmberg, p.118.

141. Annates were fees extracted by the pope from newly beneficed incumbents to spiritual livings. It had been calculated that since about 1486, between £160-180,000 had been paid into Roman coffers. Ogle (pp.299-300) suggested that the basis of the bill had been formed in the king's mind by the costs involved in the two Episcopal promotions of his almoner and his secretary (Lee and Gardiner). These calculations also suggest that the bill was intended to shock the pope into a realisation of just how much he had to lose through continued defiance.

142. Elton, *Constitution*, pp.176-7; J.J. Scarisbrick, 'Clerical Taxation in England, 1485-1535', *JEH* xi (1960), pp.41-54.

143. *CSP*, i/ii, xix (p.410).

144. G.R. Elton, 'The Commons' Supplication of 1532: Parliamentary Manoeuvres in the Reign of Henry VIII', *EHR* lxiv (1951), pp.216-32.
145. Lehmberg, p.137.
146. Elton, *Constitution*, pp.324-6.
147. It was 'not only to the diminution and derogation of your [the king's] imperial jurisdiction and prerogative royal but also to the great prejudice, inquietation, and damage of your said subjects'. See, Tanner, p.21.
148. Hall, ii, pp.784-5.
149. Lehmberg, pp.141, 145.
150. Wilkins, iii, pp.748-52.
151. Thomas F. Mayer, 'Thomas Starkey, An Unknown Conciliarist at the Court of Henry VIII', *JHI* xlix:2 (April-June 1988), pp.207-228 (at pp.207-8, 214-5).
152. Ogle, p.331.
153. Henry Gee and William J. Hardy (eds), *Documents illustrative of English church history* (London, 1896), p.162.
154. *Ibid*, pp.157-8.
155. PRO, SP 6/7, fols.239-84, also printed in Gee and Hardy (eds), pp.154-76.
156. Hall, ii, p.788; Macklem, p.138.
157. Wilkins, iii, p.754; *LP*, v, 1023
158. Redworth, pp.36-7; *LP*, v, 1013, 1058.
159. *LP*, iv/iii, 5416.
160. Muller (ed.), *Letters*, pp.48-9 (no.36); Wilkins, iii, p.752.
161. Kelly, 'Submission', pp.112-3.
162. Lehmberg, p.149.
163. James W. Joyce, *England's Sacred Synods: A Constitutional History of the Convocations of the Clergy* (London, 1855), p.342.
164. PRO, SP 6/6, fols.108-9.
165. *LP*, vii, 57; Joyce, pp.343-5.
166. Joyce, p.346; Wilkins, iii, p.749; Gee and Hardy (eds), pp.154-76.
167. *LP*, vi, 1486-7.
168. *CSP*, i/ii, 20.
169. *LP*, vi, 1487; Guy, *Tudor England*, p.135; Elton, *Reform*, p.179.
170. *LP*, iv, 5827; v, 1109.
171. *LP*, v, 707.
172. E.g., *LP*, v, 207, 378, 460, 492, 546.
173. E.g., *LP*, iv/iii, 6199, 6757; v, 62; vi, 160.
174. *LP*, vi, 1164, 1249; Scarisbrick, 'Conservative Episcopate', pp.272*ff*.
175. *CSPS*, iv/ii, 1153.
176. L.E. Whatmore, 'The Sermon against the Holy Maid of Kent, delivered at Paul's Cross, 23 November, 1533, and at Canterbury, Dec.7', *EHR* lviii:ccxxxii (October 1943), pp.463-75; Alan Neame, *The Holy Maid of Kent* (London, 1971), pp.266-8.
177. *CSPS*, iv/ii, 1153; *LP*, vi, 887.
178. John Bruce, 'Observations on the circumstances which occasioned the Death of Fisher Bishop of Rochester', *Archaeologia* xxv (1834), pp.61-99.
179. *LP*, vi, 1379 (i, ii, v).
180. *Ibid*, vi, 62; Scarisbrick, 'Conservative Episcopate', pp.278-80.
181. Scarisbrick, 'Conservative Episcopate', p.283; PRO, KB. 29/164, ro.33; 27/1085, ro.23.
182. E.g., KB. 29/151, ro.30; 29/154, ro.15ff, ro.25; 29/161, ro.44.
183. KB. 29/166, ro.42; 27/1091, ro.13.

184. *LP*, vii, 158 (2).

185. *LP*, vii, 262 (18); Rymer (ed.), xiv, p.484.

186. *LP*, vii, 296; *Statutes*, iii, p.486.

187. *CSPS*, iv/i, 250.

188. Scarisbrick, *Henry VIII*, p.326.

189. Bowker, *Longland*, p.72.

190. Wilkins, iii, p.718.

191. See Christopher Haigh, 'Anticlericalism and the English Reformation', *History*, 68:224 (October, 1983), pp.391-407; Margaret Bowker, 'The Henrician Reformation and the Parish Clergy', *BIHR* l:cxxi (May, 1977), pp.30-47; Felicity Heal, 'The Parish Clergy and the Reformation in the Diocese of Ely', *Cambridge Antiquarian Society Proceedings* lxvi (1975-6), pp.141-63.

192. For details see, GLRO, MSS, DL/C/330, fols.265-66r; Thompson, 'Pastoral Work', p.36. Also see, Colin A. McLaren, 'An Early 16th Century Act Book of the Diocese of London', *Journal of the Society of Archivists* iii (1965-1969), pp.336-41; *idem*, 'An Edition of Foxford: A Vicar-General's Book of the Diocese of London, 1521-39', 2 vols. (unpublished M Phil thesis, University of London, 1973); Brigden, p.62; Peter Heath, *The English Parish Clergy on the Eve of the Reformation* (London, 1969), pp.73-4.

193. Ann Foster, 'Bishop Tunstall's Priests', *Recusant History* ix (1967-68), pp.175-204 (at p.176); Thompson, 'Pastoral Work', pp.23, 59-61, 179-80.

194. E.g., *LP*, v, 1132; SRO, Ep 1/10/5, fols.80-90.

195. *LP*, iv/ii, 4627; Foxe, viii, p.430.

196. SRO, Ep 1/10/5, fols.5, 7-8; Lander, p.17.

197. Thompson, 'Pastoral Work', pp.233, 377.

198. SRO. Ep1/10/3, fols.31-2, 35-6, 38, 40; Ep 1/10/4, fol.12; Lander, pp.66-7.

199. Lander, pp.210-12, 215-6, 62-71, 281-2, 311, 241-4.

200. A. Hamilton Thompson (ed.), 'Visitations of Lincoln 1517-1531', in *LRS* xxxv (1944), p.207.

201. Bowker, *Longland*, p.27.

202. *Ibid*, pp.22-3; A. Hamilton Thompson (ed.), xxxv, p.208.

203. Bowker, *Longland*, pp.24-5; *LP*, v, 1158; PRO SP 1/70, fol.171.

204. *LP*, v, 1175.

205. *LP*, iv/iii, 6385.

206. Thompson, 'Pastoral Work', p.132.

207. Lehmberg, p.100; Wilkins, iii, pp.719-21.

208. *LP*, v, Appen. no.768 (xviii); John Stowe, 'Historical Memoranda', in James Gairdner (ed.), *Three Fifteenth Century Chronicles* (London, 1880), p.89; Charles C. Butterwoth, *The English Primers, (1529-1545), their publication and connection with the English Bible and the Reformation in England* (Philadelphia, 1953), p.16; William A. Clebsch, *England's Earliest Protestants, 1520-1535* (New Haven, 1964), pp.266-7.

209. Stowe, pp.88-90; *TRP*, i, pp.181-86, 193-7.

210. Foxe, iv, p.681; Margaret Aston, 'Lollards and the Reformation: Survival or Revival?', *History* xlix:lxvi (June, 1964), pp.149-70 (at p.150).

211. J.F. Davis, p.54.

212. *Ibid*; Foxe, iv, pp.683-5.

213. Foxe, iv, pp.683-5.

214. *Ibid*.

215. *Ibid*, pp.705*ff*.

216. Henry R. Plomer, *Wynkyn De Worde & His Contemporaries from the Death of Caxton to 1535* (London, 1925), p.207.

217. E.G. Duff et al (eds), *Hand-lists of Books Printed by London Printers 1501-1556* (London, 1913), n.p.; *idem, The Printers, Stationers and Bookbinders of Westminster and London from 1476 to 1535* (Cambridge, 1906), p.148. Also see, *idem, A Century of the English Book Trade* (London, 1905).

218. J. Harrison (*alias* John Bale), *Yet a course at the Romish Fox* (Zurich, 1543), sig. G7r.

219. *LP*, vi, 934 [PRO. SP 1/78, fol.85r]; Duff, *Printers*, p.149.

220. Block, p.41.

221. Barnes, p.4.

222. *Ibid*, p.5; Clebsch, p.236 (n); Also see Andrew M. McLean, 'Detestynge Thabomynacyon: William Barlow, Thomas More and the Anglican Episcopacy', *Moreana* xiii:xlix (February, 1976), pp.67-77 (at p.69).

223. E.G. Rupp, *Studies in the Making of the English Protestant Tradition (mainly in the Reign of Henry VIII)* (Cambridge, 1947), pp.66-72.

224. McLean, p.75 (n.7).

225. I.B. Horst, *The Radical Brethren: Anabaptists and the English Reformation to 1558* (Nieuwhoop, 1972), p.45.

226. Thomas Becon, *The Catechism of Thomas Becon*, ed. by John Ayre (Cambridge, 1844), pp.424-5; Clara H. Stuart, 'Hugh Latimer: Apostle to the English', *Christianity Today* xxiv (1980), pp.17-19 (at p.18).

227. Foxe, vii, p.454; Arthur G. Chester, *Hugh Latimer: Apostle to the English* (Philadelphia, 1978 Octagon Books edn.).

228. Foxe, vii, p.485.

229. *Ibid*, pp.484-5; Corrie (ed.), *Sermons*, i, p.322.

230. Foxe, vii, pp.489-90.

231. *Ibid*, p.498. For Crome see, *LP*, v, 148.

232. *Ibid*, iii, 382; Corrie (ed.), *Sermons*, i, pp.vii-viii.

233. Corrie (ed.), *Sermons*, ii, pp.294-5.

234. Guildhall MSS 9531/10, fol.142 [BL, Harleian MSS. 425, fols.13-14].

235. Wilkins, iii, p.747; Corrie (ed.), *Sermons*, ii, pp.353-4.

236. Eleven stated that anyone who had been forbidden by the bishops ought not to preach until purged by his superiors and lawfully restored. Fourteen affirmed that consecrations, sanctifications and benedictions received in the church are laudable and useful. Cf. MSS 9531/10, fol.142 and Wilkins, iii, p.747.

237. Wilkins, iii, p.747.

238. Corrie (ed.), *Sermons*, ii, pp.356-7 [BL, Harleian MSS. 6989, fol.158].

239. PRO, SP 6/1. fol.19 [*LP*, vi, 433 (vi)].

240. Wilkins, iii, p.748.

241. *LP*, v, 607, 703; vi, 1214 (i, ii); vii, 923 (xxxix); Wilkins, iii, p.756 [SP 6/9 fols.82v-84v]. For details of the Bristol sermons see, Chester, pp.84-93.

242. Foxe, v, 39; Brigden, p.206 (n. 13).

243. Foxe, v, pp.34-5; BL, Harleian MSS 425, fol.15r.

244. *LP*, v, 982.

245. Guy, *Career*, p.167; Brigden, p.207.

246. Foxe, v, 37; *LP*, vii, 923; viii, 1063.

247. Bowker, *Longland*, pp.145-6; Wharhirst, pp.169-70.

248. BL, Sloane MS. 1207, fols.1v-4v.

249. *Ibid*, as quoted in Wharhirst, pp.170-71.

250. Dickens, *Lollards*, p.19.
251. *Ibid*, pp.23-4.
252. E.g., *LP*, viii, 1005; Strype, *EM*, i/ii, p.274.
253. Gladys Hinde (ed.), *The Registers of Cuthbert Tunstall Bishop of Durham 1530-59 and James Pilkington Bishop of Durham 1561-76* (Durham, 1952), p.xxvii.
254. E.g., *LP*, v, 1132; SRO, EP 1/10/5, fols.80-90.
255. Lander, p.17; Thompson, 'Pastoral Works', p.122; Foxe, viii, p.430.
256. SRO, EP 1/10/5, fols.5, 7-8.
257. C.E. Welch, 'Three Sussex Heresy Trials', *Sussex Archaeological Collections* xcv (1957), pp.59-70 (at p.61).
258. SRO, EP 1/10/5, fol.9v.
259. Welch, p.64.
260. Elton, *Tudor Constitution*, pp.214-5.
261. J.F. Davis, 'Lollards, Reformers and St Thomas of Canterbury', *University of Birmingham Historical Journal* ix:i (1963) pp.1-15 (at p.11).
262. PRO, SP 2/P, fol.11r; *LP*, vii, 155.
263. *CW*, ix, pp.126-7.
264. *LP*, vii, 155.
265. BL, Harleian MSS 421, fol.13r; *LP*, iv/ii, 4029.
266. *LP*, vii, 155.
267. *Statutes*, iii, pp.545-6; Lehmberg, pp.186-7.
268. *LP*, xiv/i, 1001; BL, Cott. MSS Cleo. E.v. fols.377-8.
269. *CW*, ix, 351. Including translations of Luther.
270. *CW*, ix, p.89.
271. *LP*, vi, 661; Cox (ed.), ii, p.246 (no. XIV); MacCulloch, *Cranmer*, pp.101-2.
272. BL, Lansdowne MSS 979, fol.92v.
273. Guildhall MSS 9531/11: Episcopal Register Stokesley: 1530-1539, fol.71r.
274. *LP*, vi, 761; Gairdner, i, p.409; Foxe, v, p.17.
275. Gairdner, i, p.406.

# Chapter Four
## The King's Church, c.1534-1547

Whereas the Act of Appeals had left England free from all external authorities, the Act of Supremacy recognised the authority of the crown over all persons and all causes in the realm. It was not particularly innovative, merely conceding claims made by the king as early as 1512. The royal headship was affirmed in its existence and, in addition, the act affirmed the royal powers of ecclesiastical visitation, reform and the king's right to decide religious orthodoxy (pre-dating the *cuius regio, eius religio* concept by several years). It was entirely consistent with previously recognised claims.[1] Obviously it was consequential for the bishops. Their authority now depended entirely on that of the crown.

The supremacy was also the end result of a long process inextricably bound to the divorce. Its foundations were in the repudiation of papal power and in the establishment of a sound and orthodox theory of royal authority. As we will see, this was based on scripture, the Church Fathers, ancient councils, late-medieval doctors and history. The working out of the supremacy was based also in part on both the conservative and radical bishops accommodating themselves to the new reality. That is, in how they dealt with the effects of the supremacy in the dioceses and with attempts to establish a workable formula of faith. First we need to look at underlying theory, its development, and acceptance (or rejection) by the bishops themselves.

\* \* \*

## 1. Removing the impediment of papal authority

Obviously, the royal headship and the movement away from Rome had met resistance by some of the bishops. Pressures had been brought to bear and, in some cases, would continue to be. Nature too had alleviated some difficulties. Bishops Blythe, Booth, Warham, Wolsey, Fisher, Richard Fox, Nix, Sherborne, Skevington, Standish and West were all dead, or dying, by 1535. Another act of 1534 deprived the Italians of their sees, with the proviso that if either Campeggio or de'Ghinucci, within four months, came into residence and took an oath to be the king's true liegemen they could retain their sees. They both declined the offer. Shortly after Catherine's death, her Spanish confessor de'Athequa resigned Llandaff, the last foreign bishop. He was kept on as the only person around Catherine who spoke Spanish. Besides which, 'the said Bushop is the man of most simplicitie, and shal do lest harme to tary'.[2]

Nature cleared the way for the promotion of men whose loyalties were undoubted. As was noted earlier, these fourteen late bishops (mostly lawyers) were replaced with men (mostly theologians) who, as diplomats, had seen the true nature of the papacy in Rome. They had experienced its intrigues, its familial politics and its religious scandals first hand and had been appalled. As a bulwark against heresy in Europe, the papacy had certainly failed. Perhaps, with a king whose anti-heretical credentials were famous, the supremacy could be a workable proposition for those concerned with the church as an institution in England.

The groundwork for the royal supremacy had been laid, perhaps unconsciously, as early as 1529 with the need to repudiate the papal power of dispensation. The king's agents had been sent to the continental libraries and archives in search of materials to help the cause. So the very question of the extent of papal authority was the first obstacle to be overcome. As papal infallibility and indefectibility did not yet exist, the king's case was almost half-made already.[3] There were two ways around an intractable pope: either emphasise English independence from Rome and develop existing royal power or appeal to a general council. Much would be made of both England's 'special circumstances', culminating in the Act of Appeals, and conciliarism, at least so long as the advantages outweighed the disadvantages. Scarisbrick has shown conclusively that there was not a great deal of evidence to be found in the papal archives with regard to England's unique position or the crown's special privileges[4], but the king's scholars, Stokesley, Fox, Gardiner, Cranmer, and ideological supporters like Latimer, had more success with conciliar theory.

Recall the work in Paris of Stokesley, Fox and Pole, treating with the conciliarists and with collecting material for what would become the source of imperial theory, the *Collectanea satis copiosa*. These would also provide the major sources for the *Glasse of Truthe*.[5] Pole showed an interest in the writings of Jean Gerson who held that 'a general council holds its power directly from Christ: everyone, whatever his degree or dignity, even if it be papal, is bound to obey it'. Gerson had made a sharp distinction between divine and human law.[6] The fact of these other investigations is one of the clearest indications that the scholars had not gone abroad merely to find others who would condemn the Aragon marriage. That these three men (less so Pole) were formulating a plan to gain the king's divorce through an appeal to a general council is made evident by the number of references and extracts from the conciliarist writers in the *Collectanea*. What had they written and why was it useful?

Jean Mair (Stokesley's contact) had written two books by this time, *Disputatio de auctoritate concilii supra pontificem maximum* and *In Mattheum ad literam expositio* (both c.1518), wherein he argued that better provision could not have been made for the civil polity than for the ecclesiastical, reflecting Almain's dispute with Cajetan (examined below). What was important, from the scholars' point of view, were Mair's answers to the two main conciliarist questions of whether or not kings are subject to popes in temporal matters and whether or not a universal council representing the whole church is superior to the pope and can judge and depose him. Both questions formed major parts of the *Collectanea*.[7]

In brief, Mair argued that kings did not hold the material sword from popes, contrary to *Unam Sanctum*, but from the consent of the people. Thereby, a king would be wrong to subject his kingdom to the authority of anyone except himself without its consent, save in very limited ways. The second question was a long-standing controversy reflecting the previous answer. Mair held with his student, Almain, that the authority of the general council must be superior to that of the pope.[8] Almain also said (and this certainly has bearing on Henry's position) that any particular church to which the necessity of assembling a general council becomes evident, should make this fact known to the remaining churches and, by naming a safe place accessible to all, should make possible a solution. If some particular church held aloof and declined to send delegates, the authority of the entire church still resided in the assembly. As a weapon against the pope, conciliar theory held out great promise, but as a general council could also be summoned by the emperor, caution had to be taken not to depend too much upon it.[9]

As other initiatives fell by the wayside and as the financial, legislative and judicial pressures applied to the church in England seemingly failed to move the pope, the threat of an appeal to a future general council became more attractive in the short term. On 29 June 1533, the king made an appeal before archbishop Lee against the pope to a future council as a precaution, should he be excommunicated.[10] Later, the royal council decided to explore the option in greater detail. Thus parliament would be asked to enact, after confirmation of the fact by convocation, that the pope was inferior to the authority of a general council.[11]

In November, Bonner was sent to Rome to make the appeal[12], while in England, the bishops 'as now be nerest unto the Courte' (Stokesley, Clerk and Longland) were to make lengthy examinations of the divine law to prove whether or not the general council was higher in authority than the pope. Sampson and Fox were also ordered to research the question and prepare to be examined by the three bishops. All this initiated a massive campaign of sermons and polemics, asserting the general council's superiority, driving home the message that the 'bishop of Rome' had no more authority in England than any other foreign bishop. From the highest to the lowest in both the spiritual and temporal realms, the word was spread that

the sayd Bisshop of Rome, called the pope, is not in auctoryte above
the Generall Counsaile, but the Generall Counsaile is above him,

and all Bisshopes; and that he hathe not, by Goddes lawe, any more
jurisdiction within this realme, then an other foreyn Bisshop . . . and
that suche auctoryte, as he before this hathe usurped within this realme,
ys bothe ayenst Goddes law, and also ayenst the Generall Counsiales.

Stokesley appointed preachers at St Paul's Cross who would continually
hammer this message home to the listeners. Great efforts were made and men
were sent as far as Poland in search of support for the king's position.[13]

One of the most interesting of the pamphlets to emerge from this new
research effort was the *Articles Devised by the holle consent of the Kynges
moste honourable counsayle* (1533). Of course, most of the articles were
divorce-related, but article four states that 'the right belief of all true Christian
people is that a general council (lawfully gathered) is superior and hath power
over all bishops and spiritual powers, not excepting the bishop of Rome'.
Moreover, anyone who doubted this was 'to be taken by all true Christian people
as an heretic'.[14] The pamphlet is nicely rounded off by article nine which states
that 'there is none authority ne jurisidiction granted more to the bishop of
Rome than to any other *extra provinciam*', labelling Clement VII a heretic
because he had disregarded these 'truths'.[15] Dangerously, Tunstal also harboured
some doubts and, while his letter of protest is not extant, we can note his
objections from the king's reply.

Tunstal was concerned that the book proved the king's intention to secede
from the Church as it did not follow traditional readings of scripture. He pointed
out that to believe 'that the pope of Rome hath no preeminence above other
churchs and mynysters of them' was a heresy condemned at Constance. There
was also a question of the validity of Basle as a precedent to justify an appeal
to a general council. The heart of the problem for Tunstal was that the council's
book argued against the idea that 'individual members of the universal body of
Christendom are required to confirm themselves to the teaching of that
universal body, not to determine it for themselves'. Thomas More would take
much the same position and lose his head for it. Tunstal also argued that no
inferior prelate of a part of the church could judge and determine the authority
of a superior prelate of a superior church. Lastly, he brought up the war against
Louis XII (whom Henry had demonised but now seemed to lionise) who had
'assisted and nurryshed a scisme'.[16]

Tunstal had hit the nail on the head, having picked up on some of the allusions
to future activity. Elton points to the mention of parliament and the obedience
due to its statutes as significant, even though after the Act of Appeals nothing
of real note attacking the old order would be enacted in the remainder of the
1533 session. Moreover, Tunstal was correct in his reading that the *Articles*
seem to contain no hint that the king would be willing to come to terms with
Rome on the issue, but clearly the attack on the pope was personal. As the acts
of Supremacy and Succession were already in the government pipeline, the
*Articles* have to be seen as a pre-emptive strike preparing the groundwork for

what was to come. Tunstal, of course, would in time be brought around, as would some others, as the option of the general council appeal would be allowed to diminish in light of the Act of Supremacy. Having, in theory, eliminated papal supremacy, the basis of the king's own authority had to be laid.

\* \* \*

## 2. The affirmation of royal spiritual power

Certainly, at this point, the idea of royal spiritual supremacy is not new. The king had been exposed to Luther's 'elevation of kingship to a divine office', the central theme of Tyndale's *Obedience of a Christian Man*[17], and he had a precedent in that the previous reign had witnessed the formulation of the idea that the king was 'a person with dual characteristics, having both lay and ecclesiastical authority'. The king united 'the laity and the priesthood' in one person.[18] The questions for the king's intellectual advisors, prior to the Act of Supremacy, had been just how much spiritual power the king actually possessed? How far could papal authority be abrogated? Such was the self-appointed task of Fox, Stokesley, Gardiner and others, who produced the collection of opinions and citations known as the *Collectanea*.[19]

In brief, the *Collectanea* examined, compared and contrasted the sources of royal and papal authority, and went on to become the source for all the bishops' later supremacy apologies and sermons. It established certain principles of royal authority based on history and precedent. For instance, in the section labelled '*Quaedem pertinencia ad regis officium*'[20] it was noted that King Edgar had reproved clerical morals and, from Augustine and Aquinas, it was asserted that Christian princes had used their coercive powers against the enemies of the church for the salvation of their subjects' souls.[21] Likewise, the section '*Non est novum Regem esse vicarium dei in terris*'[22] referred to such thinkers as Bracton and Britton to form an argument that the king was himself God's vicar, and therefore, could have no equal in his own kingdom (as Henry had claimed in 1515). This section laid the foundation of his *imperium* or final authority on both temporal and spiritual issues.[23] *Collectanea* ranged further afield than history[24] but, for propaganda value there was nothing to beat the example of Lucius, the first (possibly mythical) Christian king of Britain who ruled in God's name, answerable to God alone.[25] Much was made of Lucius, who shows up in Sampson's supremacy apology *Oratio*[26], which emphasised that Lucian's God-given power over the spiritual realm could be 'lent' out to the priesthood. This led into a discussion of the 'two swords' theory.[27] The twist for the king's scholars was that no power was needed in the spiritual sphere save discipline, which was clearly a matter for the king.[28]

Thus, based on such sources as Malmesbury, Gervase of Tilsbury, Hugo of St Victor and Origen; accepted authorities all, the clerical powers of legislation of new canons, administration and sacerdotal function were acquired from the temporal ruler. Even the papacy itself classically derived its own wealth and power from a temporal ruler, the Emperor Constantine, through his donation to Pope Sylvester. The importance of this material, from the Act of Appeals, is that 'the Englisshe church . . . is sufficiently endowed by the kingis most noble progenitours . . . their auctorities and iurisdiccionis ys deryved and dependyth from and the same Imperiall crown of this realme'.[29] Much of this was used to justify the argument that the king could not, therefore, submit himself to the pope in Rome, but the material was also used as the fountainhead of supremacy apologies.

This was the central issue of a number of polemics in circulation by 1531[30], the most notable of which was that one delivered to convocation on 10 February by George Boleyn.[31] Clearly based on the *Collectanea*, the tract was intended to bolster the king's claims to supremacy and his power to repress heresy and error. In brief, the central argument was that the king held a

> supreme auctorite grounded on God's worde [which] ought in no case
> to be restrayned by any frustrate decrees of popish lawes or voyed
> prescriptes of humane tradtions, but that he maye both order and
> minister, yea and also execute the office of spiritual administration in
> the church whereof he is heed. . . .[32]

– a clear implication that the *potestas ordinas* could be ascribed to a temporal ruler.

Evidence was brought together to show that when Christ had chosen his Apostles it was a king, not a priest or bishop, who had been placed highest in both temporal and spiritual matters.[33] While bishops had provided leadership, only a temporal ruler, who could leave a legitimate heir, provided continuity. 'Favour [him] who satisfying his vocation [is] agreeable [with] the sending of Christ and in that no other determination or answer to be admitted than the affirmation of scripture'.[34] This 'right order' drew support from the oft-cited evidence of ancient Hebrew kings like Melchisedech, Saul, Jehoshaphat, Josias and David[35], all of whom exercised both spiritual and temporal powers.

Although merely hinted at, the tract did not in fact ascribe the *potestas ordinis*, the truly sacerdotal, sacramental power to the king, although the threat was clear. It did accredit the *potestas jurisdictionis*. This was an administrative and judicial power over the church as a corporate body. Although a restricted power, it was still useful, as it was understood to provide moral and disciplinary authority.[36] This was a position that the king's humanist-intellectual bishops could easily maintain without compromising their religious scruples. Of course, some were willing that the king should go further.

In 1540, for instance, Cranmer would go so far as to hint that it was not forbidden in divine law that a king should 'make Bishops and Priests'. This depended, however, on the rather extraordinary circumstances of a king finding himself in an infidel country without a Christian clergy.[37] Neither of the two chief moderates, however, would go that far. Stokesley recognised the king's supremacy but suggested in 1535 that he should name a clerical deputy to carry out his instructions and perform necessary ordinary functions, much as Wolsey had done in the 1520s.[38] Fox almost pre-dated Cranmer by six years when, in his edition of the *Collectanea* (entitled *De vera differentia regiae potestatis et ecclesiasticae*), he cited examples of earlier English kings investing bishops and higher clergyman. He did not mention consecration, however, nor did he examine these other examples too closely.[39]

In any case, such papers were submitted to convocation as a means of preparing the clergy for future developments. Another paper in circulation in late 1531, called *Glasse of Truthe*[40], picked up the arguments where these others left off, disseminating them to a wider audience. Although written anonymously, the tract was obviously influenced, if not written, by Stokesley and Fox. In brief, the *Glasse* rehearsed some of the evidence from the Blackfriars' trial in the form of a dialogue between a jurist and a divine who were both partisans of the king.

It began with the divine's accusation that jurists had ascribed all manner of powers to the pope and this, in turn, had delayed the settlement of the king's marriage and confused the true meaning of divine law.[41] It took divine-right theory as its basis, and outlined a plan to accomplish the king's cause in more concrete terms, much as *Articles* had, hinting at future policy directions and parliamentary action:

> Marry, I think that the way might be found well enough, if the whole head and body of the parliament would set their wits and good wills unto it; for no doubt but that it ought to be determined within this realm, as plainly enough. . . .

Alternatively, the divine points out that 'the king's highness and his parliament should earnestly press the metropolitans of this realm . . . to set an end shortly in this'[42] If nothing else this showed that the king had options.

Such tracts were also written to popularise the entire range of arguments against the Aragon marriage and in support of the English clergy's jurisdictional independence from Rome. The longer they remained under the usurped papal authority, the further put off was that day 'when Englishmen can enjoy a stable future insured by the birth of a male heir'.[43] Taking somewhat different perspectives on the matter were two other polemics justifying the abrogation of papal jurisdiction. These are also central to an understanding of the position of the king's intellectual brigade. They are Fox's *De Vera Differentia* (the earlier) and Sampson's *Oratio*, the first supremacy apology to receive widespread continental distribution.

With the royal headship firmly established, papal authority increasingly questioned in light of conciliar theory, and with a plan already underway to remove papal jurisdiction altogether, it had to be shown in a convincing and orthodox manner that the Roman primacy was itself mythical and without basis in scripture or theology. The *Glasse* had gone some way toward laying the groundwork for this, blaming jurists for granting the papacy too much power as a convenience. Fox wanted to make a distinction in his polemic between royal and papal power, referring back to Gerson's conciliarism and Marsilius' writings.

The arguments themselves are familiar; current papal claims are unsupported by early church evidence. St Paul had equal authority with St Peter, the Nicaean council had met and acted in light of the absence of papal representation, and Fox proved that '*plenitudo potestatis*' is, in actual fact, nothing more than a corruption of Christian theory. As in the *Glasse*, jurists come in for a bit of a pounding. So many canon laws, some unenforceable, some incoherent and some even contradictory, are little more than an intolerable and certainly unhelpful burden.[44] As for the power of the king, the Jews were trotted out once again, as was the fact that the apostles and Christ himself had placed themselves under civil authority. For Fox, the power of the king was best summed up by the example of Justinian, who placed all spiritual authority at the king's feet.[45] Papal authority also came in for a brisk lambasting by the pen of Sampson.

Like his intellectual colleagues, Sampson (a jurist) recognised the need to provide his readers with an ideal and deep-rooted traditionalism (i.e. a firm historical foundation) for the royal ecclesiastical supremacy. This he readily found in Marsilius. He not only provided a plausible alternative interpretation to the scriptural texts upon which had been based the papal claims to '*plentitudo potestastis*', but he also offered an in-depth re-examination of the papal supremacy's historical development.[46] In short, Marsilius provided a ready-made case against papal supremacy, which Sampson fully exploited.

For example, Marsilius made much of the idea that all the apostles were of equal status[47], a claim repeated by both Fox and Sampson.[48] Marsilius also quoted Christ's claim that 'my kingdom is not off this world', also echoed by both scholars.[49] Indeed, that both men echoed Marsilius is easy to show. His central examination of the 'coercive jurisdiction' was also employed. This was the power to make and enforce laws, which belonged to the temporal authority alone. Marsilius was supported by right reason (i.e. Aristotelian logic) through the popular 'body/state' analogy and by Revelation itself. These all provided the scholars with obvious polemical points.

In the event, Fox was altogether too wrapped up in the king's marriage crisis to stray too far from that particular issue and, in any case, was merely stressing the differences between papal and royal claims to *potestatis*. This could easily be seen as just another in the long series of threats which the king's scholars and ambassadors had already made against the pope. This is made especially clear in that, despite the seemingly endless rehearsal of source materials, Fox ultimately compromised his argument by continually referring to the pope by his traditionally accorded title and ending with an explicit plea for the pope to resolve his differences with the king.[50] Fox was giving the pope one more chance to comply. Sampson would not.

Recall that Sampson had been Wolsey's vicar-general and the king's proctor at Tournai between 1513 and 1517. He had therefore witnessed, if not participated in the king's development of new refinements to his ideas concerning the nature of his kingship and what this meant in practical terms. Mayer wrote that this was the development of 'a concept of state . . . [as] ultimate repository of all claims on allegiance' and, as such, necessitated a radical shift in royal sovereignty. The king claimed authority over all the inhabitants, both laity and clergy, in a process that strictly limited the pope's authority although which, in the end, left unconsidered the 'amalgam of *auctoritas* and *potestas*' which needed to be fully examined.[51] Then, Sampson had harboured doubts about the king's plans, worrying whether a secular power could interfere in spiritual matters. He had doubted that the population would show the king the proper fealty and he worried about the possibility of schism.[52] Sampson had convincingly advised Wolsey against a temporal assumption of spiritual authority but that was in 1515 when the king was surrounded by politicians and diplomats. Now, in 1533, Sampson set himself the task of providing the solutions to his earlier concerns.

As a jurist he called less upon theology and more upon law and his experiences in Tournai. The result was that the basic intellectual substance of the *Oratio* was the soon to be clichéd theory of absolute obedience to the king based on divine law: '*quia verbum Dei praecipit*'[53], supported by an argument against papal supremacy. He was uninterested in deep-seated theology, making instead a straightforward appeal to scripture and the laws of nature. He did this to give the king as firm a foundation in devotional life and moral duty as was possible. In the *Oratio*, therefore, to accept the king's new title of supreme head was indicative of filial obedience to God, acceptable in law and consistent with the king's supremacy in his own kingdom.[54]

Sampson began with a discussion of divine and mortal law from which sprang three sub-types – moral, judicial and ceremonial – echoing Stokesley's arguments against Fisher and Abel in the on-going divorce controversy. Nor was there anything innovative in his discussion of man's early state of grace, his fall and his redemption. But this was followed up by a surprisingly simple yet devastating discussion of concepts of love, taking the text of John 13.34 as a guide: 'A new commandment I give unto you, That ye love one another; as I have loved you, that ye also love one another'. From this he extrapolated three types of love: God's love towards man, man's love towards God and man's love towards man. Of these, the second is central to his argument. Man shows his love of God by obeying his commands: 'if you love me, keep my commandments' (John 14.15) which, for Erasmus, was the

hallmark of the true Christian. For Sampson, these commandments were
found in the '*civiles mores, natura docente*' and in the wisdom of God.
Thus, personal dignity and power came in the wake of obedience to those
deserving of it, that is, kings.

Using Romans 13.7 Sampson made the leap between man's natural love
of God and obedience due to the king. St Paul's message to the Romans
had been a simple one: 'Render therefore to all their dues: tribute to whom
tribute is due; custom to whom custom; fear to whom fear; honor to whom
honor'.[55] He took this as a statement of the Christian duty to obey the
governing authority, the representative of God, who existed to serve God
for the sake of the entire community.[56] St Peter echoed St Paul when he
used 'Honor the king' (I Peter 2.17) as the ultimate part of a discourse on
good citizenship and Christian duty. Between these citations was the focal
point of Sampson's argument: 'Obey those to whom you are bound by the
law of God to obey and do not obey he who has no right to be obeyed'.[57]

While his contemporaries, Fox, Cranmer and the king himself[58] were
making forays into establishing a spiritual duty, Sampson remained rooted
in the temporal as his earlier doubts and training necessitated. 'Therefore,
you are subject to all humane ordinance for the sake of the Lord; whether
it be to the King as supreme head . . . it is the will of God.'[59] This was the
core of his argument, supplemented by additional but largely rhetorical
questions that were more or less challenges to other scholars to prove
him wrong. To these was added a brief appeal to natural reason.[60] Having
established that subjects owe obedience to kings, he went on to append
the converse injunction that no obedience was due to the bishop of Rome.

The scriptural evidences employed on behalf of papal supremacy are
familiar and Sampson offers only a routine review of them. Elsewhere, he
attacked the historical basis of the papal claims, citing the ancient Fathers,
Cyprian and Jerome. Over the interpretation of one letter, however,
Sampson deviates from the familiar. Where Jerome had written '*extra hanc
domum qui Agnum commoderit, profanus est*'[61], Sampson construed '*extra
hanc domum*' as 'outside the faith', whereas the more typical translation was,
after Erasmus, to take '*domum*' as meaning the 'primacy of the Church of
Rome'.[62] To avoid being dismissed as simply wrong here, Sampson appealed
to the bugbear of all papists, conciliarism. This brought him back into line
with both his colleagues and with Marsilian political theory.

* * *

The fifth session of the so-called Reformation parliament met in January
1534. The most important piece of legislation to emerge was the first Act
of Succession that embodied much of the detail underpinning the Dunstable
decision. It recognised Catherine's reduction in rank and placed the king's

children by Anne Boleyn firmly at the top of the chain of succession. The act was accompanied by an oath (although the wording was not specified) and a commission led by Cranmer, Audley, Norfolk and Suffolk was set up on 20 March to implement it. There was, except for the well-known cases, little or no opposition to the oath in the country as a whole.[63] Cranmer addressed parliament, just after the passage of this and the other important acts of the session, on the matter of general councils from which we can glean his opinions on the supremacy.

Much of what he said is already familiar. He used St Peter's relationship with the other apostles and a rather conventional view of the duties of the godly prince to mould the supremacy question into a matter of 'princely oversight of the Church', talking up the supremacy as a church reform. Yet we have to be careful of Cranmer's opinions as he often merely acted as a mouthpiece for the king's own views.[64] What about the other bishops? While there seems to be little indication that Gardiner would refuse to take the oath and support the king, he was after all the commissioner for the oath in Winchester[65], it was suspected that he, Tunstal and Lee would soon be joining Fisher in the Tower for refusing.[66]

We noted earlier that Tunstal had reservations about the king's actions. Although the king had written him a cordial enough reply, in light of More and Fisher, any further opposition would be viewed more seriously. The first sign of trouble was when Tunstal and Lee received orders from both the king and Cromwell to remain in the north during the parliamentary sessions of 1534.[67] After the passage of the act, Tunstal was ordered south to make his declaration in support of it, whilst agents of the crown moved north to search his residences for any evidence of duplicity.[68] Tunstal had been warned about this, however, and had made a thorough sweep of any suspicious letters. In London he was pressured to take the oath and, with his goods in custody, he buckled.[69] That was not the end of the matter, however. Both Lee and Tunstal would be forced to prove themselves, first in public with Chapuys at Westminster and then with that rather distasteful private interview with Catherine and Mary.[70]

Chapuys' letter of 19 May described this special council meeting in which the king's chief ministers were gathered to explain his recent initiatives. The letter is a good indication of who was at the centre of royal matters. Besides Lee and Tunstal, Cranmer, Stokesley, Goodrich (now bishop of Ely), Sampson and Fox were all in attendance as representatives of both the clergy and the chief political theorists. Also in attendance were Norfolk, Exeter and Wiltshire (for the nobility), Cromwell and the major law officers. Of course, the ambassador refused to be impressed by this collection of the great and the good, and he was certainly not convinced that the king was acting with justice on his side. By the same token, the members of the council could not have been surprised by the ambassador's response. That they went through the motions at all is more indicative of the fact that the meeting was not meant to convince Chapuys, but more as a show of English unity. The clerical, noble, judicial, legislative and executive branches of government all backed the king to the full.

As noted, Chapuys argued against their theories and he made some valuable points, if only enough to give the king and his ministers pause. By appealing to a general council, did the king not thereby recognise the authority of the pope's sentences and jurisdiction, if only by default? In any case, whatever the king's thinking on the matter had been, he would begin to change his mind on general councils too, shortly after the passage of the Act of Supremacy and the Act Extinguishing Papal Authority. Still, a recently published propaganda treatise makes it clear that an appeal was still very much the preferred option for the time being: 'he hath appealed unto the General Council and is herein like a true Christene and catholike prince'[71]

* * *

## 3. The abandonment of conciliarism

The king's enthusiasm for general councils died down for two reasons. First, Charles V was reluctant to summon one without papal compliance but, even so, his political difficulties in Germany were more to Henry's advantage. Second, it was realised that there was nothing stopping the pope from summoning a council himself. For these reasons, the logic of an appeal lost its compelling force and, by autumn 1535 the king and his ministers were actively seeking to prevent a general council being called. There was some urgency behind the new initiative; they were no longer dealing with the timid and indecisive Clement VII, but with the dynamic Paul III. Moreover, the site of a projected council had been named as Mantua, and preparations for it were underway. With Almain's conclusions very much in mind, English diplomats were sent out to stall, and the king's Episcopal scholars were consulted for a means of combating this new threat.

Gardiner was sent to Paris to convince Francis I to boycott the council. This could not have been too difficult an assignment as a council would be even more detrimental to his position than to Henry VIII's.[72] Fox, Nicholas Heath, Edmund Bonner and Robert Barnes were sent to Germany to 'dissuade' the Lutheran princes from attending.[73] We will discuss the Fox mission to Germany in more detail later because of its implications with regard to the religious settlement in England. From a theoretical point of view, although the general council option was now actively opposed, it was still very much the case that the scholars attacked papal supremacy as a separate issue.

A propaganda campaign in favour of the royal supremacy (focused primarily against the pope) got underway in 1534 and culminated at St Paul's Cross two years later. Between February and March 1536, seven successive Sundays saw a bishop preaching to the London crowds. The first sermon, of 6 February, was made by Cranmer who took for his theme the pope as Antichrist, based on the materials gathered by the royal scholars.[74] Cranmer was followed by Hilsey, Latimer, Tunstal, Shaxton, Latimer again, and finally Capon, all taking issue with papal authority.[75] There were several other good sermons preached by non-bishops as well.

The opening of convocation of 1536, that one summoned to find a solution to religious difficulties, considered the papal and general council questions. It is clear from their report on the matter that the bishops were divided along religious lines, but with regard to general councils they seemed to retain a clear Catholic element in their expressions. The general council was 'necessary for the establishment of our faith, for the extirpation of heresies, and the abolishing of sects and schism; and finally, for the reducing of Christ's people unto one perfect unity and concord in religion'. This sounded orthodox enough, mixed with a plea for a neutral setting – a current Henrician catchphrase. The influence of the radical bishops, however, is clear in the next few lines. The bishops made note of an awareness that, 'ne can be any thing in the world more pestilent and pernicious to the Commonweal of Christendom' producing more 'contention . . . discord and other devilish effects' than a general council.[76] The bishops also put forward some pertinent questions, but only really expounded on the matter of who had the authority to convoke a general council.

They agreed that neither the pope 'ne any one prince, of what estate . . . may by his own authority . . . indict any general council, without the express consent . . . of the residue of Christian princes, and especially such as have within their realms . . . *imperium merum*'.[77] This became the basis of a focused argument against general councils and was used by Cranmer, Tunstal, Clerk and Goodrich, 'forsomoche that the Empire of Rome, and the monarchie of the same, hath no suche generall dominion, but many Princes have absolute power in thair awn realmes, and a hole and entire monarchie, no one Prince', clearly meaning the emperor:

> may, by his aucthoritie, call ay Generall Counsaile; but if that any one or moo of theise Princes, for the establisshing of the faith, for the extirpation of scismes, &c. lovingly, charitably, with a good syncere intente, to a sure place, require any other Prince, or the reste of the great Princes, to be content toaggre, that for the wealthe, quyetnes, and tranquillite of all christen people, by his or ther fre consent, a Generall Counsaile myght be assembled.[78]

The agreement of all of the rulers was a clear prerequisite but there were wider, more divisive, issues of basic religious questions now dividing the prelates. As they were too divided on these issues to be of much use, the government took the initiative on the general council question with two tracts, the so-called 'Hatfield manuscripts', both written anonymously (and likely by different men).

The difference between the two tracts is clear. The first attacked papal authority on the basis of canonist tradition, pointing out that many institutions once considered of divine origin had, in fact, grown through common consent. It clearly advocated a conciliarist position, marshalling the now standard arguments (e.g. the rebutting of the Petrine justifications) and, in line with the times, concluded with doubts about general councils as well: 'that only the word of God was the rule of faith'. While such phrasing suggests evangelical thinking (Cranmer?), the writer also made the proviso that the 'authority of Church doctors must not be rejected, but accepted if corroborated by Scripture'.[79]

The second tract, 'A Treatise concernynge generall councilles &c' (1538), tried to show the divine origin of kingly powers and how these had been usurped by popes. It also noted the ordering of 'indifferent things', the *ius concilium convocandi* and the *potestas confirmandi ac administrandi decrata concilii*, depending for these arguments almost exclusively on biblical authority. Here, the argument was that the clergy owed their 'mynystration' to 'the lawe of god, and . . . the lawe of man'.[80] If it is obvious that there is still a note of conciliarism in the air and in the council, it is also clear that the writer of the first tract owed a debt to Parisian nominalism and conciliarism as the source of his arguments. The writer of the second seemed to rely more on Lollard based ideas, like the separation of the human from the divine, in his argument that matrimony, confirmation, confession and penance were not of divine origin. Mantua, of course, brought the entire problem to a head. The evangelical prelates no doubt agreed over the 'evil . . . when in provincial, yea, or yet General Councils men have gone about to set forth any thing . . . with apparent reasons not infallibly deduced out of the word of God'.[81] Catholic conservatives could look to Stokesley, Tunstal and Clerk for guidance.

Tunstal and Clerk are jointly attributed with a slim position piece wherein they wrote, 'in matiers of the Faith and interpretacion of Scripture, no man made diffinitive subscription, but busshopes and preistes; for somoche as the declaration of the Wourde of godde perteignyth unto them', mooting sacerdotal monarchy. Their argument was based on John 20.21 ('*Sicut misit me Pater, et ego mitto vos*') of which, they noted, 'hath no respecte to a kynges or a Princes power, but onely to shewe, how that the ministers of the Worde of God, chosyn and sent for that intente, are the messengirs of Christ'. Moreover, in Acts 20.20-22, St Paul admonished bishops and priests, 'to be diligent pastores of the people'. They allow that, although powerful, it was the real duty of the king to see to it that bishops and priests minister and teach the word of God, punishing them if they are negligent.[82]

Stokesley and Tunstal continued to stand by the authority of general councils in another joint effort wherein they wrote, 'thuniversall consaills of all countrese in one place, and at oon tyme assembled, to thintent all heresies troubeling the church myght be ther exturped'.[83] Here, they were referring to the power of emperors to summon councils and they assigned a like power to the king. The rule of the church was a royal prerogative most effectively exercised through such councils. This was a rather unsatisfactory conclusion after 1534, however. Moreover, the problems with the councils, their disputed authorities and the relative position of the pope and princes proved far too difficult and divisive for the Henricians to solve to everyone's satisfaction. By 1535, the effort to bolster the settlement, the succession and the royal supremacy had fallen out of the conciliarists' hands, the focus becoming more clearly the king's own authority.

* * *

Like their arguments in opposition to papal jurisdiction and in favour of general councils, the bishops' arguments justifying the royal supremacy were not especially innovative. They used their theological and scholarly attributes to good effect, however, even if, as Janelle noted, they did little more than update Marsilius.[84] Of course, not all of the bishops had the necessary literary expertise of a Fox or a Sampson, but they were all given the opportunity, at least to make their peace with the king's position.

Of the Episcopal bench of 1534, Sherborne was perhaps the most suspect of duplicity. One of his prebends in Chichester had written that he,

> might have sympathised with a reformation wrought under the influence of . . . men like Erasmus, Colet, and More by a natural process of piety and learning, but to accept a system alike in doctrine and ceremonial manufactured under the superintendence of such a man as Cromwell was more than he could endure.[85]

Of course, at age 81 he was too much a creature of habit to resist the king under great pressure, but his acceptance of the supremacy was not unequivocal. Roland Lee wrote to Cromwell that Sherborne capitulated with 'no little dissimulation which is not to be forgotten'. Sherborne wrote to Cromwell himself on 28 June 1535,

> after such small talent as God hath lent me, I preached the work of God openly in my Cathedral . . . and also published there the king's most dreadful commandment concerning (with other things) the uniting of the supreme head of the Church of England unto the Imperial Crown of this realm

asking to be excused of further involvement. He retired in 1536, clearly exhausted.[86]

Most of the other bishops renounced papal authority and accepted the royal supremacy with less difficulty. Clerk, Rawlins, Tunstal, Veysey, Nix and Booth in 1534, Cranmer, Gardiner, Stokesley, Goodrich, Longland, Kite, Edward Lee, Capon, Roland Lee and Standish in 1535.[87] The first of the bishops to tackle the new position in a treatise was Gardiner. Although under suspicion of duplicity, he had been given a chance to redeem himself by spearheading the government's effort to obtain the submission of the noted intellectual brethren of Syon Abbey. Although he presented the king's case well, it is clear from his two treatises of 1535, *Si sedes illa* and *De Vera Obedientia*, that his commitment to the supremacy was less than wholehearted.[88]

The first tract was a rather slender piece written for two reasons. It was an apology for the execution of Fisher and a refutation of Paul III's attempt to drive a wedge between Henry and Francis I, by his calling on the latter to rise up in the papacy's defence.[89] The tract not only neatly divided Paul III and Francis I with references to diplomatic necessities and Francis's reluctance to comment on the matter of the supremacy, it also rehearsed the familiar arguments for the divorce and against usurped papal authority. The most interesting aspect, however, was Gardiner's contention that separation from Rome did not constitute a schism with universal Christendom, 'we knowe none, ne euer meanyd any suche'[90] This was a problem which would plague the Henrician intellectuals for some time to come. Could an independent national church adjudicate and proclaim true doctrine and legitimately remain within the corps of Christendom?

Gardiner's solution was that since 'wee knolegyng Christe, the first begoten amonge many brothern, desire to bee receyuyd in to thatt noombre, by his grace, and to be fed norishyd and conteyned within the vniuersall churche', there should be no difficulty. This led him into a rather clever historical review. He wrote that in the past, 'the Realme of Englonde, hath gyven many thynges to the Roman churche . . . annates . . . prestations . . . the price of many lawes . . . honor' but also maintained that, while it might appear by these past errors in judgement that England was merely 'tributary' of Rome, this was not, and never had been, the case.[91] England remained a Christian realm due to its confirmation of God's ultimate supremacy against the dictates of Roman canon law. Later, Stokesley and Tunstal would approach the same question but answer it in a less legal manner. They focused instead on the commonality of the priesthood.

Wher the office and dutie of all good christen men and, and, namely of us that be priests, sholde be to bring all commotion to tranquillite, all troble to quietness, all discorde to concorde, and

in doyng the contrary we show ourselfe to be the ministers of Satan,
and not of Criste, who ordeygned all us that be prests to use in all
places, the legacion of peas and not of dyscorde.[92]

We will look at these writings shortly. On the main question, in contrast
to *Si sedes illa*, Gardiner's *De Vera Obedientia* is well known.

Its main thrust was a fine-tuned discussion of what constituted
obedience. Gardiner took the reader on an intellectual roller-coaster ride
through various justifications of the supreme headship, the familiar
arguments against papal authority and a brief examination of the divorce
and marriage controversies. From there he continued with a comparison
of divine law and human tradition, an analysis of how the bishops of Rome
had gained authority in England in the first place, how this was thrown off
and why unlawful oaths can be legitimately ignored. Gardiner quickly
established his orthodoxy in his discussion of obedience by writing that

God is the truthe (as scripture recordeth) wher in he geveth his chief
lighte vnto vs so muche that who so euer seketh it in any other place
and goth about to fette it out of mennes puddles and quallmyres and
not out of the most pure and cleare fountayne it selfe.[93]

His familiarity with the works of previous apologists meant that his
arguments were fairly routine and easily anticipated, obedience owed to
civil magistrates, the king as God's true vicar in his own kingdom, etc.

*De Vera Obedientia* only became innovative, and thus truly interesting,
when Gardiner departed company with his intellectual brethren. Where
Fox held out the possibility of *rapprochement* with Rome, and where
Sampson stuck to interpretations and divisions of divine and human law to
justify the king's claims, Gardiner did not hesitate to name the king 'in
earthe the supreme headde of the churche of Englande'.[94] He did this on
the simple premise that the king is, without question, the fountainhead of
authority in all parts of the realm, whether clerical or temporal. After
this, however, ambiguities crept in. For example, in typical, perhaps even
archetypal legalese, Gardiner wrote that 'wherin surely I see no cause why
any man shoulde be offended that the kinge is called the headde of churche
of Englande rather than the headde of the realme of Englande', the church
being only the 'multitude of people which beinge vnited in the profession
of Christ is growne in to one body' while the realm. They 'comprehendeth
all subiectes of the kinges dominions who so euer they be'. Thus,

seinge the churche of Englande consisteth of the same sortes of
people at this daye that are comprised in this word realme of whom
the kinge his called the headde: shall he not beinge called the headde
of the realme of Englande be also the headde of the same men whan
they are named the churche of Englande?

It is the strength of his writing, however, which allows the reader to almost
visualise his performance in court:

> What a folye were it than for a man to confesse that al one man (if
> ye lust to call his Iohan) dwelling in Englande is in subieccion to
> the kinge as vnto the headde: and if ye call him a christian of the
> same sorte to saye that he is not a subiecte? . . . the churche of
> Englande is nothing elles but the congregation of men and women
> of the clergie and of the laytie vnited in Christe profession.[95]

Thereafter Gardiner returned to the well-established arguments in support
of the supremacy and against papal authority. After 1535, the real impetus
behind supremacy apologies passed over to Cromwell's propaganda
machine. The intellectual bishops became more aware of the threat to
Catholic orthodoxy from their more radical colleagues who, with the
exception of Cranmer, failed to produce anything of singular note apart
from urging the king on to more radical doctrinal reform.

In 1535, Cromwell ordered the 'conservative' bishops, meaning
Stokesley, Longland, Nix, Tunstal and Gardiner, to preach on successive
Sundays at St Paul's Cross. It was his thinking that, 'their avowed approval
of the schism might have a greater propaganda effect than all the invective
of the reformers against the usurped powers of the Pope'.[96] It was from
these sermons (and those presented at court during Lent) that most of the
new publications emerged, sermons by Longland and Tunstal (Stokesley
refused to have his published) adding to the supremacy canon. O'Grady
judged that these publications offer little beyond the familiar arguments,
but because they also focus attention on, and warned of the alarming rise
of radicalism in England, we will examine them later.

* * *

## 4. The meaning of royal supremacy

Previously we have used the terms jurisdiction and authority as almost
interchangeable. A distinction needs to be made, however, as after 1535,
supremacy thinking took a great deal of foreign criticism on this very
point. It is clear that the bishops were arguing that all jurisdiction
proceeded from the crown and that, therefore, all jurisdiction must be
exercised by virtue of appointments made by the crown. Indeed, Stokesley
would enter into a wide-ranging controversy with Cranmer on just this
point. The royal supremacy meant, essentially, that final jurisdiction in
all matters, spiritual and temporal, rested with the crown.

In practical terms this meant that the king had a duty to chastise the
morals of the clergy (i.e. to discipline them) although it was not his place
to order doctrinal belief (i.e. argue theology) or to assume sacerdotal
function. Fox cited examples where earlier English kings had 'invested'
bishops and higher clergyman[97], Gardiner had cited Justinian as an example

of a temporal ruler who 'put forth' laws concerning the faith in the form of 'coercive enactments' of established canon[98], and Sampson had argued much the same thing.[99] For whatever reason, the basic point seems to have been lost on the king's foreign critics, particularly his own cousin Reginald Pole. It was left to the two most doctrinaire bishops, Stokesley and Tunstal, to settle the point in a largely ignored, but nonetheless influential, letter to the man himself.

Pole had served the king's interests in France but had changed his mind on the issue and withdrew his intellectual services in the early 1530s.[100] At the time the king was in a generous mood, but this had changed by 1535. With the acts of Supremacy, Succession and Treason, the deaths of More and Fisher, and with Cromwell's propaganda campaign in full swing, an English intellectual of Pole's stature could not be allowed to remain silent.[101] The first step was to have his former student, the royal chaplain Thomas Starkey make contact.[102] It is clear from his letters that Stokesley, Cromwell and Tunstal (a recent supremacy convert) were giving him guidance.

In brief, the standard Henrician position was exhibited. The arguments underlying the divorce and the Boleyn marriage were recapped[103] and papal authority summarily rebutted as although perhaps convenient for the preservation of spiritual unity, clearly it was not conducive at all to political unity. All the usual criticisms were trotted out: papal involvement in territorial conquest, papal concern for personal or family wealth and position over the welfare of the church, how often popes had involved the church in open warfare to the detriment of Christianity, etc.[104] Pole's reply reached England on 4 September 1535, but the *Pro Ecclesiasticae Unitatis Defensione* was less than the intellectual consent which had been expected.[105] Moreover, it arrived during the very height of the tensions of the sensitive summer of 1536. A committee 'which both have learning to judge and would weigh the matter indifferently' was assembled to examine it and formulate an immediate response. The committee was Stokesley, Cromwell, Tunstal and Starkey.[106]

Although Pole's letter addressed four issues – Sampson's supremacy polemic, papal supremacy, the king's affair with Anne Boleyn and an exhortation to the king to do penance and give up his mad scheme – the second point was central. Pole noted that papal primacy, as given by Christ to St Peter and his successors, was based on the evidence of scripture and church tradition and thus unassailable.[107] He denied both the natural reason arguments of Sampson and the humanist exegesis of Fox and Gardiner.[108] Starkey's letter, partially drafted by Tunstal and edited by Stokesley, was the first official response, dispatched on 13 July 1536.[109] It was, however, only a prelude to the second, fuller response of the two bishops.

The Episcopal letter, in fact, does not really add much to the established supremacy canon. The bishops, for example, discussed the scriptural foundations of papal supremacy in a rather familiar way. Where Pole had used Matthew 16.16 to stress St Peter's 'special hidden knowledge' and 'unshared higher awareness'[110], for instance, the bishops opted to interpret his strong faith and recognition of Christ as the foundation of the church.[111] Moreover, 'and oon thing is specially to be noted, and also merveled, that the bisshoppe of rome doo challenge this primacie all only by peter', while St Paul, who was his equal in the scripture and his superior among the gentiles also suffered at Rome and was 'commenly in all the church romani ioygned with St Peter in all appellations and titles of preeminence, booth be called *principes apostolorum*, upon booth equally founded *ecclesia romani*'.[112] The ramifications of such arguments are obvious and familiar enough, but a mere trade off of scriptural passages was futile.

In his letter, Pole made it clear that he would never accept any argument whereby supreme authority was vested in a temporal ruler. 'If the soul is superior to the body, then faith is superior to reason, thus spiritual to temporal, and church over state'. By such reasoning a pope must be superior to a king and therefore a sacerdotal monarchy could not legitimately exist.[113] This was a lucid enough argument but, in making it Pole had wandered on to ground with which the Henrician intellectuals were very familiar. While neither Stokesley nor Tunstal, nor indeed Henry himself, would accept sacerdotal monarchy, the ancient kings of Israel, the early Roman Emperors and Saxon chiefs, all provided debate-worthy material on the issue. The bishops chose to answer the specific point in more philosophical terms. 'It is not requisite in any body naturall, that the hedd shall exercise eyther all maner of office of the body, or the chief office of the same, for albeit that the hedde is the highest and chief member of the naturall body'.[114] Headship of the church, therefore, need not necessitate sacerdotal function. Continuing the body analogy of the whole community, they noted

> Yet the distribution of life to all member of the body, as well to the hedd as to other members cometh frome the harte, and ministering of lief to the hole boody is the chefe acte of the body. Wherfor that reason, as it [the head performing all functions] hath no place in an naturall body, so it hath no place in a misticall bodye.[115]

Pole's argument that as the king could not perform all clerical functions he could not be head of the church was rendered untenable, especially as Henry was not claiming so much as the ancient Hebrews. Just as the king is the head of the mystical body, 'the office deputed to the bishoppe . . . is to be as eyes to the hoole body'.[116] Bishops use their position as the eyes to 'shew unto it [the body] the right way of lyving'. Just as the eyes draw power from, and translate information to the head, so too do bishops claim a like authority from and responsibility to the king. The bishops could do nothing else, 'wher for if the eye will take upon him the office of the hoole hedd, it may be answwerede unto it, it cannot soo doo, for it lacketh bryayns'.[117]

Even this, however, was not particularly new material. Stokesley and Fox had made a similar argument in the presentation copy of *Censurae*. Bishops must be prepared to stir the king and the kingdom away from a wrong-headed pope. Here, as 'head', the king must be prepared to follow the advice of his bishops, 'his eyes'. As in other cases,

> We may se in a navie by see, where thadmirall, who is capytayn over all, dooth not medle with stering or governing of every shypp, but every maister particularly must directe the shipp to passe the see in breaking the waves by the sterring and governance, which thadmirall, hedde of all, doth not him self nor yet hath not the facultie to doo, but commandethe the maistres of the shipp to doo it.

And just as in conciliarist thinking, the authority of the king was grounded on community consent, which makes his power just and legitimate.[118] The commander's obedience to the admiral gives his authority justice and legitimacy, else the navy would fall apart. 'And likewise many a capytayne of great armies, which is no hable nor never coulde shoote or breake a speare, by his wisdome and commandement onely obteygneth' lawful authority.[119] Such claims were backed up with references to Augustine, Theophylact, Chrysostom and Tertullian.

We need not rehearse them all in full. Augustine, for example, had written on the subject of imperial authority that

> One there is, who saith, that a bishop ought not to have been put to his purgation before the judgement seat of the deputy, as though he himself procured it, and not rather the emperor himself caused this inquiry to be made; to whose jurisdiction (for which he must answer to God) that cause did specially pertain.[120]

Chrysostom added that imperial authority 'hath no peer at all upon the earth' and that the emperor was thereby 'head of all men upon earth'.[121] Tertullian noted that all honour and reverence was due to the emperor, 'as is lawful to us, and expedient to him; that is to say, as a man next and second to God, from whom he hath received all the power he hath, and also inferior to God alone'.[122] He added elsewhere that emperors know, 'who hath given to them their government; they know that God is he alone, under whose only power they be; and take themselves as second to God, after whom they be chief above all others'.[123] Theophylact noted that if the apostles were subjected to princes then surely so too are all bishops. St Paul had not written 'let him obey' the authority of the prince, but the much stronger 'let him be subject' [Romans 13.1-7]. There was no real option.[124]

Scripture provided the bishops' final arguments and thus established their orthodox credentials. These arguments are familiar enough and need not detain us. Thus, for the bishops, Fox, Sampson, Gardiner, Stokesley and Tunstal, the king 'dooth nether make innovation in the church, nor yet troble the ordere therof, but dooth as the chefe and the best of the kings of Israell dide, and as all good Cristian kings ought to doo'.[125] Tunstal would repeat much of this material in his Palm Sunday sermon of 1539, making clear his support of the king once and for all.[126]

* * *

Tradition was the key word for the bishops in their discussions of the royal supremacy. Henry did nothing innovative in his actions nor, consequently, were they advancing startling new theories in his defence. Ecclesiastical jurisdiction sprang from the crown, but spiritual authority was the preserve of the bishops and clergy acting for the crown. They were the 'eyes' directing the 'head'. Moreover, and as a result of this, the strong emphasis that each bishop laid on obedience could only be expected and, on this point at least, there was no difference between conservative and radical. Where Stokesley and Tunstal depart company from the others, however, was in their more overt political thinking.

Gardiner, Fox, Sampson and Pole nowhere considered that the temporal and spiritual spheres were distinct societies. The argument had always been that both clergy and laity were of the 'realm'. The realm was England and they were all subject to one king in a straightforward hierarchy. While the other bishops made much of the clergy's duty to obey civil authority, Pole turned the equation upside down and insisted on the differences in nature and dignity between civil and sacerdotal duties, assigning each a pre-determined domain with prejudice toward the sacerdotal. Stokesley's and Tunstal's concept of society clashed with both these models. The bishops envisioned two distinct, but interacting societies, with the king at the top of a triangular structure encompassing both.

This discussion indicated that there was still a considerable attachment to conciliarist theory, at least for these two bishops, in 1537. We have already seen Stokesley's use of the works of Jean Mair in parliament in 1531 and that Tunstal had advised Pole to consult the 'said councils in Greek' on the matter, thereby establishing his own conciliarist credentials.[127] Although we have touched upon this already, and have been largely satisfied that the king had abandoned conciliarism altogether in favour of some national solution to his problem, it is obvious that the loyal Catholics of his court and council had not yet abandoned the accommodation which conciliarism provided.

In his *Editio Ionnis Maioris doctoris Parisiensis super Tertium*

*Sententiarum quaestiones*, Mair specified the ruler as the source of law.[128] It was the ruler's business to give law its binding force and adjust it to meet the needs of the distinct community. The ruler can do this as he possesses a particular and exceptional kind of wisdom. In his discussion of Mair's political ideas, Burns noted that the ruler's wisdom is not the same as the ordinary 'political wisdom' of the citizen (characteristically manifest in obedience) or of the good subordinate magistrate (concerned with particular problems). The king is the architect of the social edifice and the subordinate officials are his labourers.[129] That is to say that it is the king's duty to make sure the others fulfil theirs.

Note also that in his *Ionnes Maior in Secundum Sententiarum*, Mair wrote that a king is morally bound to follow the advice of wise counsellors, those political creatures concerned with specific issues. So long as real authority, with wide discretion, remained in the king's hands, and so long as the king's power is perpetual (meaning that it is not held precariously) Mair maintained that it retained all the advantages he held to be in monarchical authority.[130] Stokesley and Tunstal reflected this with the body analogy. Just as Mair's subordinate magistrates dealt with particular problems, the bishops used their position as the 'eyes', which 'lacketh bryayns' (that special wisdom granted to kings alone). Moreover, we know that for Mair there is a certain duty of the king to be guided by his counsellors, particular in the most serious crises by special representatives of the entire community. The two bishops echoed this point in the examples of the admiral and the general. And just as, for Mair, the authority of the king was grounded on consent, making his power just and legitimate[131], the ship commander's obedience to the admiral gave his authority justice and legitimacy too.

Stokesley and Tunstal carried on the diplomatic effort to secure Pole's repatriation just as their arguments were advanced at court and in government. Doctors Wilson and Heath, royal chaplains, were dispatched to Flanders with documents prepared by the Pole committee (including sermons, letters and books and the bishops' letter) to counter Pole's own efforts to stir up opinion against the king.[132] Christopher Mont used the letter as the official exegesis of the royal supremacy when the king was making another overture to the German princes.

In theory, therefore, the royal supremacy was orthodox, historically consistent and agreeable with both Bible and canon law. It was the issue that finally brought the medieval clerical order to an end, and was also the one religious issue in the 1530s with which both conservatives and radicals could agree. It is another issue entirely, however, to say that what was good in theory was also good in practice. We shall see that, although the bishops were being taken rapidly out of the political picture once again and divided by the religious settlement, at least in the dioceses their authority was maintained pretty much as it had always been. The supremacy did not have as great an impact on the bishops' diocesan authority as one might have expected.

* * *

## 5. The role of the bishops in the king's church

The theory and the reality of the royal supremacy were not one and the same thing. When the king and his ministers abolished papal supremacy in favour of royal authority they had not merely established 'Catholicism without the pope'. The king had wanted and had taken an active position, assuming *potestas jurisdictionis* over the church. If, as Scarisbrick wrote, the king firmly believed that the spiritual men were ministers of the crown and therefore the clergy exercised delegated authority, then this had to be firmly established beyond question everywhere.[133] Thus, it needed to be shown that he was at the head of two not quite related hierarchies. A hierarchy of spiritual ministers from archbishop to humblest curate matched a descending scale of civil ministers (chancellor to lowliest sheriff). He needed the first because he was inexpert in the niceties of bureaucracy. He needed the second because he could not perform certain clerical functions and because no cleric had authority over the entire English church. The question was just how this second would be established and how much it would affect Episcopal activity?

This was a question the bishops faced up to in 1534. Then, most of the prelates were conservatives, elevated under the assumption (*de iure* if not *de facto*) that their powers sprang from God *through the pope*. To be consistent with the royal supremacy and, in order to avoid the penalties of *praemunire*, Episcopal authority had now to spring from God *through the king*. The granting of the headship, the anti-papal acts of the Reformation parliament, the acts of Supremacy and Succession had been only the start of the change. The intellectuals, Stokesley, Longland and Gardiner, raised germane questions over their actual authority, as MacCulloch speculated, possibly in an effort to gain power at the expense of the archbishop. The answers were gradually worked out through such events as the metropolitan visitation of 1534, the promotion of Cromwell to vicar-general status, the royal visitation of 1535 and other subsequent events. It was not the result that the conservative bishops wanted, however. By 1540, the relationship between the crown and the bishops was one in which whatever autonomy the bishops had once had was now gone. In fact, during the final decade of the reign, the bishops would clearly re-emerge as they once had been, either strictly political civil servants (e.g. Richard Fox) or diocesan shepherds (e.g. Hugh Oldham).[134]

In any case we have already seen that there were some difficulties in establishing the theoretical extent of the king's new jurisdiction. As Bowker pointed out, this was the reason that the oath of succession was accompanied, for the clergy, by a formal renunciation of papal authority.[135] We have also seen how the intellectuals had been employed to prove that the pope had no more authority than any other foreign bishop and, in light of recent acts that the clergy were required to preach to this effect. It had been the problem of administering the clerical oath that initiated the first real difficulties. The oath of succession was statutory, whereas the new anti-papal clerical oath was not. The king decided, mistakenly, that the traditional ecclesiastical administrative machine was adequate to needs. Left alone, the bishops might well have achieved the desired result, as events at the London Charterhouse and at Syon Abbey show.

Those two monasteries in the diocese of London were known trouble spots. Both had strongly resisted the dissolution of the Aragon marriage and both had shown themselves unwilling to conform to the royal supremacy.[136] Syon Abbey was a particular problem, having gained notoriety through its association with Elizabeth Barton. Otherwise, it had a solid reputation for good observation of religious ceremonies. As Barton's prophesy and revelations had been unveiled to several important members there, this prompted frequent visits to the Abbey by government officials and their ordinary, Stokesley, early in January 1534.

As ordinary, the king depended on the bishop to bring the two houses to conformity. Stokesley preached a sermon to the community of Syon against the legality of the first marriage, a favourite and important topic, to which he wanted them to subscribe. Cromwell's watchdog, Bedyll, optimistically reported that converting the monastery to the king's will would follow, and in due course a first draft of the bishop's paper was signed.[137] This probably would have been the end of the matter had the Privy Council not subsequently altered the text to make it a clearer statement of approval for the Boleyn marriage. The new draft was submitted, but the brethren would not sign it and advised the nuns to do likewise.[138] This raised alarm bells and Stokesley was sent in again in August 1535 to smooth over the situation.

Two months later, with the execution of Richard Reynolds a recent event, the bishop returned to Syon to ascertain the degree of support for the supremacy and the second marriage. Bedyll's initial report was cautious but favourable; the confessor (Fewterer) had apparently produced two sermons in favour of the king's position since Stokesley's last visit. A report by David Curson, another respected monk, echoed Bedyll but, however positive this appears, another named Whitford refused to include the king's new titles in his sermons and another named Ricot maintained that he complied with the supremacy order only under duress. When he was finally persuaded to include the king's titles without qualifications, nine of the brethren walked out of his next sermon. Bedyll listed their names and Stokesley removed two of them for private instruction. Through these two, he hoped to bring the rest of the community into conformity.[139]

Meanwhile Bedyll attempted to scare Whitford into submission with a verbal assault in the Abbey's garden. When this failed, he forbade Whitford from hearing the nuns' confessions and then summoned the nuns' families in the hope that they might convince them to subscribe to the supremacy order. When this failed, Stokesley was sent back in and, with Fewterer to help him, made another attempt. By emphasising the 'peril of their souls' should they not consent he appeared to have prevailed.[140] Cromwell's agents, Bedyll and Layton, then alienated the nuns once again when they came to take an official recording of the submission, perhaps because they were temporal officers with doubtful authority.[141] One nun, Agnes Smith, went so far as to condemn them, convincing the others not to put their common seal to any official documentation.

This question of governmental authority in diocesan matters was one that would haunt the king's advisors for some time. With regard to Syon, however, Stokesley had some success with his two detainees. Some time after he had removed them from the community he wrote to Cromwell of his 'continual labouring' with them and of his growing optimism.[142] He had convinced them with reasonable arguments and wrote that they were eager to return and persuade others to give up their resistance. According to Bedyll, with 'the conversion of these two, the others are sure to follow'. He wrote that 'My Lord of London declared reasons for the confirmation of the king's title of supreme head, and for the infirmation and extinction of the Bishop of Rome's jurisdiction and power within the realm, in such a manner and fashion as was excellent and singular'.[143] Indeed, the two monks would later distinguish themselves with their own arguments against those holdouts at the Charterhouse.[144] Of course, by April 1535, we know the effort was wasted.

These events highlight the confusion over authority. Cromwell's agent there, Sir John Whalley, wrote that although his predecessor had been unable to make any headway, he had a plan. He wanted 'honest, loyal men sent to stay with them' (i.e. planted). He also wanted men like the 'Vicar of Croydon, Dr Buckmaister, Symonds and others of the popish sort.' In other words known conservatives. These actions might work but, if they did not, send in the bishops. 'Lee, Gardiner, Tunstal, Longland, Clerk and Stokesley' could be sent to preach against the pope and, if this failed, 'Cromwell should call them before the whole nobility, temporal and spiritual, and sentence them publicly according to law'.[145] Cromwell, however, had learned a lesson from Syon and let the diocesan authorities handle it.

Some time later, as a result of a letter from Copynger and Lache to the Charterhouse, Bedyll received a plea from the members there, requesting that Stokesley be sent to them as they were 'ready to be brought to good conformity'.[146] Stokesley, with Cranmer, was able to convince the brethren to take the oath with the familiar qualifying clause. Later, with Roland Lee, Stokesley met with Houghton and Middlemore, two members of the Charterhouse who had been placed in the Tower for their extreme obstinacy.[147] These trouble spots had been cleared up through the work of the concern diocesan authority.

Stokesley, who was a supporter of the king, had shown where proper authority lay and what could be achieved where this was recognised. This obviously begs the question, however, of those bishops whose loyalty to the new order was less sure. Could the foreign bishops, for instance, be trusted to conform to and enforce the new order in their dioceses? The king decided that they could not and steps were taken to remove them. Certainly Cranmer could be trusted. A metropolitan visitation was ordered to take stock of the situation in the southern province, leaving the not so trusted Lee and the northern province for later consideration.[148]

* * *

## a. The metropolitan visitation of 1534

It seemed a practical solution. One problem was that there had not been a metropolitan visitation for quite some time. As was traditional, the bishops' individual jurisdictions would be inhibited for the duration and procurations would be taken. The oath would also be administered in a special court of Audience. The sheer size of the task, however, made a uniform approach across the province unfeasible. Gardiner, for example, was allowed to make his own arrangements for the administration of the oath in Winchester, while Nix handled part of the process in Norwich and Sherborne in Chichester.[149] The visitation itself was scheduled for 10 May.[150] Cranmer wrote to Stokesley summoning the London clergy to appear at Lambeth Palace for examination and for the administration of the oath[151], and here was where problems began.

Stokesley was a staunch defender of Episcopal rights and foresaw potentially dangerous problems that led him to make early appeals. One problem was administrative. Cranmer had warned the southern prelates of the inhibition of Episcopal authority for the duration and had also inhibited the minor authorities of their clerical officers. While this was standard procedure, Cranmer had given no indication as to how long the inhibition would be enforced. This vagueness clearly annoyed the bishop of London, as well as his colleagues at Lincoln, Exeter, Norwich and Winchester.[152]

The unspecified length meant that the clergy could not correct, institute to benefice, confirm elections, consecrate churches, celebrate orders, hold probate or perform any number of minor duties seemingly indefinitely. All told, this was a bureaucratic and financial nightmare.[153]

A second, and more interesting, objection was to Cranmer's title and what it implied. Stokesley argued that the archbishop laid claim to an authority that his office no longer possessed, and he was correct.[154] Cranmer had set up his court of Audience under the authority of an '*apostolice sedis legatus*'[155], a title with widespread negative implications for the bishops. While the supremacy legislation had not reduced the archbishop's metro-political powers, Cranmer apparently assumed legatine authority in establishing his court, authority now defunct. Stokesley protested that 'no archebishop within Christendome hath nor never hade any auctorytie to kepe any suche courte by the reason of hys Archebishoprike'. Only papal legates had ever had this power, and he reminded Cranmer of

> what vexations and oppressions they [legates] have doon by the pretense therof not onely to ordynaries but also to the laytie by calling of poore men from the farthest parte of the Realme to London for an halfpeny candle or for a litill obprobriouse worde, as was declared and proved playnely in this parliament, which was a greet cause of making of a statute to remedy that before the statute of thabolisshment of the Bisshope of Rome auctoritie . . . no Archebisshop can exercise this auctoritie except he implieth to all the worlde though he speke it not nor write it not, that he ys a legate of the See of Rome.[156]

Stokesley summoned his officers into the Chapter house of St Paul's prior to the visitation, and once again at its commencement, to make an official objection. They would

> neither accepte hym as suche a Legate, nor admytte or obeye his visitation, Jurisdiction, or any thing that he wolde attempte by the pretexte or color of that name of Legate or otherwyse agaynste the crowne of our sovereigne, his regalitie, statuts or customes of his realme[157]

and he petitioned Cranmer to note the objection in his register. Stokesley obviously took these precautions to avoid a repeat of the trouble that had resulted from the clergy's acceptance of Wolsey's legatine authority. That had led to the *praemunire* charge and the bishops' indictment for exercising spiritual jurisdiction.

Cranmer, however, misunderstood the complaint. Nor, it seems, did he understand how the recent acts of parliament abolishing papal authority applied. Stokesley noted 'that all men lerned and books of the canon lawe dothe agree that noo metropolitane or primate may thus by any Lawe written suspende' Episcopal jurisdiction during their visitations, simply '*jure metropolitico*'. Cranmer acknowledged the argument, but claimed that common law was on his side.[158] Stokesley's reasoning can be found in the letter to the king. He noted that

> it semeth that he [Cranmer] never rede the said acte, nor yet can dyscerne bytwen a thing absolute that may endure without a dependence, as an advowson in grose, and a thing that standeth in a contynuall dependence, as service to the Signorie. Ffor exemptions and dispensations and suche other be absolutes, depending nothing of the graunter after his grant; but legacyes be but respectyves and as no longer lorde, no longer service. So no longer bisshop of Rome lorde here, no longer hys vicare, which was but hys servante as appereth by the text of hys legacy.[159]

The recent act simply did not insure the continuity of such an office. Stokesley pointed out that Cranmer already had in London a court of Arches authorised to deal with all causes pertaining to archiepiscopal authority. Why establish a court that contravened the recent act? Such a court would result only in the vexation of the clergy and laity for no good reason. His suspension of Episcopal jurisdiction was 'against holy scripture and thauctoritie given unto theym [bishops] by god', as well as all precedent. Not even Wolsey had held such a visitation! Stokesley also challenged the legal basis of Cranmer's claims, but the archbishop would not or could not produce the evidence.[160] There was another problem.

Stokesley rather cleverly added an objection that some former legates of Rome had also been chancellors, muddying the waters a little further. Some of Cranmer's predecessors had used the suspect title and had performed acts during their visitations that they could not perform as primates alone (which Cranmer was):

> Item it is to be remembred that in case it shall appere in any booke of tharchbisshopp that his predecessours have attempted any of the premysses first that his predecessours were Legates, and though they did visite Jure metropolitico, yet they myght peradventure as Legates attempte some things which they had had no right nor colour to doo if they had be onlye metropolitans and primates. Secundarilye in this behalf and case it is to be remembred that many of this Archbisshops of Canterburie were not oonlye Legates But also Chauncellers of Englonde, by which auctoritie they peradventure did enforce and mayntagne many things attempted against the Lawe as the Late Cardinall did. And therfor it is to be disseverd what they did as Legate, and whate as metropolitans, and whate by force after repelled, and whate by right peasiblye enioyed, and not to knytt now Jure metropolitico soche things as were doon by his predecessours as Legate nor to callenge prescription nowe, the auctoritie of the

see of rome repelled and here extinguisshed, in soche thinges as
were attempted oonlye by the pretexte of the auctoritie of that see
or els after were appealid repellid or resisted.[161]

Stokesley had clearly put some thought into his objection as he also
referred to the question of the very foundations of legatine authority.

He now advanced the idea that a metropolitan who was not a legate
should not exercise any of the claims to which objections had been made.
In so doing, it would appear that the Bishop of Rome had renewed
jurisdictions in England:

Item it is to be considred whedre any metropolitane in odre christen
realmes being noo Legate dothe exercise the premysses after the
fourme nowe here pretendid in his visitacion and encase they doo
not as it is said, they doo not attempte any such thinges but oonlye
in their visitacions prouincially useth that the common Lawe giveth
theym then here to be repelled and extinguisshed for euer to thentent
that the bisshopps of Roome hereafter shall have no colour to
maynteigne and Justifye that they kepe here yet and continuallye
the possession of their auctoritie and of our subiection by their
Legate saying that although tharchebisshop doo relynquysshe the
name of a Legate yet neverthelesse he exerciseth soche Jurisdiction
as the Lawes never gave to metropolitane nor too noo Archbisshopp
in Christendome dothe exercise (Legates of the see of Roome onely
excepted).[162]

Stokesley had an interesting and clever case.

It apperath by the ancient Registers of the Bisshops and their
churches, that when the predecessours of tharchebisshopps did
attempte any of these cases aforesaid, the bisshops and their clargies
did appeale to the See of Rome (and dyverse tymes they obteigned
sentence and executions agaynst him, and some remaigned
unredressed by the reason of the dethe of tharchbisshop or bisshop's
complaynant).[163]

Thus it was quite unfair and unjustified for the archbishop to base his
authority on the pope, as this left the bishops with no authority to which
they could appeal against any erroneous judgements. This reflected badly
on the royal supremacy. Was the archbishop denying royal authority,
perhaps?

Stokesley then asked the king to consider whether in other countries,
metropolitans, who were not legates of Rome, carry out visitations on the
same pretences as Cranmer? Did they not, in fact, limit themselves to the
powers granted to them according to the common law? Had the king's
councillors not all agreed that the authority of the bishop of Rome was
limited to that of any other foreign bishop and, that being the case, how
was it justified that his authority was being used by Cranmer? Stokesley's

final objection focused on more mundane financial matters. Although the London clergy would obey the visitation of the archbishop as their metropolitan, and pay him all proxies due and accustomed, it seemed that Cranmer was demanding more than the act which limited proxy sums allowed.[164] Of course, for Stokesley this was itself a legitimate concern having already faced riot conditions over 'excessive' fines in 1532. Stokesley's was not the only objection. Most of his southern colleagues joined him in protest.

Longland and the clergy of Lincoln had been advised of the upcoming visitation in June 1534. It appeared to the bishop that the king was overstepping his authority by intruding into unique Episcopal jurisdictions. Longland, on his own behalf and for the Cathedral dean and chapter, protested 'that neither the visitation nor the taking of procurations was customary' and proctors were thereby appointed for an appeal to Chancery.[165] According to Longland, the visitation was illicit in light of the king's coronation oath and the laws of the land.[166] He also objected that the visitation denied the basic equality of all bishops and repeated Stokesley's objections to the implied authority of the archbishop's chosen title. Longland also feared the *praemunire* implications.

As Bowker wrote, Longland was also concerned with the practical implications of this 'unique' visitation on his own powers as ordinary. Cranmer's representative in Lincoln, Richard Gwent, had been empowered by the king to visit 'dyvers Abbeys and other Collegial and cathedral churchys' in order to 'procure the chapter seale of every spirituall incorporacion . . . the subscription of every mann of that chaptre . . . [and to] procure the subscriptyon of every priest'[167] As stated above, no archiepiscopal commissioners had been sent into Winchester, Norwich or Chichester (at this point) and we can only wonder why Longland had been so treated?

There was a real clash of authorities on this issue. Despite the objections, protests and appeals, the visitation and the administration of the oaths proceeded while, at the same time, Stokesley, Longland, Nix and their suffragans carried out their normal functions.[168] In Lincoln, for example, Gwent had gone so far as to admit John Gilden to benefice; an action for which Longland appealed, based on his traditional jurisdiction in the matter. This was a right that the admission of Gilden violated. Longland thereafter took particular interest in ordination ceremonies and continued to admit priests to benefices; as noted, actions aimed at Cranmer. Moreover, he proceeded with his appeal. This forced the king and his advisors to focus on the issues involved.

In London, Cranmer had summoned the priests to Lambeth and made an extensive examination of their opinions. This contravened what Stokesley saw as his own power, as ordinary. One such case was that of the aged and outspoken Rowland Philips, vicar of Croydon. He had been a persistent critic of evangelical doctrine, Anne Boleyn and probably Cranmer too. Although he swore the oath of supremacy[169], he remained vocal in his criticisms. During the visitation he was summoned to Lambeth for examination[170] and was subsequently held over for additional questioning. Stokesley intervened, protesting the archbishop's interference to Cromwell, who engineered Philips' release.[171] Of course, men like Longland and Stokesley could depend on the king's support for their decisive participation in the dissolution of his first marriage (a seemingly bottomless well of gratitude from which Stokesley would draw repeatedly in the 1530s). Nix, old and blind and without that royal good will was eventually brought to heel through a summons into Star Chamber.[172]

Cranmer decided thereafter to visit only those parts of the southern province where he was unlikely to 'face any embarrassing personal challenge from a resident bishop'. He visited Rochester in June (Fisher was in the Tower) and he spent late summer in the west midlands (Worcester and Salisbury were vacant after the removal of the Italians).[173] In February and March of 1535 he moved into Exeter where the elderly Veysey had not made any protests. Even so, Longland and Stokesley kept up the pressure against the visitation. Stokesley ignored the inhibition and held an ordination ceremony in February; Longland's suffragan following suit in March. MacCulloch related further problems faced by the archbishop, like Gardiner's protest over the visitation of Corpus Christi College. This was a pre-emptive strike against Cranmer's projected visitation of other parts of Winchester.[174] Surrey was also one of the archbishop's target areas, but it was thought that Sherborne would fall in line.

Sherborne was known to be opposed to the fundamental changes brought about by the royal supremacy. His views had been kept to himself and he had been living in quiet isolation since 1530. He was also known to have been sympathetic to the queen's cause, so could not depend upon royal support if any problems arose.[175] In 1534, he had issued new statutes for vicars to improve the quality of the services in the Cathedral. He laid particular reference on Bible reading at meal times and on the good repair of living quarters and the Episcopal estates.[176] Sherborne had, however, proved himself resistant to any other reforms. In the diocese of Chichester, however, the problem went beyond mere Episcopal obstinacy.

Even under the later, more devoted royal supporters Bishops Sampson and Day, the enforcement of royal orders was difficult and the clergy of Chichester put up great resistance. This was exacerbated by the failure of succeeding bishops to back the new order whole-heartedly. The problems the metropolitan visitation raised were thus not only *praemunire* related. Conflicting jurisdictions, and even spiritual matters, had been raised in

the minds of the conservative bishops. They not only worried that they
would be indicted, as in 1531, for having exercised spiritual jurisdiction
but they also wanted clarification as to precisely how spiritual jurisdiction
was to be exercised. What were the new limits on their own authorities?
As the cornerstone of their own power was the archbishop, they had to
know for certain whether his jurisdiction (and thus theirs) was in derogation
of the king's.[177] They recognised that the metropolitan's power could not
be papal, which meant that its source had to be royal. But Cranmer adopted
an ambiguous title, obedience to which invited *praemunire* charges and
which left the exact delineation of his authority unclear. The continual
protests against the archbishop and the visitation finally forced a
governmental rethink.

The real crux of the problem was that the king's counsellors had failed
to make provision for the spiritual needs of the new reality. If royal power
was only nominal and symbolic, then the king needed a spiritual officer
to oversee the *potestas ordinis* much as the chancellor oversaw legal and
temporal matters. Henry did not have such an officer. If royal power was
real, then a specific royal commission for the exercise of authority was
needed, a commission Cranmer did not have. If there were to be no more
Wolsey's, no officers who could dominate both realms, what was to be
done and how were the bishops to know their limitations? When they had
asked for a precise definition of *praemunire* they had not been given one.
Now it was clear that they could not continue effectively without it.

Moreover, by 1535 this was more than merely a theoretical inquest.
Older members of the bench, those consecrated by papal authority, were
dying out and replacements were being made without reference to the
papacy. Under what authority had Roland Lee (Coventry and Lichfield),
Thomas Goodrich (Ely), Nicholas Shaxton (Salisbury) and Hugh Latimer
(Worcester) been consecrated? If their appointments had been 'wholly
and only' of the king's gift[178], where did this leave the earlier appointees,
Cranmer or Gardiner? Stokesley had written that

> no Archbisshop can exercise this aucthorite except he implieth to
> all the worlde thoughe he speke it not nor write it not, that he ys a
> legate of the See of Rome. And in case it shall please the kings
> grace to gyve like aucthoritie incommodities to his gracs subiects
> proved by the use therof and not oone commoditie at all to abyden
> by, yt shuld seme better to gyve yt to some other by specall
> commission at hys gracs pleasure, wherby yt shalbe known
> certeynely to com fro hys grace, rather then to yonye it to
> tharchbisshops See wherby tholde poyson myght still lurke, and
> breke out on day agayne if yt shuld chance some to be Archebisshop
> of Canterbery that wold change theyr copie, as hath ben in tymes
> past. And more over if his grace shuld make hym his legate, it shuld

peradventure derogate the power of his gracs genrall vicare, and if
both shuld occupie, then shall the people so moche the rather take
occasion to think and say that hus gracs vicare exerciseth the power
of a legate by his gracs aucthoritie and the Archebisshop of
Canterbery by aucthoritie of the bisshop of Rome.[179]

Clearly, what he and his colleagues wanted was a precise explanation of
the relationship between royal jurisdiction and sacerdotal function, and
this is what they got.

\* \* \*

## b. The royal visitation of 1535

The king could not extend his jurisdiction over the church through his
archbishops in real terms, without granting a clear-cut commission.
Without it, the bishops and clergy would fear obeying dubious authorities,
in light of the statute of *praemunire*. A royal commission, however, raised
difficult questions and implied a novel relationship between king and
archbishop. Was the archbishop empowered by the king (implying that
spiritual authority was received at the king's hand) or was he merely
permitted to act by the king (which left the source of spiritual authority
in doubt)?[180] Stokesley no doubt had a member of the clergy in mind when
he described the position of king's 'genrall vicare', so it must have come
as a blow when Cromwell was appointed in January 1535.[181]

In terms of administrative efficiency, Cromwell was a good choice and
had already been planning a visitation of the monasteries. On 16 April
1535, he sent out a circular letter to all spiritual and lay authorities, putting
them on their guard against any members of the clergy who were still
adhering to the old ways. Such persons were to be registered and taken
into custody at royal pleasure.[182] The bishops were addressed again on 3
June and ordered to preach every Sunday, not only the word of God but
also the king's new title and, moreover, to enforce similar preaching and
compliance by the rest of the clergy. In a like manner, schoolmasters were
to teach their charges the new details and the word 'pope' was to be erased
from all books. Indeed, any expression appearing to continence papal
claims or to encroach upon the king's authority was similarly to be struck
out.[183]

The bishops, for their parts, promised appropriate action. Again, there
were certain difficulties. Even Cranmer, for instance, was not particularly
enthusiastic. He replied, on 4 June, that he would 'satisfy the king's grace's
express commandment in every point to the most of my power'. This was
an adequate response in light of his doubts about certain aspects of the
circular, but he wanted Cromwell to advise him.[184] Ridley speculated that

Cranmer resented the implications of Cromwell's appointment. Having been Primate of all England, he was now (and would be for the next five years) effectively reduced in rank to 'little more than a Bishop in his diocese'.[185]

Longland also had some difficulties enforcing the king's orders, particularly with regard to preaching and bidding prayers. Preachers had been ordered not to discuss the handling of the supremacy controversy and other unsettled topics in their sermons, but there was widespread contempt shown to the order. In 1536, therefore, the bishop ordered a special record kept in every church with a note of the subject touched upon in each sermon. Each sermon was also to be preceded by a bidding-prayer asking the congregation to pray for the person, or the souls of persons, departed. The format of the bidding-prayer was left to the preacher. Names of the obstinate were recorded. 'All curates frome hensforthe to noote in a bill the names of euery oon that shall hereafter preache within ther churches, and by whose authorytie they doo come, and how they doo vse ther selues in ther sermondes'.[186] Problems would come to a head when Cromwell proceeded to his own visitation later in the year. As earlier, Stokesley was a prime opponent, although clearly Cromwell was a more worthy adversary. The two would clash most seriously over the scheduling of preachers at St Paul's Cross.[187]

The circular was received with somewhat more enthusiasm, as might be expected, by the new bishops, Shaxton and Roland Lee, both committed reformers. Lee returned to Coventry and Lichfield and began implementing them immediately, actually preaching in person.[188] Goodrich also reacted much as expected, promulgating the new orders on 27 June.[189] Like Cranmer, however, a more neutral tone was evident in the responses of Tunstal, who made only a token acknowledgement, and Clerk, who more or less merely repeated the contents to the clergy of Bath and Wells.[190] The reply of Sherborne (as seen earlier) was cautious in the extreme as was Edward Lee's, but for a different reason. Lee had, of course, let the king down during the divorce crisis and could not, thereby, draw from the well of royal gratitude. He was, from 1531 onwards, also perceived as untrustworthy and Sir Francis Bigod, Cromwell's agent in the north, had been asked to keep an eye on him. Lee wrote to the king on 14 June[191] defending himself against accusations of inactivity by referring to contradictions in recent orders.

In the summer of 1534, a royal directive had been issued to all the bishops (after the example of Cranmer, Gardiner, Longland and Stokesley who had been enforcing a similar measure in their respective sees) making certain restrictions on what, among other things, could and could not be used as subject matter for sermons. Cranmer's letter of 24 May makes it clear that Thirlby and Shaxton both had a hand in the drafting of the order, which was finally issued in June 1534.[192] Prayers were to address the 'whole catholic church of Christ, as well quick as dead . . . [and] no preachers for a year shall preach neither with nor against purgatory, honouring of saints, that priests may have wives, the faith only justifieth, to go on pilgrimages, to forge miracles'[193], etc. New Episcopal preaching licenses had to stipulate that preachers were 'in no wise to touch or intermeddle themselves to preach or teach any such thing that might slander or bring in doubt and opinion the Catholic and received doctrine of Christ's Church, or speak of such matters as touch the Prince, his laws or succession'.[194] Cranmer's orders concerning preachers, moreover, wanted them to inveigh against the pope. Rather than calm the situation down, however, the orders raised a new storm. Conflicts grew between those who defended traditional practices, those who attacked them and those who supported or defended the pope.

In the north, Lee wondered just what these divisive opinions were. He entered into what can only be described as a damage limitation exercise by composing a lengthy set of articles combining, as best he could, all recent orders. These were then to be declared and, if possible, expanded upon by the clergy of York.[195] Although the substance was similar to the king's late circular, the archbishop appended the royal apologists' many anti-papal arguments. This was a shrewd move. While suspicions against him were not entirely eradicated, Cromwell took the material and revised it for use in sermons by less well-learned clergy and advised the king to take the next step.[196]

With the help of some of the bishops an inhibition of more general incidence was drafted.[197] The council was drawn into the consultative process with the archbishop's injunctions as a basis for the project.[198] In many ways, of course, this new draft more or less re-addressed the same issues as the former one. In their sermons, emphasis was to be placed on the 'usurped' power of the papacy, there was to be no undue railing against other preachers and there was to be a moratorium on preaching about purgatory, saints, miracles, clerical marriage and the like for a year. This would stand until a definitive royal pronouncement later. The *Ten Articles* was to have been that statement. The order effectively muzzled both sides of the argument and indeed, there was only limited controversy following it. The next year would also pass before the bishops had to press for another statement on the matter.[199] When that year passed, however, incidents of incendiary preaching grew more frequent because of official confusion.

Like Lee, Longland had also experienced problems with the new royal instructions. Cromwell had sent the bishops examples of the 'right sort' of declaration to be preached, amended somewhat by Lee's arguments, but Longland's doubts had more to do with the practical considerations of spreading the new message across his vast diocese (although he had done his best by 19 June).[200] The bishops did what they could as best they could, no doubt spurred on by the fact that Cromwell had set the sheriffs and justices as watchdogs over them with a further circular letter of 9 June.[201]

June and July 1535, therefore, were key months in the royal supremacy saga, seeing out the executions of the major opposition. The example of More made silence a suspicious position and the bishops, particularly the conservatives, were not allowed this option. Brigden suspected that Cromwell now appointed the bishops to preach at St Paul's Cross for the propaganda effect this would have and this is no doubt correct.[202] Although historical orthodoxy suggests that the conservatives disapproved of the schism and royal policy, that they were thus forced to defend what they 'must have once, or indeed still, found anathema'[203], this conclusion is more open to question.

For example, we know that Stokesley launched the sermon campaign with a vigorous defence of the king's divorce and an attack upon papal misuse of dispensations.[204] Elton wrote that as these subjects were settled, Stokesley had simply elected to avoid a 'crisis of conscience'.[205] Yet, it seems clear that the king's matrimonial difficulties were still near the top of the political agenda. The Boleyn marriage had never been particularly popular in London and Stokesley was known to have played a major role therein. While the average Londoner may well have been unaware of the larger political and ideological issues, there had been the recent public executions of Fisher and More to spark their imaginations and raise doubts. More's execution had only been the week prior to this sermon, so to choose that particular topic at that particular moment and defending the king in uncomfortable circumstances and at the same time avoiding unorthodox opinion, seems both controversial and shrewdly calculating.

In the event, the sermon was judged by Cromwell to have been a spectacular success. He told Chapuys that he would have given 'a thousand marks for the Emperor to have heard' it.[206] Stokesley was persuaded to preach it again shortly thereafter but, famously, could not be persuaded to publish it.[207] In any case, Thompson's study has made it plain that some of the bishops, like Longland, Veysey and Tunstal, had also carried out the command with enthusiasm[208], eager to demonstrate their loyalty. Others preached in favour of the supremacy with certain misgivings, like Sherborne.[209] Others still, like Rugg, were unsure just what to preach.[210] A problem not considered at the time was the unique one experienced by the bishops of the Welsh dioceses. Capon found, in June 1535, that he could not make himself understood in Bangor as he did not speak Welsh, and Roland Lee said that he would be glad to preach throughout his diocese of Coventry and Lichfield, even though he had never preached before.[211] Even with Episcopal backing, the message was still meeting resistance. Cromwell, therefore, determined to take a more direct course.

The vicar-general's plan to hold a royal visitation was known officially by 18 September 1535 and would inhibit the exercise of Episcopal jurisdiction for the duration. Longland received his order on 6 October; four days after Veysey and Stokesley had received theirs.[212] The upcoming visitation was anticipated by some of the bishops who, perhaps, feared for their own particular authorities. Longland visited the cathedral; Sherborne visited the monastic houses at Aldingbourne, Selsey and Chichester; Lee carried out a series of monastic visitations in York in the summer and autumn of 1534, and carried on his visitation throughout 1535 right up to the inhibition itself.[213]

The new inhibition raised all the usual administrative and spiritual difficulties for the bishops. The fact that these new instructions had not been issued by a cleric, however, raised an additional and more serious theoretical problem. Could the king inhibit the bishops from necessary sacerdotal functions he himself could not perform? Longland spotted this deficiency first, and asked Cromwell 'to give me lycence for the good ordre of my dioces'.[214] Episcopal authority was returned almost immediately (seventeen days in Stokesley's case, nine in Longland's), thereby clearly establishing the king's authority. The bishops could ordain, admit to benefice, prove wills valued less than £100 and hear cases that arose out of either instance or correction, but now these ordinary powers depended on the will of the king.[215] Cathedral deans and chapters also received licences but not until some time later (19 December in the case of Lincoln), thus making lesser ecclesiastical authorities also dependent on the will of the king. Provided the bishops recognised the king's authority, there seemed to be no problems. Of course, all was not well. Some of the bishops thought that the crown was hindering their diocesan administration too much.

Archbishop Lee, for example, complained to Cromwell on a number of occasions that he did not have the freedom to give prebends to men of his own choosing. In February 1535, the bishops were told that they were not to perform any institutions or collations until Cromwell had appointed a commissioner to supervise such appointments.[216] Lee objected strongly to royal nominations and felt that he was being singled out for particularly harsh treatment. Similarly, on a number of occasions, the crown appointed prebends in the London diocese despite Stokesley's protests. The bishop of London was not a man to be ignored, however. He adopted an exasperating habit of dissimulation in order to frustrate what he saw as the vicar-general's grasping.

In 1537, for instance, the king demanded the collation of that London prebend left vacant by the death of Richard Wolman. On 19 September Stokesley explained to Cromwell that Wolman had been prebendary of Finsbury and that the appointment had already gone to John Spendlove (the bishop's cousin) the day before. Spendlove had been prebendary of Islington and had already paid the first fruits on Finsbury. Stokesley offered the king the presentation to Islington rather than Finsbury and, shortly thereafter, Eliseus Ambrose was instituted.[217] This obfuscation was matched with objections. The bishop complained that governmental interference prevented him from presenting his own chaplains to prebends, so he had no learned men around him – a complaint echoed by Lee, Veysey and Longland.[218] Even Sampson, now bishop of Chichester, wrote to Cromwell on this issue:

> A buyshop off a Cathedral Church neyther having dignities, prebendes, nor benefices in his disposition, wherso by the kynes acte he may have 6 chaplains ffor his necessarie ministration without fayle shall neyther have lerned man with hym not Commisarie officiall or any other person meate to serve.[219]

In other Episcopal matters, however, Thompson has shown that the bishops carried on much as before.

The majority of bishops instituted and examined their clergy in person, although many of them were fighting a losing battle against a dwindling supply of new priests. This led to an alarming reduction in necessary qualifications. At York, for example, only eighteen percent of Lee's institutions had degrees, while the figures were somewhat better in the London and Ely dioceses (fifty percent). Thompson has calculated that only an average thirty percent of all newly collated individuals held degrees. Such inadequacies led Edward Lee to despair of his priests' learning and their preaching abilities. In November 1537, he reminded Cromwell of his suit for more preachers, having discovered that there were little or no preachers in Nottinghamshire and several preachers were not even licensed by Lee. When he prosecuted them for preaching 'novelties', they claimed to have either Cromwell's or Cranmer's licences.[220]

Cranmer, at least, had somewhat better prospects, unconcerned as he was with radical opinion. Of his 220 collations at least ninety were graduates. That is not to say he too did not face governmental interference. In November 1538, he had to ask Cromwell to give his chaplain, Richard Campion, the rectory of Shepton Mallett. As a native of the region, Campion could settle local disputes and could preach well.[221] Latimer also tried to put his reforming ideals into practise but ran up against an obstacle in the person of the master of Stratford collegiate church, a non-resident Cromwell nominee. Latimer wanted his resignation or wanted Cromwell to persuade him to 'keep house in it and about it the reformation of that blind end of my diocese'.[222]

Longland too recognised the need to uphold quality, particularly in the face of religious reformation. He told Cromwell that, if not for him, he would have given a chantry (in 1534) not to Cromwell's nominee but to an M.A. who was a known preacher.[223] After 1534, selective interference allowed the crown a directing influence over Episcopal patronage. Thompson has shown, however, that while this affected only a small proportion of the total of cathedral and parochial livings, the bishops managed to maintain the quality of their clergy, whether conservative or radical, by responding more fully to their pastoral and spiritual needs.[224] The royal supremacy had spawned better pastoral shepherding perhaps because bishops were no longer particularly politically active and there was more concern to appoint unimpeachable clergymen.

Turning back to 1535, one of the powers not immediately returned to the prelates had been the right of monastic visitation. This indicated to Bowker that the king and Cromwell had 'very special intentions' for the houses. By the time Episcopal power of visitation was returned there were fewer religious houses left to visit. There was little or no evidence of radicalism, however, and after 1540, the case of bishop Wakeman of Gloucester shows that visitation had become largely a brief ceremonial affair.[225] In what other ways had the supremacy impacted upon diocesan authority?

At some point during the royal visitation, Cromwell and his agents determined a need for censorship. On 1 January 1536 (a month earlier in London), a proclamation was issued requiring the surrender of all of Fisher's divorce writings and for 'diverse and sundry writings and books in derogation and diminution of the dignity and authority royal of the king's majesty and his imperial crown'. These were to be handed over to Cromwell, or to Audley, within forty days.[226] For whatever reason, the new order also attacked papal indulgences and pardoners. It has been noted that the terms of the order were somewhat confusing and Stokesley used the occasion to test Cromwell's poise.[227] It seems, in fact, that he proved quite an opponent for the vicar-general, giving him quite a contest.

Elton noted that,

3there need be no doubt that the attack on him originated in the difficulties encountered in the imposing of the new order on a diocese whose Bishop, an expert canon lawyer, was adept at putting up passive resistance.[228]

In any case, Stokesley resisted the new initiative and excused himself as having had only a second-hand report of it. He wrote to Cromwell on 16 January for additional clarification, noting:

I would have sent you my books of the canon law and schoolmen favouring the Bishop of Rome; but as I am informed by those to whom you have declared the king's proclamation in this behalf, it is not meant but the Bishop of Rochester's books and sermons, and of these to have lately written in defence of the said primacy against the opinion of the Germans, I do not send them until I know your further pleasure; which known otherwise, I shall forthwith send them and all other books that I have rather than keep one that peradventure (me unawares) does defend or maintain that intolerable and exorbitant primacy.[229]

Elton suggested that this book collection was connected with the ongoing propaganda campaign, but it seems clear that seditious preaching and ecclesiastical divisions were behind the measure. The king had, after all, left the preaching problem for Cromwell to solve.

Cromwell, with the support of Cranmer, encouraged reformist preaching. This had the rather unfortunate, but foreseeable consequence of putting the bishops into difficulties. Archbishop Lee, for example, had assumed that the former order held sway even after the time limit expired, while Stokesley assumed a lapse and that preaching was once again subject to the regulations of the bishops themselves.[230] In August 1535, for example, Thomas Corthope, the curate of Harwich, although cited by Cromwell for preaching in favour of purgatory, was able to claim Stokesley's support:

now, I dare boldly spech of it and preach of it, too. For I have spoken with mine ordinary the bishop of London of late and he hath showed me so that it be not against no thing that is granted by act of Parliament we may preach as we have done in time past.[231]

Cromwell issued similar letters reiterating Cranmer's earlier order, but this was not matched by support for the bishops' efforts in any real concrete fashion and problems continued.

In York, for example, Lee took the step of summoning a conservative friar to account for the content of his sermons and was also troubled by certain radical preachers too.[232] In Lincoln's diocese, Longland was having similar difficulties with such individuals as Thomas Garret and Thomas Swynnerton, particularly the 'social impact' of the latter, which would blow up spectacularly soon enough.[233] In Worcester, Latimer was less concerned to suppress radical preaching. He left such enforcement to the conservative sheriff of Gloucester, Thomas Bell (no relation to John), who created a hornet's nest by writing to Stokesley and to the duke of Norfolk about the situation in the west midlands and the marches, labelling Latimer a 'horesone heretycke'.[234] As much as the situation might have troubled him, Stokesley was having problems of his own in London.

As noted, the task of appointing preachers to St Paul's Cross had been taken out of his hands during the parliamentary sessions of November–December 1534, although this had not seemed to bother him too much. He lodged no complaints against any of Cranmer's appointments, nor had he lodged any objections with subsequent royal appointments (having taken part himself). He would not, as Elton wrote, put up with being 'shamed to his face by having to attend a sermon hostile to his theology', however.[235]

Elton was referring to the appointment of John Hilsey, the Dominican Prior of Bristol, who was scheduled to preach by Cromwell in December.[236]

Stokesley objected to Hilsey's preaching and had summoned him to submit to an examination of his opinions prior to his sermon. The bishop asked him to subscribe to the same articles as Latimer and Crome had subscribed or be forbidden to preach at both the Cross, and throughout the diocese. Stokesley's powers of discipline had not been inhibited by the royal visitation. Hilsey, however, refused to subscribe to the orthodox doctrine of purgatory, and thus, the bishop substituted Simon Matthew into his place. He asked that Cromwell re-appoint Hilsey to preach some other time. Stokesley worried that Hilsey would 'rail this Sunday, not only in reproach of me and my order, but also to maintain his indiscreet fashion of remembrance of the souls departed'.[237]

Matthew's sermon was everything for which the bishop could have hoped. There was an explicit repudiation of the Roman primacy and a justification of the recent executions.[238] There was an objection to recent evangelical advances and there was an appeal to the audience to make prayers for the dead, 'though the laste sonday the preacher coude not fynde in his conscience to pray for the soules departed, saying that he thought his prayer shuld nothynge auayle them'.[239] All told, however, the preaching problem was not going away and the king had to step into the breach once again. On 7 January, a royal letter was sent to all of the bishops addressing the issue.

The one extant letter was addressed to de'Athequa (perhaps never sent)[240], noting the king's regret at the continual spread of divisive and extreme views in preaching and placing the blame for this on the bishops' shoulders. This censure was unfair, of course, as the king himself had promised them a decisive statement on what doctrine could be preached but had, at this point, failed to produce it. In any case, he warned them to 'consider the persons authorized by them to preach' and gave them powers to revoke former commissions if necessary. Presumably, this included metropolitan and vice-gerential commissions as well, but the main targets were those who had exhibited a lack of 'good judgement'.[241] In an appendage to the royal letter, Cromwell warned the bishops to be particularly mindful of the 'overmany novelties' he thought calculated to 'engender division' rather than remove papist corruption.[242]

As Elton noted, the bishops carried out new examinations for licenses and some even continued monastic visitation. Hilsey, for instance, was visiting Dominican houses in London (as provincial of the order) and in Fulham and Rochester[243], and this might indeed have had some effect. Nothing really could be accomplished, however, until disputed points of doctrine were examined and decided upon, and the lead for this could only come from the king. What would become the *Ten Articles* was delayed for the parliamentary sessions that saw through the first Act of Dissolution. The dissolutions progressed into the summer and the *Ten Articles* eventually saw the light of day, but proved disappointing. Not long afterwards, the royal visitation was brought to an end and, as with any other Episcopal visitation, the issue of injunctions followed.

In brief, these were fairly standard instructions dealing with the usual problems of administration, morals and spiritual reform. For example, clergy were to stay away from alehouses, were to teach the Ten Commandments, the Lord's Prayer, the articles of faith and reverently administer the sacraments. In reforming terms, the royal injunctions forbid the clergy to 'set forth or extol any images, relics, or miracles for any superstition or lucre, nor allure the people by any enticements to the pilgrimage of any saint.' As one might expect, the injunctions also referred once again to the ongoing difficulty in enforcing obedience to the royal supremacy. Every Sunday for the next three months, and twice every quarter thereafter, the clergy were enjoined to preach against papal authority and confirm the king's jurisdiction. Although a 'well-considered start' to reform and obedience, the bishops were called into play again shortly thereafter.[244]

Yet another circular was issued to the bishops on 16 November 1536. This one was in reference to the apparent failure of the *Ten Articles* to impress the nation and also as a result of the recent northern uprisings.[245] In light of these events the bishops were to personally declare the *Ten Articles* every holy day that they spent in their diocese, travel throughout, and every holy day preach plainly from a proper scriptural text and proclaim the supremacy. Cromwell revoked all preaching licences yet again and made the bishops responsible for new ones. What is new here is that the bishops were also required to search for priests who had married.[246]

At least four bishops took the king's requirements to heart and carried out new visitations. Latimer, Roland Lee, Edward Lee and Fox followed up the royal injunctions with matching injunctions based on their own subsequent visitations. Latimer visited his diocese of Worcester in 1537, paying particular attention to Bristol and to the Convent of St Mary's, to see to the condition of the clergy in light of perceived abuses and rumours. In Bristol, however, seditious preaching was rampant, as were conservative attacks on the evangelical bishop. With Latimer a distant bishop at best, and with confusion evident over local authority, little could be done. It was left to Cromwell's agents to handle the matter themselves.[247] Latimer's actions at the convent were somewhat more extensive and personal.

In the period of the dissolutions, the usual problems of monasticism are all evident. Latimer's injunctions for Worcester, however, were based very closely on the king's own injunctions and repetitive of his injunctions for St Mary's and, therefore, rather lacklustre.[248] His attitude to visitation was neatly summed up in his letter to the authorities:

> forasmuch as in this my visitation I evidentlie perceive the ignorance and negligence of dyvers religious persons in the monasterie to be intollerable and not to be suffred, for that thereby doth reign idollatrie and manie kinds of superstition and other enormities'[249]

Roland Lee's injunctions for Coventry and Lichfield were much the same as Latimer's (and thus the king's) although more detailed. He added one with regard to clerical dress, noting that he had become aware that 'certain priests in my diocese go in habit dissimuled more liker of the temporalty'. This seemed to encourage inappropriate behaviour on the part of both clergy and laity and so more appropriate apparel was ordered.[250] The bishop also had his injunctions printed so that there would be no excuse for not having read them or not having displayed them in the parishes.

Archbishop Lee's articles for the Collegiate Church of St Wilfrid Ripon were, unlike these others, based on a lengthy investigation of the difficulties caused there by one Christopher Dragley. The treasurer had been a thorn in Lee's side since 1534. Then, the archbishop's commissioner, William Clyff, had visited St Wilfrid's and as a result had brought charges against the canons and against Dragley specifically. Among the many charges brought against him was one that said he had been making appointments to vacancies among the canons and choir on his own authority. He was charged with abetting the neglect of the divine service, with having ignored required corrections to prayers for the pope and the king and that he had kept the doors to the chapter house closed. If these were not enough, it seems he also hindered his fellow officers from performing their own duties.[251]

The archbishop's injunctions of 2 October 1537 severely limited Dragley's actions with regard to church business and his own personal life (too much of which seems to have been spent in the company of Joan Calverley). Although the royal injunctions of 1536 do not have a clear influence over Lee's own set, they do show that the archbishop was alert to the problems that had earlier forced the king's hand. His injunctions to the vicars-choral, limited though they were, do at least address the issues highlighted by the king's orders. Like Latimer's tenth and eleventh injunctions for St Mary's, Lee's second decree ordered daily readings from scripture, while his third addressed the common problem of morality, particularly gambling and womanising.[252] Fox took similar cognisance of the king's injunctions when he issued his orders for the Augustinian house, St James's Wigmore. The main problem for Fox, however, was his own suffragan, John Smart, who was not an effective administrator. His orders addressed all the usual problems.[253] Clearly, at least some of the bishops were making an effort to administer their charges after the king's example. There were some problem areas, however.

In London, for example, it seems that Cromwell recognised that he had made a mistake in appointing Hilsey to handle preaching appointments at St Paul's Cross. He had thought to teach Stokesley a lesson by removing his right of appointment, but the bishop was not considered a worthy opponent for nothing. He took exception to both Hilsey and to the calibre of his recent appointments and used his reputation, both as a scholar with a penetrating mind and as a crusader against heresy, to intimidate as many of Hilsey's appointments as he could. His disapproval scared off many preachers.[254] Cromwell found that he had to back off and turn to the bishop for his advice on making more appropriate selections. Cromwell asked Stokesley to prepare a list of preachers he thought appropriate and, with those scheduled by Hilsey, he tried to choose a convenient mixture of opinion. What emerged for the remainder of the year was a blending of mildly reformed and conservative preachers, including both Edward Lee and Matthew Parker.[255]

This was one of the first indications that reform was moving faster than the king was willing to allow. In fact, Cromwell was not able to address the situation again until late in 1538, when further royal injunctions were issued. Although more or less the same as the earlier set, the details are much more interesting. They were published on 5 September, printed and dispatched to the bishops by the end of the month. What was particularly noteworthy was the well-known injunction calling for 'one boke of the whole Bible of the largest volume, in Englyshe' to be provided and 'sett up in summe convenyent place within the said church that ye have cure of.'[256]

The bishops were, however, to ensure that the Bibles were read with all due sobriety and to be sure the laity were referring obscure passages to trained theologians.[257] We will look at the problem of producing an acceptable translation later. Here, it is enough to note that the requirement that readers avoid contention and altercations over the material proved too much for the bishops and other authorities and, in time, the effort was aborted. A second innovation was the requirement for parish registers of baptisms, marriages and burials, much easier to implement.[258] These injunctions were to be enforced by the bishops with further injunctions of their own. As per instructions therefore, archbishops Lee and Cranmer (for the vacant diocese of Hereford), and bishops Shaxton and Veysey issued new orders. More often than not, however, these merely parroted the new royal set.[259]

* * *

## c. Specific reformation issues

Shaxton's injunctions, like Roland Lee's, were subsequently published. In the royal set it was clear that abuse of images, pilgrimages and offerings to saints would no longer be tolerated. There was also a warning of the impending destruction of abused images.[260] Shaxton obviously approved of this. His repetition of this order was expanded to cover any possible interpretation of 'adornment', such as 'decking of images with gold, silver, clothes, lights, or herbs . . . nor offer candles, oats, cake-bread, cheese, wool, or any such other things'. Parishioners could, in the meantime, still look at them. The clergy were warned not to allow their parishioners 'to be envious about works invented by their own foolish devotion', that is 'idle pilgrimages', 'vain confidence [in] this prayer and that prayer', 'superstitious observations, in fastings, praying, and keeping of old foolish customs', and later in the injunctions, false 'relics' such as 'stinking boots, mucky combs, ragged rochets, rotten girdles, pyld purses, great bullocks' horns, locks of hair, and filthy rags, gobbetts of woods'. It appears, however, that Shaxton was willing to be open-minded. So-called relics and any written provenance were to be sent 'unto me at mine house at Ramesbury, or other-where . . . to the intent that I and my council may explore and try them what they be, and those that be esteemed and judged to be undoubtedly true relics' would be returned. Those that proved authentic could be 'glorified, lauded, and praised'.[261] Even the most conservative of the bishops, Stokesley, engaged in relic de-bunking[262] and one has to wonder just how Shaxton proposed to verify a relic's power.

Another of the evangelical bishops that we can assume would have approved of the late injunctions, at least those sections on the abuse of images and relics, was Hilsey of Rochester. On 24 February 1538, he had preached at St Paul's Cross against relics and abuse of images using a display of 'the Rood of Grace' as evidence of just how far fakers were willing to go. The rood was dismantled so that the crowd could see that it was operated by a series of hidden gears and pulleys.[263] Similarly, on 24 November, Hilsey returned to the same subject, this time with a display of the relic known as 'Hale's Blood'. Hilsey had examined this one on a previous occasion (like Shaxton?) and had preached that it was nothing more than duck's blood. It appeared that he had been mistaken, however, as further investigation had proved that it was not any kind of blood at all, but a mixture of honey, clarified and coloured with saffron.[264]

Of the conservative bishops, less is known about their reaction to the royal injunctions as a whole. Edward Lee, in a rather verbose and long-winded manner, repeated Shaxton's orders in some instances and made equally wide considerations. With regard to images, for instance, he was direct: 'In no wise yield worship to any images, lowtinge or bowing down, or kneeling . . . ne offering to them any money, or wax light or unlight, or any other thing'. In contrast to Shaxton, however, he also drew out more interesting additions to the royal injunctions. For example, 'although they see the image of the father represented as an old man, yet they may in no wise believe, that the heavenly Father is any man, or that he hath any body or age; but that he is nature and substance.' He also reinforced traditional beliefs in justification by faith and good works and as a true intellectual theologian, expanded upon the laws of God and nature.[265] Gardiner too seemed best pleased with the new orders.

We know, indirectly, Gardiner's opinion of the royal injunctions having been faced by Thirlby on the issue when returning to England from France. Thirlby reported the meeting to Wriothesley. On the recent injunctions, he said, '[Gardiner] liked them well'. It seems that the bishop was particularly pleased 'where it is appointed that curates should advise their parishioners, in confession.' Gardiner also 'misliked not' the dismantling of abused shrines like Becket's at Canterbury. According to Thirlby, the bishop said that 'if he had been at home he would have given his counsel to the doing thereof, and wished that the like were done at Winchester'.[266] Of course, the like had already been done. St Swithin's shrine had been dismantled shortly before his return, so just as well that he would have had no objections.[267] We have already noted that Stokesley too had no ideological objections to dismantling objects of abuse, but his opposition to the use of English vernacular scripture is very illustrative of the difficulties supporters of a translation faced.

* * *

The first official notification making provision for the production of an English Bible was the royal injunctions of 1536.[268] There had been a great deal written by the humanists that was positive and in favour of vernacular scriptures much earlier than this of course. Tunstal himself had examined the arguments in favour almost a decade before. Indeed, as a humanist theologian, Stokesley no doubt shared these views. His objection was to the sources of the vernacular version rather than to the idea itself. Even so, he was none too convinced that even a sincere translation would make much difference, having little trust in human nature and intellect. In his sermon of 1535 he had said that 'love to Godd and to ther neyghbors [should be] engrave[d] and emprynte[d] the saam inwardly in ther harts [not just] in your bookys aloon'.[269] The opinion that a vernacular translation was little more than a mere stop-gap to the real problem of human virtue was one that was largely shared by his two senior colleagues, Tunstal and Longland.

In 1538, when the second set of injunctions ordered the placing of an English Bible in all churches, Longland noted with some scepticism that, 'we haue all the scrypture in Englyshe, and we haue knowledge of god and [of the] lawes, and yet doo we not lyue thereafter'[270] while, for Tunstal, the Bible had become less a book of living laws and more 'a boke of problems to dispute vppon, and care not to amede our lyuynge.'[271] The movement towards a vernacular translation was generally supported by the reform-minded bishops and latter-day conservatives like Bonner.[272] Despite his intellectual worries, Longland was positively gushing with praise when the production of another version was finished. He wrote, 'we have it in out owne mother tongue. We ioye and reiose moche and soo may we, that we soo have it in our own vulgar speche, that we here it, that we reede it, that we have it in out bosomes', perhaps hoping that his and his companions' worries would be addressed.[273] Of the three senior conservatives, Stokesley found himself alone in the actual fight against the Bibles, but he carried on with a firm mental resolve, enduring both ridicule and recrimination.

Briefly, the problem was that English vernacular Bibles had been in existence for some time, all having failed to win clerical approval. Several of them were still in circulation and more were entering the country every day. This was the problem the king and Cromwell had hoped to address in the injunctions. The king was intending to resolve it by having the scriptures translated by 'great, learned and Catholic persons'.[274] This in mind, October 1535 saw the production of the Miles Coverdale version under the patronage of Cromwell. It raised almost immediate opposition from the conservative prelates, however, as it had been based on Tyndale and Luther, rather than Erasmus.[275]

Stokesley ignored altogether the injunction that required this Bible be placed in every church. Hooker, the Elizabethan intellectual, tells the story. Coverdale, on leaving England,

> passed over into low Germany where he printed the bibles of his translation and sent them over into England, and thereof made his gain whereby he lived. But the bishops, namely Dr. Stokesley bishop of London, when he heard hereof, and minding to prevent that no such bibles should be dispersed within this realm, made inquiry where they were to be sold, and bought them all up supposing that by this means no more bibles would be had, but contrary to his expectation it fell out otherwise: for the same money which the bishop gave for these books was sent over by the merchant unto this coverdale, and by that means he was of that wealth and ability that he imprinted as many more and sent them over into England.[276]

An anecdotal tale written fifty years after the fact has the ring of truth, if not a little embellishment, about it. Bonner, elevated to Hereford in 1538 and who would succeed Stokesley in London in 1539, wrote that,

> to tell you Mr Grafton, Before God . . . the greatest fault that I ever found in Stokesley was for vexing and troubling of poor men as Lobley the bookbinder and other, for having the scripture in English; and God willing he did not so much hinder it but I will as much further it.[277]

Stokesley's campaign was a decisive part of the reason why the Coverdale project had to be shelved.[278] Evidence for this can be found in a letter of Richard Grafton to Cromwell over his difficulties distributing the Coverdale Bible. He singled out the London diocese as the bishop and his agents had managed to ferret out all the booksellers Grafton used, as Bonner indicated.[279]

Later, Stokesley also led the opposition to Matthew's Bible, although now it was less a question of jurisdiction and more one of ideology. Matthew's was more or less a compilation of Tyndale's (the New Testament and his Old Testament as far as II Chronicles), Coverdale's (his New Testament after II Chronicles) and Rogers' Bible. The bishop so exasperated Cranmer that he recommended to Cromwell that he try to get the king's license to publish it and place it in churches and allow men to read it that way. The archbishop complained that, while the Matthew's version was undoubtedly full of errors and would have to be corrected, it should be used until the bishops could produce a better translation themselves.[280]

To this end, he had taken Tyndale's translation of the New Testament and had divided it into nine or ten parts, then distributed it to the 'best learned bishops' for correction. He gave Gardiner Luke and John and gave Stokesley the Acts. Cranmer himself took Matthew and Mark, which between the three of them accounts for more than half the work.[281] By June 1535, Gardiner had finished his portion, Cranmer no doubt his, but Stokesley had refused to do it, believing that the project would be undermined by the variety of opinion that would result and that this, in turn, would 'infest the people with more heretical opinions'. He added,

> I marvaile what my lorde of Canterbury meaneth, that thus abuseth the people in gyvyng them libertie to reade the scriptures, which doith nothing else but infecte them with heryses. I have bestowed never an hower apon my portion, nor never will; and therefore my lorde shall have his boke againe, for I will never be gyltie to bring the symple people into errour.

The accusation took Cranmer by surprise and his messenger, Thomas Lawney, tried to diffuse the tension with humour. He said,

> I can tell your grace whie my lorde of London will not bestowe any labour or payne this wey. Your grace knoweth well that his portion ys a pece of Newe Testament; and than he, being persuaded Christe had bequeth hym nothing in his testament, thought it mere madnes to bestowe any labour or payne where no gayne was to be gotten. And besided this, it is the Actes of the Apostells, whiche were symple poore felowes; and therfore my lord of London disdayned to have to do with any of thair actes.[282]

Stokesley's opinion won the day and Cranmer wrote to Cromwell that he despaired of the work ever appearing because of Stokesley, and that the Bible would not be finished until 'a day after doomsday'.[283] He asked Cromwell to reconsider using Matthew's Bible.

In the event, Stokesley's worries that contention would result were borne out by occurrences in the parishes, which forced another governmental rethink. This led to the abandonment of the Matthew's Bible in favour of the so-called 'Bible of the Largest Volume' in the 1538 injunctions.[284] Matthew's had been used unofficially in the parishes and had led directly to a rise in complaints about impromptu scripture discussions in pubs and taverns, which is exactly what the king had set out to discourage. Such debates often led to brawling, much as Stokesley had predicted they would.[285] We will return to the issue of Bibles in due course.

* * *

Besides the Bible, the 1538 injunctions had also been issued to alert the bishops to an alarming increase in Anabaptist activity. Stokesley had been an outspoken critic of the sect earlier in the decade and he and Cranmer were to spearhead a commission to find and eliminate the threat. On 1 October they were commissioned to seek out, examine, and destroy both Anabaptists and their books.[286] Subsequently, the publication, importation and selling of all English books brought into the country from abroad was also prohibited. Any such books would now require a royal licence and would first have to be 'examined by the Privy Council or someone appointed by the King'.[287] Not only Bibles; all works of scriptural criticism would have to be approved in this way and Henry forbade all discussion of the Eucharist and rites and ceremonies, which had previously been neglected. The general attack on 'superstitions' was now to be strictly observed 'till the king please to change'.[288] This was a substantial victory for the conservatives and a turning point in doctrinal reformation, although the problem of diversity plagued the kingdom still. This might have been avoided, however, had the king been more willing, or able, to settle the religious question. For political reasons, the king had engaged in a kind of ongoing flirtation with Lutheran princes and theologians, reviving a question of religious orthodoxy time and time again. This, as we have seen, forestalled the bishops' efforts to instil spiritual stability in the country at large.

* * *

## 6. The problems of spiritual disunity

The Episcopal bench had been transformed by the aftermath of the divorce and the rise of the intellectuals. What had been an independent body of jurists was now a dependent corps of royal ministers specialising in theology (expressing a wide variety of opinion). The changes took place within the space of only six years and gave the bishops a new and particularly important role in the development and implementation of a workable doctrinal settlement for the kingdom. Before, they followed where Rome had led. Now, they had been given options from which to choose.

The king wanted to be advised from many different points of view. From these, he could select a convenient mixture. That this was the case is evinced by an examination of the various formularies of faith and other related materials and brings two ideas into clearer focus. First, to a degree, the individual bishops and the king had different agendas and concerns. For the bishops it was extreme religious movements (e.g. Anabaptism), the appropriate degree of reform and the preservation of as much of their Episcopal authority as they could manage. The king also disliked extreme movements and wanted to find the appropriate level of reform as well as balancing the needs of international security and domestic stability. Second, religious dispute and faction troubled both bishops and king, necessitating the search for genuine middle ground (*via media*).

Two issues, which became interrelated, brought these differences into sharp focus. In England, in the post-1534 period, there was an ever-increasing dilemma of divisive preaching for which the bishops looked to the king for leadership and resolution. On the international front, the king was making overtures to the Lutheran princes of Northern Germany in order to ease his isolation, hoping to create some kind of association with them without having to submit to their religious pre-conditions. The two efforts overlapped with the creation of the *Ten Articles* in 1536.

*  *  *

After 1534, we know that a real problem existed in the need for preachers to inveigh against the pope. This invited in any number of ideological innovations, as questioning papal power lead to similar questions on all related traditional matters. This in turn created divisions between those who defended the traditional practices, those who attacked them and those who still defended the pope and all that that entailed.

The king reviewed the problem with the help of some of his bishops and an inhibition was drafted after the example of Lee's injunctions.[289] From Cranmer's letter of 24 May, it seems clear that Thirlby also had an interest in the new inhibition, as did Shaxton, who was in close proximity to the archbishop.[290] The order was finally issued through Cranmer for the southern province in June.

Cranmer hoped that it would combat the spread of further divisions and thus give the bishops breathing space. Although preachers were still to 'preach . . . against the usurped power of the bishop of Rome', it was also ordered that 'no preachers shall content openly in pulpit one against another, nor uncharitably deprave one another in open audience'. Any issues of contention were to be ruled upon by the king, the archbishop or the bishop of the diocese in which the dispute occurred. Moreover, 'no preachers for a year shall preach neither with nor against purgatory, honouring of saints, that priests may have wives, the faith only justifieth, to go on pilgrimages, to forge miracles, considering these things to have caused dissension amongst the subjects of this realm already', which indeed they had.[291] The rest of the order was largely a reiteration of familiar anti-papal arguments.

In collaboration with his senior bishops, Stokesley, Gardiner and Longland, Cranmer made further moves to combat divisions by issuing an inhibition to preachers and curates designed to induce calm.[292] Here, the archbishop called for grants of new licenses and repeated the king's letter. Preachers were,

in no wise to touch or intermeddle themselves to preach or teach any such thing that might slander or bring in doubt and opinion the catholic and received doctrine of Christ's church, or speak of such matters as touch the prince, his laws or succession.

All of these matters, it was expected, were to be addressed by a conclusive royal statement within the year.[293] While this pronouncement was eagerly anticipated, the impetus for stability was laid firmly at the feet of the individual bishops.

The problem was that they were themselves just as divided on these matters as were the preachers, some ignoring the issue altogether. Latimer, for example, seemed unconcerned that his preachers were not conforming to the orders, leaving enforcement of the matter in the hands of Worcester's temporal authorities.[294] Even given such apparent apathy, the order effectively gagged both sides of the argument, if only briefly. There was some limited controversy over the rest of the year but it would be another year entirely before the bishops would come together to make a statement on these issues at the king's bidding. Unfortunately, incidents of divisive preaching did not go away. The king, more concerned with the perceived wisdom and implementation of the royal supremacy[295], however, left the preaching problem to Cromwell, a man who already had too much on his plate. MacCulloch has shown that while Cranmer worked hand in glove with Cromwell, he was definitely the junior partner and that neither he, nor the other bishops were ever given as free a hand as they needed. In the event, Cromwell initially only tinkered, leaving the bishops on the spot (we have seen that Lee and Stokesley took different directions).[296] The bishop of London could not desist from making some subtle commentary on these issues.

In July, at St Paul's Cross, he fronted a defence of the Aragon divorce and an apology for the royal supremacy with a subtle digression amounting to a defence of the traditional doctrine of justification. He made a standard introduction on the lack of human virtue in pre-Christian days when man's condition was 'frayle and miserabyll' needing 'the mercifull goodnes off Godd' who would 'show hys mercy to all'. Man was in such a state as to be unable to 'thynke or do any good thyng . . . [man was] oonhabyll he was off himselff to ryse agayn to any parte off hys native perfection'.[297] For the bishop, therefore, men must maintain verity, familiarise themselves with God's laws and love truth, 'and so doyng Godd shall reward youe wyth eternall glory'. Faith was a necessary pre-condition before man could 'do any good thyng' beneficial to himself and make a return to grace.[298]

In any case, by early 1536 the king had to once more step into the breach created by his failure to give clear guidance as supreme head. Another circular admonishing the bishops to revoke licenses and censor sermons was issued.[299] Cromwell matched this letter with one of his own, reiterating Cranmer's earlier orders. It was not, however, matched by support for the bishops' efforts in any real, concrete fashion, and problems developed in York, Lincoln, London and Worcester, as we have already seen above. Now, of course, they faced the added problem of dissolution of the monasteries.

Intellectually, both radical and conservative bishops earnestly supported the effort and advised the king to carry on. We know that Gardiner had written a few words in contempt of monks and friars over the years[300], and Aldrich had criticised the immoderate veneration of relics (although when the time came he voted against the dissolution[301]). Latimer was absolutely scathing in a sermon of 1536 on the abuse of relics. He wrote, 'I think ye have heard of St Blesis's heart which is at Malverne, and of St Algar's bones, how long they deluded the people: I am afraid, to the loss of many souls'.[302] Even so, it was Stokesley, 'the least resilient but the most resourceful of the conservative bishops', who was most enthusiastically involved in the dissolution of monastic houses. Indeed, it was he who called for the dissolution of the larger houses a full two years before the government took up the option.

Hall noted that the 'great and fatts abbottes' had surrendered the smaller houses in the hope of assuring the continuity of the larger ones. It was maintained in the Lords that the smaller houses were 'as thornes, but the great abbottes were putrified olde oaks and they must nedes followe & so will do other in Christendom qt Doctor Stokesley bishop of London or many yeres be passed'.[303] Stokesley's enthusiasm can be explained by the fact that he had little use or sympathy for the regular clergy and he understood and recognised the great need for reform in their communities. Moreover, as monastic houses were customarily outside the control of the diocesan, Stokesley and his fellows might well have looked forward to putting their reforming tendencies to good use in the king's name. Of course, in the wake of the acts of Appeals and Supremacy, the idea that members of a religious order owed allegiance to a parent institution outside England was dangerously anachronistic.

As we have already noted, there is evidence enough to support an argument that the monks no longer contributed much in the way of spiritual leadership anyway. Their houses were purgatorial institutions and as such served to offer prayers and masses for their founders and benefactors and their families: services that could be performed in colleges and almshouses.[304] And, as Hoyle stated in a recent examination, the religious houses were increasingly unwilling to fulfil this duty. The later medieval practice was for masses and prayers for the souls of the departed to be said, not in perpetuity, but over a fixed period at the end of which the provision would lapse. Doubts about the purpose of monasteries could thus be held without a challenge to the doctrine of purgatory itself. That is not to say such questions were not raised.

Latimer noted that 'the founding of monasteries argued purgatory to be; so the putting them down argueth it not to be.'[305] Of course, he was having difficulties with the recent preaching orders and noted the inconsistency of an act of parliament that appeared to deny purgatory while preachers in sermons could not so much as speak a word about it. Even so, he was moved to write on behalf of the virtuous Benedictines of Great Malvern in 1538, stressing the prior's commitments to hospitality and 'to maintain teaching, preaching, and study with praying'.[306] Such was the domestic scene. The bishops lacked guidance from the centre and, consequently, there was no religious continuity between the sees. Meanwhile, the king was pre-occupied with international matters.

* * *

## 7. Flirtations with Lutheranism

The best that can be said about the king's relations with the various Lutheran princes was that they were strained, disingenuous and over-cautious on both sides. We need not rehearse all the well-known details again, however. Suffice to say that the king dispatched several embassies over the 1534-40 period, all of which made the same noises against the pope and general councils, but none of which ever satisfied the king with what little achievements could be made. Obviously, this was because John Frederick, duke of Saxony, had been plain that an alliance depended on the king's subscribing to the Augsburg Confession, which Henry was loath to do. The king did hold out a diplomatic carrot of sorts in that he would negotiate if top theologians, like Melanchthon, were sent. If nothing else, at least some future bishops earned their diplomatic credentials over these otherwise fruitless years, including Heath, Fox and Bonner.[307] Indeed, little of any interest happened before Fox made a keynote address to the League of Schmalkald on 24 December.[308] This was noteworthy only because the next day, the duke, and Philip, Landgrave of Hesse, presented him with a petition to the king known as the *Christmas Articles*. These listed fourteen conditions under which England and the League could ally. As these have some bearing on the *Ten Articles* they are worth a brief look.

The first condition, upon which all the others depended and which the king would not do, was to accept Augsburg. Articles two through six concerned joint participation in a general council, while seven stated that Henry would be named 'defensor and protector of the said leage'. The remaining articles offer no surprises – abuse of the pope, mutual defence, money, etc. The final article was not a condition as such, but more a promise that if all the previous conditions were met, the Germans would send theologians to London.[309] These were forwarded to the king, and Cromwell forwarded them on to Gardiner, possibly as a political test. That Gardiner would reject the conditions outright could surely not have been a surprise.[310] The king, however, paid no heed and responded to each of the articles in turn, neatly side-stepping the real issue of subscribing Augsburg. He wrote rather 'to conferre and conclude . . . to the intente to have a parfaite concorde and unyon in faith'[311], whatever this meant short of Augsburg. Upon this vague basis, conversations and discussions continued for another year.[312] With patience wearing thin, mid-March 1536 saw the conclusion of discussions and the drawing up of the *Wittenburg Articles*, but any further meetings relied upon the king admitting 'the Gospel according to the Confession', the *sine qua non* of German alliance.[313] Fox must have thought this could be achieved and, in the summer of 1536 he attended convocation with an eye to presenting the articles.

* * *

Convocation would prove a real theological testing ground for the bishops as the king demanded they maintain 'unity, quietness, and good concord' in the dioceses, without having given any real lead in the months running up to the gathering.[314] The men of evangelical persuasion were expecting a great deal but the conservatives were not sitting idly by either. They always had at least one ace up their collective sleeve to prevent too-radical a reform in the ever-increasing threat of religious minority interests, namely, the Anabaptists.

Clearly, the Anabaptists were considered a threat worthy of individual attention. This is suggested by a draft article written by the bishops and intending to deal with salvation and the seven sacraments.[315] In the event, however, only Baptism was considered. The document contains eight articles, each dealing with one controversial doctrine or practice that needed official clarification. This, as a whole, suggests a wider concern for Anabaptism than was once recognised. The draft deals with salvation, the salvation of children, justification, images, honouring saints, praying to saints, rites and ceremonies, and purgatory, all contested doctrines[316] and all those which Cranmer had forbidden preachers to discuss back in 1534[317] but for which, as yet, the king's promised decisive statement was still forthcoming.

As the need grew for some kind of solution, a group of bishops gathered at Lambeth in March 1536 to resolve the issue and produce a statement providing authoritative guidelines for the preachers.[318] We know that Cranmer had singled out certain issues, four of which – purgatory, the honouring of saints and two articles on justification by faith – were dealt with in two draft papers. The bishops did not, however, deal with clerical marriage, pilgrimages and faked miracles, issues which Cranmer had promised some kind of statement later. They did deal with four issues not specifically mentioned earlier – the salvation of children, images, praying to saints, rites and ceremonies. This suggests that they were trying to produce a 'stop gap to gloss current doctrinal controversies, rather than a systematic doctrinal formulary' (which was now the king's prerogative). Five of these statements would end up in the bishops' draft of the *Ten Articles* (images, honouring saints, prayers to saints, rites and ceremonies and purgatory) in the section of non-essential articles. MacCulloch has shown, however, that even here there was contention. Cranmer and Tunstal differed over the honouring of saints – superstitious or scriptural – while Longland had stated in his Lenten sermon of this year that Jesus and Mary were 'perpetual intercessors' on men's behave.[319]

If nothing else, it seems clear that some of these draft articles were aimed at the rising tide of Anabaptist activity, explicitly mentioned in an article relating to the salvation of children:

> shall styll persevere & contynew as a very necessarie thnge for us of thys worlde. And all the Anabaptistes opynions contrary to hit, or any other manes opinione in oney thynge to the Anabaptistes agreable therein or aney parte thereof, to reputed amonge us hereses erroneous & detestable.[320]

That Anabaptism was perceived as a threat also led to Stokesley's wide dissemination of the Barlow book. As we have seen, however, in spring 1536 there were diplomatic realities making a widespread dissemination of the draft statement rather more controversial that the king needed.

Of course, the Anabaptists were open targets, which at least partially explains the king's own statement against them of March 1535.[321] Stokesley, in the capital, had been sufficiently fearful to release Barlow's book under the protection of his own office and his anxieties had infected the others. Kreider, based on Horst, suspected that Stokesley and Barlow were behind the new concerns[322] as well, more anxious about this in 1535-6 than over

Sacramentarianism or over the debate on the celestial flesh of Christ. In any case, the bishops' concerns about any particular heresy were overlapped by the need for a wider statement to settle domestic disparity, so the Lambeth sessions were abandoned.

* * *

## a. The Ten Articles, 1536

The convocation of 1536 is of central importance as it was here where the many strains of English religious policy came together. Fox presented the *Wittenburg Articles* in order to show where the continental theologians stood on the issues while, at the same time, the lower house presented the prelates with a collection of articles known as the '*dogmata mala*'. This was basically a list of some fifty-nine heretical opinions, then current in the realm, some of which were contained in Fox's paper. The conservative bishops held that such a doctrine, as listed, had been 'preached and discoursed to the slander of this noble realm, the disquiet of the people, and to the hindrance of their salvation.'[323] While considering these statements, the bishops were now ordered by the king to initiate an investigation into the essential questions of the faith. He wanted them to produce a statement that would, in theory, eliminate the promiscuity of conflicting dogma and ease religious tension in the realm. The result is certainly well known and we need not produce yet another detailed study here.[324] Suffice it to say that the Augsburg statements were taken apart, modified with borrowings from Melanchthon (famously moderate) and then considerably weakened with strict Catholic qualifications.

Factional strife between the conservatives and evangelical prelates led to much delay and, as MacCulloch noted, also highlighted the difficulty inherent in the provincial system. If one province (southern) decided a doctrine, how could the other province (northern) be forced to use it? All subsequent doctrinal examinations would therefore be carried out in either vice-gerential synods or private committees of invited theologians.[325] In any case, despite the work of Cranmer and Fox, the time was not yet ripe for rapid doctrinal movement. The conservative bishops were still in the ascendancy and the recent death of Anne Boleyn had, if anything, given them a much-needed confidence boost.

In any case, as Rex noted, the only essentially non-Catholic statements to emerge from convocation's discussions (possibly developed in the sub-committee) were restrictions on the doctrine of purgatory and on the cult of saints.[326] At best, what emerged was only a moderate reform package[327] but, even so, parts of it were further undermined when a sub-committee of conservative bishops subscribed a separate statement in defence of saint worship. It stated that 'the Bodies of saints, and, namely, the relicks of holy martyrs, are to be honoured most sincerely, as the members of Christ'.

Likewise, other practices were supported, like 'pilgrimage to places where
Almighty God sheweth miracles, may be don by them that have therunto
devotion'. Such statements make clear a kind of Erasmian stance on certain
late controversial issues.[328] Given such obstructionism (if that is what it
was) it is difficult to see why agreement with the Germans was
optimistically expected or that anything resembling a useful formulary
would be forthcoming. The bishops made their considerations and passed
their conclusions over to the king.[329]

The resulting *Ten Articles* was seen into print by Fox and offered to
convocation on 11 June 1536. Although more than 100 members
subscribed to it, it pleased no one and, as seen, injunctions were needed
to enforce its use at the parochial level.[330] The evangelical bishops were
disappointed because the statement did not go far enough in embracing
the German confession while the conservatives believed that, in some
cases, it favoured the confession far too much. The fact that it failed to
deal with four of the sacraments is said to prove the king's desire to win
over the German princes. It must be acknowledged, however, that the
statement had not reduced the number of sacraments to three, but had
merely failed to address the other four. The statement stayed on sure and
common theological ground. This impression is illustrated by the orthodox
explanations of Baptism, Penance and the Eucharist. Indeed, with regard
to Baptism (over which there was little or no conflict between the
Lutherans and Catholics), the *Ten Articles* provides a lengthy exposition
at one-seventh of the total document, largely repeating the familiar
orthodoxy.[331]

Even if no one else did, at least the king and, perhaps, also Thomas
Starkey assumed that the *Ten Articles* would prove to be the last word on
the subject. For Starkey it was 'a tempered doctrine . . . purged from the
old abuses and foolish superstitions and also defends from the errors of
this time, and from all false religion'.[332] The king hoped it would forestall
further divisive preaching and ordered the bishops to grant new licenses
based on it.[333] While the conservatives at least made an attempt to
implement royal policy, the more radical bishops appealed to Cromwell
to put a stop to it.[334]

* * *

## b. The Bishops' Book, 1537

A number of events conspired to force the king into further attempts at
doctrinal reform. His isolation in Europe was less of a problem as a war
had broken out between Valois France and the Habsburgs, and this lasted
throughout most of 1536-37. Balancing this, however, were the internal

tensions brought on by the Pilgrimage of Grace and the planned general council at Mantua. The German princes, equally hostile to the upcoming council, wrote to Fox assuring him of their loyalty and faith in their treaty and reminded the king that he had agreed to further talks.[335] Like his German partners, Henry also submitted a personal rejection of the call to the council to Paul III, and dispatched envoys to Germany again. In England, a state of religious adversity still existed. A variety of opinions were still being preached and the king had been taken aback at how little regard had been shown towards his previous statement.[336] The prelates were ordered to re-address the problems and produce a better one.

The bishops and twenty-five or so junior clerics were summoned to meet in the first vice-gerential synod. This combined representation from both provinces was to arrive at a definitive exposition of the faith. It is clear that the king wanted them to address specific points primarily, like prayers to saints, purgatory, clerical celibacy and penance, those which were most in dispute with the Germans. In fact, he sometimes sent in trusted advisors, like Richard Layton or Thomas Starkey, to confer with delegates and spur them on.[337] The bishops, it will become clear, had their own agendas and, by splitting themselves into committees along religious lines, impaired a project which already had too many objectives and diplomatic hopes attached to it.

In any case, the new deliberations started in mid-February 1537.[338] Attendance on the part of the bishops was variable. Whoever could attend did. We do know that the two most doctrinaire bishops, Stokesley and Tunstal, attended the committees most often, aiming to give this new confession as strong a Catholic constituency as they could, manfully (if ineffectively) opposed by the two radicals, Fox and Cranmer. The result was a much clearer compromise than the *Ten Articles* had been. Indeed, the *Bishops' Book* has a distinct but moderate evangelical essence, but this, as in the case of the former, owes much more to royal future plans than to current spiritual needs.[339] Although such items as the inclusion of all seven sacraments was trumpeted by some as a noteworthy accomplishment[340], for instance, and other statements removed identifiable Catholic or Lutheran aspects, we see from the only eye-witness report that the basic question was now the source of authentic spiritual authority. For the evangelicals, this was the word of God as expressed in scripture – *sola scriptura*. For the conservatives, the basis of authority was different – partially scripture, partially the ancient Fathers and church canons and partially the 'unwritten or unspoken' word of God often found in traditional ceremonies and rites. With the determination of modern-day parliamentary whips, Stokesley and Tunstal set out to secure the support of the undecided like Sampson. In his own words, Sampson discussed the lengths to which these two were willing to go:

[In] the tyme off the late buisshop off London when we ware busyed with the germans, and also with the boke. And to bring it to my Lord off durhams remembrance, I wold he shuld call to his memore, that he hath an old boke in greke and in that boke are dyvers things off the old usags and traditions off the old churche. . . . The late buisshop off London also browt other bokes off greke and so they conferred togethere ther bokes . . . how that the late buisshop off london wold be very ernest with me ffor thos old usages off the church, and such as are called old traditions, and that my lord off durham advysed me to the same . . . that he and my late lord off london ware fully bente to mayntayn as many off the old usags and traditions as they myght, and so they seyd it was necessarie to do especially when they appeared by the greke chirche. And as I remember oon especall thing was 'for praying for soules' and that by prayers they ware delyvered from paynes and jn this matir was Seynt augustin browt in for both parties and the messe in greke was browt jn for that purpos . . . that he with the late buisshop off London, was very diligent to serch out jn greke the old canons, as well such as we called 'canones apostolorum', as others.[341]

From this we can discern the conservative plan, a blitz of scholarly texts and Greek canons.[342] Stokesley's own efforts were similarly attested by the eye-witness account of one of the meetings (perhaps the opening session) made by the Scottish Lutheran writer and preacher Alexander Alesius, a guest of Cromwell's.

If there was any residual doubt that the bishops were now entirely dependent upon the king for their legislative authority it was dispelled by the description of the synod's design. According to Alesius, meetings were held at 'the parlamèt housse' (the sub-committees subsequently met also at Lambeth Palace[343]), where 'all the bisshops gathered to gether . . . did rise up and did obeisance unto him [Cromwell] as to their vicar general and after he had saluted them he sate him down in the highest place', after which the usual hierarchy followed around a table.[344] The bishops were told to put aside their differences and 'frindly & louingly dispute among your selues and to cóclude all things by the word of god with out al brauling or scolding'[345] MacCulloch suggests that the king wanted Cromwell to ensure a quick result.

The committee procedure was simple enough. The prelates were to agree collectively on each exposition under their terms of reference, after which Cranmer would pass out a series of questions to the entire synod which he had drafted, dealing with the essentials in dispute based on their answers. The participants were then to write out their reasons and a clear majority would decide each issue.[346] To speed matters along (and no doubt to undermine conservative obstruction), Cromwell had warned them that the king would not suffer the scripture to be wrested & defaced by any glosus, any papistical lawes or by any auctoryte of doctors or councels and moch lesse wil he admit any articles or doctrine not conteyned in the scripture but approued only by cótynuance of tyme and old custome and by unwritton verytes.[347]

According to Alesius, the first item on the agenda was the sacraments. Debate quickly settled the bishops into two opposing camps.

Alesius tells us that his personal *bête noire*, Stokesley, set out to argue the case for all seven sacraments with the encouragement of Lee, Longland, Clerk, Sampson and Rugg. Against him sat Shaxton, Goodrich, Fox, Latimer and Cranmer. The debate went on for quite some time until finally Cranmer resolved to put an end to it. He deplored the petty bickering that the meeting had dissolved into and hoped to restore order by outlining three objectives:

which be the good workes and the true service and honor which pleaseth god . . . whether vane servyce and false honoryng of god and mans tradicyons do bynd mens consciences or no . . . whether the ceremonis of confirmacyon of orders and of annealing and soch other (which can not be proued to be institute of christ nor haue any word in them to certifye us of remissyon of sinnes) ought to be called sacramentes and to be cópared with baptism and the supper of the lord or no.[348]

Cranmer's admonition pleased Alesius and, afterwards, Cromwell asked him to say a few words on the subject.[349]

Alesius suggested that the way forward was to agree first 'of the significacyon of a sacramèt', whether they are ceremonies instituted by Christ in the gospel signifying special or singular virtues or every ceremony in general which might be a token or a sign of a holy thing. If the latter was the case, it followed that there were seven, if not dozens of sacraments. If the former, however, then there were only two – Baptism and the Eucharist. Next he discussed the scriptural evidence.[350] In essence, his argument was that all sacraments must be 'institute of christ or to haue the manifest scripture to prove them or that all sacramentes must haue a significacyó of remissyon of sinnes', standard evangelical opinion.[351] Stokesley vigorously objected and Fox warned Alesius off of further dispute.

At this session, Fox too gave an oration objecting, as had Cranmer, to petty bickering. So pleased was Alesius that he once again began to recite his reasons, although Stokesley interrupted him at several points, defying Cromwell by referring to the Church Fathers:

let us grát that the sacramentes may be gathered out of the word of god, yet are you sarre deceyved if ye think that there is no nother word of god but that which euery sowter and cobler do reade in their mother tong. And if ye think that nothing perteyneth unto the Christen faith but that only that is writton in the byble, than erre ye playnly with the Lutheranes. For S.Johan saith that Jesus did many things which be not writton. And S.Paul commandeth the Thessalonians to obserue and kepe certé unwritton tradicyons and ceremonys.ii.Thessa.ii. Moreover, he him self did preach, not the scripture only by euen also the tradicyons of the elders Act xvi. Finally we haue receyued many things of the and councels by tymes which although thei be not writton in the bible, yet for as mosh as the old doctors of the church do make mencyon of thè, we ought to grant that we receiued them of the apostles, and that thei be of like autoryte with the scripture, and finally that thei may worthily be called the word of god unwritton.[352]

Alesius noted much muttering and smiling among the evangelical bishops, but that the old campaigner defied the vicar-general to his face over such evidence and justified it with biblical sources was worrisome.[353]

Indeed, as Alesius attested, Cromwell concluded this session shortly thereafter, perhaps fearing a further degeneration of the discussion.[354] Alesius resolved to study the issues and return the next day with more arguments against the conservative position, but Cromwell forbade it. He asked him not to return, but said that Alesius could leave any further arguments with him and that these would be addressed to Stokesley directly. Alesius later discovered that the points Stokesley had made about unwritten traditions and word of God were subsequently conceded.

Although self-serving, his book (addressed to the duke of Saxony) well illustrates the struggle that was to face the bishops over every point. This is also shown in what little documentation survives. Much of the evidence, be it concerned with committees or the synod itself, shows how debate had polarised around Stokesley on the one hand, and Fox on the other, the two most intellectually-gifted, but stubborn, prelates. Gardiner, in his own (second-hand) description of what had occurred, noted 'much stoutness' between these two but that, after a fashion, progress was made on whatever issue was at stake: 'Bishop Stokesley would somewhat relent in the form, as Bishop Foxe did the like. And then, as it were in a mean, each part, by placing words by special marks, with a certain understanding protested, the article went forth; and so to a new article, and so from one to another'. Any contradictions were recognised as such and allowed to stand, 'as if . . . saved by a proviso'.[355] Even so, some committee issues were not ultimately included, like the conservative statement on pilgrimages and shrines or the evangelical statement on purgatory.

If, as Rex noted, there is a mild evangelical flavour to the end result, it is clear from the reaction that the conservatives were better pleased by it. The evangelicals tended to excuse their participation. Clerk wrote, for example, that 'in mine opinion it is the most plain, sincere, and solemn doctrine that ever was set forth'.[356] Compare this to Fox's bemoaning of the fact that Cromwell had been unable to attend the final meetings and that they had 'doon . . . the best they coulde'.[357] Similarly, on 21 July, Latimer wrote his apology to Cromwell, noting that

> for, verely, my partt, I hade lever be poor parson of poore Kynton a yen then to contynee thus Busshope of Worcester; natt for ony thynge, that I hade to doo therin, or can doo, but yett, forsoth, it ys a trubulosse thynge to agre uppon a doctryne, every man (I truste) meanmynge well, and yett natt all meanyngye won way. Butt I dobwght natt, butt now, in the ende, we shall agre both won with a nother, and all with the truthe, thowgh sum wyll then mervell

and hoped that despite 'any thynge ether uncerten or unpure' the king would 'att lestway gyffe it sum notte that ytt may apere he percevyth it, thowgh he doo toleratt it for a tyme; so gyvynge place, for a ceason, to the freylte and grosse capacite of hys subjectes'.[358] Audley tried to put a cheerful spin on it, asking Cromwell to 'set forth' this formulary to 'impress it on the minds' of the people, for it 'will do much good for quietness'[359] (probably thinking of the northern rebels). Cranmer must have agreed with Audley, for he issued a mandate that parts of the book be read aloud from the pulpit every Sunday.[360]

Of the result, all seven sacraments were included but not all of them were recognised as equal. Transubstantiation was glossed over and old traditions were accepted but were given less influence on 'those things necessary for salvation' than scripture. The king was no longer impressed with such close argument, however. Over the later months of 1537, and with the expert advise of (soon to be bishops) Day, Heath, Thirlby and Skip (another mixture of evangelical and conservative opinion), he inserted 246 changes. This placed him at the receiving end of Cranmer's indignation[361] but albeit the book was far too long to ever be popular. So, despite Cromwell's repeated admonitions, it was not submitted to either convocation or parliament for ratification and never received the king's official sponsorship. It was led through publication by Fox, just prior to his death, and was rested on the authority of the signatory bishops and theologians. Perhaps for these reasons its significance was unfortunately minimal. This is a shame as it represents a considerable body of theological thought and exegesis. The exposition of the seven sacraments alone is noteworthy.

Cranmer's preoccupation with idolatry and the abuse of images perhaps explains the combination of the first two commandments into one, and elsewhere it is also clear that the bishops had in mind particular targets. As Tjernagel noted, the last two traditional commandments were combined into one and dealt with at length, thereby addressing the Anabaptists' rather lax attitude toward law and private property. Sabbatarianism was disavowed in an admonition against being 'over-scrupulous, or rather superstitious, in abstaining from bodily labour on the holyday'.[362] In the end, a philosophy emerged which drew a distinction between immutable divine law and mutable human legislation or what was actually necessary for salvation and what was indifferent or politically expedient. It created a two-tier exposition of the sacraments, dividing them into those based on the gospel and those based on unwritten verities. This use of Catholic doctrine, based on divine sanction and human expediency, lost the document the pre-eminence it was due but helped the conservatives retrench, which accounts for their praise of it.

The resulting book divided Episcopal and priestly power into the now familiar concepts of *potestas ordinis* and *jurisdictionis*. The bishops were agreed on this one point that, by traditional authorities (now subject to the supreme head) and by the authority of God, the right to make and ordain rules or canons concerning holy days, fasting days and the manner and ceremonies to be used in the ministration of the sacraments, was theirs.[363] There were some valuable formulations and, in fact, the king congratulated them on doing as well as they had 'nothing doubting but that you [being] men of such learning and virtue [as we know you to be] have indeed performed in the whole work . . . worthy and commendable', and accompanied its publication with royal injunctions to at least ensure distribution and compliance.[364] Here we run head long into the problem of foreign events once again.

* * *

## c. The Thirteen Articles, 1538

Caution had to be taken with this new statement, as re-negotiation with the German princes was about to be undertaken. This explains why the royal injunctions of 1538 deal only with the reforming aspects of the *Bishops' Book*. As noted, the Germans requested further talks but, as in 1536, they required additional details about the king's actual commitment to religious reform, his views on the *Augsburg Confession* and *Apology* before they would agree to come to England. Moreover, they wanted Fox sent to them to explain the king's stand on Mantua and his plans for the advancement of God's word at home. To the king, this smacked of having to commit his plans to foreign approval.

He therefore set limits on how far his envoys would be allowed to go. For example, no objections to the official justification of the royal supremacy, the Pole letter, would be permitted. The letter was familiar to the Germans; Henry had instructed his former envoys to take it with them, with copies for circulation on the continent. Despite these conditions the Germans agreed to send three delegates: Franz Burkhardt, Georg von Boineburg (a Hessian scholar) and Friedrich Myconius (a high-ranking churchman of Gotha). While hardly on par with Melanchthon, these second-rank theologians were competent enough and, perhaps, all Henry could have expected. They arrived on 31 May 1538.

After a number of preliminary meetings, the diplomatic niceties were performed and discussions were transferred to Lambeth under Cranmer's chairmanship.[365] Delays ensued and problems formulated which raised questions over the king's commitment. The Germans did not trust the men he had commissioned to assist Cranmer, which included Heath, Sampson and Stokesley (much to Cranmer's dismay[366]). Day was also included, as was Nicholas Wilson (another conservative and royal chaplain) and later Tunstal was added to the English side. The inclusion of hard-line conservatives was only one of several difficulties, however, and one suspects the king was again looking for a variety of views. Even so, the German envoys took up discussions in earnest on several contentious points armed with a summary of their thirteen most important beliefs. These included views on the Trinity, original sin and on the dual nature of Christ and, with their English counterparts, examined the doctrine of justification, the nature of the Church, Baptism and much else.

Initial reports back to their German masters were favourable, but setbacks were inevitable. The English could not ratify anything without first committing their opinions to paper and afterwards ascertaining the king's views. The Germans noted that while Henry had 'promised all his study to the correction of the church'[367], in reality this meant he would only take further council.[368] Cranmer indicated to Richard Morison that he would have been content to settle on several issues but Stokesley proved maddeningly immovable and, moreover, seemed to be pursuing a hidden agenda. Whether he had the king's expressed approval for his stalling actions is unknown, but he appeared determined to debate the Germans to a standstill on every point (nor did the king seem too upset by this). By the same token, the king brought Tunstal along on his summer progress through the southern ports, so all the reports from Lambeth were being filtered through another doctrinaire theologian. By 5 August, the Germans thought that they had accomplished everything they could reasonably expect. They drew up their conclusions and sent these off to the king, requesting permission to go home within ten days.[369] Cranmer blamed Stokesley for the sluggish pace of the talks and for their eventual failure to produce anything significant.[370] In reality, the Germans recognised early on that three key issues – the sacrament in both kinds, private masses and clerical celibacy – were unlikely to have been resolved in any case as the king was clearly unwilling to negotiate.

The personal appeal in their letter on these issues, however, in a seventy-two-page document outlining their views, was a mistake.[371] Henry replied with a statement of his own, filtered through Tunstal, which basically devastated their arguments and put off their criticisms to such a time as he could meet with his own divines once again at some unspecified future date.[372] At the end of September, when the Germans finally left, the king sent along a letter to the duke that, 'the embassy had given evidence of sound erudition and Christian piety'. It was clear that he would accept no one less than Melanchthon himself if negotiations were to have any real meaning for him.[373] That is not to say that the negotiations had been a complete waste of time.

One tangible, if largely ignored, result was a document of thirteen articles agreed by both sides, much after the *Augsburg Confession* but less clearly Lutheran. Officially, it was ignored by both England and Germany, accepted by neither king nor convocation[374], but that was not where its significance lay. This document reveals that the agenda of the English bishops was still specifically on minority radical religious views (i.e. Anabaptists and Sacramentarians), prevalent at the time. Like the two formularies preceding it, the articles modified further the Lutheran doctrine of justification, stating that, while men could only be justified by grace obtained through faith, 'good works are necessary to salvation'. Later, the Act of Six Articles went much further in addressing the problem of minority religions.

The *Thirteen Articles* dealt only with doctrinal issues and the only tangible action taken in the immediate aftermath was the capture and banishment of some Anabaptists by the combined efforts of bishops Stokesley and Cranmer. For the king, concerned still with his international position, all thoughts were turning to Cromwell's idea of a foreign-born princess bride.[375] By sending Barnes, now described not as 'royal chaplain' but as mere 'household servant'[376] to Saxony, the king betrayed his own waning interest in religious negotiation. The Lutheran princes' continuous demand that he agree to their own confessional position undermined what little interest remained, not to mention the need for a workable settlement in England itself. Moreover, the world had turned once again in 1538 and it was made clear to Henry that neither Charles V nor Francis I had any real designs for conflict with him. If the flirtation with the Germans had ever been anything more than that, it was now clearly over; the Act of Six Articles put paid to it.

* * *

## d. The Act of Six Articles, 1539

The king had a particular agenda. This was to have been that long awaited definitive statement on disputed religious issues and international security. Moreover, certain bishops, Tunstal, Stokesley, Gardiner, Cranmer and Latimer included, took a very close and keen interest in the development of this act along predictably factional lines.[377] This being the case, neither the king, nor any of the bishops, got what they wanted. The act was not a statement of unadulterated Catholic dogma, but the conservative bishops did get the most out of it. This begs the question of whether one of these men was now directing the king's thinking.

Redworth certainly thought so. He speculated, in a magisterial article devoted to the act, that the close connection in timing between the new negotiations with the Lutheran theologians and the act itself, not to mention the subject matter, suggested Tunstal had captured the king's ear. This is certainly a logical conclusion. The bishop had shown himself opposed to the 1538 negotiations, had advised the king throughout the summer months, had been present at the 1539 talks and, indeed, had been appointed to the 5 May committee in the lords developing the act. One minor problem with this speculation, however, is that Tunstal was not a theologian.[378]

I have speculated elsewhere that perhaps it was Stokesley who had captured the king's ear. That bishop had been present at the 1538 negotiating table (at the king's command), possibly representing the king's own arguments. He seemed, at least, to have *carte blanche* to pursue his own agenda. He had sat on the heresy commission of the same year, had saved the king's propaganda trial against Lambert and, in addition, had laid the groundwork for the 1539 convocation. His letters summoned the clergy for June, 'to treat matters relating to the security and defense of the church'.[379] Most important, however, was that he was a theologian and someone the king had depended on in the past. Indeed, Stokesley was, with Gardiner, the driving force behind the act in both the lords and in convocation.[380]

Again and again these two bishops were accused by the German commentators as the chief sponsors of the act through the lords. Burkhardt named them in his letter to Melanchthon[381] who, himself, commented on the ability of these two bishops to keep all of the Roman abuses in the church as if they had been 'brought down as new philosophies from heaven', roughly upbraiding Cranmer for not having done enough to stop them.[382] In a joint letter with Hans von Dolzig to the elector of Saxony, he branded Stokesley an enemy of the gospel, the culprit moving the bill through parliament.[383] This opinion was echoed in a joint letter of Melanchthon, Luther, Jonas and Bugenhagen to the elector on 23 October 1539.[384] Indeed, three years later, Gardiner's critic William Turner reminded him of his and Stokesley's joint responsibility for the framing of the act.[385] None of this means Redworth was wrong. Indeed, whether any one individual influenced the king is ultimately beside the point. All three bishops (as we shall see) had obvious influence over the finished product. The direction of the king's thinking is clear from early 1538 in any case.

On 5 May, Audley addressed the lords, relaying the king's desire for religious unity, informing the members that 'they should choose a committee of themselves to examine into these different opinions'.[386] What emerged was another vice-gerential synod manned by a precise division of conservative and evangelical bishops, including both archbishops and bishops Latimer, Goodrich, Capon, Tunstal, Clerk and Aldrich. The chance to claim the support of all shades of theological opinion was obviously too useful to forgo. It is widely suspected, however, that Henry had already concluded on the matter and was now merely going through the motions. As the evangelicals were in the minority on the Episcopal bench, their equal representation on the committee of inquiry suggests it was formed at the king's bidding. Still, only Cranmer, Latimer, Tunstal and Lee were scholars of note and they are roughly equally matched, so perhaps it does not matter. The committee argued, discussed and debated until only 16 May; eleven days in which no headway was made and in which little could reasonably have been expected.

Thomas Howard came in to order its discussions with six specific questions having an obvious Catholic bias[387] and moved the discussions back into the lords[388] proper, while the king informed Cranmer that the debate would be widened to include the entire upper house (with its in-built conservative majority). Surviving records show only sporadic attendance among the senior clerics, however.[389] This suggested to MacCulloch, logically enough, that the conservatives and evangelicals were hiving themselves off into private huddles and brainstorming sessions. The king's frequent participation in the meetings and clear favour for the conservatives, however, put Cranmer and the radicals on the defensive and led to some unusual parliamentary proceedings.

Cromwell, who on the surface could do nothing but support the king, introduced a money bill into the lords to divide their time and attention between the two issues. In this way he could hamper the religious discussions and put off for a time the seemingly inevitable loss of the reformation initiative. Audley, perhaps in response, asked the king for a prorogation (which would have cancelled both bills). Seeing this for what it was, and fearing this flanking attack, the conservatives might well have appealed to the duke of Norfolk, who requested that there should be only a week-long recess. Cromwell convinced the king to grant the prorogation with a special clause allowing both bills to continue. While the king and Cromwell carried on with another German representation to no avail and to Cromwell's utter annoyance, the clerics of southern convocation (with some northerners observing) met at St Paul's to continue the religious discussion.

In this pseudo-vice-gerential synod, points of doctrine were argued out and voted upon (with the king's frequent participation) and finally hammered into a final format. When parliament reassembled on 30 May, Audley informed the peers that the king and the lords spiritual were in agreement '*nunc Unio in eisdem confecta sit*'.[390] Some conservative wag (possibly from the lords) also took note of these proceedings and made light of the evangelicals' hard efforts. Although Cranmer, Goodrich, Shaxton, Latimer, Hilsey and Barlow (evangelicals all) 'defended the contrary long time' they were finally 'confounded' by the king's own wisdom. On the other hand, 'York, Durham, Winchester, London, Chichester, Norwich and Carlisle have shewed themselves honest and well learned men'.[391] The faction struggled, apart from the operation of the two committees established to hammer out the punishments (wherein Gardiner took a leading role[392]), which had been completed and won by the conservatives. Our comedian tells us that Shaxton could not accept it and 'continueth a lewd fool'. If not a rout, just how clear a victory was the act for the conservatives?

In its final form, the first article, a statement on the sacrament of the Altar, reads: 'By the strength and efficacy of Christ's mighty word, it being spoken by the priest, is present really, under the form of bread and wine, the natural body and blood'. Catholic dogma depended on the philosophical acceptance that there were two aspects to the reality of objects: 'accidents' (the substance immediately apparent to the senses) and 'essences' (the intangible quality which marked out the identity of an object). Article one thus affirmed Catholic thinking: 'after the consecration there remaineth no substance of bread or wine, nor any other substance but the substance of Christ, God and man'. The fact that the word transubstantiation was not inserted was a concession to Cranmer but mattered very little otherwise. On the same doctrinal matter, the second article held that communion of both kinds was unnecessary, affirming concomitance, an issue to which Stokesley's stubborn adherence had been the subject of evangelical broadsides.[393]

If it is necessary to look for figures to praise (or blame?) for any particular doctrine outlined in the new act, the third article rejecting clerical marriage could give us one good clue. It would surely have come as no surprise to the German negotiators, seeing as they had been so recently in close quarters with Stokesley, that he, more so than anyone else, had made his thinking on this issue crystal clear. During the Patmore heresy trial, the bishop had been quoted as saying to a married priest that he 'had better have a hundred whores than be married to his own wife'.[394] On a similar subject, the fourth article stated that 'vows of chastity or widowhood by man and woman made to God advisedly ought to be observed by the law of God'. The fifth article, on private masses, recognised them as 'meet and necessary (to be) continued and admitted in this the king's English Church and Congregation', a doctrine which had also been defended before the German theologians. The sixth article, despite its ranking, was possibly the most contentious and over-laden with faction overtones. It recommended that 'auricular confession is expedient and necessary to be retained and continued'.

When the convocation had considered this issue in the presence of the king, Tunstal, Gardiner and Lee had tried to persuade him and their fellows that divine law required auricular confession. They had taken this position against Cranmer and those of their less dogmatic brethren who had taken a less binding view. In fact, Tunstal could not relinquish the point after the king had declared himself with the archbishop, and unwisely sent him further evidences gleaned from the Fathers and scripture. As Redworth noted, the king was not impressed with this and continued to deny that auricular confession was divine law. He sent Tunstal a rather harsh, but well thought-out, written reply:

> Since methought (my lord of Durham) that both the bishops of York, Winchester, and your reasons and texts were so fully answered this other day in our House as to my seeming and suppoal the most of the House was satisfied, I marvel not a little way estsoons you have sent me this now your writing, being in manner few other texts or reasons then were declared both by the bishop of Canterbury and me to make smally or nothing to your intended purpose.[395]

The king's position reflected the *Ten Articles*, which Tunstal and Stokesley had both tried to amend through the *Bishops' Book*. On this point at least, the more radical bishops had got their way; a minor victory. On the other hand, justification by faith alone was nowhere hinted.

Attached to the articles were enforcement provisions establishing penalties for transgressions. The most severe was the first which enacted that 'any who after 12 July 1539 in words, writing or printing "publish, preach, teach, say, affirm, declare, dispute, argue or hold" contrary to the first article, as well as their supporters, shall be guilty of heresy and burned'. Transgressions of the remaining articles were considered felony offences. Enforcement of the provisions was given to 'special periodic commissions directed by the king to archbishops and bishops', as had that one set up so recently against the Anabaptists. The king also now affirmed the 'ordinary power of the ecclesiastical courts to enquire into offences', thus mitigating the provisions of the 1533 Heresy Act.

Though not a complete conservative victory, the implied humiliation of Cromwell in front of the Germans, the ending of his domination of religion and the arrests and forced resignations of Cranmer's ideological allies (Latimer and Shaxton) must have given them no small satisfaction, however.[396] Indeed, they were both replaced by conservatives. If Capon, who replaced Shaxton at Salisbury, was somewhat watered-down, at least John Bell, who replaced Latimer at Worcester, was a more solid traditionalist. Indeed, the punishment provisions allowed the most doctrinaire of them all, Stokesley, to make immediate moves against subversives in London.

Hall recorded that nearly 500 people were almost immediately presented to the bishop on heresy charges. The speed of this effort took even Cromwell aback: 'in short time after scourged a great number in the city of London, where the first quest for the inquiry of the offenders of the said statute sat at a church called Becket's house', with members hand-picked by the bishop. Stokesley also brought forth measures against the reading of the Bible in English and rounded up those who possessed a copy. Moreover, he ordered the detainment of several preachers who had supported reading vernacular scripture and other book, as well as those who had spoken out against private masses, those who seldom attended them, and in particular, harassed those who had questioned the doctrine of the Eucharist. It seems clear that he had anticipated every possible outcome to the recent parliamentary session, as he rounded up those

> who held not up their hands at sacring time, and knocked not on their breasts, And they not only inquired who offended in the six articles, but also who came seldom to the church, who took no holy bread nor holy water, who read the Bible in the church, or in communication condemned priests or images in the churches and many others, with a great number of such branches, that in fourteen days space there was not a preacher or other person in the city of name which had spoken against the supremacy of the Bishop of Rome but he was wrapped in the six articles, insomuch as they indicted and presented of suspicion to the number of five hundred persons and above.

Hall noted Audley's report that even before anyone really knew the extent of Stokesley's actions, 'a great many of them which already was in prison, had been shortly after scourged at Smithfield with fiery faggots'.[397] The bishop had been well prepared to act, had anticipated the new atmosphere and had carried out as much activity as he could before the almost inevitable royal change of heart which precedent said was sure to come. Lucky for him he died believing that orthodoxy had been restored. That this was an optimistic assumption became clear almost immediately. By the end of 1539 the king was once again flirting with the Lutheran princes, and by April 1540 (when the use of the *Bishops' Book* officially expired), he appealed to the bishops once again to examine the issues.

* * *

## 9. The final years of the reign

In the 1530s it had been the case that the king had stood slightly to the ideological right of his bishops. This was due to both domestic and international needs and to the search for a theology of accommodation. Whereas renewed warfare with France, resignations, natural deaths, executions and statutes (like the Act concerning True Opinions) would mould the Episcopate into a conservative body once again (with obvious limited exceptions), events of the 1540s make it clear that the king now stood slightly to their ideological left in his desire for a balanced doctrinal stance. Along with this, the 1540s were less theologically charged than had been the 1530s. Obviously, the deaths of Stokesley, Kite, Clerk, and the removal of Latimer and Shaxton explain this but that said there was some ideological conflict still and again the king appealed to his bishops for spiritual advice.

Evangelical leadership would soon (with the fall of Cromwell) be firmly settled on the shoulders of Cranmer, with Barlow and Goodrich in support (all three were theologians). Conservative leadership was more in question. Stokesley's replacement at London was the former bishop of Hereford, Edmund Bonner, whose opinions, although changing fast were at this time mildly evangelical. Either side could not rely upon Sampson and Tunstal was in exile once again in Durham. He had concerns of his own in the north and was again not trusted by the regime, as was the case with Lee. Gardiner emerged as the new leader. While he did not enjoy the same royal support as Cranmer (the Prebendaries' Plot of 1543 should prove this to anyone's satisfaction), the king often walked a balance between their views because he could not do without Gardiner's savvy diplomatic skills. Although the Plot and the war with France will not be part of our discussions, they will be kept in the background as explanations for the rapidly shifting ideological sands upon which the bishops stood.[398] This shifting is most apparent in the king's response to the prelates' answers to the seventeen questions and in the subsequent drafting of the king's own book of 1543.

* * *

## a. The Seventeen Questions, 1540

The king appointed two committees in April 1540 to deal with religious issues. One was a group of bishops and theologians established to examine doctrine, while the other was a group of bishops established to assess the need for liturgical ceremonies.[399] The second group set about the examination of seventeen set questions[400] dealing with a limited selection of issues. Numbers one to seven (and seventeen) dealt with the scriptural foundation, definitions and purposes of the sacraments, number eight dealt with confirmation, nine to twelve dealt with clerical and Episcopal authority and the link to royal authority, thirteen and fourteen dealt with whether a king could perform sacerdotal function and create priests and bishops, number fifteen dealt with confession and sixteen with excommunication.[401] The middle six questions are by far the most interesting as they betray 'a propensity to underline monarchical power at the expense of ecclesiastical authority'.[402]

The documentary evidence offers up a unique opportunity to position certain bishops (and a number of other theologians and future bishops). We can do this according to their theological beliefs and how they dealt with the inevitable problem of the validity of unwritten tradition. Recall that this question had dogged Episcopal discussions since 1537. Cranmer, Lee, Bonner, Heath and Aldrich, along with future bishop Day, agreed that there was no specific definition of a sacrament in scripture. They also agreed, against other theologians (but with Thirlby), that a sacrament, according to ancient writers, was a 'visible form of invisible grace' of which there are potentially several more than the traditional seven. Edward Lee stood apart on this point, maintaining that the seven traditional sacraments could be ascertained through the works of the ancient authors and in scripture, to which Barlow agreed with regard to only Baptism, the Altar, Matrimony and Penance. Indeed, of the traditional seven specifically, only Lee, Heath, Aldrich and Day maintained them all. Cranmer and Barlow were willing to subscribe only those three agreed in 1536 and Matrimony. On the question of penance, however, Cranmer broke with tradition by denying the power of confession and absolution, while Bonner, for whatever reason, seemed unable to clearly address the issue.

The fifth question, on whether the word 'sacrament' ought to be applied only to the traditional seven and whether these are found in the ancient authors, caused the first real stir. Cranmer, Skip, Barlow, Day, and future bishop Cox, provided the dissenting view. They wrote that the word ought not to be attributed to the traditional seven, but were opposed by the majority, including Lee, Bonner, Heath, Aldrich and other theologians who had no difficulties accepting traditional views. Whether or not the number of sacraments was a doctrinal matter caused a similar division. Cranmer, Tunstal, Skip, Barlow, Heath, Thirlby and Day wrote that the prescribed number of sacraments is nowhere found, while Bonner, Lee and some of the theologians dissented (no scriptural citations given, however). As to whether the number of sacraments was a doctrinal matter and to be taught as such, Skip, Barlow and Cox disagreed while Lee, Bonner, Aldrich and Day agreed that it was. On the most important question with regard to the sacraments, the traditional interpretation of the Eucharist, the bishops and theologians agreed to the traditional Catholic form. Even Cranmer, who was prepared to question confession and absolution, as yet expressed the traditional view. The next series of questions, dealing with priestly and royal power, were answered largely as one might now expect from a group of royal servants.

Cranmer was willing to go furthest and stated that 'all Christian princes have committed unto them . . . the cure of all their subjects', including the creation of priests and the consecration of bishops.[403] The others were unwilling to go so far. Barlow wrote that bishops did not have the power to create priests without the permission of the ruler. Heath modified this by agreeing that the bishops had the power, but could not use it without the prince's permission. Lee, Tunstal, Heath, Aldrich, Thirlby and Day held that only bishops have this authority and that a king cannot ordain. The panel was split along the same lines over the question of the necessity of consecration, with Bonner joining Lee, Tunstal and Aldrich on the positive side according to scriptural evidence, with Heath and Day dissenting on the scriptural evidence but holding consecration to be consistent with established tradition. Similarly, question thirteen asked whether a layman could ordain within the special circumstance of being in an infidel land. Cranmer, of course, was willing to accept this idea. Perhaps surprisingly Tunstal accepted it too, as did, less surprisingly, Barlow and Thirlby. Lee would not hear of it, and Bonner, Aldrich and Heath accepted the proposition provided there was evidence of some special divine intervention (as in the case of St Paul).

Question fifteen explored the very important point of auricular confession. We know from the debates in 1539 the opinions of Cranmer, Lee, Tunstal and Gardiner. The act had made it clear that confession was properly retained and considered useful, but not that it was scripturally justified. This was still the majority view. Bonner, Heath, Aldrich and Day supported the more traditional position while Barlow swung in behind Cranmer. It would appear from the answers to the most relevant points that the bishops, with the exception of Cranmer, had indeed become more traditionally minded.

What is amazing is that these doctrinal committees ever managed to get anything done. Ignoring the fact that what emerged was ultimately of little use, the atmosphere in which they worked could not have been less conducive to success. Only a week after it was set up, the synod was re-established as a heresy commission to examine Alexander Seton.[404] Moreover, the meetings took place in a very hostile political and religious atmosphere. They sat during the ultimate rise to the peerage and rapid fall of Cromwell, through the dissolution of the Cleves' marriage and the new Howard marriage (which both necessitated all new committees) and amidst the Gardiner-Barnes-Cranmer doctrinal disputes at St Paul's Cross.

These matters, and the experience of past committees, should render the fortunes of this mini-synod unexpected. In the end, the work was taken out of the hands of the larger committee and delegated to a smaller group of six: bishops Thirlby, Heath and Day, and theologians Redmen, Cox and Thomas Robertson. It is also possible that bishops Capon and Skip had a hand in the new committee, but this is unreliable information.[405] As we shall see, rather than do anything very original with the material, when the time came the committee merely recopied the *Bishops' Book* using heavily Catholic amendments and presented it to convocation in April 1543 as the *King's Book*.

Although there was an in-built conservative majority on the bench and in convocation, as Rex pointed out most of the religious events of the period reflected more the bishops' so-called 'Henrician' leanings. Use of the vernacular in sermons, prayers, catechises and primers were largely accepted by the bishops (although it did meet some popular resistance), while the traditional liturgy remained much as it had always been. A new edition of Coverdale's translation was released in a cheaper edition in 1540, as was a new edition of the Sarum Breviary. In 1542, southern convocation agreed that the Sarum Use would be the official liturgy of the province with a thorough revision of all Sarum service books following in 1543. All was in line with Henrician thinking in the 1530s and all based on the need for uniformity.[406] If these events represented religious change in favour of evangelicals, the conservative leadership still had one or two cards up their collective sleeve.

We saw Bonner's problem with people using the vernacular Bible to their own ends. This underpinned an initiative of Gardiner's against the Great Bible in a convocation of 1542. The more traditionally-minded prelates worked on the king's hatred of discord among the laity over spiritual issues until he agreed to allow the convocation to examine the question of errors in religion. This included that revision of canon law, which Cranmer had long desired, errors in the vernacular Bible and the creation of a collection of official homilies.[407] These were initiatives which divided the prelates once again and which were ultimately undermined by the development of the *King's Book*.

* * *

## b. The King's Book, 1543

For the events in the convocation of 1543 we have no better explanatory source than Lehmberg. On 21 February, Cranmer announced that the king wanted service books examined and revised and he assigned Capon (a moderate conservative) and Goodrich (a moderate evangelical) to oversee the project. There were some other initiatives (as referred to earlier) over which no one seemed particularly put out. This was not the case when the convocation reconvened following the Easter recess. Those materials produced by the committees in 1540 were reintroduced along with the long-awaited order to revise the *Bishops' Book*. There is some confusion, however, as to the exact chronology of events.

It seems that the convocation, as a whole, examined several new proposals made by a royal committee of Heath, Thirlby, Day and Capon.[408] These new proposals were based on a revision of the old formulary over a number of sessions between 20 and 30 April, along with a series of sub-committees examining individual items (MacCulloch mentions at least five examining the Lord's Prayer, the Hail Mary, the Ten Commandments, the Creed and the Sacraments[409]). By 5 May, a new formulary was ready for publication, having been approved by both convocation and king. It was entitled *A Necessary Doctrine and Erudition for any Christian Man*, more widely known as the *King's Book*.

We need not reiterate the many examinations of the book here. Certainly, it was a more conservative statement than its predecessor[410] of 1537 in that, for example, it affirmed the intercessionary power of saints while the *Bishops' Book* had referred only to Christ's power. Moreover, it reaffirmed the traditional beliefs with regard to the sacraments. For example, the Act of Six Articles was echoed in that, with regard to transubstantiation, the 'bread and wine do not remain still in their own substance, but by virtue of Christ's word in the consecration be changed and turned to the very substance of the body and blood of our Saviour Jesu Christ.'[411] Similarly, it reaffirms the place of satisfaction in the sacrament of penance: 'to the obtaining of the which absolution or sacrament of penance be required contrition, confession, and satisfaction, as ways and means expedient and necessary to obtain the said absolution'.[412] As Rex pointed out, the articles on the place of free will, justification and good works all took on a 'decisively anti-Protestant line'. Perhaps Cranmer had lost the debate on salvation in committee?[413] The only less-traditional section was the last one on prayers for souls departed. The word 'purgatory' was dropped from the text and, similarly, all mention of 'pain' was deleted from the tradition. The article enjoined prayers for the dead not because of their pains (as had been mentioned in the *Ten Articles*), nor because of uncertainty about their state (for only God knows their 'estate and condition'[414]) but because they are part of the mystical body of Christ in which all members, both quick and dead, are bound by charity to intercede for one another.[415]

This has been seen as a great conservative triumph and, perhaps, it was. In reality, little could be made of it. Gardiner would see more of the continent than his see over the remainder of the reign, only to return to England, make a monumental political error (in refusing certain land-exchanges with the king) and be excluded from political influence until the mid-1550s. Gone too was Sampson. Although never a mainstay of the conservatives, his translation in 1542 to the diocese of Coventry and Lichfield (making him president of the Council of Wales into the bargain), effectively removed him from London and theological events. Similarly, Tunstal was increasingly engaged in affairs for the Council of the North, and Longland, still bishop of Lincoln and royal confessor, was fearful after his arrest in 1541 and, subsequently, too old to have had much further impact.[416]

True, ideologically, the conservatives had won the battles, but the war had moved on to the political front. There, the evangelicals had entrenched themselves into superior positions around the king and court early on, positions from which they could not be extracted by their conservative opponents. In 1544, for instance, the more severe penal aspects of the Act of Six Articles and the Act for the Advancement of True Religion were relaxed. Cranmer sponsored the bill, opposed by Gardiner but, surprisingly enough, supported in the later stages by Heath, Day and Holbeach, men upon whom Gardiner had once depended.[417] In 1545, the chantries and collegiate endowments were surrendered over to the king, dissolutions ordered ostensibly for monetary reasons. Although no mention was made in the bill, with regard to prayers for the souls of the dead, these dissolutions would have a negative impact. This ideological nod toward evangelical theory was spin-doctored to great effect by Crome in his sermon of Passion Sunday, 1546.[418] The articles he had signed in the early 1530s were long forgotten.

MacCulloch suggested that this was, in fact, a thought balloon floated to gauge reaction. No doubt the king's brief flirtation with the papal nuncio, Gurone Bertano, should be seen in a similar light. Would Henry VIII, at this late stage, really arrange a new accommodation with Rome? We can never know for certain, although he did briefly consider sending delegates to the next session of Trent. This was followed almost immediately by a suggestion to the French peace envoy, the Admiral Claude d'Annebaut, that if Francis I was amenable to the idea, the two kings should 'change the mass in both the realms into a communion'. Shortly hereafter, the king was once again making friendly overtures to the Schmalkaldic League with regard to opposing the emperor.[419] Despite these odd perambulations, the reign of Henry VIII drew to a close in 1547 with the conservative leadership in exile, in prison or dead, and the evangelicals firmly lodged at court around the young new king, Edward VI.

* * *

## c. The last few Episcopal appointments

Clearly, the last years of the reign witnessed a more indeterminate attitude on the extremes of ecclesiastical matters. The king turned his attentions more and more towards foreign policy and war with France. He maintained equilibrium in spiritual affairs between the extremes of Gardiner and Cranmer; some have termed this *via media*. His waning interests, however, seem amply demonstrated by the calibre of those men he nominated to the Episcopal bench in the 1540s (mostly conservative non-entities and men who would not cause trouble).

Arthur Bulkeley, for example, was a jurist by education and had spent the majority of his clerical career in the relative obscurity of Wales. When he was promoted to the see of Bangor in 1541, he was not heard from thereafter and never left the diocese. Likewise, Paul Bush, a theologian and sometime royal chaplain, having been displaced from his Edington priorship at its dissolution in 1537, sank into obscurity until his creation as bishop of Bristol in 1542. In her study, however, Martha Skeeters made very little of his Episcopate and another writer made it clear that Bush more or less followed whatever current religious trend there happened to be. That said, in this way he lasted until 1553, forced out for having married under Edward VI.[420] There is not a great deal more that can be written about John Chambers either. Like Bush, he was a theologian by training, displaced from his position as abbot of Peterborough. He too became a royal chaplain for a time and was created bishop of Peterborough in 1541 only to be unheard from thereafter. This career path becomes a tedious pattern.

If Thirlby, Day and Knight were at least well-known prior to their Episcopal promotions, they are balanced by the likes of Henry Holbeach (who replaced Heath at Rochester), Robert King (first bishop of Oseney and Thame in 1541, renamed Oxford in 1545), Anthony Kitchen (bishop of Llandaff in 1545) and John Wakeman (bishop of Gloucester in 1541) men who, more or less, conform to the Bush-Bulkeley standard. Wakeman, for instance, merely rode the tides of ecclesiastical change, holding a couple of rather mechanical visitations (in 1542 and 1547), and was conscientious without being inconvenient.[421] There can be little surprise that not much is known of these other men, as they rarely participated in the events of the period.

Of the bishops still hanging on from the 1530s, however, most were given little opportunity to make trouble. Gardiner was dispatched to the emperor in 1540 and attended the diet of Regensberg. Also in 1540, Aldrich of Carlisle was ordered to return north, 'there to remain for the feeding of the people both with his preaching and good hospitality'.[422] Tunstal spent most of his time in Durham. Cranmer, who had played second fiddle to Cromwell, found his position not much improved by the vicar-general's death. He remained in Canterbury, promoting mildly reformed measures, dealing with image-breaking iconoclasts in Kent and a serious, but ultimately minor, plot in his own Cathedral. If the men themselves were not particularly famous, it is also the case that the events of the 1540s have received short shrift too.

The royal injunctions of 1538 were still very much in force in the early 1540s and most of the bishops were happy enough to enforce them or to issue new injunctions which did not depart too far from them. The king's tour of the north brought the message home that abuses in the church were still apparent, and he wrote to Cranmer in October of 1541 to draft injunctions against them. As a result, Goodrich, who was growing more conservative by the minute, issued his own injunctions for Ely dealing almost entirely with the abuse of images (a safe subject). Cranmer had sent out a letter to the southern prelates after the king's orders and Goodrich did little more than his duty, repeating parts of the 1538 injunctions *verbatim*.[423] Cranmer, in fact, did little more than this in his own injunctions for All Souls College, Oxford.[424] Of somewhat greater interest, however, were Bonner's activities in the London diocese.

Bonner, as we have seen, was accounted a reformer in religion and a supporter of Bible translations in the 1530s. He had promised that he would do as much as he could to further the cause of the evangelicals and had placed six copies in St Paul's before he departed on another diplomatic mission to France in early 1540.[425] That said, he soon discovered what Stokesley had known all along; that the common folk could not be trusted to read the scripture with the reverence it deserved. By May 1541, he had issued an order threatening the removal of the Bibles if certain 'insolent and indiscreet' persons did not restrain from 'brabbling' the gospel.[426] As Brigden wrote, these orders fell on deaf ears and the heresy problem in London grew dangerously violent as a result.[427] Consequential to Cranmer's letter, Bonner set up an inquisition that same month, the results of which were negligible.[428] He produced an index of forbidden works, much after Stokesley's index of 1531, and secured a new commission to make inquiries under the Act of Six Articles, much as Stokesley had done in 1539.[429] The upshot of such activity was that the king was forced to admit that perhaps more restrictions on reading of the Bible needed to be enforced across the board.

In order to consider action, southern convocation was held on 20 January 1542. The conservative prelates had now come around to Stokesley's thinking that a vernacular scripture was more trouble than it was worth, particularly the Great Bible with its dangerous errors and evangelical slant. According to Lehmberg's account of these parliamentary and convocational sessions, Cranmer put the question before the bishops on 3 February whether the Great Bible could be retained 'without scandal, error, and manifest offence to Christ's faithful people'. The majority of those present voted that it might be revised to good effect.[430] Their examinations were widened shortly thereafter to consider all 'errors in religion'. It seems clear that this was leading up to a repeat of the earlier attempts to revise the Bible in that, on 13 February, individual bishops and theologians were assigned certain scriptures to examine and revise.

Gardiner was particularly enthusiastic for the project and incurred out of pocket expenses to have the Great Bible 'devided into quieres in the Convocation Howse', in order to compile a list of controversial English terms.[431] Cranmer went so far as to name two committees on the project. The New Testament was assigned to Tunstal, Gardiner, Skip, Heath and Thirlby (with some other theologians) and the Old Testament to Lee, Goodrich and others expert in the original Biblical languages.[432] The effort, if we can take it seriously, ultimately led to nothing as Cranmer announced on 10 March that the king had decided to take the matter out of the prelates' hands and leave the examination and revision to the universities.

The senior clerics (save Cranmer, Barlow and Goodrich) objected to the idea that the universities were better suited to the project then themselves, but to little avail. They persisted, and finally in 1543, the king allowed himself to be persuaded on the need for an act of parliament to prohibit Bible reading among women and the lower orders. According to MacCulloch, however, the conservative bishops took some more immediate petty revenge in strenuously arguing for more traditional translations of key biblical texts, and in the wrecking of Cranmer's initiative to allow married civil lawyers to hold positions in the ecclesiastical legal machinery.[433] By 1546, in fact, a list of forbidden books would include the Bible in English. The arguments of the past two years did have a wider impact than on vernacular scripture, however.

Bonner issued injunctions for the London diocese in 1542, very much after previous ones but not without some interest. He reinforced the use of the royal injunctions of 1538, but now forbade preachers from reciting the sermons of those doctors of the church who were only some two or three hundred years old, preferring the works of ancient writers. Also, he ordered the clergy to familiarise themselves with the Bible as fully as they could manage, perhaps in an effort to take the initiative away from certain radicals.[434] Bonner also evinced his interests in educational reform. After the example of Shaxton's injunctions for Salisbury, he directed his attention towards instructions in reading, religion and virtue for the illiterate and semi-literate masses.[435] He also recognised the needs of the preaching ministry and pursued the matter as late as 1545. Bonner wrote a letter to Matthew Parker at Cambridge enquiring about why so few members of the university had come to preach at St Paul's Cross. He wanted to see more of them in the future and he assigned special preachers to refute condemned doctrine.[436]

Bonner's injunctions, according to one of his biographers, had been designed to reform the religious and social ills that plagued the diocese in the mid-1540s. All members of the clergy were to have and employ copies of the 1538 and 1542 injunctions and the *Bishops' Book*. He also tried to act against plurality by the requirement of licensing curates, and all who were absent at the time of the injunctions (April 1542) were to be in residence permanently before Michaelmas or else exhibit royal dispensations for their absenteeism. The injunctions also evince his attempt to introduce certain social reforms.

For example, people were to refrain from marriage with the previously married, unless a document existed asserting the death of the former spouse, priests were to mediate disputes between their parishioners, keepers of alehouses and taverns were to close on Sundays, holidays and in times of divine service or preaching, confessions would be enforced and all priests were to be vetted by the bishop and his officers before they could carry out their duties.

Bonner was not the only active diocesan by any means, and 1543 seems to have been a pivotal year. Nicholas Heath, for instance, also issued injunctions for Rochester.

This was Heath's last act in Rochester (translated to Worcester that same year) and the injunctions were wide-ranging, thorough and innovative. They mark him out as one of the most diligent resident bishops. Indeed, as Thompson wrote, some of his provisions were incorporated into the royal injunctions of 1547.[437] Heath ordered the dean and chapter to ensure that all offices were filled as quickly as possible (after the candidates were sufficiently tested and examined of course) and that all church materials were inventoried and maintained, all leases examined, and he ordered regular chapter meetings every Saturday to discuss all issues. They would, for instance, prepare a preaching rota and turn their attention to the grammar school.[438]

In the Lincoln diocese, Longland visited at least one archdeaconry in person in 1543 to ensure that the *Bishops' Book*, the 1538 injunctions and the Act of Six Articles were all being enforced. In 1545, he issued a set of injunctions for Oriel College, Oxford.[439] In Worcester, Bell was also an active enforcer of the Act of Six Articles. With the formulation of Gloucester in 1541, however, Worcester was halved to about 227 parishes, and this eased his burden somewhat. In January 1541, Bell had written to the king's secretary, Wriothesley, asking for full jurisdiction from the king in all places that were formerly exempt, as he had heard that these were in 'grete nede of visitation and reformation'. Accordingly, he held a visitation in person, wherein at least twelve people were charged with speaking against transubstantiation and other issues. On at least seven occasions, according to Thompson, Bell charged priests to appear before him, enjoining them to preach at least three sermons apiece in support of the Six Articles.[440]

As we have seen, the *King's Book* of 1543 more or less put an end to spiritual disputes between conservatives and evangelicals, at least for the rest of Henry VIII's reign. Elton summed up the period quite distinctly, in that 'superstition continued to be frowned upon, Erasmian reform . . . remained active, Cranmer continued his work on an English liturgy'.[441] As the bishops, of whatever religious leaning, lacked leadership at court, they remained largely in their dioceses and in the background. If they wanted to search out heretics, for instance, a royal licence was necessary but easily obtained. Religious conflict after 1543 largely, therefore, had degenerated into more personal confrontations between Gardiner and Cranmer, and their supporters. The king indulged this (or at least he did not seem too upset by it). Gardiner was politically and administratively too important to censor, while Cranmer was probably the king's most loyal supporter. In any case, there was little or no wider impact to their bickering and both men survived into the reign of Queen Mary.

## Notes

1.  Tanner, pp.46-8.
2.  *CSP*, i/ii, xxi (at p.417).
3.  *LP*, vi, 1489.
4.  Scarisbrick, 'Vatican Library', pp.211-6.
5.  Nicholson, p.116; *idem*, 'The Act of Appeals and the English Reformation', in C. Cross, D. Loades and J.J. Scarisbrick (eds), *Law and Government Under the Tudors* (Cambridge, 1988), pp.19-30 (at pp.25-6).
6.  O'Grady, p.24.
7.  E.g., Cleo. E vi, fols.26r*ff*.
8.  The controversy centres on Cajetan's *De comparatione auctoritatis papae et concilii* (taking the pope's side) and Almain's *Tractatus de auctoritate ecclesiae et conciliorum generalium*. Cajetan wrote that a pope has no superior on Earth, but conceded that the inferior power of the general council could remove a 'heretical' pope, and made a clear distinction between office and office-holder. Almain (and subsequently Mair) routed Cajetan by examining the source of royal authority in secular political societies, simple community consent (presupposing a right to withdraw support were the king to act in bad faith). The Church, however, as the mystical body of Christ, divined its power from God alone and exceeded all human powers, from which followed two propositions: one, supreme ecclesiastical power was conferred directly by Christ on Peter, and two, Christ conferred this power directly on the church (the body of all the faithful, the body of all the greater and lesser prelates as represented by the general council). Almain concluded that the Church (represented by the general council) must be superior to the pope. St Peter had accepted the keys from Christ 'as a sign and figure of the Church'. In other words, the keys were conferred upon the Church through St Peter. Thus, if power over the church, or the general council representing it, had been conferred upon the pope in such a way that the entire church could not punish him if he acted in bad faith, then ecclesiastical polity was inferior to civil polity, which was clearly absurd.
9.  E.g., *LP*, vi, 1488. This is probably a letter to Cromwell from one of his propagandists. What is interesting is the caution it advises when dealing with general councils: 'the court of Rome . . . has destroyed many ancient writings and hid the rest, so that it is difficult to discover the truth about all things'
10. *LP*, vi, 721.
11. *Ibid*, 1381 (3).
12. *Ibid*, 998, 1425; vii, 2-3.
13. *CSP*, i/ii, xx (at pp.411-4) [BL, Cott. MSS. Cleo. E, vi, fol.313; Burnet, iii, p.71; *LP*, vi, 1486-7]. *LP*, vi, 1489 is a catalogue of papers and books on the subject.
14. Pocock, *Records*, ii, pp.523-31 (at pp.526-7); *LP*, vii, 1, 318, 462.
15. *Ibid*, p.530.
16. Scarisbrick, 'Conservative Episcopate', p.307.
17. E.g., Strype, *EM*, i, p.172; Elton, *Reform*, p.126; Scarisbrick, *Henry VIII*, pp.247-50; Steven W. Haas, 'Martin Luther's "Divine Right" Kingship and the Royal Supremacy: Two Tracts from the 1531 Parliament and Convocation of the Clergy', *JEH* xxxi:iii (July 1980), pp.317-25 (at p.319).
18. Geoffrey de C. Parmiter, 'A note on some aspects of the Royal Supremacy of Henry VIII', *Recusant History* x (1969-70), pp.183-92 (at p.185).
19. BL, Cleo. E vi, fols.16-216.

20. PRO. SP 1/236 fols.204*ff*; Nicholson, 'Act of Appeals', p.21. Nicholson wrote that this was an earlier paper transcribed into the collection around 1530.
21. Nicholson, 'Act of Appeals', p.22.
22. PRO. SP 1/238, fols.238*ff*.
23. Nicholson, 'Act of Appeals', p.22.
24. Old Testament kings too had much to offer. The kings of Israel had been judges over the divine law, had made and unmade high-priests, had reformed the clergy and had put down ecclesiastical abuses. Hezekiah had destroyed the bronze serpent which Moses had erected at God's command (II Kings 18) as it had become an object of idolatry and abuse, while Jehosaphat had led the people of Israel back from apostasy by appointing judges in each city to hear spiritual cases, and appointing priests to decide disputed cases and hear appeals at Jerusalem (II Chronicles 19). See, Nicholson, 'Function and Nature', pp.82*ff*; Cleo. E vi, fol.24.
25. Cleo. E vi, fol.27rv.
26. Richard Sampson, *Oratio quae docet hortatur admonet omnes potissimum Anglos regiae dignitati cum primis ut obediant . . .* (London, 1534). References will be taken from the most readily available edition, Strype, *EM*, i, pp.162-74 (at p.173 for Lucian).
27. The usual interpretation being that the lay power held sway over all things pertaining to the earthly life, while the clerical power was given all things pertaining to the spiritual life.
28. Cleo. E vi, fol.61v.
29. As quoted in Nicholson, 'Act of Appeals', p.23.
30. Harpsfield, *Treatise*, p.197.
31. PRO, SP 6/2, fols.94-6; Lehmberg, p.114.
32. SP 6/2, fol.96, as quoted by Lehmberg, p.114 and Haas, 'Divine Right', p.322.
33. E.g., SP 6/2, fol.95r.
34. *Ibid*, as quoted by Haas, 'Divine Right', p.323.
35. E.g., SP 6/2, fol.96r.
36. Ernst Kantorowicz, *The king's Two Bodies: A Study in Medieval Political Theology* (Princeton, 1957), pp.211-2; Francis Oakley, 'Edward Foxe, Matthew Paris, and the Royal "Potestas Ordinis"', *SCJ* xviii:iii (1987), pp.347-53 (at p.349).
37. Burnet, iv, 128-30; Oakley, 'Fox', p.350.
38. E.g., BL, Cott. MSS. Cleo. F.i, fol.93.
39. Edward Fox, *De vera differentia regiae potestatis et ecclesiasticae, et quae sit ipsa veritas ac virtus utrusque*, in Melchior Goldest (ed.), *Monarchia S. Romani Imperii . . .* (3 vols., Frankfurt, 1613), iii, pp.22-45 (at pp.35-6); *idem, The true dyfferis between y regall power and the ecclesiasticall power, etc.*, trans. by Henry, Lord Stafford (London, 1548, Amsterdam, 1973 edn), sigs.lviiia, lixa-lxviia, lxxxv. See also, P. Janelle, *L'Angleterre catholique à la veille du schisme* (Paris, 1935), pp.271-2, 281.
40. *The Glasse of Truthe* (London, 1531) or STC 11919. Another edition is Pocock, *Records*, ii, pp.385-421. A good, but rather dated, examination is Steven W. Haas, 'Henry VIII's Glasse of Truthe', *History* lxiv:ccxii (October 1979), pp.353-62.
41. Pocock, *Records*, ii, p.385.
42. *Ibid*, ii, pp.418-19.
43. Haas, 'Glasse', p.354.
44. Fox, *The true dyfferis*, sigs.xff, as quoted in O'Grady, p.49.
45. Fox, *The true dyfferis*, sigs.xlii, xlvii.
46. O'Grady, p.45.

47. He wrote, 'for just as Peter had no power over the rest of the Apostles; so too Peter's successors in the episcopal seat at Rome have no power over the successors of the other Apostles'. See, C.W. Previté-Orton (ed.), *The Defensor Pacis of Marsilius of Padua* (Cambridge, 1928), p.279; Alan Gewrith (ed. and trans.), *Marsilius of Padua: The Defender of Peace* (2 vols., New York, 1928), ii, p.246.

48. Cf. Fox, *The true dyfferis*, sigs.xxi, xxxiii, and Strype, *EM*, i, p.168.

49. Gewirth (ed.), p.115. On this point Fox was somewhat more specific, see Fox, *The true dyfferis*, sig.xxxiiii.

50. Fox, *The true dyfferis*, sigs.lxxxxii ('we beseeche your holines with meke and humblye prayers that ye ponder the primissis in ye balaunce of right Judgement with abundas of paciens and deuocion'), c ('ye wyll louingly suffer him quietli & peacably to possesse & to remaine incorrupt al his riches, libertes, customes & lawes without ani dimunicion & dysquietnes').

51. Mayer, 'On the Road to 1534', p.12.

52. Mayer, 'Tournai', p.26; *LP*, i, 3545, 3546.

53. Strype, *EM*, i, p.162.

54. This theme is touched upon to good effect by B.V Walker, 'Cardinal Reginald Pole; Papal Authority and Church Unity 1529-1536' (unpublished M.A. thesis, University of Dublin, 1972), pp.107*ff.*

55. Strype, *EM*, i, pp.163-4; Romans 13.7. For a discussion of *Oratio* see Chibi, 'Sampson'.

56. Walker, p.108.

57. Strype, *EM*, i, p.164. '*Et sis cautus oportet, eo ne spreto, cui Dei praecepto obedire teneris, illi obedias, cui nullam obedientiam debes*'.

58. BL, Cottonian MSS. Cleo. E, v, fol.42.

59. Strype, *EM*, i, p.166. He wrote '*Ut simus ergo Regi et ejus potestati ejus legibus subditi in omnibus, quae ad hujus saeculi negotia pertinent, mandat Deus ipse*'.

60. Chibi, 'Sampson', p.554. For additional commentary see, Walker, p.111 and O'Grady, p.51.

61. Jerome, 'Epistolae S Hieronymi in quatuor classes divisae secundum ordinem temporum', in *PL*, i, pp.235-1182 (at pp.355-8 (Ep. xv)). For an English translation, see Jerome, 'Letter to pope Damasus concerning the hypostases', in *NPNF*, vi, pp.18-20 (Letter xv).

62. *CWE*, lxi, pp.194-200 (at p.198).

63. Rex, *Henry VIII*, p.22.

64. O.P. Rafferty, 'Thomas Cranmer and the Royal Supremacy', *Heythorp Journal* xxxi:ii (1990), pp.129-49 (at p.131); Cox (ed.), i, pp.76-8.

65. Muller (ed.), *Letters of Gardiner*, p.56.

66. E.g., *LP*, vii, 522.

67. Strype, *EM*, pp.190-1; *LP*, vii, 121; *CSPS*, v/i, 8.

68. Sturge, *EM*, p.196; *LP*, ix/ii, 750 (p.279).

69. *LP*, vii, 690; *CSPS*, v/i, 58 (p.159).

70. Lee and Tunstal's report of the meeting is found at PRO. SP 1/84, fols.71-72r (*CSP*, i/ii, xxiii).

71. *A Litel Treatise ageynste the mutterynge of some papistis in corners* (London, 1534). The quote is taken from the edition in Pocock, *Records*, ii, pp.539-52 (at p.546).

72. *LP*, viii, 823.

73. *Ibid*, ix, 213.

74. MacCulloch, *Cranmer*, pp.149-50.

75. C. Wriothesley, *Chronicle of England* (2 vols., London, 1885 edn), i, pp.33-5; Ridley, *Cranmer*, p.98.
76. Burnet, iv, pp.300-02.
77. *Ibid.* Italics are mine.
78. *CSP*, i/ii, lxxxiv (p.544); Lambeth MSS 1107, fol.163; Wriothesley, i, pp.52-3.
79. Burnet, i, pp.287-8; P. Sawada, 'Two Anonymous Tudor Treatises on the General Council', *JEH* xii (October 1961), pp.197-215 (at p.202).
80. *A Treatise Concernynge generall councilles, the Byshoppes of Rome, and the Clergy* (London, 1538), sig.Aii.
81. Burnet, i, p.298.
82. *CSP*, i/ii, lxxxiv (at p.544).
83. PRO, SP 1/113, fols.10rv; John Stokesley and Cuthbert Tunstal, *The true copy of a certain Letter written by Cuthbert Tonstal, Bishop of Durham, and John Stokesley, Bishop of London, to Cardinal Pole, proving the Bishop of Rome to have no special superiority above other Bishops*, in Foxe, v, pp.90-99 (at p.97). This was published as *Letter to Cardinal Pole* (London, 1575). All references will be to the original in the record office.
84. Janelle, p.275.
85. Stephens, pp.206-7; Steer, p.13.
86. Stephens, pp.205-6; *LP*, vii, 759 [SP, 1/84, fol.119]. Also see *LP*, viii, 190, 941; ix, 509; Strype, *EM*, i/ii, p.205.
87. *LP*, vii, 1024 (6, 10); viii, 190, 293, 311, 494, 803, 854.
88. Fox suspected this as well. See *LP*, xi, 403.
89. O'Grady, p.55.
90. Janelle, p.37, as quoted in O'Grady, p.56.
91. Janelle, pp.37-45.
92. SP 1/113, fol.4r.
93. Janelle, p.73.
94. *Ibid*, p.91.
95. *Ibid*, pp.93-5.
96. Brigden, p.233
97. Goldest (ed.), iii, pp.35-6; Fox, *The true dyfferis*, sigs.lviiia, lixa-lxviia, lxxxv. Also see Janelle, pp.271-2, 281.
98. Janelle, p.117; O'Grady, p.59.
99. Strype, *EM*, i/i, p.239.
100. Cox (ed.), ii, pp.229-31.
101. J. Ridley, *Henry VIII* (London, 1984), p.282. Pole was to be 'educated'. See A.M. Qurini (ed.), *Epistolarum Reginaldi Poli S.R.E. Cardinalis et aliorum ad ipsum* (5 vols., Farnborough, 1967), i, p.428; *LP*, x, 7.
102. BL, Cott. MSS. Cleo. E, vi, fols.367rv. Starkey assured the king that Pole would offer 'hys grace true and faytheful servyce'. For additional details, see W. Schenk, *Reginald Pole, Cardinal of England* (London, 1950), pp.63ff.
103. E.g., BL, Cott. MSS. Cleo. E, vi, fols.368rv, 375.
104. Schenk, pp.63-4.
105. Qurini (ed.), i, pp.434 [*LP*, x, 420], 450. It was written to render 'Peter's bark safe against any piratical attack', a counterbalance to the 'flattery and temporizing' This had been a source of trouble, and Pole's solution was to expose 'the naked truth'. For more on this, see T. Starkey, *England in the Reign of Henry VIII*, ed. by J.M. Cowper (2 vols., London, 1871-8), i, p.xxxii.
106. T. Starkey, i, xxxv; Thomas F. Mayer, 'A Diet for Henry VIII: The Failure of Reginald

Pole's 1537 Legation', *JBS* xxvi (July 1987), pp.305-31 (at p.305). The king likely saw only Richard Morison's brief abstract. See D.S. Berkowitz (ed.), *Humanist Scholarship and Public Order: Two Tracts Against the Pilgrimage of Grace by Sir Richard Morison, with Historical Annotations and Related Contemporary Documents* (London, 1984), p.25; T. Maynard, *The Crown and the Cross* (New York, 1950), pp.188-92; *LP*, xi, 1354.

107. E.g., Reginald Pole, *Pro Ecclesiasticae Unitatis Defensione* (c.1537), sig.xxxi[v].

108. Walker, p.139.

109. BL, Cott. MSS. Cleo. E, vi, fols.379-83v; T. Starkey, i, p.xxxv; Mayer, *Starkey*, p.232. At fol.379v, Stokesley added an appeal to the consent of the English clergy to test Pole's *consensus ecclesiae*, an argument left unpursued in the course of the matter.

110. Pole, sigs.xlvii[rv].

111. SP 1/113, fols.4rv, based on I Corinthians 3.11.

112. *Ibid*, fols.5v-6.

113. Pole, sigs.xxii[rv], xxiv.

114. SP 1/113, fol.8v.

115. *Ibid*.

116. Ezekiel 3.17.

117. SP 1/113, fol.8v.

118. J. Mair, *Ionnis Majoris Doctoris Theologi in Quartum Sententiarum quaestiones* (Paris, 1516), fol.lxxxvi (r°A).

119. SP 1/113, fol.9r.

120. Augustine, '*Epistolarum Classis III, Epistolae Quas Scripsit Reliquo Vitae Tempore (ab anno 411 ad 450)*', in *PL*, xxxiii, pp.471-1024 (at pp.704-8 (Ep.clxii)).

121. I. Barrow, *A Treatise of the Pope's Supremacy* (Cambridge, 1859), pp.66-8.

122. Tertullian, 'Liber Ad Scapulam', in *PL*, i, pp.697-706 (at p.700); SP 1/113, fol.9v.

123. Tertullian, 'Apologeticus', in *PL*, i, pp.257-536 (at p.441 (ca.30)); SP 1/113, fol.10r.

124. Theophylact, 'Chronographia', in *PG*, cviii, pp.1038-1164 (at pp.1134-5).

125. SP 1/113, fol.10r.

126. Cuthbert Tunstall, *A Sermon . . . made upon Palme Sondaye last past* (London, 1539), but see Foxe, v, pp.80-90, for an abridged version.

127. Burnet, vi, 182.

128. J. Mair, *Editio Ionnis Maioris doctoris Parisiensis super Tertium Sententiarum quaestiones* (Paris, 1517), fol.lxxxv (r°B). '*Lex non est bona nisi a prudenti viro lata*'.

129. J.H. Burns, '*Politia Regalis et Optima*: The Political Ideas of John Mair', *History of Political Thought* ii:i (January 1981), pp.31-61 (at p.35).

130. *Ibid*, pp.36-7; J. Mair, *Ionnes Maior in Secundum Sententiarum* (Paris, 1510), fols. c (r°B-v°A).

131. Mair, *Quartum Sententiarum*, fol.lxxxvi (r°A).

132. *LP*, xii (ii), 620; Roger B. Merriman (ed.), *Life and Letters of Thomas Cromwell* (2 vols., Oxford, 1902), ii, p.85 (no.217).

133. *LP*, vi, 332.

134. This is the central focus of Margaret Bowker's excellent article 'The Supremacy and the Episcopate: The Struggle for Control, 1534-1540', *HJ* xviii:ii (1975), pp.227-43.

135. E.g., *LP*, viii, 190.

136. Cook, p.32.

137. *LP*, viii, 441.

138. PRO, SP 1/82, fols.12 [*LP*, vii, 15], 40 [*LP*, vii, 22]; *LP*, vii, 8, 12; viii, 229; ix, 332.

139. BL, Cott. MSS. Cleo. E, iv, fol.109 [*CSP*, i/ii, 24; *LP*, vii, 1090].

140. *LP*, ix, 986; T. Wright (ed.), *Three Chapters of Letters relating to the Suppression of Monasteries* (London, 1843), p.49.

141. BL, Cott. MSS Cleo. E, iv, fol.168 [*LP*, viii, 1125].

142. *LP*, viii, 77.

143. Wright (ed.), pp.45-6 [BL, Cott. MSS. Cleo. E, iv, fol.168; *LP*, viii, 1125].

144. *Ibid*, p.78.

145. *LP*, viii, 600.

146. *CSP*, i/ii, 24.

147. William Hunt et al (eds), *The Political History of England* (12 vols., London, 1906), v, pp.344-5.

148. Presumably, when northern convocation concluded unanimously against papal authority on 5 May 1534 this was considered adequate. Kite was firmly the king's man, while Lee and Tunstal were approached individually and shown what the penalties of disobedience might be. See 'Records of the Northern Convocation', pp.232-3; Wilkins, iii, pp.782-3; *LP*, viii, 190 (7, 8), 311, 854.

149. E.g., Muller (ed.), *Letters*, p.56; *LP*, vii, 690; ix, 25; Bowker, 'Supremacy', p.230.

150. E.g., Guildhall MSS. 9531/11, fols.59r-60r (London); Wilson, *Visitations*, p.357 (Worcester); Cox (ed.), ii, p.304 (no.cxlv for Winchester).

151. Guildhall MSS. 9531/11, fol.60r.

152. E.g., 'The Appeal of Stokesley, Bishop of London to the king, Against the Archbishop's Visitation', in John Strype, *Memorials of Thomas Cranmer* (2 vols., Oxford, 1812), ii, pp.704-8 (at pp.704-5); BL, Cott. MSS. Cleo. F, ii, fol.124r.

153. Guildhall MSS. 9531/11, fols.67r-68r; BL, Cott. MSS. Cleo. F, ii, fol.124rv.

154. Two letters of protest are extant at BL, Cott. MSS. Cleo. F, ii, fol.124r-127r and F, i, fols.93-4. On the second letter, see Stanford E. Lehmberg, 'Supremacy and Vice-Gerency: A Re-Examination', *EHR* cccxix (April 1966), pp.225-35 (at p.231). Also see Cox (ed.), ii, pp.304-6 (no.cxlv).

155. Wilkins, iii, p.769.

156. BL, Cott. MSS. Cleo. F, i, fol.93.

157. *Ibid*, F, ii, fol.124r.

158. *Ibid*, fol.124v.

159. *Ibid*, F, i, fol.94rv.

160. *Ibid*, F, ii, fols.125rv.

161. *Ibid*, fol.124.

162. *Ibid*, fol.126. Also see, Churchill, i, pp.582-4.

163. Cleo. F, ii, fols.126rv.

164. *Ibid*, fol.127.

165. Bowker, 'Supremacy', p.231; *idem, Longland*, p.73.

166. *LP*, viii, 1044; Bowker, 'Supremacy', p.232.

167. Bowker, *Longland*, p.74.

168. E.g., *LP*, vii, 665, 921; 'Original Acknowledgements of the Royal Supremacy', in *Deputy Keepers Reports of the Public Records*, Seventh and Eighth reports (London, 1846), pp.279-306; MacCulloch, *Cranmer*, p.127.

169. *LP*, ix, 583.

170. Brigden, pp.261-3; *LP*, xi, 1424; Morice, p.276.

171. *VCH:London*, i, p.265.

172. MacCulloch, *Cranmer*, pp.128-9; PRO, SP 1/89, fol.130 [*LP*, viii, 159].

173. MacCulloch, *Cranmer*, pp.127-8.

174. *Ibid*, p.132.
175. PRO, SP 1/93, fols.63, 71; *LP*, viii, 859 (32, 33).
176. S. Thompson, 'Pastoral Works', pp.145-7; Mumford, pp.87-8; G. Oliver, *Lives of the Bishops of Exeter* (Exeter, 1861), pp.117-20.
177. Bowker, 'Supremacy', p.233.
178. Elton, *Policy and Police*, p.227; Burnet, vi, pp.290-1; *LP*, vii, 427.
179. BL, Cott. MSS. Cleo. F, i, fol.93r [*LP*, viii, 705].
180. Lehmberg, 'Supremacy', p.227.
181. F. Donald Logan, 'Thomas Cromwell and the Vicegerency in Spirituals: A Revisitation', *EHR* ciii:ccccviii (July 1988), pp.658-67 (at p.658).
182. Cranmer's letter is extant, see *LP*, viii, 623.
183. *TRP*, i, pp.230-21; Ellis (ed.), iii/ii, pp.324-6.
184. Cox (ed.), ii, pp.306-7 (no.cxlviii); *LP*, viii, 820.
185. Ridley, *Cranmer*, p.92.
186. Andrew Clark (ed.), *Lincoln Diocese Documents, 1450-1544* (London, 1914), pp.194-7.
187. Elton, *Policy*, p.214; Brigden, p.233.
188. *LP*, viii, 821, 834.
189. Elton, *Policy*, p.233.
190. *LP*, viii, 849, 293 (i).
191. Ellis (ed.), iii/ii, pp.324-32; *LP*, viii, 869.
192. Cox (ed.), ii, pp.293, 460-2.
193. *Ibid*, pp.460-2.
194. *Ibid*, pp.283-4; *LP*, vii, 463.
195. Ellis (ed.), iii/ii, pp.337-42; *LP*, viii, 292 (i), 963.
196. Elton, *Policy*, p.235.
197. Cox (ed.), ii, pp.292-3; Cleo. e.v., fols.294-7.
198. Ellis (ed.), iii/ii, p.326; *LP*, viii, 869; S. Thompson, 'Pastoral Works', p.105.
199. S. Thompson, 'Pastoral Works', p.107; *LP*, viii, 480, 570, 625, 626.
200. Clark (ed.), pp.188-91 (no. xlvi).
201. *TRP*, i, p.232.
202. Brigden, pp.233-4.
203. Elton, *Policy*, pp.214-5; Millar Maclure, *The Paul's Cross Sermons 1534-1642* (Toronto, 1958), pp.185-6.
204. *LP*, viii, 1019.
205. Elton, *Policy*, p.189.
206. *LP*, viii, 1105.
207. *Ibid*, 1043, 1054 [PRO, SP 1/94, fol.98rv]; PRO, SP 1/94, fol.50r.
208. *Ibid*, 922 (Longland), 1005; ix, 183.      (Tunstal); x/ii, 83 (Veysey).
209. *Ibid*, viii, 941.
210. *Ibid*, xiv/i, 865.
211. *Ibid*, viii, 823, 839.
212. Wilkin, iii, p.797; *LP*, ix, 517; Cox (ed.), ii, p.463.
213. 'Visitations in the diocese of York, Holden by Archbishop Edward Lee (A.D. 1534-5)', pp.424-58; S. Thompson, 'Pastoral Works', p.377; Bowker, *Longland*, p.90
214. *LP*, ix, 569.
215. E.g., Wilkins, iii, pp.797-8.
216. *LP*, vi, 399, 400, 1451; vii, 879; viii, 284; ix, 30-1, 933.
217. *LP*, xii/ii, 720; Hennessy, p.34.
218. *LP*, xii/ii, 720; xiv/ii, 177; ix, 349, 453-4.

219. S. Thompson, 'Pastoral Works', pp.53-4.

220. *Ibid*, pp.63-5; *LP*, viii, 963; x/i, 716; xii/i, 1093.

221. *LP*, x, 120; Cox (ed.), ii, pp.366-7; S. Thompson, 'Pastoral Works', p.65.

222. Corrie (ed.), *Sermons and Remains of Hugh Latimer*, p.384 (no.xxiii).

223. Bowker, *Longland*, pp.44-5, 171-2.

224. S. Thompson, 'Pastoral Works', p.77.

225. Bowker, 'Supremacy', pp.237-8; S. Thompson, 'Pastoral Works', p.117.

226. *TRP*, i, p.236-7.

227. Elton, *Policy*, p.220.

228. *Ibid*, p.161.

229. *LP*, viii, 55 (mis-dated) [PRO. SP 1/89, fol.32r].

230. SP 1/98, fols.103rv, 194; *LP*, ix, 742, 704.

231. SP1/99, fols.202v-203 [*LP*, ix, 1059]; S. Thompson, 'Pastoral Works', p.109.

232. S. Thompson, 'Pastoral Works', p.110; BL, Cott. MSS Cleo.E.v., fols.101rv [*LP*, x, 172].

233. SP 1/103, fols.234-5 [*LP*, x, 804]; *VCH: Buckinghamshire*, iii, p.109. For Swynnerton, see *LP*, vii, 1067 (2), 923 (7); SP 1/113, fol.108v [*LP*, xi, 1424]. For Longland's complaints, see SP 1/103, fol.274, 304 [*LP*, x, 850, 891]; SP 1/104, fol.157 [*LP*, x, 1099]; SP 1/113, fols.108v-09 [*LP*, x, 1424].

234. SP 1/104, fol.157 [LP, x, 1099]; S. Thompson, 'Pastoral Works', p.112. Latimer and his preachers were 'disorderly and colourable', bringing 'disquiet' to the people. See, Caroline Litzenberger, *The English Reformation and the Laity: Gloucestershire, 1540-1580* (Cambridge, 1997), p.36.

235. Elton, *Policy*, p.214.

236. *LP*, vii, 616, 1643.

237. *LP*, viii, 1054 [SP 1/94, fol. 98v].

238. S. Mathew, *A Sermon made in the cathedrall churche of Saynt Paul at London* (London, 1535), sigs.Bii, Cvii.

239. *Ibid*, sigs.Avi-vii.

240. *LP*, x, 45; vii, 750 (a mis-dated draft). De'Athequa's authority in Llandaff had been effectively suspended the previous November [*LP*, ix, 606].

241. *LP*, x, 45.

242. *Ibid*, 46; Burnet, iv, pp.394-5; Merriman (ed.), ii, pp.111-3.

243. S. Thompson, 'Pastoral Works', p.233.

244. Gee and Hardy (eds), pp.269-74; Elton, *Policy*, p.251; W.H. Frere and W.M. Kennedy (eds), *Visitation Articles and Injunctions of the Period of the Reformation* (3 vols., London, 1910), ii, pp.1-11.

245. Burnet, iv, pp.396-9.

246. E.g., GLRO, DC/L/330, fol.242v (for London).

247. Skeeters, pp.48*ff*.

248. Frere and Kennedy (eds), ii, pp.12-18; Corrie (ed.), *Sermons and Remains of Hugh Latimer*, pp.242-4.

249. Wilson, *Visitations*, p.358.

250. Burnet, vi, pp.206-9 (at p.209); Frere and Kennedy (eds), ii, p.23.

251. Frere and Kennedy (eds), ii, p.25.

252. *Ibid*, p.29.

253. *CSP*, xii/i, 742; ; Frere and Kennedy (eds), ii, pp.30-3; A.T. Bannister (ed.), *Registrum Edwardi Foxe, Episcopi Herefordensis A.D. MDXXXV - MDXXXVIII* (London, 1921), pp.372-4.

254. *LP*, x, 462.

255. Maclure, p.187.

256. Gee and Hardy (eds), pp.275-81.

257. Wilkins, iii, p.815; Frere and Kennedy (eds), ii, p.36.

258. Wilkins, iii, p.816.

259. E.g., Cox (ed.), i, pp.81-2; Wilkins, iii, p.837. For Veysey's injunctions see, Frere and Kennedy (eds), ii, pp.61-64.

260. Merriman (ed.), ii, p.153.

261. Burnet, vi, pp.210-15 (at pp.213, 215); Frere and Kennedy (eds), ii, p.57.

262. BL, Harleian MSS. 604, fol.96v.

263. *LP*, xiii/i, 339.

264. Wriothesley, p.90; Maclure, p.187.

265. Burnet, vi, pp.195-200.

266. *CSP*, viii, 51.

267. *LP*, xiii/ii, 401.

268. PRO, SP 6/6, fols.39-42v.

269. *Ibid*, fol.91.

270. John Longland, *A Sermonde made before the Kynge his maiestie at grenewiche upon good Frydaye* (London, 1538), sig.Gii. There is an incomplete abridgement of this sermon in Foxe, v, pp.171-9.

271. Cuthbert Tunstal, *A Sermon . . . made upon Palme Sondaye last past* (London, 1539), sigs.Evii-viii. There is also an incomplete abridgement of this sermon in Foxe, v, pp.80-89.

272. *LP*, xiii/ii, 336, 537, 1085; Guildhall MSS 9531/12, fols.25v-27; S. Thompson, 'Pastoral Works', p.167.

273. John Longland, *A Sermonde made before the Kynge his maiestie at grenewiche upon good Frydaye* (London, 1538), sig.Gii.

274. James Gairdner, 'Henry VIII', in *The Cambridge Modern History* i, pp.416-73 (at pp.464-5).

275. G.W.H. Lampe (ed.), *The Cambridge History of the Bible* (2 vols., Cambridge, 1960-70), ii, pp.428*ff.*

276. J.F. Mozley, *Coverdale and His Bibles* (London, 1953), pp.117-8.

277. A.F. Pollard (ed.), *Records of the English Bible: The Documents Relating to the Translation and Publication of the Bible in English: 1525-1611* (London, 1911), p.225.

278. PRO, SP 6/6. fol.40v; Frere and Kennedy (eds), ii, p.3; David C. Douglas (ed.), *EHD* (12 vols., London, 1953-81), v, p.807.

279. *LP*, xii/ii, appendix no.35; Lewis Lupton (ed.), *A History of the Geneva Bible* (12 vols., London, 1979), xi, p.101.

280. G.E. Duffield (ed.), *The Work of Thomas Cranmer* (Appleford, 1964), pp.257-8; *CSP*, i/ii, xciv (at p.561).

281. Mozley, p.38.

282. Morice, pp.277-8; Muller (ed.), *Letters of Gardiner*, p.66; Foxe, i, pp.277-8; Strype, *Memorials*, ii, p.48.

283. Duffield (ed.), pp.258-9; *CSP*, i/ii, xxx (at p.430), xciv (at pp.561-2). Also see PRO, SP 1/223, fols.198-9; Cox (ed.), ii, p.344.

284. PRO, SP 6/3, fols.1-3.

285. Frere and Kennedy (eds), ii, pp.35-6, 35 (n.1).

286. *LP*, xiii/ii, 498.

287. *TRP*, i, pp.270-1; *LP*, xiii/ii, 848.

288. *LP*, xiii/ii, 848; Elton, *Policy*, p.256.

289. BL, Cottonian MSS, Cleopatra E.v., fols.294-7; Ellis (ed.), iii/i, p.326; *LP*, viii, 869.

290. Cox (ed.), *Works*, ii, p.293.

291. *Ibid*, pp.460-61.

292. *Ibid*, p.283, addressed to an anonymous bishop.

293. *LP*, vii, 871.

294. Cox (ed.), *Works*, ii, pp.296-7 (no.cxxvii). This is a letter alerting Latimer to the difficulties in Worcestor diocese that some of his appointments caused. Also see Skeeters, pp.46-7.

295. Cox (ed.), *Works*, ii, p.307; *LP*, viii, 849, 821, 832, 833, 835, 836, 839, 869; Strype, *EM*, i/ii, p.210 (*LP*, viii, 921); Ellis (ed.), iii/ii, pp.324-32, 338-9 (*LP*, viii, 869, 963).

296. PRO, SP 1/98, fols.194, 103rv (*LP*, ix, 742, 704).

297. PRO, SP 6/6, fols.90v-91.

298. *Ibid*, fol.98v.

299. Only that letter to Llandaff survives. See, PRO, SP 1/101, fol.53 (*LP*, x, 45); SP 6/2. fols.126-9 (*LP*, vii, 750 wrongly dated).

300. E.g., Muller (ed.), *Letters of Gardiner*, pp.170, 305.

301. *LJ*, i, p.10.

302. Hugh Latimer, 'Sermon to the convocation of 9.      June 1537', in *Sermons by Hugh Latimer Sometime Bishop of Worcester* (London, n.d.), pp.30-53 (at p.51).

303. Hall, ii, p.819; M. St C. Byrne (ed.), *The Lisle Letters* (6 vols., London, 1980), iii, p.221.

304. R.W. Hoyle, 'The Origins of the dissolution of the monasteries', *HJ* xxxviii:ii (June 1995), pp.275-306 (at p.276).

305. Corrie (ed.), *Works*, ii, p.249; John K. Yost, 'Hugh Latimer's Reform Program, 1529-1536, and the Intellectual Origins of the Anglican *Via Media*', *Anglican Theological Review* liii (April 1971), pp.103-14 (at p.109).

306. Corrie (ed.), *Remains*, pp.410-11; Hoyle, p.277.

307. A good basic account of these diplomatic efforts is Neelah Serawlook Tjernagel, *Henry VIII and the Lutherans: A Study in Anglo-Lutheran Relations from 1521 to 1547* (St Louis, 1965), pp.139*ff.* A more detailed examination is R. McEntegart, 'England and the League of Schmalkalden 1531-1547: Faction, foreign policy and the England Reformation' (unpublished Ph.D., London School of Economics, 1992) or *idem*, *Henry VIII, The League of Schmalkalden and the English Reformation* (Woodbridge, 2002). Specific embassies can be found discussed at *LP*, vi, 19-21, 337, 1115, 1212; viii, 213, 385, 433, 892; ix, 294, 355; Burnet, iii/ii, pp.133-6; and C.G. Bretschneider et al (eds), *Corpus Reformatorum* (101 vols. to date, Halle, 1834 to present), ii, pp.939-45, 1008.

308. *Ibid*, p.1028.

309. Burnet, iii/ii, pp.141-45; *LP*, ix, 1018.

310. Strype, *EM*, i/ii, pp.236-9.

311. Burnet, iii/ii, p.145.

312. E.g. *LP*, x, 63, 81, 118.

313. *LP*, x, 771.

314. PRO, SP 1/111, fol.163; *LP*, xi, 1110.

315. PRO SP 6/1, fols.1-5; cf. SP 6/11, fols.147-53 (a preparatory draft of the former).

316. Alan Kreider (ed.), 'An English Episcopal Draft Article Against the Anabaptists, 1536', *Mennonite Quarterly Review* xlix (1975), pp.38-42 (at p.38).

317. Cox (ed.), *Works*, ii, pp.460-1; BL, Cottonian MSS, Cleopatra E.v., fol.294v.

318. *LP*, x, 601.

319. John Longland, *A Sermond Spoken before the Kynge his maiestie at Grewiche,*

*uppon good Fryday* (London, 1536), sig.Bi.
320. PRO, SP 6/1, fol.2; 6/11, fols.147rv.
321. Horst, p.38.
322. Kreider, p.41.
323. Tjernagel, p.164.
324. For opposing points of view, cf. H.E. Jacobs, *The Lutheran Movement in England During the Reigns of Henry VIII and Edward VI* (London, 1890), p.58; Constant, *Reformation*, i, p.394. Rex, *Reformation*, pp.145*ff* and MacCulloch, *Cranmer*, pp.162*ff* both present good, if varying, modern examinations.
325. MacCulloch, *Cranmer*, p.165.
326. Rex, *Reformation*, p.146.
327. *Ibid*, p.145; Haigh, *Reformations*, p.129.
328. BL, Cott. MSS. Cleo. E, v, fol.5 [Strype, *EM*, i, p.388].
329. E.g., BL, Cott. MSS. Cleo. E, v, fols.48-50 [*LP*, xi, 60] which deals with Holy Orders; fols.51-52v, which deals with other questions of doctrine; PRO, SP 6/1, fols.2-5v [*LP*, xi, 59 (ii)] is a tract on the evangelical view of the requirements for salvation.
330. BL, Cott. MSS. Cleo. E, v, fol.72.
331. BL, Cott. MSS. Cleo. E, v, fols.64r-65v [Jacobs, pp.89-90; C. Lloyd (ed.), 'Articles Devised by the king's Majestie, to Stablyshe Christen Quietnes and Unitie amonge us' in *Formularies of Faith put forth by authority during the reign of Henry VIII* (Oxford, 1825), pp.xiii-xxxii (at pp.xviii-xx)].
332. BL, Cott. MSS. Cleo, E, vi, fols.384v-5 (*LP*, xi, 138); S. Thompson, 'Pastoral Works', p.125.
333. Wilkins, iii, pp.807-8.
334. For Longland, see PRO, SP 1/105, fols.102-3 (*LP*, xi, 136-7); fol.104 (*LP*, xi, 138); 1/123, fols.145v-46 (*LP*, xii/ii, 374); Sherwin Bailey, 'Robert Wisdom under Persecution, 1541-1543', *JEH* ii (1951), pp.180-9. For Stokesley, see PRO, SP 1/104, fol.198 (*LP*, xi, 186); 1/106, fols.21rv (*LP*, xi, 325).
335. *LP*, xii/i, 432.
336. Burnet, iv, pp.396-7.
337. *LP*, xii/ii, 289, 295, 1089; Tjernagel, p.172.
338. *LP*, xii/i, 457, 708, 1068, 1187; xii/ii, 289, 293, 410, 703; A.F.S. Pearson, 'Alesius and the English Reformation', *Records of the Scottish Church History Society* x:ii (1949), pp.57-87 (at p.79).
339. Rex, *Reformation*, p.152.
340. E.g., *LP*, xii/i, 789.
341. BL, Cott. MSS. Cleo. E, v, fol.308-9 [Strype, *EM*, i/ii, pp.381-3 (at pp.381-2)].
342. *LP*, xv, 758; Strype, *EM*, i/ii, p.381.
343. *LP*, xii/i, 457. John Husee wrote to Lord Lisle, on 18 February, that 'most part of the bishops have come, but nobody knows what is to be done'
344. Alexander Alesius, *Of the Authority of God against the Bishop of London. . .*, (n.d.), sigs.A5ab. Probably published c.1537 or as soon after he was asked to remove himself as possible.
345. *Ibid*, sigs.A6ab.
346. Ridley, *Cranmer*, pp.118-22.
347. Alesius, sigs.A7ab. There is another edition of this work in Alexander Alesius, *An Epistle of the Most Mighty and Redoubted Prince Henry VIII* (Leipzig, 1541), and his work is discussed by J.T. McNeill, 'Alexander Alesuis, Scottish Lutheran (1500-1565)', *AfR* lv (1964), pp.161-91.
348. Alesius, sigs.A7b-8a.

349. *Ibid*, sig.B1. It should be noted that there is only Alesuis' word for the events which follow.
350. *Ibid*, sigs.B1b-2.
351. *Ibid*, sig.B3.
352. *Ibid*, sig.B6b. Foxe [v, p.383] made certain additions to Stokesley's speech.
353. O'Grady, p.145 (n. 26); *LP*, iv, 394.
354. Alesius, sig.B7.
355. Muller (ed.), *Letters of Gardiner*, p.351.
356. *LP*, xii/ii, 834.
357. *CSP*, i/ii, xc (at p.556) [*LP*, xii/ii, 289].
358. *CSP*, i/ii, xcvi (at p.563) [*LP*, xii/ii, 295].
359. *LP*, xii/ii, 329.
360. Tjernagel, p.174.
361. PRO, SP 1/126, fol.193v (*LP*, xii/ii, 1122 (2); BL, Titus, B.1. fol.472 (*LP*, xiii/i, 187)]; Cox (ed.), *Works*, ii, pp.358-9; *CSP*, i/ii, pp.574-5.
362. C. Lloyd (ed.), 'The Institutions of a Christian Man', in *Formularies of Faith Put Forth By Authority During the Reign of Henry VIII* (Oxford, 1825), pp.23-211 (at p.145); S. Thompson, 'Pastoral Works', p.174.
363. Lloyd (ed.), 'Institutions', pp.101-21.
364. PRO, SP 6/2, fols.155-56v.
365. MacCulloch, *Cranmer*, p.215.
366. *LP*, xiii/i, 1296.
367. *LP*, xiii/i, 1437.
368. *LP*, xiii/ii, 498.
369. *LP*, xiii/ii, 38.
370. Ridley, *Cranmer*, p.162.
371. Tjernagel, p.182.
372. *LP*, xiii/ii, 165; BL, Cott. MSS. Cleo. E v, fols.228-38.
373. Doernberg, p.114; *LP*, xiii/ii, 497.
374. Cox (ed.), *Works*, ii, pp.472-80.
375. E.g., *LP*, xiv/i, 1198.
376. *Ibid*, 441.
377. E.g., C.S.L. Davies, *Peace, Print & Protestantism: 1450-1558* (London, 1976, 1982 edn); Ridley, *Cranmer*, pp.178-9; S.E. Lehmberg, *The Later Parliaments of Henry VIII: 1536-1547* (Cambridge, 1977), pp.57-8.
378. Glyn Redworth, 'A Study in the Formulation of Policy: The Genesis and Evolution of the Act of Six Articles', *JEH* xxxvii:i (January 1986), pp.42-67.
379. *LP*, xiii/ii, 845; W.D. Hamilton (ed.), *A Chronicle of England ... by Charles Wriothesley, Windsor Herald* (2 vols., London, 1875, 1877), i, p.94.
380. *LJ*, i, p.104; Byrne (ed.), v, pp.459-60.
381. *LP*, xiv/ii, 423.
382. *Ibid*, 631.
383. Thüringisches Staatsarchiv Weimar, Reg H, fols.171-3 (fol.172), as quoted by F. Pruser, *England und die Schmalkaldener, 1535-1540* (Leipzig, 1929), p.315.
384. *LP*, xiv/ii, 379.
385. W.Turner, *The Rescuing of the Romish Fox* (Basel, 1542), sig.Aiii.
386. *LJ*, i, p.105; Redworth, 'Formulation', p.55.
387. *LJ*, i, pp.109, 113; *LP*, xiii/ii, 1040. These were *An Eucharistia verum sit Corpus Dominicum, asbque Transubstantione; Utrum Eucharistia sit communicanda Laicis sub utraque specie; An Vota Castitatis, per Viros aut Mulieres facta, sint*

*observanda, de Jure Divino; An private Misse sint observande, de Jure Divino; Utrum Auricularis Confessio sit necessaria, de Jure Divino.*

388. Byrne (ed.), v, p.354.

389. *LJ*, i, pp.109-10.

390. *Ibid*, p.113.

391. *Ibid*; *LP*, xiv/i, 1040.

392. Lehmberg, *Later Parliaments*, pp.70*ff*; Burnet, i, pp.189-90.

393. E.g., William Turner, *The Huntying and Fyndung out of the Romish Fox which more than Seven Years hath been hyd among the Byshoppes of England, after the Kynges Highnes, Henry VIII, had commanded hym to be dryven out of hys Realme*, ed. by Robert Potts (Cambridge, 1851), pp.11-2.

394. James Sawtry (*alias* George Joye), *The defence of the mariage of preistes: agenst Steuen Gardiner* (Antwerp, 1541), sig.Aiii.

395. BL, Cott. MSS. Cleo. E, v, fols.131-2, as quoted in Redworth, 'Formulation', p.62.

396. Hamilton, i, p.103. Latimer went into the custody of Sampson and Shaxton went into the custody of Clerk, there to remain as prisoners 'at the king's pleasure'.

397. Hall, i, p.828; Holinshed, iii, pp.945-6; Foxe, v, p.654. Foxe was concerned to list some of the names of the victims rather than make a general accounting. It is interesting to note, however, that at least two of the immediate victims were of the king's own guard, Giles Germain and Lancelot.

398. There are three modern examinations of the Plot, the comparisons of which should satisfy any scholarly interest. Cf. Michael L. Zell, 'The Prebendaries' Plot of 1543: a Reconsideration', *JEH* 27:3 (July 1976), pp. 241-53; Redworth, *Gardiner*, chap.8; MacCulloch, *Cranmer*, pp.297-308.

399. MacCulloch, *Cranmer*, pp.268-80. This is the most current account, and offers a most useful disentanglement and examination of the documentary evidence. I have followed it for the events, if not for the interpretations.

400. BL, Cott. MSS. Cleo. E v, fols.40-47v; (Burnet, vi, 443-96).

401. Cox (ed.), *Works*, ii, pp.115-7 (for the Archbishop's responses); *LP*, xv, 697, 766, 860; xvi, p.951.

402. O.P. Rafferty, 'Thomas Cranmer and the Royal Supremacy', *The Heythrop Journal* xxxi:ii (1990), pp.129-49 (at pp.131-2).

403. Burnet, vi, pp.338, 347.

404. MacCulloch, *Cranmer*, p.268; *LP*, xv, 485-6.

405. Muller (ed.), *Letters of Gardiner*, p.365; *LP*, xviii/i, 365 (for Capon and Skip).

406. Rex, *Reformation*, p.129.

407. MacCulloch, *Cranmer*, p.290.

408. PRO, SP 1/126, fol.193v (*LP*, xii/ii, 1122).

409. MacCulloch, *Cranmer*, p.308; *LP*, xviii/i, 365.

410. But see Scarisbrick, *Henry VIII*, pp.534, 540 and 543 for commentary.

411. T.A. Lacey (ed.), *The king's Book or A Necessary Doctrine And Erudition For Any Christian Man, 1543* (London, 1932), p.51.

412. *Ibid*, p.45.

413. Rex, *Reformation*, pp.157-8; Muller (ed.), *Letters of Gardiner*, pp.336-7.

414. Rex, *Reformation*, p.164.

415. S. Thompson, 'Pastoral Works', p.151.

416. *LP*, xvi, 449.

417. *LJ*, i, pp.252*ff*; MacCulloch, *Cranmer*, p.328; O'Grady, pp.101-3.

418. He later was forced into a recantation of his sermon, see Gardiner, *Lollardy*, ii, pp.434*ff*.

419. MucCulloch, *Cranmer*, pp.356-7.

420. 'Paul Bush', at p.98.
421. Litzenberger, pp.45-6.
422. *VCH: Cumberland*, ii, p.58.
423. Cox (ed.), ii, p.490; Wilkins, iii, p.857; Frere and Kennedy (eds), ii, pp.67-9.
424. Frere and Kennedy (eds), ii, pp.70-81.
425. Foxe, v, p.412; McConica, pp.18-9.
426. Guildhall MSS 9531/12, fol.26v; Foxe, v, appendix, xiv; Burnet, iv, p.139; Lansdowne, MSS 938, fol.224.
427. Brigden, pp.330*ff.*
428. Guildhall MSS 9531/12, fols.33r-v.
429. Brigden, p.339.
430. Lehmberg, *Later Parliaments*, p.163.
431. Muller (ed.), *Letters of Gardiner*, p.313 (no.124).
432. Wilkins, iii, p.861.
433. *LP*, xvii, 176; Lehmberg, *Later Parliaments*, p.224; MacCulloch, *Cranmer*, pp.291-2. The bill was revised and passed through the lords in 1545.
434. Wilkins, iii, p.866; Merrill F. Sherr, 'Bishop Bonner: A Quasi Erasmian', *Historical Magazine of the Protestant Episcopal Church* xliii (1974), pp.359-66 (at p.362).
435. Frere and Kennedy (eds), ii, p.85; Wilkin, iii, p.866; Guildhall MSS 9531/12, fols.38v-40.
436. *LP*, xx/ii, 557.
437. S. Thompson, 'Pastoral Works', p.86.
438. Frere and Kennedy (eds), ii, pp.92-3 (Items 9, 10 and 13).
439. *Ibid*, pp.99-102; Bowker, *Longland*, pp.167-8
440. S. Thompson, 'Pastoral Works', p.134.
441. Elton, *Policy*, p.301.

# Conclusions
## Henry VIII's Bishops

It is obviously somewhat arbitrary to draw this examination to a close at the end of the reign of Henry VIII in 1547, especially as the influences that conspired to create the uniqueness of his Episcopal bench originated well before the advance of the Tudors themselves. Not only had a great deal been made of events in the reign of Henry VII (and earlier) but, of course, the 'Henrician' bishops did not forfeit their positions with the accession of the new king. Quite a few of them went on to serve Mary I, and a couple even survived into the reign of Elizabeth I (see Table 9). They survived, but not without problems and set backs in their careers. Their activities and fates under the remaining Tudors are briefly discussed in the Appendix, as this did not form part of our earlier discussion. Nor was the decision to draw the discussion to an end at this point a frivolous one.

The fact of the matter is that this book was only partially aimed at the members of the Episcopate specifically. At least two other areas have been explored. These were the influence of the Episcopate on the reign of Henry VIII and the influence of the reign on the Episcopate as an elite social and ecclesiastical unit. In an effort to determine what those reciprocating influences had been, this study drew certain general conclusions about the Henricians as a starting point. These were based on their social and regional origins, on their educational and intellectual backgrounds and achievements, and on their service records to both church and state. Some of what we discovered about the Henricians was interesting and unexpected, while some was just as we would expect to find out about a group of early modern bishops.

In social terms, for instance, it was discovered that the Henricians were quite a diverse and idiosyncratic group. All ranks or 'sorts' of people were represented in some way with no obvious bias toward any one group exhibited at any point in the reign, except as population percentages would dictate. Combining this small piece of data with others, we extrapolated the fact that in Henrician England, social degree was not an obstruction to social mobility. This was quite unlike much of contemporary early modern Europe. It also underlined other historians' findings that the Tudors had a certain affinity with the middle-classes. Staying with this theme, it was also found out that the Henricians were largely representative of England's regional schematic. As with the social distribution, this did not colour their careers to any statistically significant degree. Northerners served in the south, southerners served in the north, midlanders served in Wales. Moreover, with the exception of certain specific instances in Wales primarily, this mingling had no serious side effects. Again, this small piece of data underlined the conclusion that Henrician England was a place where regionalism was over-shadowed by national concerns, and a place where the church was a non-regionalist blanket unifying all parts of the realm. These prosopographical considerations gave us a good basic understanding of the men with whom we were dealing.

The first conclusion, therefore, is that the 'ascribed status' of the bishops who served Henry VIII was not overly influential on their 'achieved status'. This means that, just as he claimed, Henry VIII was more interested in what a man could bring to the job than with traditional social connections or political concerns. It would be interesting to discover if this was the case with some of the king's other appointments – political, judicial, household, etc., or why not? As such traditional justifications were ignored, we had to ask what the Henricians had to offer instead. Historical orthodoxy suggested that the bishops were not dedicated churchmen as such, but rather worldly lawyers and civil servants. It seems that they offered not much expertise beyond these important areas. This tells us that the cure of souls entrusted to them was unimportant and, indeed, that the bishops were not effective pastoral shepherds.

The second conclusion, therefore, is that historical orthodoxy has misrepresented the Henricians to a great degree. The unflattering view of the bishops was put to the test in such a way as to uncover the facts (the talents, skills and interests of the bishops, if any) and let these speak for themselves. This was also done in order to discover any 'typical' characteristics or 'common' career paths. We focused on their academic performances, their ecclesiastical service records, and their services rendered to the crown prior to their gaining Episcopal promotions. What data was uncovered was somewhat novel, particularly when a comparison was made with Episcopates in contemporary Europe or in medieval England.

We found the Henricians, as a group, very well educated and academically cosmopolitan. They had exhibited interests in everything from law to music, theology to mathematics, and we found that a sizeable proportion of them had studied abroad. In these ways they gained unique experiences and insights into the minds and lives of other Europeans. They also gained insight into the workings of the church as a pan-European force. More than this, however, we found that with regard to academia, the Henricians were also effective teachers and researchers, considerate pastoral guardians of their younger colleagues and skilled governors of their schools. They gained experience in matters financial, pastoral, administrative and legal, thus setting themselves up for future success. This showed us that the bishops were capable in many fields.

The third conclusion is that the Henricians served God and king equally well, as is evinced by their service records. In their service to the church (which could be termed 'Episcopal apprenticeships') we found an average of sixteen years between first spiritual appointment and Episcopal consecration. In this time the Henricians distinguished themselves at every level in the church hierarchy, as humble curates and chaplains and as lordly deans. If service to God had been the only criteria for Episcopal elevation, then we would have to call them distinguished indeed. Add to this their educations and crown services, and we find an Episcopal bench with members both spiritually strong and bureaucratically fit. One would think that in the hands of such men the church was safe (and, largely, it was). There is, however, the old canard that as they served both God and crown, whenever considerations in the latter proved the more immediate, elements in the former suffered.

The fourth conclusion is that this was not the case to any debilitating degree. When such thinking was put to the test, we found that historical orthodoxy had failed the Henricians yet again. The bishops (as a group and as individuals) had a surprisingly limited involvement in the 'temporal' kingdom prior to their Episcopal promotions but, where they had been involved, the spiritual welfare of the nation had not suffered too much. This means that worldly considerations were not as singularly important to Henry VIII in choosing his bishops as historical orthodoxy suggests. Such matters as training, education and ecclesiastical experience were at least as important to him, if not more so. This is by no means to claim that the bishops were uninvolved in temporal affairs. They served the king personally, they served him administratively and they served him diplomatically in offices at all levels. Far from unimportant, these temporal services were valuable in terms of character evaluation and in that they engendered loyalty and a sense of duty to the secular state. This was experience that the bishops would need as members of the lords and as the heads of diocesan administrations.

All told, from the first part of this study we found out several interesting facts. The men who became Henrician bishops were career-minded social climbers, diplomats, ecclesiastical administrators, government functionaries, spiritual leaders and matchless intellectuals who served the crown and the church in several ways. We found out that, for the most part, secular service was joined to considerable spiritual experience. The combination of this with superior academic attainments and intellectual pursuits gave the king a pool of talent from which to draw. This was that 'extra-something' for which he looked. Having uncovered this information we went on, in the main body of this study, to put our conclusions to the test. As bishops, had they fulfilled the promise they seemed to exhibit in their earlier careers? How influential were they on the king and on the events of the period and, conversely, how influential were the events and the king on them?

The fifth conclusion is that influence was reciprocal. In 1509, Henry VIII was untried, inexperienced and untrained for his new role. His closest companions were mostly young noblemen with whom he searched for martial glory. Luckily, the men who dominated the council were seasoned administrators and diplomats, well trained in the previous reign, but used to having a king personally involved in affairs of state taking a leadership role. They managed to gain for the new king what he most wanted while limiting the damage on the rest of the nation. If, as in one famous case, the diocesan cure of souls seems to have suffered, at least there was a peaceful domestic *status quo* maintained. In this early period the king observed the perplexing nature of sovereignty and learned that he could not match Francis I or Charles V in the pursuance of arms or wealth. He also found that he was better suited to a supervisory role in governmental terms (setting the wider agenda) rather than, as had been his father, to handling the intricate details. He found that it is true, no matter what else might be so, that lawyers cannot leave well enough alone and, therefore, that the bishops needed some kind of supervision. He also found that he could outdo his continental rivals as a renaissance-prince by surrounding himself with scholars of varied experience. Finally, he discovered that he could effectively rule all manner of men with least trouble to himself through one minister. The upshot of all this is that due to the early influence of politically-minded bishops, the Episcopate itself was altered by the king. What had been a body dominating the government as lawyers and politicians, slowly evolved into one dominating society and the court as thinkers, pundits and intellectuals.

Consequently, when in the 1520s Henry VIII faced up to the dynastic problem that his marriage created, the solution was formulated not by Episcopal diplomats and lawyers but by humanist intellectuals and scholars. These men produced a useful, almost unanswerable curative (unanswerable in that they had no love for the pope or for papal authority) and they showed the king just how uncaring the papacy was when its own interests were threatened. In so doing, they laid the foundation for a national church shielded (or dominated if you like) by the king himself, he becoming a true *fidei defensor*. By providing the king with a theoretical basis for his annulment, they planted the seeds of an imperial kingship (which Cromwell developed to such a startling effect) and nurtured to full growth the royal supremacy. The result of this was, of course, schism, the drawing up of the old medieval orders and the development of a unique 'English' church organisation.

To be schismatic in early modern Europe was easy enough. To combine anti-papal thinking with orthodox dogma was much more difficult. To do this, the king needed religiously devoted, but anti-papal, disciples. If it is true that lawyers cannot leave well enough alone, it is equally true that intellectuals cannot deal in practicalities. To be schismatic was one thing. To be secure from outside threats, however, the king needed the support of the entire nation. To convince the people of his righteousness he needed the message drummed into them by clerical and temporal officers alike. He also needed church leaders who would be sincere in attacking *all things* papal.

This created another split. This time, a three-way division of the Episcopal bench itself. Those who supported *all things* papal condemned those who pursued radical change. Against both stood those who resisted radical change but who supported the king. As supreme head it was Henry VIII's role to lead. It was his role to determine all of those intricate details, to keep an eye on the bigger picture, an exercise we know he found odious. In the absence of the king's leadership, the bishops did the best they could and, all told, it must be said they did rather well.

By the 1540s, after almost a decade of religious experimentation, the king had grown older and more conservative. He increasingly found theology a nit-picking discipline, and intellectual theologians too stubborn in their views. He thus increasingly turned his mind back towards the missed military glories of his youth and began to surround himself not with theologians, not with lawyers, but with a select few administrators and statesmen (now increasingly lay figures). The men who now became bishops were diplomats (like Knight), administrators (like Thirlby) or non-entities who rarely left their diocesan posts. The Episcopal bench, with few exceptions, had become a body of dedicated pastoral shepherds.

The bishops influenced the king and events, and vice-versa. Of course, this simple synopsis leaves out many of the other determining factors and as such, appears *a priori*. Rather than make too much of a cause and effect argument, however, I have been a little more cautious and have tried throughout this study to include other determining factors. Be these factors issues of political context, diplomatic relations or social influences, all were considered if only as a backdrop. In so doing I have shown that the bishops were promoted because they had all the necessary intellectual, moral and practical 'stuff' to face these matters effectively. I have also shown that they had a clear and concise impact on the events of the reign and that the events of the reign had a clear, concise and corresponding impact upon them.

Finally, the sixth conclusion is that not only was Henry VIII an important and leading figure, not only did he use his authority with clear ends in mind, but that he also selected as bishops (the points of contact between the temporal and the spiritual and between the crown and the commons) men who could serve well and who did serve well. He chose men who could focus on day-to-day matters without losing sight of the larger picture. He picked men who at once cushioned him against the niggling minutiae of authority and shielded the laity from the sometimes harsh realities of reformation and politics. Significantly, Henry VIII and his bishops did this during one of the most unsettled periods of British and European history, the consequences of which we still face today.

# Tables

## Table 1: Social Degree

| Period | Nobles | Lesser Nobles | Esquires | Gentlemen | Yeomen | Commons |
|---|---|---|---|---|---|---|
| 1509 | | Audley<br>Stanley | de'Gigli | Fitzjames<br>Oldham<br>Owain<br>Smith<br>Warham<br>Blythe<br>Nix<br>R Fox | Fisher<br>Bainbridge<br>Mayew<br>Penny<br>Salley<br>Sherburne<br>Vaughan | e'Castellesi |
| 1510s | | | Booth | de'Athequa<br>Skevington<br>Ruthal<br>Veysey | Atwater<br>Birkhead<br>Kite<br>Standish<br>West<br>Wolsey | |
| 1520s | Campeggio<br>de'Ghinucci<br>de'Medici | | | Longland<br>Tunstal | Rawlins<br>Clerk | |
| 1530s | | | Cranmer | E Fox<br>Gardiner<br>E Lee<br>R Lee<br>Rugg<br>Stokesley<br>Holgate<br>Goodrich | Bonner<br>Aldrich<br>Barlow<br>Bell<br>Bird<br>Capon<br>Heath<br>Hilsey<br>Sampson<br>Shaxton<br>Skip<br>Wharton | Latimer |
| 1540s | | | | Bulkeley<br>Kitchen<br>Thirlby | Bush<br>Chambers<br>Day<br>Holbeach<br>King<br>Wakeman | Knight |

# Table 2: Shire Origins

| Shire | 1509 | 1510-1519 | 1520-1529 | 1530-1539 | 1540-1547 |
|---|---|---|---|---|---|
| Northumberland | | | | R Lee | |
| Westmorland | Bainbridge | | | | |
| Yorkshire | Fisher | | Tunstal | | Holgate |
| Lancashire | Smith<br>Oldham<br>Stanley | Booth<br>Standish | | | |
| Derbyshire | Blythe | | | | |
| Nottinghamshire | | | | Cranmer | Kitchen |
| Lincolnshire | R Fox | | | Goodrich | Holbeach |
| Shropshire | | | | Rugg | Day |
| Staffordshire | Audley<br>Sherborne | | | | |
| Leicestershire | | | | Latimer<br>Skevington | |
| Norfolk | | | | Shaxton<br>Skip | |
| Warwickshire | | Veysey | | Bird | |
| Northamptonshire | | | | Stokesley | |
| Cambridgeshire | | | | | Thirlby<br>Chambers |
| Suffolk | | Wolsey | | Gardiner | |
| Worcestershire | | | | Bonner<br>Bell | Wakeman |
| Gloucerstershire | Ruthal | | | E Fox | |
| Oxfordshire | | | Longland | | King |
| Buckinghamshire | | | | Aldrich | |
| Essex | | | | Capon | |
| Wiltshire | | | | Bush | Bush |
| Berkshire | | | | Hilsey | |
| Surrey | | West | | Sampson | |
| Kent | | | | E Lee | |
| Hampshire | Warham<br>Mayew | | | | |
| Somersetshire | Fitzjames<br>Nix | Atwater | | | |
| Wales | Owain<br>Vaughan | | | Barlow | Bulkeley |
| Unknown | Salley<br>Penny | Birkhead | Rawlins<br>Clerk | Wharton | |
| London | | Kite | | Heath | Knight |
| Italy | de'Giglis<br>de'Castellesi | Campeggio | de'Medici<br>de'Ghinucci | | |
| Spain | | de'Athequa | | | |

# Table 3: Education

| Bishop | Institutions Grammar | College | Highest Degree Foreign | |
|---|---|---|---|---|
| Aldrich | Eton | King's | | DD (1530) |
| Atwater | Eton | Magdalen | | DD (1493) |
| Audley | | Lincoln | | MA (1471) |
| Bainbridge | | Queen's | Ferrara Bologna | LLD (?) |
| Barlow | | Wadham | | DD (?) |
| Bell | | Balliol | ? | LLD (?) |
| Bird | | Carmelite's | | DD (1513) |
| Birkhead | | Cambridge (?) | | DTh (1503) |
| Blythe | Eton | King's | ? | ? |
| Bonner | | Pembroke | | DCivL (1525) |
| Booth | | Pembroke | Bologna | DCivL (?) |
| Bulkeley | | New Inn | | ? |
| Bush | | Wadham | | DD (c.1519) |
| Capon | | Benedictine's | | DD (?) |
| Chambers | | Oxf/Camb. | | BD (1539) |
| Clerk | | Cambridge (?) | Bologna | LLD, DCanL (1510) |
| Cranmer | | Jesus | | DD (?) |
| Day | | Cambridge (?) | | ? |
| Fisher | | Michaelhouse | | DTh (1510) |
| Fitzjames | | Merton | | DD (1481) |
| Fox, Edward | Eton | King's | | DD (?) |
| Fox, Richard | Winchester | Magdalen | Louvain Paris | DCanL, DCL |
| Gardiner | | Trinity | | DCL, DCanL (1521) |
| Goodrich | | Oxf/Camb. | | DD (c.1529) |
| Heath | St Anthony's | Oxf/Camb. | | DD (1535) |
| Hilsey | | Dominican's | | DD (1532) |
| Holbeach | | Buckingham | | DD (1534) |
| Holgate | | St John's | | DD (1537) |
| King | Cistercian's | St John's | | DD (1519) |
| Kitchen | | Gloucester | | DD (1538) |
| Kite | Eton | King's | | BCanL (1495) |
| Knight | Winchester | New College | Ferrara | DCL (1507) |
| Latimer | | Clare | | BD (1524) |
| Lee, Edward | | Magdalen | Bologna Louvain | DD (1530) |
| Lee, Roland | | St Nicholas's | | DDecrees (1520) |
| Longland | | Magdalen | | DD (1511) |
| Mayew | | Magdalen | | DTh (1478) |
| Nix | | Trinity | Ferrara Bologna | LLD, DCanL (1483) |

| Bishop | Institutions | | Highest Degree |  |
|--------|-------------|---------|-------|---|
|        | Grammar     | College | Foreign |  |
| Oldham | Stanley Household | Queen's |  | BCL (1493) |
| Owain |  | ? |  | ? |
| Penny | Austin Canon's | Lincoln |  | DCL (?) |
| Rawlins |  | Merton |  | DD (1495) |
| Rugg | Norwich Priory | Caius |  | DD (1513) |
| Ruthal |  | Oxf/Camb. |  | DCanL (1499) |
| Salley |  | ? |  | ? |
| Sampson |  | Trinity | Paris | DCL, DCanL (1520) |
|  |  |  | Perugia |  |
|  |  |  | Siena |  |
| Shaxton | Gonville | Gonville |  | BD (1521) |
| Sherborne | Winchester | New College |  | MA (?) |
| Skevington | Cistercian's | St Bernard's |  | ? |
| Skip |  | Gonville |  | DD (1535) |
| Smith | Stanley Household | Lincoln |  | DCanL (1496) |
| Standish | Hereford (?) | Oxf/Camb. |  | DTh (1502) |
| Stanley | Stanley Household | Oxf/Camb. | Paris | DCanL (1506) |
| Stokesley | Magdalen | Magdalen | Rome | DD (c.1515) |
| Thirlby |  | Trinity |  | DCanL (1530) |
| Tunstal |  | Oxf/Camb. | Rome | DCanL, DCivL (?) |
|  |  |  | Padua |  |
| Vaughan |  | Cambridge (?) |  | DCL/CivL (1482) |
| Veysey |  | Magdalen |  | DLaws (1492) |
| Wakeman | Benedictine's | Gloucester |  | BD (1511) |
| Warham | Wykeham's | New College |  | LLD (1500) |
| West | Eton | King's |  | LLD (c.1486) |
| Wharton |  | Cambridge (?) |  | BD (1525) |
| Wolsey | Magdalen | Magdalen |  | DD (?) |

# Table 4: Academic Services

| Bishop | Institution | Services | |
|---|---|---|---|
| | | **College Offices** | **University Offices** |
| Aldrich | King's College | Master, Eton (1515-20) | preacher (1523) |
| | | Provost (Eton - 1534) | Proctor (1524-7) |
| Atwater | Magdalen College | bursar | Vice-chancellor (1500-02) |
| | | | Temp. Chancellor (1500) |
| Bainbridge | Queen's College | Provost (1495) | |
| Blythe | King's College | | Master of King's Hall |
| Cranmer | Jesus College | reader in divinity | common reader |
| | | | public examiner |
| Day | Cambridge (?) | | public orator |
| | | | Master (St John's) |
| | | | Vice-chancellor (1537) |
| | | | Provost (King's -1538) |
| Fisher | Michaelhouse | Master (1497) | Senior proctor (1494) |
| | | | Vice-chancellor (1501) |
| | | | Chair of Divinity (1503) |
| | | | Chancellor (1504) |
| Fitzjames | Merton | bursar | Senior proctor (1473) |
| | | Warden of Merton | Principal (St Alban's) |
| Fox, Edward | King's College | Provost (1528) | |
| Fox, Richard | Magdalen | | Master of Pembroke |
| Gardiner | Trinity | Lecturer (1524) | Statute revisions |
| | | Master (Trinity) | |
| Goodrich | King's College | | Proctor (1515) |
| | Corpus Christi College | | |
| | Jesus | | |
| Latimer | Cambridge (?) | | preacher |
| Lee, Edward | Magdalen | | Proctor (1515) |
| Longland | Magdalen | bursar | |
| | | Principal (1505) | |
| Mayew | Magdalen | President | Senior proctor (1469) |
| | | | Chancellor (1503) |
| Rawlins | Merton | bursar(s) | |
| | | Dean(s) | |
| | | Warden (1508-21) | |
| Ruthal | Oxf/Camb. (?) | | Chancellor (Camb. 1503) |
| Shaxton | Gonville | President (Gonville) | preacher |
| | | Inceptor in Divinity | |
| Sherborne | New College | | Secretary (1480-86) |

| Bishop | Institution | Services | |
|---|---|---|---|
| | | **College Offices** | **University Offices** |
| Skip | Gonville | Master (Gonville) | |
| | | President (Gonville) | |
| Smith | Lincoln | | Keeper of the Hanaper |
| | | | Chancellor (Oxford) |
| Stokesley | Magdalen | usher (1497) | Northern proctor (1503) |
| | | Prelector in logic | |
| | | Preston Chaplain (1506) | |
| | | Principal (1498) | |
| | | bursur (1502) | |
| | | Dean of Divinity | |
| | | Prelector in Philosophy | |
| | Vice-president (1505) | | |
| | | Act. President (1510) | |
| Thirlby | Trinity | commissary (1528-34) | |
| Warham | New College | | moderator of civil law |
| West | King's College | | Proctor |
| Wolsey | Magdalen | Master | |
| | | Jnr. burser (1498-9) | |
| | | Snr. burser (1500) | |
| | | Dean of Divinity | |

# Table 5: Secular Offices (Lower)

| Bishop | Vicarages | Offices / Rectories | Prebends |
|--------|-----------|---------------------|----------|
| Aldrich | Stanton Harcourt 1528 | Cherton 1531 | Centum Solidorum 1528 |
| | | | Decem Librarum 1528/9 |
| | | | Windsor 1534 |
| Atwater | Cumnor | Piddlehinton | Wells 1498 |
| | | Spetisbury | St George's 1504-14 |
| | | St Nicholas | Ruscombe 1512 |
| | | Hawkridge 1498 | Liddington 1512 |
| | | Ditcheat | St Stephen's 1512 |
| | | | Salisbury |
| | | | Llangan in St David's |
| Audley | | Mackworth 1465 | Colwall 1464 |
| | | Berwick St John 1465 | Windsor |
| | | Bursted Parva 1471 | Iwern 1467 |
| | | Llanaber | Farrendon 1472 |
| | | Preston 1473 | St George's Chapel 1474 |
| | | | Gaia Minor 1474 |
| | | | Codeworth 1475 |
| | | | Mora 1476 |
| | | | Givendale 1478 |
| Bainbridge | All Cannings 1498 | St Leonard's 1475 | South Grantham |
| | | Pembridge 1485 | Chardstock 1485/6 |
| | | Aller 1497-1505 | Horton 1485/6 |
| | | Meonstoke 1497 | North Kelsey 1495-1500 |
| | | Farindon 1498 | Exeter 1499 |
| | | Wroughton 1499 | Strensall 1503 |
| Bell | | Subedge 1518 | Lichfield |
| | | | St Paul's |
| | | | Lincoln |
| | | Southwell | |
| Blythe | | Corfe 1494/5 | Strensall 1493 |
| | | | Sneating 1496 |
| | | | Stratton 1499 |
| Bonner | | Cherry Burton 1529 | |
| | | Ripple 1529 | |
| | | Bledon 1529 | |
| | | East Dereham 1534 | |
| Booth | | Normanton 1493 | St Helen's 1495 |
| | | | St James' Garlick 1495 |
| | | | St Mary's Altar |
| | | | Beverley 1501 |
| | | | Clifton 1501 |
| | | | Farendon 1504 |
| | | | Reculverland 1505 |

| Bishop | Vicarages | Offices Rectories | Prebends |
|---|---|---|---|
| Bulkeley | | Llanddeusant 1525 | St Asaph 1525 |
| | | St James' Garlick 1531 | |
| | | Llangeinwen 1537 | |
| Clerk | | Hothfield 1508 | |
| | | Rothbury 1512 | |
| | | Portishead 1513 | |
| | | Ditcheat 1513-17 | |
| | | Ivychurch 1514 | |
| | | West Tarring 1514 | |
| | | Charlton 1514 | |
| | | South Molton 1519 | |
| | | Coltishall 1519 | |
| Cranmer | | Bredon 1530 | |
| Day | All Hallow's 1537 | | |
| Fisher | | Lythe 1499 | |
| Fitzjames | Minehead 1484 | Spetisbury 1472 | Taunton 1474 |
| | | Trent 1476 | Portpoole 1485 |
| | Aller 1485 | | |
| Fox, E. | | Combemartin 1528 | Osbalswiche 1527 |
| | | SS Mary and George | |
| Fox, R. | Stepney 1485 | | Bishopstone 1485 |
| | | | Nunnington 1485 |
| | | | Brownswood 1485 |
| | | | Grantham borealis 1486 |
| Gardiner | | St Michael's Gloucester | |
| Goodrich | | St Peter Cheap 1529 | St Stephen's 1529-34 |
| Heath | Hever 1531 | Bishopsbourne 1537 | |
| Kite | | Wolferton 1496 | Stratton 1517 |
| | | Boscombe 1499 | Exeter c.1507 |
| | | Harlington 1510 | Chichester 1507 |
| | | Weye at Weyhill 1510 | Crediton 1509 |
| Knight | | Barton 1504 | Farrendon 1516 |
| | | Sandhurst 1508 | Horton 1517 |
| | | Stowting 1513 | Chamberlainwood 1517 |
| | | All Hallow's Bread Street 1515 | Llavair 1520 |
| | | Bangor Monachorum | Westminster 1527 |
| | | Romald Kirk 1527 | |
| Latimer | | West Kington 1531 | Exeter 1509 |
| Lee, Edward | | Freshwater 1509 | Rothfem 1510 |
| | | Odiham 1530 | Welton Beckhall 1512 |
| | | | All Cannings |
| | | | Donnington 1530 |
| | | | St Stephen's 1530 |
| Lee, Roland | | Banham 1520 | Norton 1512 |
| | | Ashdon 1522-33 | Curborough 1527 |
| | | Fenny Compton 1526 | Ripon 1533 |
| | | St Sepulchre's 1532 | Wetwing 1533 |

| Bishop | Vicarages | Rectories | Offices Prebendaries |
|---|---|---|---|
| Longland | Thorverton 1508 | Woodham Ferrers 1504 | North Kelsey 1514 |
| | | Lifton 1518 | Alton Borealis 1514 |
| | | | St Stephen's |
| | | | St George's 1519 |
| Mayew | | Wolverton 1466 | Combe 1475 |
| | | Weston-super-Mare 1471 | Ramsbury 1500 |
| | | St Thomas 1471 | St Stephen's Altar 1504 |
| | | St Pierre Calais 1472 | |
| | | Brightwell 1480 | |
| | | West Meon 1482 | |
| Nix | Stokenham 1492 | Ashbury 1473 | St Crimtock 1489 |
| | | Cheddon 1490 | Woodburgh 1493 |
| | | Chedzoy 1490 | Huish 1494 |
| | | Bishop Wearmouth 1496 | Friday Thorpe 1494 |
| | | High Ham 1499 | St George's 1497 |
| | | South Moulton 1499 | Westbury on Trym 1498 |
| | | | Yatton 1498 |
| | | | Merymouth 1498 |
| Oldham | | St Mildred 1485 | St Stephen's 1492 |
| | | Lanivet 1488 | Exeter 1494 |
| | | Swineshead 1493 | Colwich 1495 |
| | | Cheshunt 1494 | Alton Borealis 1495 |
| | | Alphington 1495 | Stoke Newington 1497 |
| | Overton 1501 | Leighton Buzzard 1497 | W a r b o y s |
| 1499 | South Cave 1499 | | Iverton 1499 |
| Crediton 1500 | | | |
| Shillington 1500 | | Freford 1501 | |
| Freechapel 1503 | | Overton 1501 | |
| | Gillingham | | |
| Rawlins | | St Mary Woolnoth 1494 | Beverley Willesden 1499 |
| | | Hendon 1504 | St Michael's Altar 1503 |
| | | Thornton 1505 | Howden 1506 |
| | | St Martin's Ludgate 1514 | St George's Chapel 1506 |
| | | | St Stephen's 1518 |
| Ruthal | | Bocking 1495 | Wells 1502 |
| | | Monks Risborough 1500 | Ruscombe 1503 |
| | | Southam 1500 | Lincoln 1505 |
| | | Barnsley 1501 | Exeter 1508 |
| | | Stratton 1502 | |
| | | Sampson | Stepney 1526 |
| | | Wheathampsted 1523 | Newbold 1519 |
| | | Hackney 1534 | Chiswick 1522 |
| | | | Langford Ecclesia |
| | | | Lichfield 1532-3 |
| Shaxton | | Fuggleston 1533 | St Stephen's 1534 |

| Bishop | Vicarages | Offices Rectories | Prebendaries |
|---|---|---|---|
| Sherborne | | Childrey 1491 | Langford Manor 1486 |
| | | Rodmerton 1496 | Milton Manor 1493 |
| | | | Langford 1494 |
| | | | Wildland 1489 |
| | | | Whitechurch and Binegar |
| | | | Warminster |
| | | | Finsbury 1493 |
| | | | Mora 1496-7 |
| | | | Milverton |
| | | | Henfield |
| | | | Leckford |
| Skip | Thaxted 1534-5 | Newington 1537-8 | St Stephen's 1535 |
| Smith | | Donington 1483 | Sadlescombe 1479 |
| | | | St Stephen's 1485 |
| | | Combe Martyn 1486 | Wherwell Abbey 1487 |
| | | Great Grimsby 1486 | Holy Trinity 1487 |
| | | Cheshunt 1492 | Tamworth 1490 |
| | | Syerscote 1492 | |
| Stanley | | Eccleston 1482 | Southwell 1479 |
| | Walton on the Hill 1485 | Beaminster 1493 | |
| Hawarden 1487 | | Givendale and Skelton | |
| Winwick 1494 | | Yetminster 1505 | |
| Rosthorne 1498 | | | |
| Stokesley | Willoughby 1505/6 | Slimbridge 1505/6 | Wherwell Abbey 1528-9 |
| | | Brightstone 1518 | St Stephen's |
| | | Ivychurch 1523 | |
| Thirlby | | Ribchester 1539 | St Stephen's 1537 |
| | | | Yeatminster 1539 |
| Tunstal | | Barmston 1506 | Stow Longa 1511 |
| | | Stanhope 1508 | Botevant 1519 |
| | | Sutton Veny 1509 | Combe and Hornham 1521 |
| | | Aldridge 1509 | |
| | | Steeple Langford 1509 | |
| | | East Peckham 1511 | |
| | | Harrow-on-the-Hill 1511 | |
| Vaughan | Islington 1499 | St Matthew Friday 1487 | Reculverland 1493 |
| | | Avening 1498 | Harleston 1499 |
| | | | Bromesbury 1503 |
| | | | Llanbister |
| Veysey | St Michael's 1507-20 | St Blaize 1495 | Darlington 1498 |
| | | Clifton Reynes 1495-9 | Exeter 1503 |
| | | Brize Norton 1497 | Crediton 1504 |
| | | Edgmond 1497 | St Stanford's 1512 |
| | | St Mary's on the Hill 1499 | Liddington 1514 |
| | | Stoke Teignheld 1504 | St Stephen's 1514-8 |
| | | Meifod 1518 | |

| Bishop | Vicarages | Offices<br>Rectories | Prebendaries |
|---|---|---|---|
| Warham | | Great Horwood 1488<br>Blenkenoll 1497<br>Barley 1495<br>Cottenham 1500 | Timsbury in Romsey |
| West | Kingston on Thames 1502<br>Merton 1508 | Yelford 1489<br>Egglescliffe 1499-1515<br>Witney 1502<br>Eltord 1502 | |
| Wolsey | Lydd 1501 | Limington 1500<br>Redgrave 1506<br>Great Torrington 1510<br><br>Llanhister | Pratum Minus 1508<br>Welton Brinkhall 1508/9<br>Stow Longa 1509<br>Windsor 1511<br>Bugthorpe 1512<br>Compton Dunden 1513 |

## Table 6: Secular Offices (Higher)

| Bishop | Archdeaconries | Offices<br>Deaneries | Others |
|---|---|---|---|
| Aldrich | Colchester 1531<br>Lewes 1509-12 | Salisbury 1509<br>St George's Chapel 1502 | Officer of Bishop Longland<br>Chancellor of Lincoln Cathedral 1506-12 |
| Atwater<br>Huntingdon 1514 | | | |
| Audley | East Riding, Yorks 1475<br>Essex 1479<br>Surrey 1501 | | Trustee, Savoy Hospital |
| Bainbridge | | York 1503<br>St George's Chapel 1505 | Treasurer of St Paul's 1497 |
| Bell | Gloucester | | Vicar-general/Chancellor 1518<br>Wolsey's commissary for Salisbury<br>Warden, Stratford-upon-Avon 1518<br>Master, St Walstan's Hospital 1518<br>Treasurer, Salisbury 1494 |
| Blythe | Cleveland 1493<br>Gloucester 1497/8<br>Leicester 1535<br>Buckingham 1505 | York 1496<br>Salisbury 1499 | |
| Bonner | | | Chaplain to Wolsey 1529<br>Treasurer of Lichfield 1495 |
| Booth | | | Chancellor/Commissary to Bishop Smith<br>Advocate - Court of Arches 1495 |
| Clerk | Colchester 1519 | St George's Chapel 1519 | Chaplain to Wolsey<br>Master - St Mary's Hospital 1509<br>Grand Penitentiary for England 1529<br>Orator to the Apostolic See 1529 |
| Cranmer | Taunton 1529-30 | | |
| Day | | | Chaplain to Bishop Fisher |
| Fitzjames | | | Treasurer of St Paul's 1483-97<br>Master - St Leonard's Hospital 1493 |

| Bishop | Archdeaconries | Offices Deaneries | Others |
|---|---|---|---|
| Fox, Edward | Leicester 1531 | Salisbury 1533 | Secretary to Wolsey<br>Master - Sherburn Hospital 1528 |
| Fox, Richard Gardiner | Norfolk 1528-9<br>Worcester 1530<br>Leicester 1531<br>Stafford 1534 | | Grammar Master - Stratford-upon-Avon<br>Private secretary to Wolsey c.1524 |
| Heath | | Shoreham 1531-2<br>South Malling 1537 | |
| Kite | | | Sub-dean of St George's Chapel<br>Archbishop of Armagh 1513 |
| Knight | Chester 1532<br>Huntingdon 1523<br>Richmond 1529 | | |
| Lee, Edward | Colchester 1523<br>Surrey 1530 | | Chancellor - Salisbury 1529 |
| Lee, Roland | Cornwall 1528<br>Taunton 1533 | | Chancellor to Bishop Blythe |
| Longland | Oxford 1493 | Salisbury 1514 | Chaplain to Bishop Smith 1488<br>Warden - Estwyke Chapel 1487 |
| Mayew  York 1501 | | St Stephen's Chapel 1497 | Vicar-general to Bishop R Fox 1493-6 |
| Nix | Exeter 1491-2<br>Wells 1494<br>Exeter 1492/3 | | |
| Oldham | | Wimborne 1485<br>St John's College 1493 | Master - St John's Hospital 1496<br>Master - St Leonard's Hospital 1500 |
| Rawlins | Cleveland 1507<br>Huntingdon 1514 | | Sub-dean of York 1504 |

| Bishop | Archdeaconries | Offices Deaneries | Others |
|---|---|---|---|
| Ruthal | Gloucester 1503<br>Lincoln 1505<br>Wimborne 1508 | Salisbury 1502 | Protonotary 1499 |
| Sampson | Cornwall 1517<br>Suffolk 1528/9 | St Stephen's 1516<br>St George's Chapel 1516<br>Windsor 1523<br>Lichfield 1533 | Chaplain to Wolsey<br>Chancellor of Tournai 1514<br>Vicar-general to Wolsey<br>Treasurer - Salisbury 1535<br>Treasurer - Salisbury 1533 |
| Shaxton |  |  |  |
| Sherborne | Buckinghamshire 1495<br>Huntingdon 1496<br>Taunton 1496 | St Paul's 1499 | Treasurer - Hereford 1486<br>Secretary to Cardinal Morton<br>Master - St Cross Hospital 1492-1508<br>Warden - Holy Trinity Hospital 1492<br>Warden - St David by Kingsthorpe 1492 |
| Skip | Suffolk 1536<br>Dorset 1539 |  |  |
| Smith | Surrey 1493 | Wimborne 1485<br>St Stephen's 1490<br>St George's Chapel 1491 | Provost of Wells<br>Arches - Judicial Reform |
| Stanley | Richmond 1500 | St Martin-le-Grand 1485 | Precentor of Salisbury 1485<br>Warden - Collegiate Church of Manchester 1509 |
| Stokesley | Surrey 1522<br>Dorset 1523 | St George's Chapel 1524 | Chaplain to Bishop R Fox 1515-7<br>Precentor - St Mary's Southampton 1518 |
| Thirlby | Ely 1534 | St George's Chapel 1534 | Official to the Archdeacon of Ely 1532<br>Prolocutor of Canterbury Convocation 1540<br>Provost - St Edmund at Salisbury 1534<br>Master - St Thomas' Hospital Southwark 1539 |
| Tunstal | Chester 1515 | Salisbury 1521 | Chancellor to Archbishop Warham 1511<br>Auditor of Causes |

| Bishop | Archdeaconries | Offices Deaneries | Others |
|---|---|---|---|
| Vaughan | Lewes 1488 | | Portioner of St Probus Cornwall 1487 |
| | | | Treasurer of St Paul's 1503 |
| | | | Precentor of Abergwili Carmarthshire 1504 |
| | | | Vicar-general to Bishop Arundel 1498-1502 |
| | | | Chancellor to Bishop Arundel |
| Veysey | Chester 1499-1515 | Exeter 1509 | Precentor of Exeter 1508 |
| | Barnstable 1503 | St George's Chapel 1514 | |
| | | Windsor 1515-9 | |
| | | Wolverhampton 1516-21 | |
| Warham | Huntingdon 1496 | | Warden - Clyst St Gabriel Chapel 1508 |
| | | | Precentor of Wells 1495 |
| | | | Proctor of Bishop Alcock 1490 |
| | | | Advocate - Court of Arches 1488 |
| | | | Proctor of Morton and Alcock in Rome |
| West | Derby 1486 | St George's Chapel 1509 | Vicar-general to Bishop Fox 1501 |
| | | | Treasurer of Chichester 1507 |
| Wolsey | | Lincoln 1509 | Rural Dean of Depwade and Humbleyard 1499 |
| | | Hereford 1512 | Parson of St Bride's Fleet Street 1510 |
| | | York 1513 | Precenter of London 1513 |
| | | St Stephen's 1513 | Chaplain to Archbishop Deane 1501 |
| | | | Bishop of Tournai 1513-8 |
| | | | Chaplain - Deputy of Calais 1503 |

## Table 7: Regular Offices

| Bishop | Priories | Abbacies | Miscellaneous |
|---|---|---|---|
| Barlow | Blackmore, Essex, 1509<br>Tiptree, Essex, 1509-15<br>Leighs, Essex, 1515<br>Bromehill, Norfolk, 1524-8<br>Bisham Abbey, 1527<br>Haverfordwest, 1534-5<br>Bisham, Berkshire, 1535-7 | | Rector, Great Cressingham |
| Bird | | | Carmelite Provincial, 1516-19<br>Suffragan of Llandaff, 1522<br>Suffragan of Penrith, 1537<br>Rector, Edington, 1537 |
| Bush | Edington, 1538 | | |
| Capon | St John's Colchester 1516 | St Benet's Hulme, 1516-7<br>Hyde, Winchester, 1529-39 | |
| Chambers | | | |
| Hilsey | Peterborough (1528)<br>Bristol, May 1533<br>London Dominicans, 1535 | | Dominican Priovincial, 1534 |
| Holbeach | Buckingham College, 1535<br>Worcester, 1536 | | |
| Holgate | St Catherine's London, 1529<br>Watton, Yorks, 1536 | | Dean of Worcester, 1540<br>Suffragan of Bristol, 1538<br>Vicar of Cudney, 1529<br>Master, Order of St Gilbert |
| King | | Brewern 1515<br>Thame, 1530<br>Osenay 1537 | Prebend, Crakepole St Mary<br>Prebend, Biggleswade 1536-41<br>Suffragan to Longland (1527) |

| Bishop | Priories | Abbacies | Miscellaneous |
|---|---|---|---|
| Kitchin | Gloucester Hall, 1526 | Eynsham, 1530-39 | |
| Owain | | Conway | |
| Penny | | St Mary de Pre, 1477<br>Bradley, 1503 | |
| Rugg | Yarmouth, 1520 | St Bennet's Hulme, 1530 | Sacrist, Norwich, 1514<br>Sub-prior of Norwich, 1526 |
| Salley | | Eynesham, 1499-1500 | |
| Skevington | | Waverley, Surrey, 1509<br>Beaulieu, 1509 | |
| Standish | | | Rector, Standish<br>Warden, London Greyfriars<br>Suffragan (?) |
| Wakeman | | Tewkesbury, 1534-9 | |
| Wharton | | Bermondsey, -1538 | |

## Table 8: Royal Service

| Bishop | Personal | Diplomacy | | Government |
|---|---|---|---|---|
| | | As Ambassador to | As Envoy to | |
| Aldrich | Divorce advocate<br>Agent to Syon (1535)<br>Queen's Almoner - Jane Seymour<br>King's Chaplain | | France (1533)<br>Rome (1534) | Registrar (Garter) |
| Atwater | | | ? | Registrar (Garter - c.1504)<br>Request Court Judge<br>Master of the Rolls (1504) |
| Bainbridge | | ? | | |
| Barlow | Divorce advocate | Scotland (1535) | France<br>Rome (1529) | |
| Bell | King's Chaplain<br>Divorce advocate | | | Councillor |
| Bird | Divorce Advocate | Germany (1539) | | |
| Birkhead | King's Preacher | | | |
| Blythe | | Bohemia (1502)<br>Rome (1533)<br>Hamburg (1535)<br>Charles V (?)<br>France (1538) | | |
| Bonner | | Councillor to Arthur | | |
| Booth | | | | Chaplain (Welsh Marches)<br>Chancellor (Welsh Marsches) |
| Bush | King's Chaplain | | | |
| Capon | Divorce advocate | | | |
| Chambers | King's Chaplain (1539) | | | |

| Bishop | Personal | Diplomacy | | Government |
|---|---|---|---|---|
| | | As Ambassador to | As Envoy to | |
| Clerk | | Rome (1521)<br>Rome (1523) | ? | Star Chamber Judge<br>Master of the Roll (1522-3) |
| Cranmer | Divorce advocate | Charles V (1532) | Rome (1529-30) | |
| Day | King's Chaplain | | | |
| Fisher | Confessor to Lady Margaret (1497) | | | |
| Fitzjames | Chaplain to Edward IV<br>Chaplain to Henry VII<br>Almoner to Henry VII (1495) | Calais (1497) | | |
| Fox, Edward | Divorce advocate<br>King's Almoner<br>Queen's Almoner (1536) | Rome (1528)<br>Francis I (1532-3)<br>Scotland (1534)<br>Germany (1536) | Paris (1529-31) | |
| Fox, Richard | Secretary | Scotland (?) | | Principle Secretary<br>Lord Privy Seal |
| Gardiner | Divorce advocate<br>King's Secretary (1529) | Rome (1528)<br>Francis I (1528) | | |
| Goodrich | Divorce advocate<br>King's Chaplain (1529-34) | Francis I (1533) | | |
| Heath | King's Almoner (1536) | Germany (1535) | | |
| Hilsey | | | | Monastic visitation (1534-5) |
| Holbeach | King's Almoner (1540) | | | |
| Holgate | King's Chaplain | | | |
| Kitchin | King's Chaplain (1539) | | | |
| Kite | King's Chaplain (1509) | Charles V (1518) | | Deputy Com. (Jewels - 1520) |

| Bishop | Personal | Diplomacy — As Ambassador to | As Envoy to | Government |
|---|---|---|---|---|
| Knight | Secretary (Henry VII); King's Chaplain (1515); Clerk (Closet - 1520); Secretary (1526) | Spain (1512); Brussels (1514); Switzerland; Charles V (1516); Rome (1527) | ? | |
| Latimer | King's Chaplain (1534) | | | |
| Lee, Edward | King's Chaplain (1520); Almoner (1523) | Aragon (1523); Charles V (1525) | Italy (1529-30) | |
| Lee, Roland | King's Chaplain (1532); Monastic Rep. (1531-4) | | | Advocate (1520); Master (Chancery - 1532) |
| Longland | King's Confessor (1519); King's Almoner (1521) | | | |
| Mayew | King's Chaplain (1484); King's Chaplain (1491); King's Almoner (1497) | | ? (1490) | |
| Nix | | | | Registrar (Garter - 1496-7); Com. of Peace (1495-1504); Almoner at Gravelines (1520) |
| Oldham | Chaplain to Lady Margaret (1509) | | | |
| Rawlins | King's Almoner (1509) | | | |
| Rugg | Divorce advocate | | | |
| Ruthal | Secretary (Henry VII and VIII) | | | |
| Sampson | King's Chaplain; Proctor (Tournai 1516-7); Divorce advocate (1536) | Brussels (1514); Bilbao (1522); Charles V (1529) | Trade commission; ? | Councillor (1502); Advocate (1514-5) |
| Shaxton | Queen's Almoner - Boleyn | | | |
| Sherborne | Secretary (Henry VII) | Rome (1502); Rome (1504) | Rome (1496); Scotland (1503) | Governor of Richmond Castle; Governor of Porchester |

| Bishop | Personal | Diplomacy | | Government |
|---|---|---|---|---|
| | | As Ambassador to | As Envoy to | |
| Skip | Queen's Almoner (1518)<br>Chaplain to Anne Boleyn<br>Almoner to Anne Boleyn | | | Heresy commission (1538) |
| Smith | King's Chaplain | | | |
| Standish | Court Preacher | | | |
| Stokesley | King's Confessor (1516-9) | Francis I (1529) | | Chief - King's Spiritual Council<br>Trier of Petitions (1523) |
| King's Chaplain (1518-20) | | Rome (1529-30)<br>Italy (1529-30) | | Councillor (1520) |
| King's Almoner (1520-24) | | Charles V (1530)<br>Paris (1529-30) | | Requests Court Judge (1520-3) |
| Divorce advocate | | | | |
| Thirlby | King's chaplain (1533)<br>Divorce advocate | France (1538) | France (1533) | Council of the North (1540)<br>Heresy commission (1538, 1540) |
| Tunstal | | Brussels (1515) | Charles V (1520) | Master of the Rolls (1516)<br>Registrar (Garter - 1515) |
| Veysey | Queen's Council (1489) | | | Enclosures Commission (1517) |
| Warham | | Antwerp (1491)<br>Flanders (1493)<br>Scotland (1497)<br>? | Aragon (1496) | Master of the Rolls (1494-1501)<br>Keeper - Great Seal (1501) |
| West | King's Chaplain (1502)<br>Councillor (1504) | Maximilian<br>Scotland (1511)<br>Scotland (1513)<br>Scotland (1512)<br>Louis XII (1514)<br>Francis I (1515) | Saxony (1505)<br>Low Countries | Adv. - Hospitallers<br>Trier of Petitions (1512) |
| Wolsey | King's Chaplain (1507)<br>King's Almoner (1509) | ? | Maximilian<br>Scotland (1508) | Registrar (Garter - 1511)<br>Councillor |

# Table 9: Episcopal Longevity

† - died   d - deprived   r - resigned   ‡ - executed

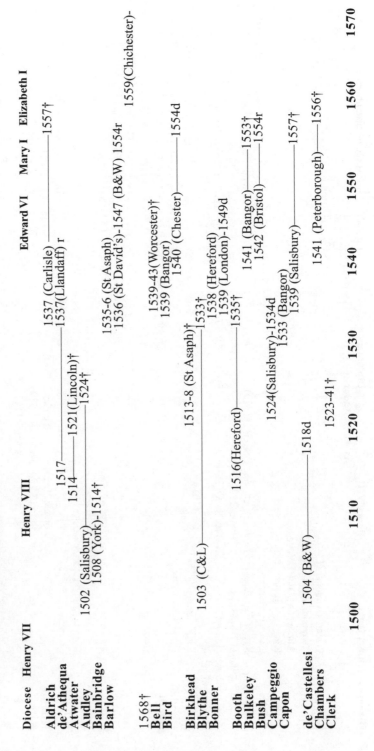

| Diocese | Henry VII | Henry VIII | Edward VI | Mary I | Elizabeth I |
|---|---|---|---|---|---|

Aldrich   1537 (Carlisle)————1557†
de'Athequa   1517 ———— 1537(Llandaff) r
Atwater   1514 ———— 1521(Lincoln)†
Audley   1524†
Bainbridge   1502 (Salisbury)  1508 (York)-1514†
Barlow   1535-6 (St Asaph)  1536 (St David's)-1547 (B&W) 1554r  1559(Chichester)-

1568†
Bell   1539-43(Worcester)†
Bird   1539 (Bangor)  1540 (Chester)————1554d

Birkhead   1513-8 (St Asaph)
Blythe   1503 (C&L)  1533†
Bonner   1538 (Hereford)  1539 (London)-1549d   1535†

Booth   1516(Hereford)
Bulkeley   1541 (Bangor)  1553†
Bush   1542 (Bristol)  1554r
Campeggio   1524(Salisbury)-1534d
Capon   1533 (Bangor)  1539 (Salisbury)————1557†

de'Castellesi   1504 (B&W)————1518d
Chambers   1523-41†
Clerk   1541 (Peterborough)————1556†

1500      1510      1520      1530      1540      1550      1560      1570

Monarch reign columns (left to right): Henry VII | Henry VIII | Edward VI | Mary I | Elizabeth I

Timeline scale: 1500　1510　1520　1530　1540　1550　1560　1570

| Diocese | Entries |
|---|---|
| **Cranmer** | 1532 (Canterbury)————1556‡ |
| **Day** | 1543-51(Chichester)d 1553-6 (Chichester)† |
| **Fisher** | 1504 (Rochester)————1535‡ |
| **Fitzjames** | 1497 (Rochester) 1504 (Chichester) 1506 (London)————1522† |
| **E Fox** | 1535-8(Hereford)† |
| **R Fox** | 1487 (Exeter) 1491 (B&W) 1494 (Durham) 1501 (Winchester)————1528† |
| **Gardiner** | 1553-5† 1531 (Winchester)————1550d |
| **de'Giglis** | 1498 (Worcester) de'Ghinucci————1521† 1522(Worcester)—1534d |
| **Goodrich** | 1534 (Ely)————1554† |
| **Heath** | 1539 (Rochester) 1543-51(Worcester)d 1553-5 1555-9(York)d |
| **Hilsey** | 1535-9 (Rochester)† |
| **Holbeach** | 1544 (Rochester) 1547-51 (Lincoln)† |
| **Holgate** | 1537 (Llandaff) 1545 (York)————1554d |
| **King** | 1541 (O&T) 1545 (O&T) |
| **Kitchin** | 1545 (Oxford)————1557† 1545 (Llandaff)————1565† |
| **Kite** | 1513 (Armagh) 1521-37 (Carlisle)† |

|  | Henry VII | Henry VIII | Edward VI | Mary I | Elizabeth I |
|---|---|---|---|---|---|

**Diocese**

Knight — 1541(B&W)-1547†

Latimer — 1535-9 (Worcester)r

E Lee — 1531(York) —— 1545†

R Lee — 1534(C&L) — 1541†

Longland — 1521(Lincoln) —— 1547†

Mayew — 1504 (Hereford) ——— 1516†

de'Medici — 1521-2 (Worcester)r

Nix — 1501 (Norwich) ———— 1536†

Oldham — 1504 (Exeter) —— 1519†

Owain — 1503 (St Asaph) — 1513†

Penny — 1504 (Bangor) 1508 (Carlisle) —— 1520†

Rawlins — 1523 (St David's) —— 1536†

Rugg — 1536 (Norwich) —— 1550r

Ruthal — 1509 (Durham) —— 1528†

Salley — 1500 (Llandaff) —— 1517†

Sampson — 1536 (Chichester) 1542 (C&L) —— 1554†

Shaxton — 1535-9 (Salisbury)r

Sherborne — 1505 (St David's)x 1508 (Chichester) —— 1536r

Skevington — 1509-33 (Bangor)†

Skip — 1539 (Hereford) —— 1552†

Smith — 1493 (C&L) 1496 (Lincoln) ——— 1514†

Standish — 1518 (St Asaph) —— 1535†

Stanley — 1506 (Ely) — 1515†

Stokesley — 1530 (London)-1539†

Thirlby — 1540 (Westminster) —— 1554-9 (Ely)d

1500    1510    1520    1530    1540    1550    1560    1570

| Diocese | Henry VII | Henry VIII | Edward VI | Mary I | Elizabeth I |
|---|---|---|---|---|---|
| **Tunstal** | | 1522 (London)-1530<br>1530 (Durham)——————————————————————————————1559d | | | |
| **Vaughan** | | 1509 (St David's)————1523† | | | |
| **Veysey** | | 1519 (Exeter)————————————————————————1551retired<br>1553-4 (Exeter)† | | | |
| **Wakeman** | | | 1541-9(Gloucester)† | | |
| **Warham** | 1501-4 (London)<br>1504 (Canterbury)—————————————————1531† | | | | |
| **West** | | 1515 (Ely)————————————1534† | | | |
| **Wharton** | | 1536 (St Asaph)——————————————————————————1554<br>1554-7 (Hereford)† | | | |
| **Wolsey** | | 1513-8 (Tournai)s<br>1514 (Lincoln)-1521<br>1514 (York)————————————1531†<br>1518-22 (B&W)r<br>1528-30 (Durham)r<br>1529-31 (Winchester)† | | | |

# Appendix
## Biographical Information

Some of the following details were taken from the *Biographical Register of the University of Cambridge to 1500*, ed. by A.B. Emden (Cambridge, 1963); *Biographical Register of the University of Oxford to 1500*, ed. by A.B. Emden, 3 vols. (Oxford, 1957-59); J. and J.A. Venn, *Alumni Cantabrigiensis: Part One to 1750*, 4 vols. (Cambridge, 1922-7); *The Dictionary of National Biography* (London, 1885-1901); Thomas Fuller, *The Worthies of England*, ed. by John Freeman (London, 1952 edn); F. Godwin, *A Catalogue of the Bishops of England* (London, 1601); G. Constant, 'Les Evêques Henriciens sous Henri VIII', *Revue Des Questions Historiques* xii (1912), pp. 384-425; L.B. Smith, *Tudor Prelates and Politics* (Princeton, 1953); William D. Macray, *A Register of the Members of Mary Magdalen College, Oxford, from the Foundation of the College*, 4 vols. (Oxford, 1904) and *Handbook of British Chronology*, ed. by E.B. Fryde *et al.* (London, 1986 3rd edn). Where available, more specific sources on the individuals have been listed below their entry.

**Aldrich, Robert** (c.1490-1556). Born at Burnham, Buckinghamshire to yeoman parents. He was educated at Eton and King's College Cambridge (B.A. 1511-2, M.A. 1515, B.D. 1529) and at Oxford (D.D. 1530). He served as schoolmaster of Eton (1515-20) and was a university preacher (1523), university proctor (1524-7) and provost of Eton (from 21 June 1534). He was vicar of Stanton Harcourt, Oxfordshire (1528) and was prebendary of Centum Solidorum (18 July 1528) and of Decem Librarum (from January 1528-9), both in Lincoln. He served **Longland** in some capacity before retiring both prebends in 1529, having gained royal favour and appointments as rector of Cherton, Winchester (3 January 1531) and as archdeacon of Colchester in the London diocese (30 December 1531). He was also canon of Windsor (3 May 1534) before his provision to the see of Carlisle (18 July 1537). As royal chaplain he was often employed by the king on official duties and was counted as a supporter of the Aragon divorce (in which regard he was sent to the troublespot of Syon Abbey in 1535). He was also sent to France with Norfolk in June 1533 and went on a commission with **Bonner** to the pope to lodge the royal appeal against the king's excommunication (1534). He served as Registrar of the Order of the Garter and as Almoner to Queen Jane Seymour. Later, under Edward VI, he opposed further clerical reforms.

**Atwater, William** (1440-1521). Born at either Cannington or Davington in Somerset, or at Downton in Wiltshire to yeoman parents. He was educated at Eton and at Magdalen College, Oxford (D.D. 1492-3) served the college as bursar, and later served the university as Vice-Chancellor (1497, 1500-02) and temporary Chancellor (1500). He was noted by Wood for his regard to 'academic discipline'. His clerical career is impressive, having held several minor offices. He was vicar of Cumnor, Berkshire and rector of Piddlehinton, Spetisbury and St Nicholas (all Berkshire), of Hawkridge in Wiltshire (1498) and of Ditcheat in Somerset. He held prebends in Wells (1498) and Salisbury Cathedrals, was canon of St George's (1504-14), of Ruscombe (1512) and Liddington (1512) in Lincoln, of St Stephen's (1512) and of Llangan in St David's Cathedral. He held higher office as archdeacon of Lewes (1509-12) and Huntingdon (1514), as dean of Salisbury (1509) and of St George's Chapel (1502), and served **Smith** as chancellor of Lincoln Cathedral (1506-12) before his provision to the see of Lincoln (15 September 1514). He also served the king as Registrar of the Order of the Garter (from 21 June 1504).

**Audley, Edmund** (c.1440-1524). Born in Staffordshire, the son of James Tucket (5th Lord Audley) and Eleanor Holland (an illegitimate daughter of Thomas Holland, Earl of Kent). He was educated at Lincoln College Oxford (B.A. 1463, M.A. 1471), a patron of the college thereafter. He held a number of positions, largely as an absentee. He was rector of Mackworth, Derbyshire (1465), Berwick St John, Wiltshire (1465), Bursted Parva (1471) and of Llanaber in Gwynedd. He was canon of Colwall in Hereford Cathedral (1464), of Windsor, of Iwern (1467) and Preston (1473), both in Salisbury Cathedral, of Faringdon in Lincoln Cathedral (1472), St George's Chapel (1474), Gaia Minor in Lichfield (1474), Codeworth in Wells (1475), Mora in St Paul's (1476), Givendale in York Minster (1478) and Tamsworth and Coton in Staffordshire (1479). He was archdeacon of the East Riding of Yorkshire (1475) and of Essex (1479) and was, for a time, a trustee of Savoy Hospital (where he gained a reputation for charity and reform). He resigned all these offices in exchange for the see of Rochester (7 July 1480). He was later bishop of Hereford (provided on 22 June 1492) and bishop of Salisbury (provided 10 January 1502). He served Edward IV as royal clerk and Henry VII as chancellor of the Order of the Garter (from 1502).

**Bainbridge, Christopher** (c.1464-1514). Born at Hilton, Westmorland to yeoman parents. He was educated at Queen's College Oxford (LL.D) which he served as provost (from 1495) and was a patron of the college in his will. His clerical career was extensive. He was vicar of All Cannings Donnington, Yorkshire (1498) and rector of St Leonard's Eastcheap, London (1475), Pembridge, Worcestershire (1485), Aller, Bath and Wells (1497-1505), Meonstoke, Hampshire (1497), Faringdon, Oxfordshire (1498) and of Wroughton, Wiltshire (1499). He was canon of South Grantham, Salisbury

(1485), Chardstock, Devon (1485-6), Horton, Salisbury (1485-6), North Kelsey, Lincoln (1495-1500), Exeter (1499) and of Strensall, York (1503). He held higher clerical office as archdeacon of Surrey (1501), dean of York (1503) and of St George's Chapel (1505 for which he resigned Aller), and was treasurer of St Paul's (1497). He was provided the see of Durham (27 August 1507) and later the see of York (22 September 1508). He was promoted cardinal in March 1511-2. He served Henry VII as master of the rolls (1504) and Henry VIII as ambassador to the pope (1509), carrying out a variety of diplomatic duties in that regard.

Further Sources: D.S. Chambers, *Cardinal Bainbridge in the Court of Rome, 1509-1514* (Oxford, 1965); W.E. Wilkie, *The Cardinal Protectors of England: Rome and the Tudors Before the Reformation* (Cambridge, 1974). Letters by and about him are featured in *Original Letters illustrative of English History*, ed. by H. Ellis, 11 vols. in 3 series (London, 1824, 1827, 1846), i/i. pp.108-12, ii/i. pp.226-32.

**Barlow, William** (d.1568). Little information is certain. Possibly born at Slebech in Wales to yeoman parents. He was educated by the Canon Regulars of St Austin at St Osyth's (Essex) and later at their house in Oxford (D.D.), and also spent some time at Cambridge. He founded free grammar schools at Caermarthen, Brecon and Christ's College. He was a regular of St Osyth's, rector of Great Cressingham, Norfolk (1524) and prior of Blackmore (1509), Tiptree (1509-15) and Leighs (1515) all in Essex, Bromehill, Norfolk (1524-28), Bisham Abbey, Berkshire (1527, 1535-7) and of Haverfordwest, Dyfed (1534-5). Under Henry VIII he was nominated as bishop of St Asaph (1535-6) but translated to St David's (10 April 1535) before consecration. He was later bishop of Bath and Wells (nominated 3 February 1548), which he resigned fromunder Mary I, and bishop of Chichester (nominated 22 June 1559). Under Elizabeth he was also prebendary of Westminster (1560). Barlow was a writer of note, targeting Wolsey with plays and poems. This, and his support of the Aragon divorce, earned him the patronage of the Boleyn family. His most noted work is *A dyaloge descrybyng the originall ground of these Lutheran Faccyons, and many of their abuses* (1553), written for the use of **Stokesley** in the 1530s. He served Henry VIII on embassies to France and Rome (1529) on divorce business, and to Scotland (1535).

Further Sources: A.S. Barnes, *Bishop Barlow and Anglican Orders: A Study of the Original Documents* (London, 1922); C. Jenkins, *Bishop Barlow's Consecration and Archbishop Parker's Register: with some New Documents* (London, 1935); A. Koszul, 'Was Bishop William Barlow Friar Jerome Barlow?', in *The Review of English Studies* 4:13 (1928), pp.25-34. His career is discussed in W.R.W. Stephens, *Memorials of the South Saxon See and Cathedral Church of Chichester* (London, 1876), pp.246-55.

**Bell, John** (d.1556). Born in Worcestershire to yeoman parents. He was educated at Balliol College Oxford (B.Civ.L., D.Civ.L. 1531) and also attended Cambridge (1503-4) and a foreign university some time thereafter. He was rector of Subedge Gloucestershire (1518), held prebends in Lichfield and Lincoln Cathedrals, was canon of Southwell in Durham and of Reculversland in St Paul's (?-1529) and was archdeacon of Gloucester. He served **de'Giglis** as vicar-general and chancellor at Worcester (1518) and **Wolsey** as commissary for Salisbury. He was the warden of the collegiate church of Stratford-upon-Avon (1518), master of St Walstan's Hospital (1518), and bishop of Worcester (11 August 1539 - 17 November 1543 resigned). He served Henry VIII as royal chaplain, as a diplomat and as a councillor, having been appointed by **Wolsey** to examine heresy (1526). He supported the Aragon divorce and served as the king's proxy at Westminster in 1527, examined the scholars of Oxford with **Longland** and **Edward Fox** (1528) and was king's council at Blackfriars (1529) and at Dunstable (1533).

**Bird, John** (d.1558). Born either in Warwickshire or in Coventry to yeoman parents. He was educated at the Carmelite houses in Oxford (B.D. 1510, DD. 1513) and in Cambridge. Although he held none of the usual clerical offices he was elected as the Carmelite provincial (1516-19 and 1522) and served as suffragen (bishop of Penrith) to both **de'Atheque** (1522) and to **Cranmer** (1537). He was elected bishop of Bangor (24 July 1539), translated to Chester (4 August 1541) but deprived (1554) due to his being married. He served as suffragen to **Bonner** in London thereafter. Bird supported the royal supremacy, and served Henry VIII as a go-between to Catherine with **Edward Fox** and Thomas Bedyl (1535) and on an embassy to Germany (1539). No publications, but he left some manuscripts on religious themes.

**Birkhead, Edmund** (d.1518). Birthplace unknown. His parents were probably of the yeoman rank. He was a Franciscan friar and had been educated at Cambridge (D.Th. 1503). One of Henry VIII's favourite preachers, Birkhead is known to have been an opponent of John Colet and to have earned promotion as bishop of St Asaph (provided 15 April 1513).

**Blythe, Geoffrey** (c.1470-1530). Born at Norton, Derbyshire to parents of the gentry class. He was educated at Eton and King's College Cambridge (1483) earning an LL.D. He served as master of King's Hall Cambridge (11 February 1498-9 to 1528) and was a patron of his schools in his will. His clerical career was limited. He was rector of Corfe, Somerset (1494-5), canon of Strensall in York (1493), Sneating in St Paul's (1496) and Stratton in Salisbury (1499). He held higher office as archdeacon of Cleveland (1493) and of Gloucester (1497-8), as dean of York (1496) and Salisbury (1499) and was treasurer of Salisbury (1494) before provision to the see of Coventry and Lichfield (3 August 1503). His service to Henry VIII was extensive. He was ambassador to Ladislaus II of Bohemia (27 May 1502) and was lord president of Wales (1512-24). Controversially, Blythe faced a treason charge in 1508-9 and was later, 1510-11, under investigation for land-fraud dealings.

Further Sources: P. Heath, 'The Treason of Geoffrey Blythe, Bishop of Coventry and Lichfield, 1503-31', in BIHR, 42 (1969), pp.101-09; *Bishop Geoffrey Blythe's Visitations, c.1515-1525*, ed. by P. Heath, 2 vols. (Stafford, 1973); P. Heath, 'Suppliments to Bishop Blythe's Visitations', in *Staffordshire Record Society*, 4th series, vol.8 (1988), pp. 47-56.

**Bonner (or Boner), Edmund** (c.1500-1569). Born at Elmley, Worcestershire. He was thought to have been the illegitimate son of a priest named George Savage, but more likely was born to yeoman parents. He was educated at Pembroke College Oxford (B.Can.L and B.Civ.L. 1519, D.Civ.L. 1525). He was rector of Cherry Burton, Yorkshire (1529), Ripple, Worcestershire (1529), Bledon, Durham (1529) and of East Dereham, Norfolk (1534, served as archdeacon of Leicester (1535) and was chaplain to **Wolsey** (1529). He was elected to the see of Hereford (26 October 1538) but translated to London (elected 20 October 1539) before his consecration. He served Henry VIII as a diplomat, on embassy to the pope (11 July 1533) to appeal against the king's excommunication, to Hamburg (1535) and to Charles V and Francis I (1538). He was involved in the heresy persecution of Anne Askew and was ambassador to Charles V (1542-43). He was imprisoned under Edward VI in opposition to the royal injunctions and the Book of Homilies (1547). Subsequently, he refused to endorse the new Prayer-Book and was imprisoned (1549-53) and deprived of his see for opposing the king's authority. He was restored to London (5 September 1553) but deprived (29 May 1559) for refusing to swear the oath of supremacy under Elizabeth I.
Further Sources: M.F. Sherr, 'Bishop Bonner: A Quasi Erasmian', in *Historical Magazine of the Protestant Episcopal Church* 43 (1974), pp.359-66; G.M.V. Alexander, 'The Life and Career of Edmund Bonner, Bishop of London until his Deprivation in 1549' (unpublished Ph.D. thesis, University of London, 1960).

**Booth (or Bothe), Charles** (d.1535). Born at Barton, Lancashire to parents of the esquire class (second son of Sir Robert Booth). He was educated at Pembroke College Oxford (B.Civ.L. 1484-5) and at Bologna (D.Civ.L. 1493). He was rector of Normanton on Soar, Nottinghamshire (1493), of St James' Garlickhithe, London (1495) and was canon of St Helen's (1495), St Mary's Altar (1501) and Beverley in York (1501), of Clifton (1501) and Faringdon in Lincoln (1504) and of Reculverland in St Paul's (1505). He held higher offices as archdeacon of Buckingham (1505) and was treasurer of Lichfield (1495) and chancellor-commissary to **Smith** at Lincoln (1501-6) before his provision to the see of Hereford (21 July 1516). He served as councillor to Arthur, Prince of Wales, at Ludlow, was an advocate in the court of Arches (1495) and was chancellor-chaplain to the Council of the Welsh Marches.
Further Sources: His register was published by the Canterbury and York Society as *Registrum Caroli Bothe, Episcopi Herefordensis AD MDXVI - MDXXXV*, ed. by A.T. Bannister (London, 1921).

**Bulkeley** (or **Bokeley**), **Arthur** (d.1553). Born at Anglesey, Wales to parents of the Welsh gentry class. He was educated at New Inn Hall, Oxford (perhaps D.Can.L.). He was rector of Llanddeusant, Anglesey (1525) and of St James' Garlickhithe, London (1531) and was prebendary of St Asaph (1525) and of Llangeinwen, Dyfed (1537) prior to his election as bishop of Bangor (18 November 1541).

**Bush, Paul** (1490-1558). Born either in Wiltshire or Somerset to yeoman parents. He was educated by the Austin Canons, possibly at Wadham College Cambridge (B.D., D.D. 1519), having also studied poetry and medicine. He was rector, provost and corrector of the Bonhomme friars of Edington (1537), prior of Edington (1538) and prebendary of Bishopston in Salisbury (1537), before his nomination as the first bishop of Bristol (4 June 1543 - June 1554 resigned). He served Henry VIII as a royal chaplain. Under Mary I he was rector of Winterbourne, Gloucestershire (1555-58). Author of some devotional tracts and some poetry.

Further Sources: Anon, 'Paul Bush, The Last Rector of Edington and First Bishop of Bristol, 1490-1558', in *Wiltshire Notes and Queries*, iv (September 1902), pp.97-107.

**Campeggio, Lorenzo** (1472-1539). Born either at Bologna or Milan to an Italian noble family. He was educated in law at the universities of Pavia, Venice and Bologna, and only took clerical orders after the death of his wife. He was *in commendam* bishop of Feltri (1512), of Salisbury (provided on 2 December 1524 - 21 March 1534 deprived) and archbishop of Bologna (1524). He was created a cardinal (1517), was papal legate to England (1518, 1529) and cardinal protector of England and the Holy Roman Empire. Campeggio famously halted the marriage trial at Blackfriars (1529) and, thereafter, was an opponent of the Aragon divorce.

Further Sources: E.V. Cardinal, *Cardinal Lorenzo Campeggio: Legate to the Courts of Henry VIII and Charles V* (Boston, 1935).

**Capon** (or **Salcot**), **John** (d.1559). Born at Salcot, near Colchester in Essex, to yeoman parents. He was educated by the Benedictines of Cambridge (B.A. 1488, B.D. 1512, D.D. 1515). He was a regular of St John's Abbey, Colchester and was later elected prior (c.1516-17). He was elected abbot of St Benet's Hulme, Norfolk (16 February 1516-7) and later of Hyde, Winchester (15 March 1529) where he remained until 30 April 1539. He held Hyde *in commendam* with the see of Bangor (elected November 1533) and after translation, with the see of Salisbury (nominated 7 July 1539). He supported the Aragon divorce and worked on an official translation of the Bible in 1542.

**Chambers, John** (d.1556). Born at Peterborough, Cambridgeshire to yeoman parents. He was educated by his order at both Oxford and Cambridge (M.A.

1505, B.D. 1539). He was a regular of the Benedictine Abbey of Peterborough where he was elected abbot in 1528 on the recommendation of **Wolsey**. One of Henry VIII's royal chaplains (c.1539), he was nominated first bishop of Peterborough (4 September 1541).

**Clerk, John** (d.1541). Birthplace unknown, his parents were probably of the yeomanry. He was educated at Cambridge (B.A., M.A. 1502, LL.D) and at Bologna (D.Can.L. 1510). He was rector of Hothfield, Kent (1508), Rothbury, Northumberland (1512), Portishead (1513) and Ditcheat (1513-17) both in Somerset, Ivychurch, Kent (1514), West Tarring, Sussex (1514), Charlton, Wiltshire(?) (1514), South Molton, Devon (1519) and Coltishall, Norfolk (1519). He was archdeacon of Colchester (1519), dean of St George's Chapel (1519), some time chaplain to **Wolsey** and master of St Mary's Hospital (1509), prior to his provision to the see of Bath and Wells (26 March 1523). He served the king as a judge in Star Chamber, as master of the rolls (1522-3), royal messenger, envoy, ambassador to Rome (1521, 1523, 1527), to France (1526) and to Cleves (1539-40). He was council to Queen Catherine of Aragon at Blackfriars, had presented the *Assertio Septem Sacramentorum* to Pope Leo X and was author of *Pro Defensione Matrimonii Henrici cum Catherina* (c.1528). Further Sources: His register was published in 1940 by the Somerset Records Society, vol.4, as *The Register of John Clerke as Bishop of Bath & Wells 1523-41*, ed. by H. Maxwell-Lyte. Two of his letters are featured in *Original Letters illustrative of English History*, ed. by H. Ellis, 11 vols. in 3 series (London, 1824, 1827, 1846), ii/i. pp.305-16, 317-24.

**Cranmer, Thomas** (1489-1556). Born at Aslacton, Nottinghamshire to parents of the esquire class. He was educated at Jesus College Cambridge in philosophy, classics and logic (B.A. 1511-12, M.A. 1515, D.D. 1526). He was a fellow (later deprived), reader in divinity, public examiner for Cambridge and common reader at Buckingham (later Magdalene College). Perhaps wisely he declined **Wolsey's** offer to become a founding fellow at Cardinal College. He was rector of Bredon, Worcestershire (1530) and archdeacon of Taunton (1529-30) prior to his provision to the see of Canterbury (21 February 1532). One of only two English bishops to hold papal appointment (the other was **Ruthal**), he was grand penitentiary for England (1529) and orator to the Apostolic See (1529). A supporter of the Aragon divorce, he secured the patronage of the Boleyns and was chaplain to Queen Anne Boleyn. He served Henry VIII as ambassador to the pope and to Charles V (24 January 1532). He was appointed to Edward VI's governing council and was responsible for the first Prayer-Book (1548) which he also revised (1552). Imprisoned by Mary I (1553) for treason, he was condemned by Cardinal Pole as a heretic (1554) and burned at the stake (1556). Author of *Reformatio Legum Ecclesiasticarum* (1550) and several theological tracts. Further Sources: *Miscellaneous Writings and Letters of Thomas Cranmer*, ed. by J.E. Cox (Cambridge, 1846); F.E. Hutchinson, *Cranmer and the Reformation*

(London, 1951); D. MacCulloch, *Thomas Cranmer: A Life* (London, 1996); J. Ridley, *Thomas Cranmer* (Oxford, 1962); C. Smyth & C. Dunlop, *Thomas Cranmer: Two Studies* (Doncaster, 1986 edn.); John Strype, *Memorials of Archbishop Cranmer*, 3 vols (Oxford, 1848); *Narratives of the Days of the Reformation*, ed. by J. Gough (Lodon, 1859), pp.218-75. Cranmer's writings are also featured in *Original Letters illustrative of English History*, ed. by H. Ellis, 11 vols. in 3 series (London, 1824, 1827, 1846), i/ii. pp.33-40; G. Burnet, *The History of the Reformation of the Church of England*, ed. by N. Pocock, 7 vols. (Oxford, 1865), vi. pp.165-6 and N. Pocock, *Records of the Reformation*, 2 vols. (Oxford, 1870), i. pp.334-99, ii. pp.130-4.

**Day, George** (c.1501-56). Born at Newport, Shropshire to yeoman parents. He was educated at Eton and St John's College Cambridge, acting as public orator (1528), as master of St John's, as vice-chancellor (1537) and as provost for King's College (1538-47). He was vicar of All Hallow's the Great, London (1537) and some time chaplain to **Fisher** and to the king, prior to his nomination to the see of Chichester (15 April 1543). He served as almoner to Queen Catherine Parr (1545). He was deprived of his see (10 October 1551) and imprisoned for contempt, but released and restored under Mary I (24 August 1553).
Further Sources: His career is discussed in W.R.W. Stephens, *Memorials of the South Saxon See and Cathedral Church of Chichester* (London, 1876), pp.220-31.

**de'Athequa (or de'Ateca), Jorge.** Born at Ateca, west of Saragossa, to parents of the Spanish gentry. He was educated by the Dominicans. He was confessor to Queen Catherine of Aragon and provided to the see of Llandaff (11 February 1517) from which he resigned in February 1537. He also served as master of St Catherine's Hospital.

**de'Castellesi (or de'Castello), Adriano.** Born at Corneto, Tuscany of an obscure family. His education is unknown, although Polydore Vergil noted that he was a poet and philsopher of modest standing. He was collector of Peter's Pence, papal nuncio, and held a prebend in St Paul's (1492) prior to his provision to the see of Hereford (14 February 1502). He was translated to Bath and Wells on 4 August 1504, but was deprived on 5 July 1518.
Further Sources: His register was published by the Somerset Records Society in 1939, vol.54, as *The Register of Hadrian de Castello as Bishop of Bath and Wells, 1503-1513*, ed. by H. Maxwell-Lyte, pp.vii-xxii, 128-191.

**de'Gigli, Silvestro** (d.1521). Born at Lucca to parents of the Italian upper gentry. He was educated in law at the expense of his uncle, Giovanni de'Gigli. He succeeded his uncle to the see of Worcester (provided 24 December 1498), which he held to his death.
Further Sources: M. Creighton, 'The Italian Bishops of Worcester', in *Historical Essays and Reviews* (London, 1902), pp.202-34. A letter to Erasmus can be found in *Collected Works of Erasmus*, various editors, 67 vols. (Toronto, 1974-1991), iv. pp.202-3.

**de'Ghinucci, Geronimo.** Born at Sienna to parents of an Italian noble family with banking interests. Provided to the see of Worcester on 26 September 1522, and held it to his deprivation on 21 March 1533. He was **Wolsey's** agent in Spain and supported the Aragon divorce.

Further Sources: K. Down, 'The Administration of the Diocese of Worcester Under the Italian Bishops, 1497-1535', in *Midland History* xx. (1995), pp. 1-20.

**de'Medici, Guilio** (1478-1534). Born at Florence to parents of the Italian nobility. He was provided the see of Worcester on 7 June 1521 and held it *in commendam* with various Italian offices until he resigned it on 26 September 1522, shortly before his election as pope (Clement VII) in 1523. He famously refused to grant an annulment to Henry VIII's marriage to Catherine of Aragon.

**Fisher, John** (1469-1535). Born at Beverley, Yorkshire to yeoman parents of modest merchantile interests. He was educated at Michaelhouse, Cambridge (B.A. 1485, fellow in 1487, M.A. 1491, D.Th. 1510) and had a considerable academic career. He was a senior proctor (1494), master of Michaelhouse (1497), vice-chancellor (1501), first Lady Margaret professor of divinity (1503), chancellor (1504), president of Queen's College (12 April 1505-08). He also supervised the founding of Christ's College (1505) and St John's College (1511). He personally founded four fellowships, two scholarships and carried out the revision of college statutes. He was rector of Lythe, Yorkshire (1499) before his provision to the see of Rochester (14 October 1504), which he held until his deprivation (2 January 1535). He had been confessor to Margaret, countess of Richmond (1497), had been nominated to attend the Lateran Council in Rome of 19 April 1512, but was never sent and, in 1523, famously opposed Wolsey over clerical taxation. He was a fierce opponent of both the Aragon divorce and the royal supremacy, and was the author of many works, the most notable of which are *Assertionis Lutheranae Confutatio* (1523), *Defensio Regiae Assertionis contro Babylonicam Captivitatem* (1525) and *De Causa Matrimonii serenissimi regis Angliae liber* (1530). Canonized in 1935.

Further Sources: M. Macklem, *God Have Mercy: The Life of John Fisher of Rochester* (Toronto, 1968); R. Rex, *The Theology of John Fisher* (Cambridge, 1991); *Humanism, Reform and Reformation: The Career of John Fisher*, ed. by B. Bradshaw and E. Duffy (Cambridge. 1989); *English Works of John Fisher, Bishop of Rochester* (Sermons and Other Writings 1520 to 1535), ed. by Cecilia A. Hatt (Oxford, 2002).

**Fitzjames, Richard** (d.1522). Born at Redlynch, Somerset to parents of the gentry class. He was educated at Merton College Oxford (fellow 1465, M.A. 1471, D.D. 1481) and at Cambridge (M.A. 1495), perhaps pursuing his interests in astrology. He served his college as bursar and warden (1483-1507), was principal of St Alban's Hall (1477-81) and founded a school in Burton. He served the university as senior proctor (1473), commissary and vice-chancellor (1481, 1491, 1492 and 1502). He was vicar of Minehead, Somerset (1484),

rector of Spetisbury, Berkshire (1472), Trent, Dorset (1476) and Aller, Bath
and Wells (1485). He also held two prebends, Taunton, Somerset (1474) and
Portpoole in St Paul's (1485). He was also treasurer of St Paul's (1483-97)
and was master of St Leonard's Hospital (1493). He served both Edward IV
and Henry VII as royal chaplain, also serving the latter as almoner (1495) and
went on a brief embassy to Calais (1497). He was, consecutively, bishop of
Rochester (provided 18 February 1497), of Chichester (provided 29 November
1503) and of London (provided 5 June 1506). He found fame for his great
restorations and reformations (e.g. he built the palace of Fulham) and carried
out several heresy investigations.

**Fox, Edward** (1496-1538). Born at Dursley, Gloucestershire to parents of
the gentry class. He was educated at Eton and at King's College Cambridge
(fellow, 1515, M.A. 1519-20, D.D. 1532) and served for a time as provost of
his college (c.1528). He was rector of Combemartin, Exeter (1528) and held
two prebends, Osbalswiche in York (1527) and Saints Mary and George at
Windsor. He held higher office as archdeacon of Leicester (1531) and as dean
of Salisbury (1533). He also served in several valuable positions, initially as
secretary to **Wolsey** and master of Sherburn Hospital, Durham (1528), and
later as royal almoner (1532) and almoner to Queen Anne Boleyn. He was a
supporter of the Aragon divorce and the royal supremacy, and had been sent to
Cambridge with **Gardiner** and to Oxford with **Longland** and **Bell** to canvas
opinion. Later, he was sent to Paris with Reginald Pole on the same matter,
and served in a diplomatic capacity in France (1532, 1533), Scotland (1534)
and on several envoys with the German powers prior to his nomination to the
see of Hereford (20 August 1536). He was the author of *De vera differentia
regiae potestatis et ecclesiasticae, et quae sit ipsa veritas ac virtus utrusque*
(1534), a comparative examination of royal and papal authority, and co-author
of *Gravissimae, atque exactissimae illustrissimarum totius Italiae et Galliae
academiarum censurae* (1530) with **Stokesley** and de Burgo, an examination
of the theological arguments against the Aragon marriage.
Further Sources: F. Oakley, 'Edward Foxe, Matthew Paris, and the Royal "Potestas
Ordinis"', in *Sixteenth Century Journal* 28:3 (1987), pp. 347-53. His register is
available as *Registrum Edwardi Foxe, Episcopi Herefordensis A.D. MDXXXV -
MDXXXVIII*, ed. by A.T. Bannister (London, 1921).

**Fox, Richard** (c.1446-1528). Born either at Ropsley or Pullock's Manor,
Lincolnshire to parents of the gentry class. Kinsman and patron of **Edward
Fox**. He was educated at either Boston or Winchester school and Magdalen
College Oxford (B.A. 1477, D.Can.L., D.Civ.L.), later studying at Cambridge,
Louvain and Paris. He served the schools as chancellor of Cambridge (1500),
master of Pembroke College, master of grammar at Stratford-upon-Avon and
as founder of Corpus Christi. A supporter of Henry Tudor against Richard III, his
early appointments can be held in some doubt. He was vicar of Stepney (1485)

and canon of Bishopstone, Salisbury (1485), Nunnington, Hereford (1485), Brownswood, St Paul's (1485) and Grantham Borealis, Salisbury (1486). He was, successively, bishop of Exeter (provided 29 January 1487), of Bath and Wells (provided 8 February 1492), of Durham (provided 30 July 1494) and of Winchester (provided 20 August 1501), although largely an absentee. He was principle private secretary to both Henry VII and Henry VIII, and served on diplomatic missions to France and Scotland. He was principle secretary of state, lord privy seal (24 February 1487 to May 1516) and was recognized as the patron of many future bishops and ecclesiastical officials. Fox translated the *Rule of St. Benedict for women* (printed in 1517) and edited the Sarum *Processional* (1508).

Further Sources: *Letters of Richard Fox, 1486-1527*, ed. by P.S. and H.M. Allen (Oxford, 1929); *The Register of Richard Fox, Lord Bishop of Durham, 1494-1501*, ed. by M.P. Howden (London, 1932); B. Collett, 'The Civil Servant and Monastic Reform: Richard Fox's Translation of the Benedictine Rule for Women, 1517', in *Monastic Studies; The Continuity of Tradition*, ed. by J. Loades (Bangor, 1990), pp. 211-28. His register has been made available as 'The Registers of Robert Stillington and Richard Fox, Bishops of Bath and Wells', ed. by H. Maxwell-Lyte, *Somersetshire Record Society*, lii (1937).

**Gardiner, Stephen** (c.1483-1555). Born at Bury St Edmunds, Norfolk to parents of the gentry class. He was educated at Trinity College, Cambridge (fellow, D.Civ.L. 1520, D.Can.L. 1521), taking an LL.D (1531) at Oxford thereafter. He served as Rede lecturer and tutor in law (1524), master of Trinity Hall (1525-1549) and was involved with the revision of statutes for Cardinal College and Ipswich for **Wolsey** (1528). He was rector of St Michael's, Gloucester (c.1528) and was archdeacon of Norfolk (1528-9), Worcester (1530) and Leicester (1531), acting as private secretary to **Wolsey** since c.1524. He excelled in the royal service on heresy commissions (c.1526) and several diplomatic missions, to the pope with **Edward Fox** (1528), to Francis I (1528 and throughout much of the reign of Henry VIII thereafter) and served as royal secretary after 28 July 1529. He was a supporter of the Aragon divorce (canvassing opinion at Cambridge with **Edward Fox**). He was provided the see of Winchester on 20 October 1531. He was the author, under Henry VIII, of *De vera obedientia* (1535), a defence of the royal supremacy which he later repudiated. Under Edward VI, he was imprisoned over his opposition to doctrinal changes and deprived his see (14 February 1551), but was restored (August 1553) and made lord chancellor to Mary I. Engaged in polemical disputes with **Cranmer**, Martin Bucer and William Turner.

Further Sources: *A Machiavellian Treatise by Stephen Gardiner*, ed. and trans. by P.S. Donaldson (Cambridge, 1975); *Obedience in Church and State: Three Political Tracts by Stephen Gardiner* (Cambridge, 1930); J.A. Muller, *Stephen Gardiner and the Tudor Reaction* (London, 1926); P. Donaldson, 'Bishop Gardiner: Machiavellian', in *The Historical Journal* 23:1 (1980), pp.1-16; G. Redworth, *In Defence of the*

*Church Catholic: The Life of Stephen Gardiner* (Oxford, 1990); *The Letters of Stephen Gardiner*, ed. by J.A. Muller (New York, 1933).

**Goodrich (or Goodricke), Thomas** (d.1554). Born at East Kirby, Lincolnshire to parents of the gentry class. He was educated at King's College, Cambridge and at Corpus Christi College, Oxford (B.A. 1510, M.A. 1514, D.D. c.1529), was a fellow of Jesus College and acted as proctor (1515). He was rector of St Peter Cheap, London (1529) and canon of St Stephen's, Westminster (1529-34). He served the king as royal chaplain (1529-34) and on an embassy to France (1533), but was more importantly an advocate of both the Aragon divorce and the royal supremacy. He was nominated to the see of Ely (6 March 1534) and was an ecclesiastical commissioner and privy councillor to Edward VI, ambassador to Henri II (1551) and lord chancellor (1552-3).

**Heath, Nicholas** (c.1501-78). Born at London to yeoman parents. He was educated at St Anthony's School, Corpus Christi College Oxford, Cardinal Wolsey College Oxford (B.A. 1519) and Christ Church Cambridge (B.A., fellow 1521, M.A. 1522, D.D. 1535), and was a fellow of Clare Hall (c.1524). He was vicar of Hever (1531), rector of Bishopsbourne (1537), archdeacon of Stafford (1534), and dean of Shoreham (1531-2) and of South Malling (1537). He served the king as almoner (c.1536) prior to his nomination to the see of Rochester (24 March 1540) and translated to Worcester (20 February 1544). He served the king on an embassy to Germany with **Edward Fox** (1535) and oversaw the official translation of the Bible with **Tunstal** (1541). He was deprived of his see by Edward VI (10 October 1551) but restored by Mary I (1554) under whom he became archbishop of York (nominated 19 February 1555) but was deprived by Elizabeth I (5 July 1559). He was, for a time, lord chancellor (1556-8), but removed from public affairs thereafter.

**Hilsey (or Hildesleigh), John** (d.1539). Born at Benham, Berkshire to yeoman parents. He was educated by the Dominicans of Bristol and at their house at Oxford (B.D. 1527, D.D. 1532), and may have studied at Cambridge. He was prior of Bristol (May 1533) and of the London Dominicans (1535), becoming provincial of the order (April 1534) prior to his election as bishop of Rochester (7 August 1535). His service to the crown was limited to a commission for monastic visitations (to friaries) (1534-5) and as press censor (1536). He was the author of *The manual of prayers, or the prymer in Englysh and Laten* (1539).

**Holbeach (or Rands), Henry** (d.1551). Born at Holbeach, Lincolnshire to yeoman parents. He entered Crowland Monastery and was educated at the Benedictine house at Cambridge, Buckingham College (B.D. 1527, D.D. 1534). He was prior of Buckingham College (1535) and of Worcester (13 March 1536), but was also rector of Bromgrove and chaplain of King's Norton, both Worcestershire. He served **Latimer** as suffragan bishop of Bristol (24 March 1538), and was dean of Worcester (1540) and royal almoner (1540) prior to his nomination to the see of Rochester (23 April 1544). Under Edward VI he was translated to the see of Lincoln (nominated 1 August 1547).

**Holgate (**or **Holdegate), Robert** (c.1481-1556). Born at Hemsworth, Yorkshire to parents of the gentry class. He was educated at St Gilbert's of Sempringham, Cambridgeshire and St John's College (D.D. 1537). He founded three grammar schools at York, Old Matton and Hemsworth by letters patent. He was a canon of St Gilbert's and a preacher (1524), prior of St Catherine's Without London (1529) and vicar of Cudney, Lincolnshire (1529), later becoming master of the Gilbertines and prior of Watton, Yorkshire (1536). He was a royal chaplain and a chaplain to Thomas Cromwell prior to his provision to the see of Llandaff (consecrated 25 March 1537) held *in commendam* with his other offices. He later became archbishop of York (nominated 5 January 1545). He served the king as president of the council of the north (1538-50). He was deprived of York (23 March 1554) for being married and was imprisoned under Mary I (1554). He endowed the hospital at Hemsworth in his will.
Further Sources: A.G. Dickens, *Robert Holgate, Archbishop of York* (London, 1955). One of his letters is available in G. Burnet, *The History of the Reformation of the Church of England*, ed. by N. Pocock, 7 vols. (Oxford, 1865), iv. pp.394-5.

**King, Robert** (d.1557). Born at Thame, Oxfordshire to yeoman parents. He was educated by the Cistercians at Rewley Abbey Oxford and later, at St John's College (B.D. 1506-7, D.D. 1518-9). He was a canon of St Frideswide's, and abbot of Brewern, Oxfordshire (1515), abbot of Thame (1530) and abbot of Oseney, Oxfordshire (1537). As suffragan bishop of Rheon to **Longland** (1527-35) he was prebendary of Crackpole St Mary (15 April 1535) and Biggleswade (28 November 1536 to 1541) prior to his nomination as bishop of Oseney and Thame (1 September 1542), and renamed bishop of Oxford (9 June 1545 - 4 December 1557).

**Kitchin (**or **Dunstan), Anthony** (1477-1566). Born at Dunstan, near Bolsover, to parents of the gentry class. He was perhaps educated at Gloucester Hall, Oxford (B.D. 1525, D.D. 1538) although Lacey Baldwin Smith questions this. Less doubtful is his clerical career. He was a canon of Westminster and was later elected prior of Gloucester Hall (1526) and abbot of Eynsham (1530), which he held until the house's surrender on 4 December 1539. He was a royal chaplain (1539) thereafter, until his consecration as bishop of Llandaff (3 May 1545).

**Kite, John** (d.1537). Born at London to yeoman parents. He was educated at Eton and King's College Cambridge (B.Can.L. 1495-6). He was rector of Wolferton, Norfolk (1496), Boscombe, Wiltshire (1499), Harlington,

Middlesex (1510), Weye at Weyhill, Winchester (1510), and much later of St Stephen's, Walbroom, London (1534), held prebends in Exeter (c.1507) and Chichester (1507) and was prebendary of Crediton, Devon (1509) and of Stratton, Salisbury (1517). He held higher office as sub-dean of St George's Chapel prior to his provision to the archbishopric of Armagh (24 October 1513) and subsequently to the see of Carlisle (12 July 1521). He served the king on an embassy to Charles V (February 1518), as deputy commissioner of the jewel office (1520) and on royal commissions of the peace with Scotland (1524, 1526).

**Knight, William** (1476-1547). Born at London to parents of the peasant class. He was educated at Winchester School (1487), New College Oxford (fellow 1492, B.Civ.L. 1504, D.Civ.L. 1507) and Ferrara, leaving money to Winchester and New College in his will. He was rector of Barton (1504), of Sandhurst, Gloucester (1508), of Stowting, Kent (1513), of All Hallow's Bread Street, London (1515), of Bangor Monachorum and of Romald Kirk, Yorkshire (1527), and held five prebends, Farrendon-cum-Balderton, Lincoln (1516), Horton, Salisbury (1517), Chamberlainwood, St Paul's (1517), Llavair, Bangor (1520) and Westminster (1527). He held higher office as dean of the collegiate church at Newark, Leicestershire (1515) and was archdeacon of Chester (1522), Huntingdon (1523) and Richmond (1529) prior to his provision to the see of Bath and Wells (29 May 1541). He had an extensive career in the royal service. He was often a diplomat and secretary for Henry VII, served Henry VIII as ambassador to Spain (1512), to Mechlin in the Low Countries (1514), to Switzerland (July 1514), to Charles V (1515, 1516), and to the pope (1527). He was, moreover, clerk of the closet (1520) and royal secretary (1526). He supported both the Aragon divorce and the royal supremacy.
Further Sources: His career is discussed in P.M. Hemby, *The Bishops of Bath and Wells, 1540-1640: Social and Economic Problems* (London, 1967) and his register is available from the Somerset Records Society, vol.55 as *The Register of William Knight, Bishop of Bath & Wells, 1541-47*, ed. by H. Maxwell-Lyte (1940), pp.90-119.

**Latimer, Hugh** (c.1485-1555). Born at Thurcaston, Leicestershire to parents of the peasant class. He was educated at Clare Hall Cambridge (fellow 1510, B.A., M.A. 1514, B.D. 1524) and was for a time university preacher. He was rector of West Kington, Wiltshire (1531) prior to his election as bishop of Worcester (12 August 1535). He held radical religious opinions but was an avid supporter of the Aragon divorce, the royal supremacy and reformation issues. He was a royal chaplain (1534) but was forced to resign from his see (1 July 1539) due to his unorthodox views. He was a popular preacher under Edward VI, but was imprisoned under Mary I (1553) and burnt as a heretic (1555) with **Cranmer** and Nicholas Ridley. He was the author of several sermons and religious tracts.
Further Sources: Robert Demaus, *Hugh Latimer, A Biography* (London, 1903);

*Sermons by Hugh Latimer*, ed. by G.E. Corrie (Cambridge, 1844); R.O'Day, 'Hugh Latimer: Prophet of the Kingdom', in *Historical Research* 65:158 (October 1992), pp.258-76; C.H. Stuart, 'Hugh Latimer: Apostle to the English', in *Christianity Today* 24 (1980), pp.17-19; *Sermons by Hugh Latimer, Sometime Bishop of Worcester* (London, n.d.). He is mentioned in a letter of 1538, see *Original Letters illustrative of English History*, ed. by H. Ellis, 11 vols. in 3 series (London, 1824, 1827, 1846), ii/ii. pp.104-6 and is the subject of a Roman Catholic satire, see N. Pocock, *Records of the Reformation* 2 vols. (Oxford, 1870), ii. pp.180-2.

**Lee, Edward** (1482-1544). Born at Lee Magna, Kent to parents of the gentry class. He was educated at Magdalen College, Oxford (fellow 1500, B.A. c.1503, B.D. 1515, D.D. c.1531), at Cambridge (M.A. 1504) and at Louvain (c.1516) and Bologna. He served his college as proctor. He was rector of Freshwater (1509) and Odiham (1530) and prebendary of Rothfem, Exeter (1510), Welton Beckhall, Lincoln (1512), All Cannings, Donnington, Yorkshire (1530) and St Stephen's (1530). He held higher office as archdeacon of Colchester (1523) and of Surrey (1530) and was chancellor of Salisbury (1529), prior to his provision to the see of York (20 October 1531). He served the king as royal chaplain and almoner and went on embassies to Ferdinand of Aragon (1523) and Charles V (1525). He supported the Aragon divorce and was the author of *Apologia Edoardi Leei contra quorundam calumnias*, critical of Erasmus's biblical translations.

Further Sources: R. Coogan, *Erasmus, Lee and the Correction of the Vulgate: The Shaking of the Foundations* (Geneva, 1992); 'Visitations in the diocese of York, Holden by Archbishop Edward Lee (A.D. 1534-5)', in *The Yorkshire Archaeological Journal* xvi (1902), pp. 424-58. His injunctions can be found in G. Burnet, *The History of the Reformation of the Church of England*, ed. by N. Pocock, 7 vols. (Oxford, 1865), vi. pp.199-205, and letters in *Original Letters illustrative of English History*, ed. by H. Ellis, 11 vols. in 3 series (London, 1824, 1827, 1846), iii/ii, and in *The Complete Works of Sir Thomas More*, vol.15 (New Haven, 1976-).

**Lee (or Legh), Roland** (d.1543). Born at Morpeth, Northumberland to parents of the gentry class. He was educated at St Nicholas Hostel, Cambridge (LL.B. 1510, D. Decrees 1520). He was rector of Banham, Norfolk (1520), Ashdon, Essex (1522-33), Fenny Compton, Warwickshire (1526) and St Sepulchre's Newgate, London (1532) and was prebendary of Norton, Suffolk (1512), Curborough, Lichfield (1527), Ripon (1533) and Wetwing (1533), both in York. He held higher office as archdeacon of Cornwall (1528) and of Taunton (1533). He served the king as a royal chaplain (c.1532) and as chancellor to **Blythe** prior to his provision to the see of Coventry and Lichfield (10 January 1534). He supported the Aragon divorce and the royal supremacy, although his service to the crown was largely law oriented. He was appointed an advocate (8 December 1520) and a master (1532) in Chancery, and was the king's representative to the monasteries (1531-34) and president of the king's council of the marches of Wales (from May 1534).

Further Sources: His injunctions to the clergy of Coventry and Lichfield can be found in G. Burnet, *The History of the Reformation of the Church of England*, ed. by N. Pocock, 7 vols. (Oxford, 1865), vi. pp.206-9.

**Longland, John** (1473-1547). Born at Henley on Thames, Oxfordshire to parents of the gentry class. He was educated at Magdalen College, Oxford (fellow, B.A., D.D. 1511) and served as a lecturer in theology, as principal of Magdalen Hall (1505) and was chancellor of Oxford (1532). He was vicar of Thorverton, Devon (1508), rector of Woodham Ferrers, Essex (1504) and of Lifton, Devon (1513), and held four prebends: North Kelsey (1514) and Alton Borealis (1514), both Lincoln, St Stephen's, Westminster and St George's, Windsor (1519). He held higher office as dean of Salisbury (1514), prior to his provision to the see of Lincoln (20 March 1521). He was one of only two bishops (the other was **Stokesley**) to serve the king as royal confessor (after 1519) and he was almoner (1521) as well. A gifted theologian, he published a sermon (1517), *Tres Conciones* (1527), *A Sermonde spoken before the kynge his majestie at Grenwiche, uppon good frydaye* (1536) and *A Sermonde made before the Kynge, his majestye at grenewiche, upon good Frydaye* (1538).

Further Sources: M. Bowker, *The Henrician Reformation: The Diocese of Lincoln under John Longland 1521-1547* (Cambridge, 1981); G.E. Wharhirst, 'The Reformation in the Diocese of Lincoln as Illustrated by the Life and Work of Bishop Longland (1521-47)', in *Lincolnshire Architectural and Archaeological Societies Reports and Papers* 1:2 (1937), pp.137-76; 'Extracts from Bishop Longland's Register', ed. by A.R. Maddison, *Associated Architectural Societies' Reports and Papers*, 15:2 (1880), pp. 161-78. His 1538 sermon can be found in J. Foxe, *Acts and Monuments*, ed. by G. Townshend and C.R. Cattley, 8 vols. (Oxford, 1837-41), v. pp.171-78.

**Mayew (or Mayhew), Richard** (c.1440-1516). Born at Edmundsthorpe, Kingsclere in Hampshire to yeoman parents. He was educated at Magdalen College, Oxford (M.A. 1467, B.Th. 1475, D.Th. 1478), served his college as president and the university as senior proctor (1469) and chancellor (after 1503). He was rector of Wolverton, Hampshire (1466), Weston-super-Mare, Avon (1471), St Thomas Winchelsea, Sussex (1471), St Pierre, Calais (1472), Brightwell, Oxfordshire (1480) and of West Meon, Hampshire (1482), and was prebendary of Combe, Wells (1475), Ramsbury, Salisbury (1500) and of St Stephen's Altar, York (1504). He held higher office as archdeacon of Oxford (1493) and of York (1501) and was chaplain to **Smith** (1488) and warden of Estwyke Chapel (1487). Interestingly, he served both Richard III (1484) and Henry VII (1491) as royal chaplain, serving the latter as almoner (1497) and sometime envoy (e.g. 1490) as well. Controversially, he was provided the see of Hereford (9 August 1504), an appointment that clashed with his presidency of Magdalen, leading to trouble at the college.

Further Sources: His register is available as *Registrum Ricardi Mayew, Episcopi Herefordensis*, ed. by A.T. Bannister (London, 1921).

**Nix (or Nykke), Richard** (c.1447-1535). A kinsman of Robert Stillington, bishop of Bath and Wells, he was born in Somerset to parents of the gentry class. He was educated at Trinity Hall Cambridge (LL.D. D.Can.L. 1483) and at Oxford, Ferrara and Bologna. A client of **Richard Fox**, he was vicar of Stokenham, Devon (1492), rector of Ashbury, Berkshire (1473), Cheddon, Somerset (1490), Chedzoy, Somerset (1490), Bishop Wearmouth (1496), High Ham, Somerset (1499) and South Moulton, Devon (1499), and prebendary of St Crantock, Cornwall (1489), Woodburgh, St Paul's (1493), Huish, Wells (1494), Friday Thorpe, York (1494), St George's, Windsor (1497), Westbury on Trym (1498), Yatton, Wells (1498) and Merymouth (1498). He held higher office as archdeacon of Exeter (1491-2) and of Wells (1494), and was dean of St Stephen's Chapel (1497). He was also vicar-general to **Richard Fox** (1493-6), prior to his provision to the see of Norwich (26 February 1501). His service to the crown was to registrar of the order of the Garter for Henry VII (1497). He opposed both the Aragon divorce and religious reform, but a *praemunire* charge in 1534 forced a change of heart on the latter.

**Oldham, Hugh** (d.1519). Born at Oldham (Oldom, Aldham) near Manchester in Lancashire to parents of the gentry class. He was educated in the household of Thomas Stanley, Earl of Derby (**James Stanley's** father) under the direction of Lady Margaret Beaufort, at Queen's College, Cambridge (B.Civ.L. 1493) and perhaps at Oxford. He founded the Manchester grammar school and became patron to both Corpus Christi College, Oxford and Queen's. He was rector of St Mildred Breadstreet, London (1485), Lanivet, Cornwall (1488), Swineshead, Lincolnshire (1493), Cheshunt, Hertfordshire (1494), Alphington, Devon (1495), Warboys, Cambridgeshire (1499), Iverton (1499), Shillington, Lincolnshire (1500), Overton, Hampshire (1501) and Freechapel, Stert, Wiltshire (1503), and prebendary of St Stephen's, Westminster (1492), Exeter (1494), Colwich, Lichfield (1495), Alton Borealis, Salisbury (1495), Stoke Newington, St Paul's (1497), Leighton Buzzard, Lincoln (1497), South Cave, York (1499), Crediton, Devon (1500), Freford, Lichfield (1501), Overton, Winchester (1501) and Gillingham, Shaftesbury Abbey. He held higher office as archdeacon of Exeter (1492/3), and as dean of Wimborne (1485) and of St John's College (1493). He held two hospital masterships, of St John's (1496) and of St Leonard's (1500) and was chaplain to Margaret Beaufort, countess of Richmond and Derby. He served Henry VII on several peace commissions (1495-1504), and was an advocate in the court of Arches prior to his provision to the see of Exeter (27 November 1504).
Further Sources: A.A. Mumford, *Hugh Oldham, 1452[?] - 1519* (London, 1936).

**Owain (Owen), Dafydd ap** (d.1513). Practically nothing is known of this most obscure Henrician. He was born in Wales, probably to parents of the gentry rank and was abbot of Conway (a Cistercian house) prior to his provision to the see of St Asaph (18 December 1503).

**Penny, John** (d.c.1520). May have been born in Wales to parents probably of the yeoman class. He was educated by the Austin Canons and at Lincoln College, Oxford (D.Civ.L.) and at Cambridge (LL.D). He was a canon of the Abbey of St Mary de Pratis, Leicester (1477), and was elected abbot on 25 June 1496, an office he held *in commendam* as abbot of Bradley, Leicestershire (14 September 1503). He was provided to the see of Bangor (30 August 1505), later translated to the see of Carlisle (provided 22 September 1508).

**Rawlins, Richard** (d.1536). Birthplace unknown, but his parents were probably of the yeoman class. He was educated at Merton College, Oxford (fellow 1480, B.D. 1492, D.D. 1495), which he also served as bursar, lecturer and warden (1508-21). He was rector of St Mary Woolnoth, London (1494), Hendon, London (1504), Thornton, Yorkshire (1505) and of St Martin Ludgate, London (1514), and was prebendary of Beverley, York (1499), Willesden and St Michael's Altar (1503) both in St Paul's, Howden, Skipworth (1506), St George's, Windsor (1506) and St Stephen's, Westminster (1518). He held higher office as archdeacon of Cleveland (1507) and of Huntingdon (1514) and as sub-dean of York (1504). He was royal almoner (1509) and almoner at the meeting of Charles V and Henry VIII at Gravelines (1520), prior to his provision to the see of St David's (11 March 1523).
Further Sources: His career is discussed in W.B. Jones and E.A. Freeman, The *History and Antiquities of Saint David's* (London, 1856).

**Rugg (or Reppes), William** (d.1550). Born in Shropshire to parents of the gentry class. He was educated at the Benedictine priory of Norwich, and at Caius College, Cambridge (B.D. 1509, D.D. 1513). He was a canon, and later sacrist, of Norwich (27 April 1514), prior of Yarmouth (1520), sub-prior of Norwich (1526) and abbot of St Bennet's Hulme (26 April 1530) prior to his provision to the see of Norwich (11 June 1536). He supported both the Aragon divorce and the royal supremacy. In 1540 he was appointed one of three commissioners for dealing with heresy, but resigned Norwich on 26 January 1550).

**Ruthal (or Rowthall), Thomas** (d.1523). Born at Cirencester, Gloucestershire to parents of the gentry class. He was educated at both Oxford (B.Can.L., B.Civ.L. 1488) and Cambridge (D.D. 1500), at which he served as chancellor (1503-04), and later made several grammer school endowments. He was rector of Bocking, Essex (1495), Monks Risborough (1500), Southam, Warwickshire (1500), Barnsley, Gloucester (1501) and of Stratton, Salisbury (1502), was a canon in Wells (1502), Lincoln (1505), Exeter (1508) and held the prebendary of Ruscombe in Salisbury (1503). He held higher office as archdeacon of Gloucester (1503), and was dean of Salisbury (1502) and of Wimborne (1508). He was also one of only two English bishops to hold a papal appointment (the other was **Cranmer**) as protonotary (1499), prior to his provision to the see of Durham (12 June 1509). He was royal secretary to both Henry VII and Henry VIII, carried out several embassies to France, was a privy councillor in 1502 and was appointed keeper of the privy seal (1516). Further Sources: One of his letters, to Erasmus, can be found in *Collected Works of Erasmus*, various editors, 67 vols. (Toronto, 1974-1991), iii. pp.63-8.

**Sally (Salley), Miles** (d.1516). Little is known for certain about this obscure Henrician. Perhaps born in Wales to parents of the yeoman class, he was probably educated in theology by his order, the Benedictines (no educational records are extent). He was elected abbot of Eynesham on 13 March 1499-1500, and held the post *in commendam* with the see of Llandaff (consecrated 16 April 1500).

**Sampson, Richard** (d.1554). Born at Bynfeld, Berkshire to parents of the yeoman class. He was educated at Clement hostel and Trinity Hall Cambridge (B.Civ.L. 1505), Paris, Siena (D.Civ.L. 1513) and Perugia (D.Can.L. 1520) but held no academic posts. A client of **Wolsey**, he was vicar of Stepney (1526), and rector of Wheathampsted (1523) and Hackney (1534). He was prebendary of Newbold, York (1519), Chiswick, St Paul's (1522), Langford Ecclesia, Lincoln and Stoffold, Lichfield (1532-3). He held higher office as archdeacon of Cornwall (1517) and of Suffolk (1528-9), and dean of St Stephen's, Westminster (1516), St George's, Windsor (1516), Windsor (1523) and Lichfield (1533). His association with **Wolsey** began in Tournai, where he served as chaplain and later as chancellor (1514) to **Wolsey's** bishop, later serving as vicar-general. He was treasurer of Salisbury (1535) prior to his election as bishop of Chichester (3 June 1536). He served the king as a royal chaplain and, after his elevation, was first co-adjutor to Richard Pace at St Paul's. After 20 July 1536 he was allowed to hold the deanery *in commendam* with Chichester. On 19 February 1543 he was translated to the see of Coventry and Lichfield. Sampson was appointed to an embassy to Brussels (September 1514) to the Lady Margaret and on 8 May 1515 he was on a trade commission with More and Tunstal there. He was admitted an advocate on 20 March 1514-15 and shortly thereafter, 12 January 1517, was made royal proctor for Tournai. Later, he was appointed to an embassy with Sir Thomas Boleyn to Bilbao (October 1522), was resident ambassador to Charles V and performed countless similar diplomatic duties. He supported both the Aragon divorce and the royal supremacy and acted for the king in the case against Queen Anne Boleyn. With Cromwell and **Edward Fox**, he sat on a commission to treat for peace in Europe. Later, post-1543, he acted as lord-president of Wales. He was the author of many theological works, his most famous being *Oratio quae docet hortatur admonet omnes potissimum Anglos regiae dignitati cum primis ut obediant . . .* (1534) in support of Henry VIII's claims of supreme headship.

Source: A.A. Chibi, 'Richard Sampson, His "Oratio", and Henry VIII's Royal Supremacy', in *Journal of Church and State*, 39 (Summer 1997), pp.543-60. Sampson's career is discussed in W.R.W. Stephens, *Memorials of the South Saxon See and Cathedral Church of Chichester* (London, 1876), pp.209-21; *Collected Works of Erasmus*, various editors, 67 vols. (Toronto, 1974-1991), xlii. pp.10-3, 71-7; *The Acts of the Dean and Chapter of the Cathedral Church of Chichester, 1472-1544*, ed. by W.D. Peckham (Chichester, 1951-2), pp.12-128 and *The Acts of the Dean and Chapter of the Cathedral Church of Chichester, 1545-1642*, ed. by W.D. Peckham (Chichester, 1959), pp.1*ff*.

**Shaxton, Nicholas** (c.1485-1556). Born at Norwich, Norfolk to parents of the yeoman class. He was educated at Gonville Hall, Cambridge (fellow, B.A. 1506, M.A. 1510, B.D. 1521). In May 1532 he was inceptor in divinity. He was the official university preacher (1520) and was president of Physick's Hostel, part of the college (1512-13). He was rector of Fuggleston, Wiltshire (1533) through royal patronage, and prebendary of St Stephen's, Westminster (1534). He served as treasurer of Salisbury (1533) and as almoner to Queen Anne Boleyn prior to his provision to the see of Salisbury (elected 22 February 1535), which he was forced to resign in 1540 due to his religious opinions. He supported the Aragon divorce at Cambridge and was appointed (May 1531) one of the twelve Cambridge divines to serve on a joint committee with twelve Oxford divines, examining English 'heretical' books. Later he was arraigned on heresy charges (1546) and condemned to burning before his recantation. He became master of St Gile's Hospital, Norwich (1546-7), held parochial charge at Hadleigh, Norwich and was suffragen to **Thirlby** (as bishop of Ely) under Mary I.

Further Sources: 'Articles (of errors) acknowledged by Nicholas Shaxton', in G. Burnet, *The History of the Reformation of the Church of England*, ed. by N. Pocock, 7 vols. (Oxford, 1865), iv. pp.531-2; *Bishop Shaxton's Injunctions to the clergy of Salisbury* (London, 1538) as seen in Burnet, vi. pp.210-15.

**Sherborne** (or **Shirburn**), **Robert** (c.1440-1536). Born at Rolleston, Staffordshire to yeoman parents. He was educated at Winchester School (c.1465) and New College Oxford (fellow 1474, B.A. 1477, M.A., B.D.) and served as secretary for the university (1480-86). Accounted a patron of education, he founded the prebends of Bursalis, Exceit Bargham and Wyndham, all to be held by alumni of New College or Winchester. He also founded a grammar school in Rolleston (c.1520). He was rector of Childrey, Oxfordshire (1491) and of Rodmerton, Gloucestershire (1496) and was prebendary of Langford Manor, Lincoln (1486 and 1494), Milton Manor, Lincoln (1493), Alresford and Essex (1494), Wildland, St Paul's (1489), Whitechurch and Binegar, Wells (resident to 1493), Warminster, Salisbury and Finsbury, St Paul's (1493), Mora, St Paul's (1496-7) and of Milverton in Exeter, Henfield in Chichester and Leckford in Winchester. He held higher office as archdeacon of Buckinghamshire (1495), Huntingdon (1496) and of Taunton (1496), dean of St Paul's (1499) and was treasurer of Hereford (1486). He also served as secretary to Cardinal Morton, master of St Cross Hospital in Winchester (1492-1508) and warden of Holy Trinity Hospital (1492) and of St David's by Kingsthorpe (1492). Controversy surrounded his provision to the see of St David's (5 January 1505) due to the apparent forging of the papal bulls, but he remained until his translation to Chichester (provided 18 September 1508). He resigned sometime between 25 May and 5 June 1536 over his opposition to the royal supremacy. He was royal secretary to Henry VII and a diplomat. He was envoy to Rome (1496, 1502, 1504), to Scotland (4 May 1503) and served as governor of Richmond Castle and of Porchester.

Further Sources: M.E.C. Wlacott, 'Bishops of Chichester, from Stigard to Sherborne', in *Sussex Archaeological Collections Relating to the History and Antiquities of the County*, 29 (1879), pp.1-39; F.W. Steer, *Robert Sherburne, Bishop of Chichester: Some Aspects of his Life Reconsidered* (Chichester, 1960); S.J. Lander, 'The diocese of Chichester, 1508-1558: Episcopal reform under Robert Sherburne and its aftermath' (unpublished D.Phil., University of Cambridge, 1974). His career is discussed in W.R.W. Stephens, *Memorials of the South Saxon See and Cathedral Church of Chichester* (London, 1876), pp.183-208.

**Skevington** (or **Skeffington**, or **Pace**, or **Patexe**), **Thomas** (d.1533). Born at Skeffington, Leicestershire to parents of the gentry class. He was educated at the Cistercian house of Merevale, Warwickshire and at St Bernard's, Oxford. He became a minor patron of the house after his death. He served as abbot of Waverley, Surrey (1509) and of Beaulieu, Hampshire (1509) *in commendam* with the see of Bangor (provided 23 February 1509).

**Skip** (or **Skyppe**), **John** (d.1552). Born in Norfolk to yeoman parents. He was educated at Gonville Hall Cambridge (fellow, B.A. 1514-5, M.A. 1518, B.D. 1533, D.D. 1535) and served as master of Gonville Hall, resigning in 1540. He also served as president of Physick Hostel (1519-21). As almoner to Queen Catherine of Aragon and later chaplain and almoner to Queen Anne Boleyn (directing her charity to poor scholars), his clerical career was limited but reflective of royal favour. He was vicar of Thaxted, Essex (1534-5), rector of Newington, Surrey (1537-8) and prebendary of St Stephen's, Westminster (1535). He held higher office as archdeacon of Suffolk (1536) and Dorset (1539) *in commendam* with the see of Hereford (nominated 13 October 1539) and the priory of Wigmore. He supported both the Aragon divorce and the royal supremacy at Cambridge and, on 1 October 1538, sat on a commission with **Cranmer** and **Stokesley** investigating Anabaptism. He resigned from his see (30 March 1552) in opposition to the *Prayer-Books* of Edward VI.

**Smith** (or **Smyth**), **William** (c.1460-1514). Born either at Farnsworth near Manchester or Prescot, Lancashire to parents of the gentry class. He was educated in the Stanley household with **Oldham**, under the supervision of

Margaret Beaufort, and at Lincoln College Oxford (B.Can.L. 1476, B.A. 1478, B.Civ.L. 1492, D.Can.L. 1496), serving the university as keeper of the hanaper of the chancery (20 September 1485-93), and chancellor (1500-3, resigned over fraudulent financial dealings). In 1507 he founded a fellowship at Oriel College, established a free school at Farnsworth and made endowments to Lincoln. On 1 June 1509 he was co-founder of Brasenose College. He was vicar of Donington (1483), rector of Sadlescombe (1479), Combe Martyn, Devon (1486), Great Grimsby (1486) and of Cheshunt, Hertfordshire (1492), and prebendary of St Stephen's, Westminster (1485), Wherwell Abbey, Winchester (1487), Holy Trinity (1487), Tamworth (1490) and of Syerscote (1492). He held higher office as archdeacon of Surrey (1493), dean of Wimborne (1485), St Stephen's, Westminster (1490) and of St George's, Windsor (1491). He served as provost of Wells and was an advocate of judicial reform in the court of Arches. As bishop of Coventry and Lichfield (provided 1 October 1493) he re-founded the hospital of St John and as bishop of Lincoln (provided 6 November 1495) he carried out extensive renovations. He served as royal chaplain to Henry VII, was a member of Prince Arthur's council in Wales and was appointed (22 August 1501) as lord president of Wales. ·

**Standish, Henry** (d.1535). Born at Standish, Lancashire to yeoman parents. He was educated at a Hereford convent (c.1489), Oxford and Cambridge (D.Th. 1502). He was a friar and eventually, warden of Greyfriars, London and Franciscan provincial, and was rector of Standish prior to his consecration as bishop of St Asaph (11 July 1518). He was one of Henry VIII's court preachers and some time chief of his spiritual council, but also served on embassies and was involved in the examination of heretics (1525). He was a judge at the trial of Bilney and Arthur (1527) and of John Tewkesbury (20 December 1531). He opposed the Aragon divorce, acting as one of Queen Catherine of Aragon's counsellors.

Further Sources: J.D.M. Derrett, 'The Affairs of Richard Hunne and Friar Standish', in *The Complete Works of Sir Thomas More*, vol.9 (New Haven, 1976-), pp.215-46.

**Stanley, James** (c.1465-1515). Born in Lancashire c.1465, the sixth son of Thomas Stanley, the first Earl of Derby. He was educated in his father's household, and later attended both Oxford (M.A., D.Can.L. 1506) and Cambridge, and spent some time in Paris with Erasmus. He took part in the countess of Richmond's foundation of St John's and Christ's College Cambridge, and compiled statutes for Jesus College, Cambridge. He was rector of Eccleston, Lancashire (1482), Walton on the Hill, Staffordshire (1485), Hawarden, Clyde (1487), Winwick, Cambridgeshire (1494) and of Rosthorne, Chester (1498), and prebendary of Southwell, Durham (1479), Beaminster, Ripon (1493), Givendale and Skelton, York (1493) and of Yetminster, Salisbury (1505). He held higher office as archdeacon of Richmond (1500) and dean of St Martin-le-Grand, London (1485), and served as precentor of Salisbury (1485) and as

warden of the Collegiate Church of Manchester (1509), prior to his provision to the see of Ely (18 January 1506).
Further Sources: His career is discussed in S. Hibbert, *History of the Foundation in Manchester of Christ's College, Chetham's Hospital, and the Free Grammar School*, 3 vols. (Edinburgh and Manchester, 1834-5).

**Stokesley, John** (1475-1539). Born at Collyweston, Northamptonshire to parents of the gentry class. He was educated at Magdalen College School, Magdalen College Oxford (fellow 1494-5, M.A. 1500, D.D. 1516) and Rome. He served the school as short-term usher (1497), prelector in logic (1498), principal of Magdalen Hall, bursur (1502), dean of divinity and northern proctor (1503), prelector in philosophy (1504-5) and vice-president of Magdalen College and Preston Chaplain (1506). He was vicar of Willoughby, Warwickshire (1505-6), rector of Slimbridge, Gloucestershire (1505-6), Brightstone, Isle of Wight (1518) and Ivychurch, Kent (1523), and prebendary of Wherwell Abbey, Winchester (1528-9) and of St Stephen's, Westminster (c.1524). He held higher office as archdeacon of Surrey (1522) and Dorset (1523), dean of St George's, Windsor (1524) and was chaplain to **Richard Fox** (1515-7) and precentor of St Mary's Southampton (1518), prior to his provision to the see of London (28 March 1530). He supported both the Aragon divorce and the royal supremacy. He served the king as a councillor (1520), royal chaplain (1518-20), as a judge in the court of Requests (1520s), royal confessor (c.1516-9), royal almoner (1520-24), parliamentary trier of petitions from Gascony and parts beyond the sea (1523) and as ambassador to Francis I (1529) and to Charles V and Clement VII (1529-30). He was co-author of *Gravissimae, atque exactissimae illustrissimarum totius Italiae et Galliae academiarum censurae* (1530) with **Edward Fox** and de Burgo, in support of the Aragon divorce, and *Letter to Cardinal Pole* (c.1537, published in 1575) with **Tunstal**, in support of the royal supremacy.
Further Sources: A.A. Chibi, *Henry VIII's Conservative Scholar: Bishop John Stokesley and the Divorce, Royal Supremacy and Doctrinal Reform* (Berne, 1997); A.A. Chibi, 'Henry VIII and his Marriage to his Brother's Wife: The Sermon of Bishop John Stokesley of 11 July 1535', in *Historical Research* 67:162 (February 1994), pp.40-56. His career is discussed in J. Foxe, *Acts and Monuments*, ed. by G. Townshend and C.R. Cattley, 8 vols. (Oxford, 1837-41), v. pp.862-7, vii. pp.165-82, 666-76; N. Pocock, *Records of the Reformation* 2 vols. (Oxford, 1870), ii. pp.369-70; G. Burnet, *The History of the Reformation of the Church of England*, ed. by N. Pocock, 7 vols. (Oxford, 1865), iv. pp.296-7; C. Wriothesley, *A Chronicle of England During the Reigns of the Tudors From AD 1485 to 1559*, ed. by W.D. Hamilton (London, 1875) and Ralph Morice, 'The Answers of Mr Thomas Lawney', in *Narratives of the Days of the Reformation*, ed. by J.G. Nichols (London, 1959), pp.276-8.

**Thirlby (** or **Thirleby), Thomas** (c.1506-70). Born in Cambridge to parents of the gentry class. He was educated at Trinity Hall Cambridge (fellow, B.Civ.L., D.Civ.L. 1521, D.Can.L. 1530), and served as a commissary (1528-

34) and an auditor (1530-31). He was rector of Ribchester, Lancashire (1539) and prebendary of St Stephen's, Westminster (1537) and Yeatminster, Salisbury (1539). He held higher office as archdeacon of Ely (1534) and dean of St George's, Windsor (1534), and served as an official to the archdeacon of Ely (1532), as prolocutor of Canterbury Convocation (1540), provost of St Edmund's, Salisbury (1534) and master of St Thomas a'Becket Hospital, Southwark (l539). He served the king as royal chaplain (1533) and was part of a commission deliberating upon sundry points of religion (1540) prior to his nomination as the first, and only, bishop of Westminster (18 December 1540). He served on a few embassies in France, was appointed to the council of the north (1536) and was ambassador to Francis I with **Gardiner** and Sir Francis Brian (2 May 1538). He also sat on a commission to investigate Anabaptist activity (1538) with **Cranmer, Skip** and **Stokesley**. Thirlby was a member of the privy council (1542), ambassador to Charles V in Spain (1542, 1545), ambassador to Scotland (May 1545) and was provided the see of Norwich, (1 April 1550) and translated, under Mary I, to Ely (nominated 10 July 1554) while serving as ambassador to the pope. He refused to swear the oath of supremacy to Elizabeth, was deprived of Ely (5 July 1559) and imprisoned (1560).

Further Sources: T.F. Shirley, *Thomas Thirlby: Tudor Bishop* (London, 1964).

**Tunstal** (or **Tonstall**), **Cuthbert** (1474-1559). Born at Hackforth, North Riding of Yorkshire, the illegitimate son of Thomas Tunstal of Thurland Castle, Lancashire. He was educated at Balliol College Oxford, King's Hall Cambridge, Padua (D.Can.L., LL.D.) and Rome (1505). He was rector of Barmston, Yorkshire (1506), Stanhope, Durham (1508), Sutton Veny, Wiltshire (1509), Aldridge, Staffordshire (1509), Steeple Langford, Wiltshire (1509), East Peckham, London (1511) and Harrow-on-the-Hill, London (1511) and prebendary of Stow Longa, Lincoln (1511), Botevant, York (1519) and Combe and Hornham, Salisbury (1521). He held higher office as archdeacon of Chester (1515), dean of Salisbury (1521), and served as chancellor and commissary-general to **Warham** (1511), auditor of Causes in the Canterbury courts prior to his provision to the see of London (16 May 1522), and translated to Durham (provided 21 February 1530). Tunstal served the crown on an embassy to Charles V in Brussels (7 May 1515), as master of the rolls (12 May 1516 - October 1522), as ambassador to Charles V (1519-20, 1526, 1527) and keeper of the privy seal (appointed on 25 May 1523). He opposed the Aragon divorce and served as one of Queen Catherine of Aragon's councillors. He was later president of the council of the north (1537) and served on various peace commissions in Scotland and France. He was co-author of *Letter to Cardinal Pole* (c.1537, published in 1575) with **Stokesley**, in support of the royal supremacy, and published *A Sermon of Cuthbert Bysshop of Duresme, made uopn Palme sondaye laste past, before the majestie of out soverayne lorde*

*kyng Henry the .VIII. kynge of England* (1539). He was executor to Henry
VIII's will, but opposed the Uniformity Act of 1549 and was accused of inciting
rebellion against Edward VI in 1550, confined to his London house and deprived
his see (1553), to be restored by Mary I and deprived again by Elizabeth I for
refusing the oath of supremacy (1559). Author of *De Veritate Corporis et
Sanguinis . . . in Eucharistia* (1550).
Further Sources: *The Registers of Cuthbert Tunstall Bishop of Durham 1530-59
and James Pilkington Bishop of Durham 1561-76*, ed. by G. Hinde (Durham, 1952);
A. Forster, 'Bishop Tunstall's Priests', in Recusant History 9 (1967-8), pp.175-204;
C. Sturge, *Cuthbert Tunstal: Churchman, Scholar, Statesman, Administrator*
(London, 1938). His career is discussed in J. Foxe, *Acts and Monuments*, ed. by G.
Townshend and C.R. Cattley, 8 vols. (Oxford, 1837-41), v. pp.80-9, 861-2 and G.
Burnet, *The History of the Reformation of the Church of England*, ed. by N. Pocock,
7 vols. (Oxford, 1865), iv. pp.400-07.

**Vaughan, Edward** (c.1450-1522). Born in South Wales to yeoman parents,
he was educated at Cambridge (B.Civ.L. 1475, D.Civ.L. 1480, D.Can.L. 1482).
He was vicar of Islington, London (1499), rector of St Matthew Friday Street,
London (1487) and of Avening, Gloucestershire (1498), and prebendary of
Reculverland (1493), Harleston (1499), Bromesbury (1503) all in St Paul's,
and of Llanbister in St David's. He held higher office as archdeacon of Lewes
(1488), and served as portioner of St Probus, Cornwall (1487), treasurer of
St Paul's (1503) and precentor of Abergwili, Carmarthenshire (1504), prior
to his provision to the see of St David's (13 June 1509), where he carried out
extensive renovations.
Further Sources: His career is discussed in W.B. Jones and E.A. Freeman, The *History
and Antiquities of Saint David's* (London, 1856).
10
**Veysey** (or **Voysey**, or **Harman**), **John** (c.1465-1554). Born at Sutton-
Coldfield, Warwickshire, the eldest son of William Harman of Moor Hall. He
was educated at Magdalen College Oxford (probationary fellow 1486, fellow
1487, D.of Laws 1494). He was vicar of St Michael's, Coventry (1507-20),
rector of St Blaize, Cornwall (1495), Clifton Reynes, Buckinghamshire (1495-
9), Brize Norton, Oxfordshire (1497), Edgmond, Shropshire (1497), St Mary's
on the Hill, Chester (1499) and of Meifod, Montgomeryshire (1518), and
prebendary of Darlington, Durham (1498), Exeter (1503), Crediton, Devon
(1504), St Stanford's in Crediton, Devon (1512), Liddington, Lincoln (1514),
Stoke in Teignhead, Devon (1504) and St Stephen's, Westminster (1514-8).
He held higher office as archdeacon of Chester (1499-1515) and Barnstable
(1503), dean of Exeter (1509), St George's, Windsor (1514), Windsor (1515-
9) and of Wolverhampton (1516-21), and served as vicar-general and chancellor
to Bishop Arundel (1498-1502), precentor of Exeter (1508) and as warden of
Clyst St Gabriel Chapel (1508), prior to his provision to the see of Exeter (31
August 1519). He was councillor to Queen Elizabeth of York (1489), registrar

of the order of the Garter (1515), commissioner in the 'inquisition of 1517' on enclosures in Berkshire and six other counties and president of the court of marches of Wales (1526). He was later deprived of his see (14 August 1551) by Edward VI and restored by Mary I (28 September 1553).

Further Sources: D.H. Pill, 'The administration of the Diocese of Exeter under Bishop Veysey', in *The Devonshire Association for the Advancement of Science, Literature and Art, Reports and Transactions*, 98 (1966), pp.262-78. His injunctions for Exeter (1538) can be found in *Concilia Magnae Britanniae et Hiberniae. . .* , ed. by David Wilkins, 4 vols. (London, 1737), iii. pp.844*ff.*

**Wakeman (**or **Wiche), John** (c.1485-1549). Born at Drayton, Worcestershire to yeoman parents, he was educated by the Benedictines at Gloucester Hall Oxford (B.D. 1511). He was prior, and later abbot, of Tewkesbury (27 April 1534 to its surrender on 9 January 1539) before his nomination to the see of Gloucester (3 September 1541).

**Warham, William** (c.1450-1532). Born at Malshanger, Hampshire to parents of the gentry class. He was educated at Wykeham's in Winchester, New College Oxford (fellow, 1475, LL.D. 1485) and Cambridge (LL.D. 1500). He served as principal or moderator of the civil law school and became chancellor of Oxford on 28 May 1506. He was rector of Great Horwood, Buckinghamshire (1488), Blenkenoll, Salisbury (1497), Barley, Hertfordshire (1495) and of Cottenham, Cambridgeshire (1500) and prebendary of Timsbury in Romsey Abbey, Hampshire. He held higher office as archdeacon of Huntingdon (1496), and served as precentor of Wells (1495), as proctor of Bishop Alcock (1490), as an advocate in the court of Arches (1488) and as proctor for Cardinal Morton and Bishop Alcock in Rome prior to his provision to the see of London (20 October 1501) and translation to Canterbury (provided 29 November 1503). He served the crown on a trade embassy to a diet at Antwerp (April 1491), to Flanders (July 1493) and to Scotland (4 July 1497). On 13 February 1494 he was appointed master of the rolls (resigned 1 February 1501) and on 5 March 1496 he was commissioned to treat with the Spanish ambassador regarding the marriage of Prince Arthur and Catherine of Aragon. On 11 August 1501 he was appointed keeper of the great seal and on 21 January 1504 he was made lord chancellor (resigned 22 December 1515). His opinions regarding the Aragon divorce and the supreme headship wavered pro and con.

Further Sources: M. Bateson, 'Archbishop Warham's Visitation of Monasteries, 1511', in *EHR* 6:21 (January 1891), pp.18-35; J. Moyes, 'Warham: An English Primate on the Eve of the Reformation', in *Dublin Review*, 114 (1894), pp.390-420; M.J. Kelly, 'Canterbury Jurisdiction and Influence during the Episcopate of William Warham, 1503-1532' (unpublished Ph.D. thesis, University of Cambridge, 1963). His letters feature in *Concilia Magnae Britanniae et Hiberniae. . .* , ed. by David Wilkins, 4 vols. (London, 1737), iii. pp.746*ff;* in *Collected Works of Erasmus*, various editors, 67 vols. (Toronto, 1974-1991), iii. pp.316-9, 424 and J.B. Sheppard, *Literae Cantuarienses* 3 vols. (London, 1889).

**West, Nicolas** (1461-1533). Born at Putney, Surrey to yeoman parents. He was educated at Eton and King's College Cambridge (fellow 1483-98, B.A., M.A., LL.D c.1486) and served his college as proctor. He was vicar of Kingston on Thames, Surrey (1502) and of Merton, Oxfordshire (1508), rector of Yelford, Oxfordshire (1489), Egglescliffe, Durham (1499-1515), Witney, Oxfordshire (1502) and of Eltord, Lichfield (1502). He held higher office as archdeacon of Derby (1486), dean of St George's, Windsor (1509) and served as vicar-general to **Richard Fox** (1501) and as treasurer of Chichester (1507). He was admitted to the order of the Friars Observant (25 January 1514), prior to his provision to the see of Ely (27 November 1515). He served the crown as royal chaplain (1502) and councillor to Henry VII (1504), as ambassador to Emperor Maximilian, three times ambassador to James IV (1511, 1513) and to Louis XII (1514). He was the king's special envoy to George, Duke of Saxony (1505) and to Francis I (1515), as well as having been Trier and receiver of petitions to parliament from Gascoigne and beyond seas (1512) and advocate for the Knights Hospitallers. He opposed the Aragon divorce and wrote two polemics, *In Dei nomine, amen. Cum ex facto* and *In Dei nomine, Amen. Ad ea qua*, outlining his opinions.

**Wharton** (or **Warton**, or **Purefoy**, or **Parfew**), **Robert** (d.1557). Probably the son of yeoman parents, but his birthplace is unknown. He was educated at Cambridge (B.D. 1535). A Cluniac monk, he was abbot of Bermondsey (? to 1538), prior to his elevation to the see of St Asaph (8 June 1536). During the reign of Mary I he was translated to Hereford (nominated 17 March 1554).

**Wolsey, Thomas** (c.1475-1530). Born at Ipswich, Suffolk (famously or infamously) son of a butcher. He was educated at Magdalen College School, Magdalen College Oxford (B.A. 1490, fellow 1497, B.D. 1510, D.D.) and served the school as master of Magdalen College School, as junior bursar (1498-9), senior bursar (1499-1500) and as a tutor. He was the founder of Cardinal's College and Ipswich Grammar. He was vicar of Lydd, Kent (1501), rector of Limington, Somerset (1500), Redgrave, Suffolk (1506) and of Great Torrington, Devon (1510) and prebendary of Pratum Minus, Hereford (1508), Welton Brinkhall, Lincoln (1508-9), Stow Longa, Lincoln (1509), Windsor (1511), Bugthorpe, York (1512), Compton Dunden, Wells (1513) and of Llanhister, Abergwili, Carmarthenshire. He held higher office as dean of Lincoln (1509), Hereford (1512), York (1513) and of St Stephen's, Westminster (1513) and served the church as rural dean of Depwade and Humbleyard, Lincolnshire (1499), parson of St Bride's Fleet Street, London (1510), precenter of St Paul's (1513), chaplain to Archbishop Deane (1501) and chaplain to Sir Richard Nanfan, the Deputy of Calais (1503), prior to his many episcopal promotions. He was bishop of Tournai (1513-8), Lincoln (provided 6 February), archbishop of York (provided 15 September 1514), *in commendam* with Bath and Wells (provided 27 July 1518), Durham (February 1523) and Winchester (provided 8 February 1529). He became a cardinal (10 September 1514) of St Caecilia trans Tiberim, papal legate *a latere* (17 May 1514), legate for life (21 January 1524) and abbot of St Alban's. He served the crown as royal chaplain to both Henry VII (1507) and Henry VIII (1509), special envoy to Emperor Maximilian (1508) and to Scotland (1508), almoner (1509), registrar of the Knights of the Garter (1511), councillor and lord chancellor (appointed 24 December 1514). He incurred a *praemunire* and indictment in King's Bench (3 November 1529), was deprived all his sees save York, and would have faced treason charges if he had not died in Leicester *en route* to London.

Further Sources: C.W. Ferguson, *Naked to Mine Enemies: The Life of Cardinal Wolsey* (Toronto, 1958); *Cardinal Wolsey: Church, State and Art* ed. by S.J. Gunn & P.G. Lindley (Cambridge, 1991); P. Gwyn, *The King's Cardinal* (London, 1990); A.F. Pollard, *Wolsey* (London, 1965 edn); J. Ridley, *Statesman and Fanatic: Cardinal Wolsey, Sir Thomas More and the Politics of Henry VIII* (London, 1982). Two of his registers are available, from the Somerset Records Society, vol.54, as *The Register of Thomas Wolsey as Bishop of Bath and Wells, 1518-1523*, ed. by H. Maxwell-Lyte (1940), pp.1-26 and from the Canterbury and York Society as *Registrum Thome Wolsey, Cardinalis Ecclesie Wintoniensis Administratoris*, ed. by H. Chitty (London, 1926).

# List of Works Cited

Manuscript Sources

London
1 Greater London Record Office
     MSS DL/C/330
2 British Library
     Cottonian MSS
            Cleopatra E, iv, v, vi, F, i, ii
            Otho, C, x
            Titus B, i
    Vespasian C, i.
            Vitellius B, ii, iv, v, xii, xiii, xx
        Lansdowne, MSS 938, 979, 980
        Harleian MSS 283, 421, 422, 425, 604, 6382, 6989
        Sloane MSS 1207
        Additional MSS 8442, 48012, 28580
3 London Guildhall Library
     MSS 9531/10: Episcopal Register Tunstal: 1522-1529/30
     MSS 9531/11: Episcopal Register Stokesley: 1530-1539
4 Lambeth Palace Library
     MSS 1107, 2341
5 Public Record Office
     King's Bench 27/1048, 27/1050, 27/1085, 27/1091, 29/151, 29/154, 29/161, 29/164, 29/166
        Requests 1/4, 3/10
        Exchequer Rolls 1/2652
        State Papers 1/1, 1/3, 1/4, 1/5, 1/7, 1/12, 1/18, 1/19, 1/23, 1/26, 1/50, 1/53, 1/54, 1/56, 1/63, 1/70, 1/78, 1/82, 1/84, 1/89, 1/93, 1/94, 1/98, 1/99, 1/101, 1/103, 1 / 104, 1/105, 1/111, 1/113, 1/126, 1/223, 1/229, 1/236, 1/238, 2/1, 2/P, 6/1, 6/2, 6/3, 6/6, 6/7, 6/9, 6/11

Chichester
1 Sussex Record Office
     ACC 5517 Box Sherb. I.
     EP 1/10/3, 1/10/4, 1/10/5
     EP I/1/5, I/52/7, I/52/9 (Bundels 1-2)
     EP VI/4/1

Cambridge
1 University Library
     Register of Nicholas West

Exeter
1 Devon Record Office
        Register of Hugh Oldham

Leeds
1 Thornton Society
        MSS Box 1/2


                        Primary Sources (Printed)


*A Litel Treatise ageynste the mutterynge of some papistis in corners* (London, 1534).
*A Treatise Concernynge generall councilles, the Byshoppes of Rome, and the Clergy* (London, 1538).
Alesius, Alexander, *Of the Authority of God against the Bishop of London* . . . , (n.d.)
        *An Epistle of the Most Mighty and Redoubted Prince Henry VIII* (Leipzig, 1541)
Allen, P.S and H.M (eds), *Letters of Richard Fox: 1486-1527* (Oxford, 1929).
Anon, *The Bishops Manifest (or, A Comparative Relation of conformitie of the English Prelates to those treacherous and deceitful ones in the Reign of King Hen. the eighth* . . . (London, 1641).
                'A Supplication to our moste Sovereigne Lorde Kyng Henry the Eight' (1544), *The Harleian Miscellany* ix (London, 1812), pp.451-66.
'Archbishop Warham's Visitation in the Year, 1511' in *British Magazine*, xxix (1847), pp.29-41, 145-63, 297-313, 391-404; 625-40; xxx (1848), pp.23-31, 151-58, 255-69, 518-33, 659-66; xxxi (1849), pp.33-40, 167-78, 267-77, 411-21, 538-51, 637-52; xxxii (1850), pp.41-7.
Aquinas, Thomas, *Summa Theologicae* (60 vols., London, 1969).
Augustine, '*Epistolarum Classis III, Epistolae Quas Scripsit Reliquo Vitae Tempore (ab anno 411 ad 450)*', in *PL*, xxxiii, pp.471-1024.
Bannister, A.T (ed.), *Registrum Edwardi Foxe, Episcopi Herefordensis A.D. MDXXXV - MDXXXVIII* (London, 1921).
        *Registrum Ricardi Mayew, Episcopi Herefordensis* (London, 1921).
        *Registrum Caroli Bothe, Episcopi Herefordensis AD MDXVI - MDXXXV* (London, 1921).
Becon, Thomas, *The Catechism of Thomas Becon*, ed. by John Ayre (Cambridge, 1844).
Berkowitz, D.S (ed.), *Humanist Scholarship and Public Order: Two Tracts Against the Pilgrimage of Grace by Sir Richard Morison, with Historical Annotations and Related Contemporary Documents* (London, 1984).
Blaauw, W.H., 'Episcopal visitations of the Benedictine Nunnery of Easebourne', in *Sussex Archaeological Collections*, ix (1857), pp.1-32.
Bretschneider, C.G. et al (eds), *Corpus Reformatorum* (101 vols. to date, Halle, 1834 to present).
Brown, Rawdon (ed.), *Four years at the court of Henry VIII* (2 vols., London, 1854).
Byrne, Muriel St Clare (ed.), *The Lisle Letters* (6 vols., Chicago, 1981).
*Calender of State Papers* . . . *King Henry VIII* (11 vols., London, 1830-52).
*Calendar of State Papers* . . . *Milan (1385-1618)*, ed. by Allen B. Hinds (London, 1912).
*Calendar of State Papers* . . . *Spanish*, ed. by G. Mattingly, Pascual de Gayangos, M.A S. Hume and R. Tyler (15 vols. in 20, London, 1862-1954).
*Calendar of State Papers* . . . *Venetian*, ed. by R. Brown, H. Brown and C. Bentinck (9 vols., London, 1864-1898).

Cavendish, George, *The Life and Death of Cardinal Wolsey*, ed. by R.S Sylvester (London, 1959).
    'The Life and Death of Cardinal Wolsey' in R.S Sylvester and D.P Harding (eds), *Two Early Tudor Lives* (New Haven, 1962).
    'The Negotiations of Thomas Wolsey, the Great Cardinal of England', *Harleian Miscellany* v (1810), pp.123-178.
Cessi, Roberto (ed.), *Dispacci Degli Ambasciatori Veneziani Alia Corte Di Roma Presso Guilio II (25 Guigno 1509 - 9 Gennaio 1510)* (Venice, 1932).
Clark, Andrew (ed.), *Lincoln Diocese Documents, 1450-1544* (London, 1914).
Cook, G.H., *Letters to Cromwell and Others on the Suppression of the Monasteries* (London, 1965).
Corrie, George E. (ed.), *The Works of Hugh Latimer, Sometime Bishop of Worcester, Martyr, 1555* (2 vols., Cambridge, 1844-5).
    *Sermons by Hugh Latimer, Sometime Bishop of Worcester, Martyr, 1555* (Cambridge, 1845).
Cox, J.E. (ed.), *Miscellaneous Writings and Letters of Thomas Cranmer* (2 vols., Cambridge, 1846).
Croke, Richard, *Orationes Ricardi Croci Duae* ([London?], 1520).
*The Divorce Tracts of Henry VIII*, ed. by Edward Surtz and Virginia Murphy (Angers, Moreana, 1988).
Douglas, David C. (ed.), *English Historical Documents* (12 vols., London, 1953-81).
Duffield, G.E. (ed.), *The Work of Thomas Cranmer* (Appleford, 1964).
Ehses, Stephen (ed.), *Ehses Römische Dokumente zur Geschichte der Ehescheidung Heinricks VIII von England, 1527-1534* (Paderborn, 1893).
Ellis, H. (ed.), *Original Letters illustrative of English History* (11 vols., in 3 series, London, 1824, 1827, 1846).
*Collected Works of Erasmus*, various editors, (67 vols., Toronto, 1974-1991).
Fisher, John, *English Works of John Fisher, Bishop of Rochester (Sermons and Other Writings 1520 to 1535)*, ed. by Cecilia A. Hatt (Oxford, 2002).
Fox, Edward, *De vera differentia regiae potestatis et ecclesiasticae, et quae sit ipsa veritas ac virtus utrusque*, in Melchior Goldest (ed.), *Monarchia S. Romani Imperii* . . . (3 vols., Frankfurt, 1613), iii, pp.22-45.
    *The true dyfferis between y regall power and the ecclesiasticall power, etc.*, trans. by Henry, Lord Stafford (London, 1548, Amsterdam, 1973 edn).
Frere, W.H. and Kennedy, W.M. (eds), *Visitation Articles and Injunctions of the Period of the Reformation* (3 vols., London, 1910).
Gairdner, James (ed.), *Letters and Papers Illustrative of the Reigns of Richard III and Henry VII* (2 vols., London, 1861, 1863).
Gee, Henry and Hardy, William J. (eds), *Documents illustrative of English church history* (London, 1896).
Gewrith, Alan (ed. and trans.), *Marsilius of Padua: The Defender of Peace* (2 vols., New York, 1928).
*The Glasse of Truthe* (London, 1531).
Gray, G.J., 'Letters of Bishop Fisher, 1521-3', *The Library* 3rd series, iv (1913), pp.133-45
Grazebrook, G. and Rylands, J.P (eds), *The Visitation of Shropeshire, 1623* (2 vols., London, 1889).
Hall, Edward, *The Union of the Two Noble and Illustre Families of Lancastre & York*, ed. by H. Ellis (2 vols., 1809 edn).
Hamilton, W.D. (ed.), *A Chronicle of England . . . by Charles Wriothesley, Windsor Herald* (2 vols., London, 1875, 1877).

Harper-Bill, Christopher (ed.), *Register of John Morton, Archbishop of Canterbury, 1486-1500* (2 vols., Leeds, 1987).

Harpsfield, Nicholas, *A Treatise on the Pretended Divorce between Henry VIII and Catherine of Aragon*, ed. by N. Pocock (Westminster, 1878).

> *The Life and Death of Sir Thomas More*, ed. by E.V Hitchcock (London, 1932).

Harrison, J. (*alias* John Bale), *Yet a course at the Romish Fox* (Zurich, 1543).

Hay, Denys (ed. and trans.), *The Anglica historia of Polydore Vergil, A D 1485-1537* (London, 1950).

Heath, P. (ed.), 'Bishop Geoffrey Blythe's Visitations, c.1515-1525', in *Staffordshire Record Society*, fourth series, vii (1973).

> 'Suppliments to Bishop Blythe's Visitations', in *Staffordshire Record Society*, fourth series, xiii (1988), pp.47-56.

Hinde, Gladys (ed.), *The Registers of Cuthbert Tunstall Bishop of Durham 1530-59 and James Pilkington Bishop of Durham 1561-76* (Durham, 1952).

Holinshed, Raphael et al (eds), *Chronicles* (3 vols, London, 1586).

Howden, M.O. (ed.), *The Register of Richard Fox, Lord Bishop of Durham 1494-1501* (London, 1932).

Isaacson, R.F. (ed.), *The Episcopal Register of the Diocese of St David's 1397 to 1518* (3 vols., London, 1917, 1920).

Jerome, 'Epistolae S Hieronymi in quatuor classes divisae secundum ordinem temporum', in *PL*, i, pp.235-1182.

> 'Letter to Pope Damasus concerning the hypostases', in *NPNF*, vi, pp.18-20.

Jessopp, A. (ed.), *Visitations of the Diocese of Norwich, A D 1492-1532* (London, 1888).

Johnson, Goddard, 'Chronological Memoranda touching the city of Norwich', *Norfolk and Norwich Archaeological Society* i (1847), pp.140-66.

*Journals of the House of Lords, 1509* . . . (10 vols., London (s.a.).

Kreider, Alan (ed.), 'An English Episcopal Draft Article Against the Anabaptists, 1536', *Mennonite Quarterly Review* xlix (1975), pp.38-42.

Lacey, T.A. (ed.), *The King's Book or A Necessary Doctrine And Erudition For Any Christian Man, 1543* (London, 1932).

Latimer, Hugh, 'Sermon to the convocation of 9 June 1537', in *Sermons by Hugh Latimer Sometime Bishop of Worcester* (London, n.d.), pp.30-53.

*Letters of Papers, Foreign and Domestic, of the Reign of Henry VIII, 1509-1547*, e d . by J.S Brewer et al (21 vols. and 2 vols. addenda, London, 1862-1932).

'Letters and Papers, Foreign and Domestic, of the Reign of Henry VIII', *The Quarterly Review* cxliii:cclxxxv (1877), pp.1-51.

'Letters and Papers Relating to the War with France 1512-13', in Alfred Spont (ed.), *Publications of the Navy Records Society* x (London, 1897).

Lloyd, C. (ed.), 'Articles Devised by the King's Majestie, to Stablyshe Christen Quietnes and Unitie amonge us' in *Formularies of Faith put forth by authority during the reign of Henry VIII* (Oxford, 1825), pp.xiii-xxxii.

> 'The Institutions of a Christian Man', in *Formularies of Faith Put Forth By Authority During the Reign of Henry VIII* (Oxford, 1825), pp.23-211.

Longland, John, *A Sermond Spoken before the Kynge his maiestie at Grewiche, uppon good Fryday* (London, 1536).

> *A Sermonde made before the Kynge his maiestie at grenewiche upon good Frydaye* (London, 1538).

Maddison, A.R. (ed.), 'Extracts from Bishop Longland's Register', in *Associated Architectural Societies' Reports and Papers*, xv:ii (1880), pp.167-79.

Mair, J., *Ionnes Maior in Secundum Sententiarum* (Paris, 1510).

*Ionnis Majoris Doctoris Theologi in Quartum Sententiarum quaestiones* (Paris, 1516).

*Editio Ionnis Maioris doctoris Parisiensis super Tertium Sententiarum quaestiones* (Paris, 1517).

*Historia Maioris Britanniae tam angliae quam Scotiae* (Paris, 1521).

*A History of Great Britain as well England as Scotland*, trans. by Archibald Constable (Edinburgh, 1892).

Marshall, G.W. (ed.), *The Visitations of the County of Nottingham in the years 1569 and 1614* (London, 1871).

Matthew, S., *A Sermon made in the cathedrall churche of Saynt Paul at London* (London, 1535).

Maxwell-Lyte, H.C. (ed.), 'The Registers of Robert Stillington and Richard Fox, Bishops of Bath and Wells', in *Somersetshire Record Society*, lii (1937).

Merriman, Roger B. (ed.), *Life and Letters of Thomas Cromwell* (2 vols., Oxford, 1902).

Metcalfe, W.C. (ed.), *Visitations of Hertfordshire, 1572 and 1634* (London, 1886).

Migne, J.P. (ed.), *Patrologiae cursus completus: series Latina* (221 vols., Paris, 1844-1903).

*Patrologiae cursus completus: series Graeca* (161 vols., Paris, 1857-1866).

*The Complete Works of St Thomas More*, various editors (15 vols., New Haven, 1976-90).

Morice, Ralph, *Narratives of the Days of the Reformation*, ed. by J.G. Nicholas (London, 1860).

Muller, J.A. (ed.), *Letters of Stephen Gardiner* (Cambridge, 1933).

'Original Acknowledgements of the Royal Supremacy', in *Deputy Keepers Reports of the Public Records*, Seventh and Eighth reports (London, 1846).

Pace, Richard, *De fructu qui ex doctrina percipitur liber* (Basil, 1517).

*The Benefit of a Liberal Education*, ed. and trans. by Frank Manley and Richard S. Sylvester (New York, 1967).

Pocock, Nicholas, *Records of the Reformation* (2 vols., Oxford, 1870).

Pole, Reginald, *Pro Ecclesiasticae Unitatis Defensione* (c.1537).

Pollard, A.F. (ed.), *Records of the English Bible: The Documents Relating to the Translation and Publication of the Bible in English: 1525-1611* (London, 1911).

Previté-Orton, C.W. (ed.), *The Defensor Pacis of Marsilius of Padua* (Cambridge, 1928).

Quirini, A.M. (ed.), *Epistolarum Reginaldi Poli S.R.E. Cardinalis et aliorum ad ipsum* (5 vols., Farnborough, 1967).

'The Records of the Northern Convocation', in *Surtees Society Publications*, cxiii (Durham 1907).

Rye, Walter (ed.), *The Visitation of Norfolk* (London, 1891).

Rymer, Thomas (ed.), *Foedera* (17 vols., London, 1704-35).

Sampson, Richard, *Oratio quae docet hortatur admonet omnes potissimum Anglos regiae dignitati cum primis ut obediant . . .* (London, 1534).

Sawtry, James (*alias* George Joye), *The defence of the mariage of preistes, against Steven Gardiner, Bishop of Winchester, William Repps, Bishop of Norwich, and against all of the bishops and priests of that false popish sect* (Antwerp, 1541).

Seyssel, Claude de, *The Monarchy of France*, trans. by J.H. Hexter (New Haven, 1981).

Sheppard, J.B. (ed.), *Literae Cantuarienses* (3 vols., London, 1889).

Skelton, John, *The Complete English Poems*, ed. by J. Scattergood (London, 1978).

Starkey, T., *England in the Reign of Henry VIII*, ed. by J.M Cowper (2 vols., London, 1871-8).

*The Statutes of the Realm* (11 vols., London, 1810-28).

Stokesley, John, 'The Appeal of Stokesley, Bishop of London to the King, Against the Archbishop's Visitation', in John Strype, *Memorials of Thomas Cranmer* (2 vols., Oxford, 1812), ii, pp.704-8.

Stokesley, John and Tunstal, Cuthbert, *The true copy of a certain Letter written by Cuthbert Tonstal, Bishop of Durham, and John Stokesley, Bishop of London, to Cardinal Pole, proving the Bishop of Rome to have no special superiority above other Bishops*, in Foxe, v, pp.90-99.

   *Letter to Cardinal Pole* (London, 1575).

Stowe, John, 'Historical Memoranda', in James Gairdner (ed.), *Three Fifteenth Century Chronicles* (London, 1880).

Strype, John, *Memorials of Thomas Cranmer* (2 vols., Oxford, 1812).

   *Ecclesiastical Memorials* (3 vols., Oxford, 1822).

Theophylact, 'Chronographia', in *PG*, cviii, pp.1038-1164.

Tertullian, 'Liber Ad Scapulam', in *PL*, i, pp.697-706.

Tertullian, 'Apologeticus', in *PL*, i, pp.257-536.

Thompson, A. Hamilton (ed.), 'Visitations in the Diocese of Lincoln 1517-1531', in *Lincoln Record Society* xxxiii (1940).

   'Visitations of Lincoln 1517-1531', in *Lincoln Record Society* xxxv (1944).

Tunstall, Cuthbert, *A Sermon . . . made upon Palme Sondaye last past* (London, 1539).

Turner, William, *The Rescuing of the Romish Fox* (Basel, 1542).

   *The huntyng and fyndyng out of the Romyshe foxe, which more then seven yeares hath bene among the bisshoppes of Englonde* (Basle, 1543).

   *The Huntying and Fyndung out of the Romish Fox which more than Seven Years hath been hyd among the Byshoppes of England, after the Kynges Highnes, Henry VIII, had commanded hym to be dryven out of hys Realme*, ed. by Robert Potts (Cambridge, 1851).

Turner, William and Blaauw, W.H., 'Injunctions given to the Prior and Convent of Boxgrove, A.D. 1518', in *Sussex Archaeological Collections*, ix (1857), pp.61-66.

Tyndale, William, 'The Practice of Prelates', in *Expositions and Notes on Sundry Portions of the Holy Scripture*, ed. by Henry Walter (Cambridge, 1849).

'Visitations in the diocese of York, Holden by Archbishop Edward Lee (A.D. 1534-5)', *The Yorkshire Archaeological Journal* xvi (1902), pp.424-58.

Wakefield, Robert, *Oratio de laudibus et utilitate trium linguarum* (London, n.d.).

Whatmore, L.E., 'The Sermon against the Holy Maid of Kent, delivered at Paul's Cross, 23 November, 1533, and at Canterbury, Dec.7', *EHR* lviii:ccxxxii (October 1943), pp.463-75.

Williams, C.H. (ed.), *English Historical Documents 1485-1558* (London, 1967).

Wilson, J.M., 'The Visitations and Injunctions of Cardinal Wolsey and Archbishop Cranmer to the Priory of Worcester in 1526 & 1534 respectively', in *Associated Architectural Societies' Reports and Papers* xxxvi:i (1921), pp.356-71.

Wood-Legh, K.L. (ed.), *Kentish Visitations of Archbishop William Warham and his Deputies, 1511-1512* (Maidstone, 1984).

Wright, T. (ed.), *Three Chapters of Letters relating to the Suppression of Monasteries* (London, 1843).

Wriothesley, C., *Chronicle of England* (2 vols., London, 1885 edn).

Secondary Sources

Aston, Margaret, 'Lollards and the Reformation: Survival or Revival?', *History* xlix:lxvi (June 1964), pp.149-70.

Bacon, F., *The History of the Reign of Henry the Seventh*, ed. by F.J Levy (New York, 1972 edn).

Bailey, Sherwin, 'Robert Wisdom under Persecution, 1541-1543', *JEH* ii (1951), pp.180-9.

Barnes, A.S., *Bishop Barlow and Anglican Orders: A Study of the Original Documents* (London, 1922).

Barrow, I., *A Treatise of the Pope's Supremacy* (Cambridge, 1859)

Baskerville, Geoffrey, *English Monks and the Suppression of the Monasteries* (London, 1937, 1965 edn).

Bateson, Mary, 'Archbishop Warham's Visitations of Monasteries, 1511', *EHR*, vi, (1891), pp.18-36.

Baumgartner, Frederic J., *Change and Continuity in the French Episcopate: The Bishops and the Wars of Religion, 1547-1610* (Durham, 1986).

Bayne, Ronald (ed.), *The Life of John Fisher* (London, 1921).

Beresford, William, *Lichfield* (London, 1890).

Bernard, G.W., *War, Taxation and Rebellion in Tudor England* (Sussex, 1986).

'The Pardon of the Clergy Reconsidered', *JEH* xxxvii:ii (April 1986), pp.258-71.

'The Fall of Anne Boleyn: A Rejoinder', *EHR* cvii:ccccxxiv (July 1992), pp.665-74.

Black, A.J., 'What was conciliarism? Conciliar theory in historical perspective', in B. Tierney and P. Lineham (eds), *Authority and Power* (Cambridge, 1980), pp.213-24.

Block, J., *Factional Politics and the English Reformation 1520-1540* (Woodbridge, 1993).

Bowker, Margaret, *The Secular Clergy in the Diocese of Lincoln, 1495-1520* (Cambridge, 1967).

'The Supremacy and the Episcopate: The Struggle for Control, 1534-1540', *HJ* xviii:ii (1975), pp.227-43.

'The Henrician Reformation and the Parish Clergy', *BIHR* l:cxxi (May, 1977), pp.30-47.

*The Henrician Reformation: The diocese of Lincoln under Bishop John Longland, 1521-1547* (Cambridge, 1981).

Bowers, Roger, 'The cultivation and promotion of music in the household and orbit of Thomas Wolsey', in S.J. Gunn and P.G. Lindley (eds), *Cardinal Wolsey: Church, state and art* (Cambridge, 1991), pp.178-218.

Bradshaw, Brendan, 'Bishop John Fisher, 1469-1535: the man and his work', in B. Bradshaw and E. Duffy (eds), *Humanism, Reform and Reformation: The Career of Bishop John Fisher* (Cambridge, 1989), pp.1-24.

Brigden, Susan, *London and the Reformation* (Oxford, 1989).

Bruce, John, 'Observations on the circumstances which occasioned the Death of Fisher Bishop of Rochester', *Archaeologia* xxv (1834), pp.61-99.

Brucker, Gene, *Renaissance Florence* (Berkeley, 1969).

Burnet, G., *The History of the Reformation of the Church of England*, ed. by Nicholas Pocock (7 vols., Oxford, 1865).

Burns, J.H., '*Politia Regalis et Optima*: The Political Ideas of John Mair', *History of Political Thought* ii:i (January 1981), pp.31-61.

Bush, D., 'Tudor Humanism and Henry VIII', *University of Toronto Quarterly* vii (1937), pp.162-7.

Butterworth, Charles C., *The English Primers (1529-1545), their publication and connection with the English Bible and the Reformation in England* (Philadelphia, 1953).

Cameron, Euan, *The European Reformation* (Oxford, 1991).

Cameron, T.W., 'The Early Life of Thomas Wolsey', *English Historical Review* iii (1888), pp.458-77.

Cardinal, Edward V., *Cardinal Lorenzo Campeggio, Legate to the Courts of Henry VIII and Charles V* (Boston, 1935).

Chambers, D.S., *Cardinal Bainbridge in the Court of Rome 1509-1514* (Oxford, 1965).

Chandler, Pretor W., 'Doctor's Commons', *London Topographical Record* xv (1931), pp.4-20.

Chester, Allan G., 'Robert Barnes and the Burning of Books', *Huntington Library Quarterly* xiv:iii (May 1951), pp.211-21.

 'A Note on the Burning of Lutheran Books in England in 1521', *Library Chronicle* xviii (1952), pp.68-70.

Chester, Arthur G., *Hugh Latimer: Apostle to the English* (Philadelphia, 1978 Octagon Books edn.).

Chibi, Andrew A., 'Henry VIII and his Marriage to his Brother's Wife, the Sermon of Bishop John Stokesley of 11 July 1535', *HR* lxvii:clxii (February 1994), pp.40-56.

 '"*Turpitudinem uxoris fratris tui non revelavit*": John Stokesley and the Divorce Question', *SCJ* xxv:2 (Summer 1994), pp.387-97.

 *Henry VIII's Conservative Scholar: Bishop John Stokesley and the Divorce, Royal Supremacy and Doctrinal Reform* (Berne, 1997).

 '"Had I but served God with half the zeal . . .": The Service Records of the Men Who Became Henry VIII's Bishops', *Reformation* 3 (1998), pp.75-136.

 'The Social and Regional Origins of the Henrician Episcopal Bench', in *The Sixteenth Century Journal*, xxix:4 (Winter 1998), pp.955-73.

 'State v Church: Implementing Reformation (Cromwell, Stokesley and London Diocese)' in *Journal of Church and State*, 41:1 (Winter 1999), pp.77-98.

 'The Intellectual and Academic Training of the Henrician Episcopacy', in *Archiv für Reformationsgeschichte*, 91 (2000), pp.354-72.

Churchill, Irene J., *Canterbury Administration* (2 vols., London, 1933).

Clebsch, William A., *England's Earliest Protestants, 1520-1535* (New Haven, 1964).

Cobban, A.B., 'Colleges and Halls, 1380-1500', in J.I. Catto and Ralph Evans (eds), *The History of the University of Oxford* (3 vols., Oxford, 1992).

Collett, Barry, 'The Civil Servant and Monastic Reform: Richard Fox's Translation of the Benedictine Rule for Women, 1517', in Judith Loades (ed.), *Monastic Studies; The Continuity of Tradition* (Bangor, 1990), pp.211-28.

Condon, Margaret, 'Ruling Elites in the Reign of Henry VII', in C. Ross (ed.), *Patronage Pedigree and Power in Later Medieval England* (Gloucester, 1979), pp.109-42.

Constant, Gustav, 'Les Evêques Henriciens sous Henri VIII', *Revue Des Questions Historiques* xii (1912), pp.384-425.

 *The Reformation in England*, trans. by R.E. Scantlebury (2 vols., London, 1939-42).

Coogan, Robert, *Erasmus, Lee and the Correction of the Vulgate: The Shaking of the Foundations* (Geneva, 1992).

Cooper, Tim N., 'Oligarchy and Conflict: Lichfield Cathedral Clergy in the Early Sixteenth Century', *Midland History*, xix (1994), pp.40-57.

Coote, Bell C., *Sketches of the Lives and Characters of Eminent English Civilians* (London, 1804).

Cowan, Ian B., *The Scottish Reformation; Church and Society in Sixteenth Century Scotland* (London, 1982).

Coward, Barry, *Social Change and Continuity in Early Modern England 1550-1750* (London, 1988, 1995 edn).

Creighton, Mandal, 'The Italian Bishops of Worcester', *Associated Architectural Societies, Reports and Papers* xx:ii (1840), pp.94-118.

    *Cardinal Wolsey* (London, 1891).

Cruickshank, C.G., *Army Royal, Henry VIII's Invasion of France 1513* (Oxford, 1969).

Daniell, David, *William Tyndale, A Biography* (New Haven, 1994).

Darby, Harold S., 'Thomas Bilney', *London Quarterly and Holborn Review* v (January 1942), pp.67-84.

Davies, C.S L., *Peace, Print & Protestantism: 1450-1558* (London, 1976, 1982 edn).

Davies, Eliza J., 'Doctor's Common, Its Title and Topography', *London Topographical Record* xv (1931), pp.36-50.

Davis, J.F., 'Lollards, Reformers and St Thomas of Canterbury', *University of Birmingham Historical Journal* ix:i (1963) pp.1-15.

    *Heresy and Reformation in the South East of England 1520-1559* (London, 1983).

Derrett, J. Duncan M., 'The Affairs of Richard Hunne and Friar Standish', in *CWTM* ix, pp.215-46.

Dickens, A.G., *Robert Holgate, Archbishop of York and President of the King's Council of the North* (London, 1955).

    *Lollards and Protestants in the Diocese of York 1509-1558* (London, 1959, 1966 reprint).

    *The English Reformation* (New York, 1976 edn).

*The Dictionary of National Biography* (London, 1885-1901).

Ditchfield, P.H. and Page, William (eds), *VHC: A History of Bershire* (4 vols., London, 1907-24).

'The Divorce of Catherine of Aragon', *English Review*, clx:cccxxvii (July, 1884), pp.89-116.

Dodsworth, William, *An Historical Account of the Episcopal See, and Cathedral Church of Salisbury* (Salisbury, 1814).

Doernberg, Erwin, *Henry VIII and Luther: An Account of Their Personal Relations* (London, 1961).

Doran, Susan and Durston, Christopher, *Princes, Pastors and People* (London, 1991).

Doubleday, H.A. and Page, William (eds), *VHC: A History of Hampshire* (5 vols., Westminster, 1900-12).

Dowden, John, *The Bishops of Scotland*, ed. by J. Maitland Thomson (Glasgow, 1912).

Dowling, Maria, 'Humanist Support for Katherine of Aragon', *BIHR* lvii:liii (May 1984), pp.46-55.

    'Cranmer as Humanist Reformer', in Paul Ayris and David Selwyn (eds), *Thomas Cranmer: Churchman and Scholar* (Woodbridge, 1993), pp.89-114.

Down, Kevin, 'The Administration of the Diocese of Worcester Under the Italian Bishops, 1497-1535', *Midland History* xx (1995), pp.1-20.

Duff, E.G., *A Century of the English Book Trade* (London, 1905).

    *The Printers, Stationers and Bookbinders of Westminster and London from 1476 to 1535* (Cambridge, 1906).

Duff, E.G, et al (eds), *Hand-lists of Books Printed by London Printers 1501-1556* (London, 1913).

Dunham, William H., 'The Members of Henry VIII's Whole Council, 1509-1527', *EHR* lix:ccxxxiv (May 1944), pp.187-210.

Edelstein, Marilyn Manera, 'The Social Origins of the Episcopacy in the Reign of Francis I', *French Historical Studies* viii (1974), pp.377-92.

'Foreign Episcopal Appointments during the Reign of Francis I', *Church History* xliv (1975), pp.450-59.

Editor, 'Paul Bush, The Last Rector of Edington and First Bishop of Bristol, 1490-1558', *Wiltshire Notes and Queries* iv (September 1902), pp.97-107.

Elliott, J.H., *Imperial Spain, 1469-1716* (Harmondsworth, 1970).

Elton, G.R., 'The Commons' Supplication of 1532: Parliamentary Manoeuvres in the Reign of Henry VIII', *EHR* lxiv (1951), pp.216-32.

    *Star Chamber Stories* (London, 1958, 1974 edn).

    *The Tudor Revolution in Government* (Cambridge, 1969 edn).

    *Policy and Police: The Enforcement of the Reformation in the Age of Thomas Cromwell* (Cambridge, 1972).

    'The Body of the Whole Realm: Parliament and Representation in Medieval and Tudor England', in G.R Elton (ed.), *Studies in Tudor and Stuart Politics and Government (Papers and Reviews 1946-1972)* (2 vols., Cambridge, 1974), pp.19-61.

    *Reform and Reformation England, 1509-1558* (Cambridge, Mass., 1977).

    *The Tudor Constitution* (Cambridge, 1982 2nd edn).

    *England Under the Tudors* (London, 1991, 3rd edn).

Emden, Alfred B. (ed.), *Biographical Register of the University of Oxford to 1500* (3 vols., Oxford, 1957-59).

    *Biographical Register of the University of Cambridge to 1500* (3 vols., Cambridge, 1963).

    'Oxford Academical Halls in the Later Middle Ages' in Alfred B. Emden (ed.), *Medieval Learning and Literature: Essays Presented to Richard William Hunt* (Oxford, 1976), pp.353-65.

Falkes, Malcolm and Gillingham, John (eds), *Historical Atlas of Britain* (London, 1981).

Farge, James K., *Biographical Register of Paris Doctors of Theology, 1500-1536*, (Toronto, 1980).

    'The Divorce Consultation of Henry VIII', in Heiko A. Oberman et al (eds), *Orthodoxy and Reform in Early Reformation France: The Faculty of Theology of Paris, 1500-1543* (Leiden, 1985), pp.135-43.

    'Paris Partisans of Henry VIII and of Catherine of Aragon', in Heiko A. Oberman et al (eds), *Orthodoxy and Reform in Early Reformation France: The Faculty of Theology of Paris, 1500-1543* (Leiden, 1985), pp.143-50.

Ferrajoli, A., 'Un breve inedito per la investitura del regno di Francia ad Enrico VIII', *Archivio della Reale Societa Romana di Storia Patria* xix (1896), pp.425-27.

Foster, Ann, 'Bishop Tunstall's Priests', *Recusant History* ix (1967-68), pp.175-204.

Foster, Joseph, *Alumni Oxonienses: 1500-1714* (4 vols., Oxford, 1891).

Frati, L., *Le due spedizioni militari di Guilio II* (Bologna, 1886).

Fuller, Thomas, *The Worthies of England*, ed. by John Freeman (London, 1952 edn).

Gairdner, James, 'New Lights on the Divorce of Henry VIII. Part One', *EHR*, xi:xlvi (October 1896), pp.673-702.

    'Henry VIII', in *The Cambridge Modern History*, ed. by A.W Ward, G.W Prothero and Stanley Leatles (2 vols., Cambridge, 1984), ii, pp.416-73.

Gasquet, Francis Aidan, *The Eve of the Reformation* (London, 1913).

Godwin, F., *A Catalogue of the Bishops of England* (London, 1601).

Gunn, S.J. and Lindley, P.G. (eds), *Cardinal Wolsey: Church, State and Art* (Cambridge, 1991).

Guy, J.A., 'Wolsey, the Council and the Council Courts', *EHR* xci:ccclx (July 1976), pp.481-505.

*The Cardinal's Court: The Impact of Thomas Wolsey in Star Chamber* (Hassocks, 1977).

'Henry VIII and the Praemunire Manoeuvres of 1530-31', *EHR* xcvii:ccclxxxiv (July 1982), pp.481-503.

'The Pardon of the Clergy: a Reply', *JEH* xxxvii:ii (April 1986), pp.283-4.

'Thomas Cromwell and the Intellectual Origins of the Henrician Reformation', in A. Fox and J. Guy (eds), *Reassessing the Henrician Age: Humanism, Politics and Reform 1500-1550* (Oxford, 1986), pp.151-178.

'Thomas Cromwell and the Intellectual Origins of the Henrician Reformation', in A. Fox and J. Guy (eds), *Reassessing the Henrician Age: Humanism, Politics and Reform 1500-1550* (Oxford, 1986), pp.151-78.

'The Privy Council: Revolution or Evolution?', in Christopher Coleman and David Starkey (eds), *Revolution Reassessed: Revisions in the History of Tudor Government and Administration* (Oxford, 1986), pp.59-85.

Gwyn, P., *The King's Cardinal: The Rise and Fall of Thomas Wolsey* (London, 1990).

Haas, Steven W., 'Henry VIII's Glasse of Truthe', *History* lxiv:ccxii (October 1979), pp.353-62.

'Martin Luther's "Divine Right" Kingship and the Royal Supremacy: Two Tracts from the 1531 Parliament and Convocation of the Clergy', *JEH* xxxi:iii (July 1980), pp.317-25.

Haigh, Christopher, 'Anticlericalism and the English Reformation', *History* lxviii:ccxxiv (October, 1983), pp.391-407.

Hallman, Barbara McClung, *Italian Cardinals, Reform, and the Church as Property* (Berkeley, 1985).

Harper-Bill, Christopher, 'Bishop Richard Hill and the Court of Canterbury 1494-96', *Guildhall Studies in London History* iii:i (October 1977), pp.1-12.

Hart, A. Tindal, *Ebor: A History of the Archbishops of York* (York, 1986).

Hay, Denys, 'The Life of Polydore Vergil of Urbino', *Journal of the Warburg and Courtauld Institutes* xii (1949), pp.132-51.

*The Church in Italy in the Fifteenth Century* (Cambridge, 1977 edn).

Heal, Felicity, 'The Parish Clergy and the Reformation in the Diocese of Ely', *Cambridge Antiquarian Society Proceedings* lxvi (1975-6), pp.141-63.

*Of Prelates and Princes: A Study of the Economic and Social Position of the Tudor Episcopate* (Cambridge, 1980).

Heath, Peter, *The English Parish Clergy on the Eve of the Reformation* (London, 1969).

'The Treason of Geoffrey Blythe, Bishop of Coventry and Lichfield 1503-31', *BIHR* xlii (1969), pp.101-9.

Hembry, Phyllis M., *The Bishops of Bath and Wells, 1540-1640; Social and Economic Problems* (London, 1967).

Hennessy, G., *Novum Repertorium Ecclesiasticum Parochiale Londiniense* (London, 1898).

Herendeen, Wyman H. and Bartlett, Kenneth R., 'The Library of Cuthbert Tunstall, Bishop of Durham', *Bibliographical Society of America Papers* lxxxv (September 1991), pp.235-96.

Hibbert, S., *A History of the Foundations in Manchester. . .* (2 vols., Edinburgh and Manchester, 1834-5).

Highfield, J.R L., 'The English Hierarchy in the Reign of Edward III', *TRHS* 5th series, vi (1956), pp.115-38.

Horst, I.B., *The Radical Brethren: Anabaptists and the English Reformation to 1558* (Nieuwhoop, 1972).

Hoyle, R.W., 'The Origins of the dissolution of the monasteries', *HJ* xxxviii:ii (June 1995), pp.275-306.

Hume, D, *History of England* (4 vols., Philadelphia, 1821-2).

Hunt, William et al (eds), *The Political History of England* (12 vols., London, 1906).

Ives, E.W., *Anne Boleyn* (London, 1986).
   'The Fall of Anne Boleyn Reconsidered', *EHR* cvii:ccccxxiv (July 1992), pp.651-64.

Jacobs, H.E., *The Lutheran Movement in England During the Reigns of Henry VIII and Edward VI* (London, 1890).

Janelle, P., *L'Angleterre catholique à la veille du schisme* (Paris, 1935).

Jones, G.Lloyd, *The discovery of Hebrew in Tudor England: a third language* (Manchester, 1983).

Jones, M.K. and Underwood, M.G., *The King's Mother Lady Margaret Beaufort, Countess of Richmond and Derby* (Cambridge, 1992).

Jones, William B. and Freeman, Edward A., *The History and Antiquities of Saint David's* (London, 1856).

Joyce, James W., *England's Sacred Synods: A Constitutional History of the Convocations of the Clergy* (London, 1855).

Kamen, H., *The Phoenix and the Flame: Catalonia and the Counter Reformation* (New Haven, 1993).

Kantorowicz, Ernst, *The King's Two Bodies: A Study in Medieval Political Theology* (Princeton, 1957).

Kaufman, Peter I., *The "Polytique Churche" Religion and Early Tudor Political Culture, 1485-1516* (Macon, 1986).

Kelly, M., 'The Submission of the Clergy', *TRHS* xv (1965), pp.97-120.

Kelly, H.A., *The Matrimonial Trials of Henry VIII* (Stanford, 1976).

Kitching, Christopher, 'The Prerogative Court of Canterbury from Warham to Whitgift', in Rosemary O'Day and Felicity Heal (eds), *Continuity and Change: Personnel and administration of the Church of England, 1500-1642* (Leicester, 1976), pp.191-214.

Knecht, R.J., 'The Episcopate and the Wars of the Roses', *Birmingham University Historical Journal* vi (1957-8), pp.108-131.
   'The Concordat of 1516: A Reassessment', in Henry J. Cohn (ed.), *Government in Reformation Europe, 1520-1560* (London, 1971), pp.91-112.

Knowles, M.D., *The Religious Orders in England* (3 vols., Cambridge, 1959).
   'The English Bishops, 1070-1532', in J.A. Watt, J.B. Morrall and F.X Martin (eds), *Medieval Studies Presented to Aubrey Geynn, S. J.* (Dublin, 1961), pp.283-96.

Koenigsberger, H.G, Mosse, George L. and Bowler, G.Q., *Europe in the Sixteenth Century* (London, 1989 2nd edn).

Koszul, A., 'Was Bishop William Barlow Friar Jerome Barlow?', *The Review of English Studies* iv:xiii (1928), pp.25-34.

Lampe, G.W H. (ed.), *The Cambridge History of the Bible* (2 vols., Cambridge, 1960-70).

Lapsley, G.T., *The County Palatine of Durham: A Study in Constitutional History* (London, 1900).

Leader, Damian R., *A History of the University of Cambridge* (2 vols., Cambridge, 1988).

Lehmberg, Stanford E., 'Supremacy and Vice-Gerency: A Re-Examination', *EHR* cccxix (April 1966), pp.225-35.
   *The Reformation Parliament 1529 - 1536* (Cambridge, 1970).
   *The Later Parliaments of Henry VIII: 1536-1547* (Cambridge, 1977).

Litzenberger, Caroline, *The Englishg Reformation and the Laity: Gloucestershire, 1540-1580* (Cambridge, 1997).

Logan, F. Donald, 'Thomas Cromwell and the Vicegerency in Spirituals: A Revisitation', *EHR* ciii:ccccviii (July 1988), pp.658-67.

Logan, Oliver, *Culture and Society in Venice, 1470-1790: The Renaissance and its Heritage* (London, 1972).

Lunt, W.E., *Financial Relations of the Papacy with England, 1327-1534* (Mediaeval Academy of America, 1962).

Lupton, J.H., *A Life of John Colet* (London, 1887, 1909 edn).

Lupton, Lewis (ed.), *A History of the Geneva Bible* (12 vols., London, 1979).

Lusardi, James P., 'The Career of Robert Barnes', in *CWM*, viii/iii, pp.1367-1415.

MacCulloch, Diarmaid, 'Two Dons in Politics: Thomas Cranmer and Stephen Gardiner, 1503-1533', *HJ* xxxvii:i (1994), pp.1-22.

    *Thomas Cranmer: A Life* (New Haven, 1996).

MacCurtain, Margaret, *Tudor and Stuart Ireland* (Dublin, 1972).

Mackie, J.D., *The Earlier Tudors, 1485-1558* (Oxford, 1952, 1992 edn).

Macklem, Michael, *God Have Mercy: The Life of John Fisher of Rochester* (Toronto, 1968).

Mackenny, Richard, *Sixteenth Century Europe: Expansion and Conflict* (Basingstoke, 1993).

Maclure, Millar, *The Paul's Cross Sermons 1534-1642* (Toronto, 1958).

Macray, William D., *A Register of the Members of St.Mary Magdalen College, Oxford, from the Foundation of the College* (4 vols., Oxford, 1904).

Maddison, A.R., (ed.), *Lincolnshire Pedigrees* (4 vols., London, 1902-4).

Mahoney, M., 'The Scottish Hierarchy, 1513-1565', in David McRoberts (ed.), *Essays on the Scottish Reformation 1513-1625* (Glasgow, 1962), pp.39-84.

Manley, Richard H., 'Pedigree of Edward Lee', *Gentleman's Magazine and Historical Review* New Series, xv:ii (1863), p.337.

Masek, Rosemary, 'The Humanistic Interests of the Early Tudor Episcopacy', *Church History* xxxix (1970), pp.5-17.

Mayer, Thomas F., 'A Diet for Henry VIII: The Failure of Reginald Pole's 1537 Legation', *JBS* xxvi (July 1987), pp.305-31.

    'Thomas Starkey, An Unknown Conciliarist at the Court of Henry VIII', *JHI* xlix:2 (April-June 1988), pp.207-228.

    'A Fate Worse than Death: Reginald Pole and the Parisian Theologians', *EHR* ciii:ccccix (October 1988), pp.870-91.

    *Thomas Starkey and the Commonwealth* (Cambridge, 1989).

    'Tournai and Tyranny: Imperial Kingship and Critical Humanism', *HJ* xxxiv:ii (1991), pp.257-77.

    'On the road to 1534: the occupation of Tournai and Henry VIII's theory of sovereignty', in Dale Hoak (ed.), *Tudor Political Culture* (Cambridge, 1995), pp.11-30.

Maynard, T., *The Crown and the Cross* (New York, 1950)

McConica, J.K, *English Humanism and Reformation Politics Under Henry VIII and Edward VI* (Oxford, 1965).

    'The Collegiate University', in J.K McConica (ed.), *The History of the University of Oxford* (3 vols., Oxford, 1986).

McEntegart, Rory, *Henry VIII, The League of Schmalkalden, and the English Reformation* (Woodbridge, 2002).

McLaren, Colin A., 'An Early 16th Century Act Book of the Diocese of London', *Journal of the Society of Archivists* iii (1965-1969), pp.336-41.

McLean, Andrew M., 'Detestynge Thabomynacyon: William Barlow, Thomas More and the Anglican Episcopacy', *Moreana* xiii:xlix (February, 1976), pp.67-77.

McNeill, J.T., 'Alexander Alesuis, Scottish Lutheran (1500-1565)', *Archiv Für Reformationsgeschichte* lv (1964), pp.161-91.

Miller, Helen, *Henry VIII and the English Nobility* (London, 1989).

Mitchell, R.J., 'English Students at Ferrara in the XV Century', *Italians Studies* i:ii, (1937), pp.75-82.

    'English Law Students at Bologna in the Fifteenth-Century', *EHR* li:ccii (April 1936), pp.270-87.

Moyes, J., 'Warham, An English Primate on the Eve of the Reformation', *Dublin Review* cxiv (1894), pp.390-420.

Mozley, J.F., *Coverdale and His Bibles* (London, 1953).

Mumford, A.A., *Hugh Oldham* (London, 1936).

Muller, J.A. *Stephen Gardiner and the Tudor Reaction* (New York, 1970 edn).

Murphy, Virginia, 'The Literature and Progaganda of Henry VIII's First Divorce', in Diarmaid MacCulloch (ed.), *The Reign of Henry VIII. Politics, Policy and Piety* (New York, 1995), pp.135-58.

Neame, Alan, *The Holy Maid of Kent* (London, 1971).

Newell, E.J. (ed.), *Llandaff* (London, 1902).

Nicholson, G.D., 'The Act of Appeals and the English Reformation', in C. Cross, D. Loades and J.J Scarisbrick (eds), *Law and Government Under the Tudors* (Cambridge, 1988), pp.19-30.

Oakley, Francis, 'Almain and Major: Conciliar Theory on the Eve of the Reformation', *American Historical Review* lxx:iii (April 1965), pp.673-90.

    *The Western Church in the Later Middle Ages* (Ithaca, N.Y., 1979).

    'On the Road from Constance to 1688: The Political Thought of John Major and George Buchanan', in Francis Oakley (ed.), *Law, Conciliarism and Consent in the Middle Ages* (London, 1984), pp.1-31.

    'Edward Foxe, Matthew Paris, and the Royal "Potestas Ordinis"', *SCJ* xviii:iii (1987), pp.347-53.

Ogle, Arthur, *The Tragedy of the Lollard's Tower: Its Place in History 1514-1533* (Oxford, 1949).

Oliver, G., *Lives of the Bishops of Exeter* (Exeter, 1861).

Ortroy, F. van. (ed.), 'Vie du bienheureux martyr Jean Fisher cardinal, évêque de Rochester', *Analecta Bollandiana* x/i (1891), pp.121-365.

Page, William (ed.), *VHC: A History of Norfolk* (2 vols., London, 1901, 1906).

    *VCH: Hertfordshire* (4 vols., London, 1902-14).

    *VCH: A History of Surrey* (4 vols., London, 1902-12).

    *VCH: Leicestershire* (5 vols., London, 1907-64).

    *VHC: A History of London* (2 vols., London, 1909).

Pantin, W.A., *The English Church in the Fourteenth century* (Cambridge, 1955).

Parmiter, Geoffrey de C., *The King's Great Matter* (London, 1967).

    'A note on some aspects of the Royal Supremacy of Henry VIII', *Recusant History* x (1969-70), pp.183-92.

Parrish, G., *The Forgotten Primate* (London, 1971).

Pearson, A.F S., 'Alesius and the English Reformation', *Records of the Scottish Church History Society* x:ii (1949), pp.57-87.

Peronnet, Michel, *Les évêques de l'ancien France* (2 vols., Paris, 1978).

Perry, George G., 'The Visitation of the monastery of Thame, 1526', *EHR*, iii (1888), pp.704-22.

    'Episcopal Visitations of the Austin Canons of Leicester and Dorchester', *EHR*, iv (1889), pp.310-13.

Pill, D.H., 'The administration of the diocese of Exeter under Bishop Veysey', *Transactions of the Devon Association* xcviii (1966), pp.262-78.

Plomer, Henry R., *Wynkyn De Worde & His Contemporaries from the Death of Caxton to 1535* (London, 1925).

Pocock, N., 'Archbishop Warham's Abortive Council, 1518', *EHR* viii:xxx (April 1893), pp.297-9.

Pollard, A.F., *Henry VIII* (London, 1905, 1951 edn).
    *Wolsey* (London, 1929).

Prodi, Paolo, 'The structure and organization of the church in Renaissance Venice: suggestions for research', in J.R Hale (ed.), *Renaissance Venice* (London, 1973), pp.409-30.

Pruser, F., *England und die Schmalkaldener, 1535-1540* (Leipzig, 1929).

Rafferty, O.P., 'Thomas Cranmer and the Royal Supremacy', *The Heythrop Journal* xxxi:ii (1990), pp.129-49.

Randell, Keith, *The Catholic and Counter Reformations* (London, 1990).

Rawlings, H.E., 'The Secularization of Castilian Episcopal Office Under the Habsburgs, c.1516-1700', *Journal of Ecclesiastical History*, xxxviii:i (January 1987), pp.53-79.

Reardon, Bernard M.G., *Religious Thought in the Reformation* (London, 1981).

Redstone, V.B., 'Wulcy of Suffolk', *Proceedings of the Suffolk Institute of Archaeology and Natural History* xxvi (1918), pp.71-89.

Reed, A., *Early Tudor Drama*, (London, 1926).

Redworth, Glyn, 'A Study in the Formulation of Policy: The Genesis and Evolution of the Act of Six Articles', *JEH* xxxvii:i (January 1986), pp.42-67.
    *In Defence of the Church Catholic: The Life of Stephen Gardiner* (Oxford, 1990).

Rex, Richard, 'The English Campaign against Luther in the 1520s', *TRHS*, 5th series, xxxix (1989), pp.85-106.
    *The Theology of John Fisher* (Cambridge, 1991).

Ridley, Jasper, *Thomas Cranmer* (Oxford, 1962).
    *Statesman and Saint* (New York, 1982).

Rosenthal, Joel, 'The Training of an Elite Group: English Bishops in the Fifteenth Century', *Transactions of the American Philosophical Society*, lx:v (1970), pp.5-54.

Rupp, E.G., *Studies in the Making of the English Protestant Tradition (mainly in the Reign of Henry VIII)* (Cambridge, 1947).

Rummel, E., *Erasmus and his Catholic Critics 1515-1522* (Nieuhoop, 1989).

Sawada, P., 'Two Anonymous Tudor Treatises on the General Council', *JEH* xii (October 1961), pp.197-215.

Scarisbrick, J.J., 'The Pardon of the Clergy, 1531', *Cambridge Historical Journal* xii:i (1956), pp.22-39.
    'Clerical Taxation in England, 1485-1535', *JEH* xi (1960), pp.41-54.
    'Henry VIII and the Vatican Library', *Bibliotheque d'humanisme et renaissance* xxiv:xxv (Geneva, 1962), pp.211-16.
    *Henry VIII* (Berkeley, 1968).

Schenk, W., *Reginald Pole, Cardinal of England* (London, 1950).

Sheppard, J.T., *Richard Croke, A Sixteenth Century Don* (Cambridge, 1919).

Sherr, Merrill F., 'Bishop Bonner: A Quasi Erasmian', *Historical Magazine of the Protestant Episcopal Church* xliii (1974), pp.359-66.

Shirley, T.F., *Thomas Thirlby, Tudor Bishop* (London, 1964).

Slavin, A.J., 'Humanists and Government in Early Tudor England', *Viator*, i (1970), pp.307-25.

Smith, H. Maynard, *Henry VIII and the Reformation* (London, 1962).

Smith, L.B., *Tudor Prelates and Politics* (Princeton, 1953).

Squibb, G.D., *Doctor's Common: A History of the College of Advocates and Doctors of Law* (Oxford, 1977).

Stanier, R.S., *Magdalen College: A History of Magdalen College School, Oxford* (Oxford, 1940).

Steer, Francis W., *Robert Sherburne, Bishop of Chichester: Some Aspects of his Life Reconsidered* (Chichester, 1960).

Stephens, W.R.W., *Memorials of the South Saxon See and Cathedral Church of Chichester* (London, 1876).

Storey, R.L. *The Reign of Henry VII* (London, 1968)

Stuart, Clara H., 'Hugh Latimer: Apostle to the English', *Christianity Today* xxiv (1980), pp.17-19.

Sturge, Charles, *Cuthbert Tunstal: Churchman, Scholar, Statesman, Administrator* (London, 1938).

Surtz, E., *The Works and Days of John Fisher* (Cambridge, Mass., 1967).

Thompson, Craig R., *Universities in Tudor England* (Washington, 1959).

Thompson, Stephen, 'The bishop in his diocese', in B. Bradshaw and E. Duffy (eds), *Humanism, Reform and Reformation: The Career of John Fisher* (Cambridge, 1989), pp.67-80.

Thomson, G. Scott, 'Three Suffolk Figures: Thomas Wolsey: Stephen Gardiner: Nicholas Bacon', *Proceedings of the Suffolk Institute of Archaeology and Natural History* xxv (1952), pp.149-63.

Thomson, John A.F., *The Transformation of Medieval England 1370-1529* (London, 1983).
        *The Early Tudor Church & Society 1485-1529* (London, 1993).

Tjernagel, Neelah Serawlook, *Henry VIII and the Lutherans: A Study in Anglo-Lutheran Relations from 1521 to 1547* (St Louis, 1965).

Underwood, Malcolm G., 'Politics and Piety in the Household of Lady Margaret Beaufort', *JEH* xxxviii:i (January 1987), pp.39-52.
        'John Fisher and the promotion of learning', in B. Bradshaw and E. Duffy (eds), *Humanism, Reform and Reformation: The Career of Bishop John Fisher* (Cambridge, 1989), pp.25-46.

Venn, John and J.A., *Alumni Cantabrigiensis: Part One to 1750* (4 vols., Cambridge, 1922-7).

Walcott, M.E.C., 'Bishops of Chichester', in *Sussex Archaeological Collections Relating to the History and Antiquities of the County* xxix (1879), pp.1-39.

Walker, Greg, 'Saint or Schemer? The 1527 Heresy Trial of Thomas Bilney Reconsidered', *JEH* xl:ii (April 1989), pp.219-38.

Weiss, R., *Humanism in England during the Fifteenth Century* (Oxford, 1967).

Welch, C.E., 'Three Sussex Heresy Trials', *Sussex Archaeological Collections* xcv (1957), pp.59-70.

Wernham, R.B., *Before the Armada: The Growth of English Foreign Policy, 1485-1588* (London, 1966, 1971 reprint).

Wharhirst, Gwenolen E., 'The Reformation in the Diocese of Lincoln as illustrated by the Life and Work of Bishop Longland, (1521-1547)', *Lincolnshire Architectural and Archaeological Societies Reports and Papers* i:ii (1937), pp.137-76.

Wharton, Henry, *Anglia Sacra* (2 vols., London, 1691).

William E. Wilkie, *The Cardinal Protectors of England: Rome and the Tudors Before the Reformation* (Cambridge, 1979)

Williams, Glanmor, *The Welsh Church from Conquest to Reformation* (Cardiff, 1976).
        *Recovery, Reorientation and Reformation Wales c.1415-1642* (Oxford, 1987).
        *Wales and the Reformation* (Cardiff, 1997).

Willis-Bund, J.W and Page, William (eds), *VHC: A History of Worcester* (4 vols., London, 1901-24).

Wilson, J. (ed.), *VHC: Cumberland* (2 vols, London, 1905).

Wood, Anthony, *Athenae Oxonienses: An Exact History of All the Writers and Bishops* (4 vols., London, 1721).
    *Athenae Oxonienses: An Exact History of All the Writers and Bishops*, ed. by P. Bliss (6 vols., London, 1813 edn).

Woodward, G.W O., *Dissolution of the Monasteries* (Blandford, 1969 edn).

Wunderli, Richard, 'Pre-Reformation London Summoners and the Murder of Richard Hunne', *JEH* xxxiii:ii (April 1982), pp.209-24.

Yost, John K., 'Hugh Latimer's Reform Program, 1529-1536, and the Intellectual Origins of the Anglican *Via Media*', in *Anglican Theological Review* liii (April 1971), pp.103-14.

Youings, Joyce, *Sixteenth-Century England* (London, 1991 edn).

Zell, Michael L., 'The Prebendaries' Plot of 1543: a Reconsideration', *JEH* 27:3 (July 1976), pp. 241-53.

Dissertations

Alexander, G.M V., 'The Life and Career of Edmund Bonner Bishop of London until his Deprivation in 1549' (unpublished Ph.D. thesis, University of London, 1960).

Fines, John, 'Studies in the Lollard Heresy. Being an Examination of the Evidence from the Dioceses of Norwich, Lincoln, Coventry and Lichfield, and Ely, during the period 1430-1520 (unpublished Ph.D. thesis, University of Sheffield, 1964).

Heal F., 'The Bishops of Ely and their Diocese during the Reformation' (unpublished Ph.D. thesis, University of Cambridge, 1971).

Kelly, M.J., 'Canterbury Jurisdiction and Influence during the Episcopate of William Warham, 1503-1532' (unpublished Ph.D. thesis, University of Cambridge, 1963).

Lander, S.J., 'The diocese of Chichester, 1508-1558: episcopal reform under Robert Sherburne and its aftermath' (unpublished D.Phil., University of Cambridge, 1974).

McEntegart, R., 'England and the League of Schmalkalden 1531-1547: Faction, foreign policy and the England Reformation' (unpublished Ph.D., London School of Economics, 1992).

McLaren, Colin A., 'An Edition of Foxford: A Vicar-General's Book of the Diocese of London, 1521-39', 2 vols. (unpublished M Phil thesis, University of London, 1973).

Murphy, Virginia M., 'The Debate over Henry VIII's First Divorce: An Analysis of the Contemporary Sources' (unpublished Ph.D. dissertation, University of Cambridge, 1984).

Nicholson, G.D., 'The Nature and Function of Historical Argument in the Henrician Reformation' (unpublished Ph.D. dissertation, University of Cambridge, 1977).

Scarisbrick, J.J., 'The Conservative Episcopate in England: 1529-1535' (unpublished Ph.D. thesis, University of Cambridge, 1963).

Sherr, Merrill F., 'Bishop Bonner: Bulwark Against Heresy' (unpublished Ph.D. thesis, New York University, 1969).

Thompson, Stephen, 'The Pastoral Work of the English and Welsh Bishops 1500-58' (unpublished Ph.D. thesis, University of Oxford, 1984).

Walker, B.V., 'Cardinal Reginald Pole; Papal Authority and Church Unity 1529-1536' (unpublished M.A. thesis, University of Dublin, 1972).

# Index